Absence of Moves

Absence of Moves
A Magical Autobiography

Ken Hawes

FIRST EDITION

Book design by Kathryn Myers

ISBNs
Paperback: 978-1-80541-434-6
eBook: 978-1-80541-433-9

Dedicated with love
to the memory of
Sam and Cassie Hawes and Clare Jones

Contents

Introduction

Dear Reader

Welcome to the story of my life. It begins in 1950 the year of my birth and ends in 2014 when I retired. Tacked onto the end of it however I write about how my time is spent during my retirement years. It is a comprehensive account of a lifetime spanning 70 years, including my childhood and teenage years in the 50s & 60s, young adulthood in the 70s & 80s, and getting on a bit in the 90s & 2000s. Intermingled with it all is my working and family life and of course the story of my times as a performing magician. Throughout the pages you will find good times and bad times, happy times, and sad times, all you would expect from a life of seven decades. In many ways it has been an ordinary life not unlike your own I suspect. Nonetheless it has been enjoyable and for the most part happy, enriching, and full. I hope you find it interesting and I'm sure there will be parts of it you can identify with and could well bring back forgotten memories of your own. Inevitably there are some sad moments in what follows, but don't get too upset as there are many happy bits as well which I'm sure will make you giggle.

CHAPTER 1

Childhood

I was born in 1950 in Fenny Stratford, an area of Bletchley in the county of Buckinghamshire some 50 miles north of London. It is situated on the main railway line (and the Grand Union Canal) about halfway between London and Birmingham. In those days it was a small and quiet country market town known for the manufacture of brushes and bricks. Now of course it is known throughout the world for Bletchley Park and the wonderful work that was done there during World War 2. My Dad grew up in the town along with his Mum and Dad and seven brothers and sisters. I did ask him if he was aware of anything going on at Bletchley Park at the time and all he could remember was some odd-looking people riding around on bicycles.

Dad spent his war in the Home Guard as he failed the forces medical due to a heart problem. He did his bit though as a member of a concert party which entertained locally in the town and surrounding villages. These were very popular during the war years and certainly helped to keep up morale and spread some cheer to families who had loved ones fighting abroad. Among other things Dad performed 'living marionettes'. His head would be visible as the head of the puppet which was attached around his neck and operated with small rods fixed to its feet. With Dad wearing black and a black velvet backdrop the illusion was complete and very effective. He worked from a booth and had all sorts of characters including a clown and even a cowboy on a horse. One of his favourites was a beautifully dressed lady. The colourful blind on the booth would rise to reveal Dad complete with wig and make up who would then regale the audience with a rendition of, 'Why am I always the bridesmaid' with the audience no doubt joining in with the familiar chorus. For years the old booth was stored in the shed at home with Dad reluctant to part with it. He assembled it for the last time when we were quite small and gave us a little show with some of it filmed for posterity, needless to say we loved it. Dad also performed various musical items often with unusual instruments including a set of sleigh bells. These worked when bells of various sizes were attached to leather straps and hung on a frame with each one emitting a different note. They were played by shaking the straps in the correct order to make popular tunes of the day. It went down particularly well at Christmas as you can imagine. Another unusual one was a strange box like stringed contraption called Fairy Bells. The strings were plucked with the thumbs as the box was swung round his head to allow the sound to travel and resonate. It was a pleasant enough sound rather like church bells, even though the performance of it was, well, different. Dad was known mainly for his "musical" saw. An ordinary wood saw that's held between the knees at the handle and notes are formed by bending it and brushing the edge with a cello bow. He was accompanied by a pianist, and it really did sound nice especially in a room with good acoustics. Dad was a gifted musician and could get a tune out of anything. He played a mouth organ in the vamp style which involves playing the rhythm and melody at the same time. He would tell me how easy it was once you knew where all the notes were! I wish.

Mum was born and grew up in Holyhead in North Wales and moved to Bletchley along with the family she worked for just after the war. Although living and working in different parts of the town I suppose there was an inevitability that Mum and Dad's paths would eventually cross. They both visited the same high street which in those days was known as Bletchley Road. It seems that Dad spotted Mum first and noticed that she called into the same newsagent at the same time each day and soon so did he. They began to chat, and over a short period of time got to know each other and the rest as they say is history. They married in 1947 in Holyhead and Miss Elizabeth Hawkins (known as Cassie) and Mr William Hawes (known as Sam) became Mr and Mrs Hawes. After a short honeymoon they moved into a small house in Fenny Stratford High Street. My sister Margaret (Maggs) was born in 1948, followed by me in 1950, and my sister Jean in 1951. In 1953 we moved to a brand-new council house on a new estate about a mile away and soon settled into family life. Mum was a housewife and Dad worked for "Beacon Brushes" which was a family run business supplying a range of brushes pretty much exclusively for Woolworths. The factory wasn't too far away, and Dad was able to cycle there and back each day quite comfortably. At the back of the premises were the gravel pits and in those early days sailing was a popular pastime as was fishing. In the summer, families would often go there for picnics. It was a nice spot by the water with a sandy almost seaside type of beach. During some of those long hot summers, children were occasionally tempted to go in for a swim, but it came to a sudden and tragic end in the early 60s when a young lad was drowned. I do remember that day with some clarity. It was the first time I saw my Dad cry.

Christmas time in the 50s and 60s were always happy occasions. When I was quite young, I would sleep in the girls' room on Christmas Eve. They shared a double-bed, and I was in a small single on the opposite side of the room. Stockings would be hung in the front room on the mantelpiece (in the form of Dad's old socks) each one held up by a brass candlestick. Empty pillowcases were already in position on the landing as we went to bed. When we woke up early on Christmas morning one of us would creep out to see if they'd been filled during the night, if they had then the loud whisper of "He's been!" would wake Mum and Dad. We then had to wait a while for Dad to get up and get his cine camera and lights sorted out so that he could film us opening our presents. It's interesting to see those old films now with us in bed all wearing cardigans and jumpers, no central heating in those days. After washing and dressing we'd go downstairs to check out the stockings. Inside would be a few chocolate coins, an assortment of nuts, and rammed into the toe section would be one of the highlights of the day, a tangerine. On the sideboard there were boxes of chocolates, a box of dates, a carton of figs, more nuts, biscuits, and a variety of fruit which included grapes and bananas. More than enough for all of us.

We didn't have a television but were quite happy playing in the front room with our new presents and toys in front of the open coke fire. Sometimes we played board games on the table in the dining room which we always called the little room. Underneath the window was a wooden sideboard with doors and drawers. Inside the cupboards were our books and comics and in the drawers were nutcrackers, old screwdrivers, bits of string and wire, an assortment of nuts and bolts, screws, pens pencils and old watches, a veritable glory hole of stuff that should have been thrown away but never was as 'it could come in handy one day'. On the opposite side of the room was a built-in cupboard with two large, panelled glass doors and underneath that a small two door cupboard where Mum would keep her knitting and supply of wool. The glass cupboard, as it was known, was the home of the rent book, bills, and school reports among other things. Many times if something was lost Mum would call out "have you looked in the glass cupboard?"

Christmas lunch was magnificent. We'd either have turkey or a large cockerel, and on one occasion a goose. In the afternoon we'd gather in the front room to open the large cardboard box sent from Mum's sister our Auntie Maudie. Every year it would arrive from Wales full of presents for all of us.

Dad would always make an effort at Christmas time even if he was tired out after working long hours or feeling unwell. He entered into the spirit of it all and was the perfect father. He bought a small Christmas tree every year which would go on the front room sideboard along with lights and a fairy for the top (which I still have.) One year he went out to buy a tree and came home empty handed, sold out everywhere. He could see our disappointment but had a brainwave. He disappeared out to the barn and found a saw and cut out a section of the garden privet hedge! Somehow, he got it to stand erect on the sideboard and strung its rather sparse foliage with lights. It was better than nothing, as I said Dad always made an effort. When I got older, I would help him put the decorations up in the front room. These consisted of lengths of coloured crepe paper twisted a few times to get the typical decoration pattern. They ran from corner to corner via the light fitting in the centre of the ceiling. My job was to stand on a chair and fix the paper upwards into each corner with a drawing pin.

"Make sure you put them in the same holes as last year boy, we don't want a ceiling full of holes," said Dad. As If anybody could see them anyway. Once fixed in the corner I had to wind the paper round the dangling cable from the light fitting and continue across and fix it in the opposite corner. When I suggested we use separate lengths and pinned them to the ceiling by the light, he said, "What more holes?"

I did as I was told but now the light fitting was being pulled across at a ridiculous angle.

"That'll be ok, it'll all pull back into shape when you put the other piece up."

Again I did as I was told and fixed the final length across the opposite corners. Now the whole system was like a coiled spring. Suddenly a drawing pin pinged out from a corner (no surprise there as it had been shoved in the same hole as previous years!). This started a chain reaction, the end result of which were rather sad looking lengths of slowly uncoiling crepe paper hanging off a gently swinging lampshade. We just laughed. After that me and the girls did it using four lengths instead of two, he never did notice the extra pin holes by the light fitting.

The infant school was directly opposite our house (which was handy). The Head Teacher was Miss Jenkins who looked quite severe, but her bark was much worse than her bite and generally speaking she was liked and certainly respected. My days there were happy enough and I got on well with my classmates, but I was quiet and rather shy particularly with the girls. How I wish I could have talked to "the twins." Two identical very pretty girls who were in my class. I was infatuated with both of them and desperate to get myself noticed in whatever way I could. Over a weekend I had an idea and hatched a cunning plan that couldn't fail to impress. On the Monday after school I ran out of the gates as fast as I could and climbed up the back gate and onto the barn roof. There I stood erect with arms folded with a serious look on my face desperately trying to look cool and impressive. It didn't occur to me that I wasn't really dressed for the part. Brown sandals, short trousers, a grey shirt, and a green sleeveless jumper was hardly the uniform of a super cool dude, but in my seven-year-old mind I was somebody to be admired. I watched as they walked out of the school and stopped to stare. There was a bit of giggling and pointing and then they skipped up the road home, no doubt with all thoughts of me posing like mad on a barn roof gone from their pretty little heads. Did I do it I wonder because I was shy and insecure and craved attention, or was I just a blatant show off? Probably a combination of both. The burning question is of course were they impressed? I like to think they were, luckily perhaps I'll never know.

The Junior school was a 15-minute walk away which our parents were happy for us to do every day. We would tend to walk in small groups of the same age and sex and luckily there were only two main roads to cross, and at the busiest there was the 'Lollipop' man, Mr. Goodman, to see us safely across.

I loved that school and still have happy memories - chanting the Times Tables, ink wells and pens with nibs, blackboards and chalk, small bottles of milk with straws, and playing marbles and conkers at playtime. In the summer we played on the large field at the back of the school, football mostly with plastic balls with little bobbles. Thanks to one of the teachers called Mr. Williams, sport was very popular at the school particularly football. with a well-supported annual tournament (Bluebirds v Robins) which involved all of the school. Even at that early age I began to realise I wasn't a team player and never did take to football. Luckily, again thanks to Mr. Williams, I discovered athletics. Here was something I could do! Running, jumping, and throwing, I loved it all.

Academically I wasn't particularly bright, "Average" appeared on my school reports quite regularly and I didn't get too much grief from Mum and Dad apart from once when the word lackadaisical was mentioned. Another one of my teachers, Mr. Vince, had the most beautiful italic handwriting. I remember one occasion when I was called up to his desk to have a passage of English explained to me. He wrote it out and was talking to me at the same time. I was so impressed by the effortless beauty of his handwriting that I didn't hear a word he said...

"You're not listening to me are you, Hawes?"

"Yes sir."

Because we had an hour for lunch, we would walk home from school for something to eat. Mondays stick in my mind because they were always the same. Monday was wash day and I hated it. As I walked into the kitchen I was greeted with the combined smell of steam and cold meat. Condensation would be running down the walls and windows, and the old copper would be bubbling away full of washing, its lid propped open with the copper stick. The hand-driven mangle would be at the side of it, which Mum had to feed the washing through to squeeze out as much water as possible before it was heaved onto the washing line. Mum would be there with sweat running down her face trying to sort the washing out and dish up the remnants of the Sunday roast and veg to three hungry children.

Mum was a good cook and we certainly had enough to eat with loads of fresh vegetables from Dad's allotment. I loved her roly-poly suet pudding with ham and onions, then there was steak and kidney pie, liver and onions, and her Sunday roasts were to die for. Her crispy roast potatoes and Yorkshire pudding were the best I've ever had. The Sunday joint would be lamb or beef and on special occasions we would have chicken. Seems strange now how that has been completely reversed. Whenever I smell the distinct aroma of mint sauce I'm transported to those childhood Sunday lunchtimes, with lovely food and the sound of Two-way Family Favourites on the radio, followed by The Navy Lark, The Clitheroe Kid, or The Billy Cotton Band Show.

The radio was always on and the music and voices from it created a wonderful backdrop to my childhood. When we were quite young the set was on the sideboard in the little room. A huge brown Bakelite valve driven thing with a series of knobs on the front and a dial that lit up. After it had beamed its final programme and suddenly stopped Dad got another one (second-hand of course and vaguely similar) and this one was put on the old table in the kitchen. It would be on during my lunch hour, and I would listen to Workers Playtime which was a variety programme beamed live from a factory somewhere in England. It would often feature early performances from the likes of Ken Dodd and Frankie Howerd.

In the fifties and early sixties the radio was an important part of our lives before we got a TV. Me and my sisters would listen to Children's Hour at teatime during the week and Children's Favourites on Saturday mornings, and on Sunday evenings the whole family would gather round and listen to the comedy programme Take it from Here with Jimmy Edwards and June Whitfield on the Light Programme and Hughie Green's Opportunity Knocks on Radio Luxembourg. At this point in my young life I did feel a bit left out because a lot of my school friends did have a TV. I would go to Cubs every Tuesday and the talk as the meeting ended was having to rush home to catch The Charlie Drake Show or Whack-O. I had no idea what they were talking about. In the summer it didn't matter so much as we would always be out and about.

Weekday evenings we played with other local children on the small green area in front of the school opposite our house. Tennis was popular along with French cricket and a type of hide-and-seek called Sixty. Just up the road was a small recreation ground with a seesaw where we would sometimes go for a change of scenery or if we got moaned at for being too noisy close to the house. Sundays were different for us though as we went to Sunday School in the morning and afternoon.

In those days the Methodist Church we went to was full every week with both morning and evening services. The Sunday School was huge with two separate groups, Primary and Seniors, and we went to both. I do remember it with some affection along with the teachers, Ernie Allen, Jim Massey, and Grace King. We would meet for an hour in 'The Hut' which was a separate building at the side of the church after which we would go into the church for the final part of the main service. The large choir sat in their own area facing the congregation and sounded magnificent when accompanied by the impressive organ which was played by regular organist Mr. Stephens. The annual Sunday School Anniversary was one of the highlights of the year with the church packed for both quite lengthy services. The downside of that was having to go to Anniversary Practice every Thursday evening for weeks leading up to the big day. It was always in June at the start of the fishing season; no wonder I was miserable.

Sunday School was an important part of my childhood, and I went along every Sunday from when I was quite young to when I was 14. It was then I was given the choice from Mum and Dad to stay or leave. It was the mid-sixties and I had other interests, and to be honest I would rather spend half the weekend doing something else with my pals, so I left. It did give me however a solid groundwork of the Christian Faith, unconditional love and forgiveness, tolerance, and kindness. Decades later I did return.

Sunday tea was usually a salad with bread and butter, homemade cake, and tinned fruit with cream. If it was a pleasant evening the whole family would go for a walk, the route would be decided by Dad, and we walked miles. Most of the time it would be along the canal or down by the river and occasionally a long trek across the fields to local villages. By the time we got home we were exhausted and ready for bed. The girls slept in the back bedroom, and I was in the small box room at the front. Sometimes if he wasn't too tired Dad would stand on the landing and sing us to sleep; he had a pleasant baritone voice and would regale us with "It's time to say goodnight", a song made popular by Henry Hall in the 1930s.

In those days of the late fifties and early sixties we were very lucky. We were well fed (and exercised), unspoilt and loved. You couldn't ask for more.

The highlight of the summer for me was June 16th. The opening day of fishing season. Invariably it would be on a school day so I'd have to wait patiently until the end of afternoon lessons before I could cast my float. To save time, preparations had been made leading up to the big day. A rod licence had been bought (three shillings) rod and tackle checked, and two shillings worth of maggots had been bought from Don Sewell's tackle shop along with a packet of No.16 hooks. When I got home from school, I would rush my tea down and then use Dad's spade to dig for worms from the garden as bait for perch, then grab a slice of bread to make up some bread paste for roach and bream. I was ready - I put the bait into my box which Dad had made from an old wooden radio, the valves and internal workings had been removed and the mesh from the speaker replaced with a piece of plywood. The strap was made from an old bicycle tyre which was nailed to the sides enabling me to hang it around my neck and shoulders. The whole thing was painted brown and yellow. The colour of this (and many of my future early magic props) was dependant on what was on the paint run in the brush factory at the time. Dad wasn't all that good with his hands but what he lacked in skill he made up with ingenuity, he was also quite talented in persuading his workmates to help out. The box was certainly practical if a little heavy but in spite of its unusual colour scheme it was always going to look like a radio. With rod in hand and box round my shoulders I would hurriedly walk the short distance up to the canal bank behind the house. Invariably there would be one or two older lads already up there (brave enough to skip school for the day). Of course they had much better equipment than I did, and they would look at my cheap and cheerful cane rod and old-fashioned wooden ratchet reel, (not forgetting the 'radio box') and just laugh. "I hope you won't be turning that radio on; you'll frighten the fish"! I ignored them and got set up as far away from them as I could. As time passed, I was joined by a lot of boys and girls spread out along the canal bank. Although we planned for perch, roach, or bream we invariably only caught gudgeon which were quite small, but it was better than nothing. Sometimes

Dad would come up and see us and offer advice and suggestions and when it was too dark to see the float we would make our way home, reeking of the smell of fish, bread, and maggots, and covered in slime. We chatted away to each other oblivious to it all, wondering if a bigger size hook with more than one maggot would attract bigger fish, or perhaps we could try moving the lead shot further up or lower down… that night I would go to bed clutching Dad's well-thumbed copy of 'Mr. Crabtree Goes Fishing' and soon to fall asleep, safe in the knowledge that tomorrow I would do it all over again.

Summer was a busy time for Dad and his allotment. He had a big plot and would grow an assortment of vegetables that would feed us all throughout the year. He grew carrots, onions, peas, runner beans, beetroot, broad beans, swede, parsnips, cabbage or sprouts and a lot of potatoes! Needless to say I would be roped in to help out. I can't remember refusing to go although there were times when I went reluctantly as I got older. I was never offered a monetary reward and it wasn't expected. It was assumed that I would go because it was what you did, as he did with his father. It was hard work and as Dad got older and his health deteriorated, he couldn't have done it on his own anyway. By the time I got to my teens, and he'd helped me so much with my magic, I felt it was the least I could do. When I was quite young, I would just play with a small bucket and spade and try and keep out of the way. If it was a Saturday afternoon, I'd often wander over to the boundary fence and look out across the football pitch to watch Bletchley Town play for a while. Often there would be a bonfire on the corner of the plot where the remains of potato foliage or sprout stalks would be burnt. When there was nothing left, I would run around trying to find something flammable just to get it going again. Sometimes

I would burn a finger, or my eyes would stream from the effect of smoke. No sympathy from Dad,

"What do you expect if you play with fire"?

He knew I was learning the hard way. Even now decades later whenever I catch the scent of a bonfire I'm transported to those long sunny and idyllic afternoons. Along with mint sauce, I often smell my childhood.

Dad was a perfectionist when It came to all things allotment. His rows of vegetables were dead straight, and the soil had been hoed to the smoothness of a snooker table. As the seedlings began to sprout, we would be on our knees picking out small weeds and thinning out so that the gap between each plant was identical. It looked immaculate. Dad taught me the technique of digging as soon as I could lift a spade. How to keep a trench and to cut and not pat, where to put each spit (a spade full of soil), how to maintain a level and which weed can go into the trench (clover & groundsel) and which shouldn't, (twitch grass and thistle) and to make sure every trace of a potato was removed. We would either dig together, or he would dig and I would follow along putting a fork full of rather ripe fresh manure into the trench. By the time I was 17 I was as good as him. Dad was never good on giving praise, but I could tell he was proud, and relieved as well. One year when I was still quite young, he had to have a spell in hospital. I went to see him, and he was concerned about getting the digging done. He told me to make a start and once the other chaps saw me, they would step up and give me a hand. That just didn't happen though, and it took me two days. Just as I was finishing off and cleaning my spade one chap did come over and compliment me on a neat piece of digging.

"Not many lads of your age would even attempt that," he said.

I would've got it done a lot quicker if you'd helped, I almost said, but didn't. If the boot had been on the other foot with *him* needing help, then Dad wouldn't have hesitated. He assumed everyone was the same - you help each other out, it's just what you do.

That evening as I was nursing blisters and an aching back, I wondered how on earth Dad did all of that digging (Spring and Autumn) for all of those years before I was old enough to help. Not only that but transporting sacks of potatoes home on his bike up a hill and going down there watering every evening in the summer after working a 12-hour shift in the brush factory, all with a heart condition. There is no doubt that Dad did love his allotment, but he also had the mindset of his generation of providing for your family whatever the cost.

During school holidays in the summer I would always be outside. If I wasn't at the allotment, I'd be off on my bike somewhere with a couple of pals or fishing on the canal or the river. Long walks in the countryside were popular with some of us too. What made those days so special was the freedom we had. As long as Mum and Dad had some idea of where we were and made sure we came home for tea or before it got dark, we could do just about anything and go anywhere. It was all down to trust and respect. Happy days indeed.

Between the ages of 11 and about 14 I was into trainspotting in a big way. This was in the last days of steam and those old locomotives were just wonderful. I would spend all day with a packed lunch close to Bletchley railway station with a few of my like-minded enthusiastic friends. Sometimes we went to Sandy or Bedford to spend the day there. We became quite knowledgeable and could even tell the class of locomotive by the sound of its whistle particularly if it was distinctive, like a Brit (Britannia).

My trainspotting highlight was a visit to Kings Cross station in London when I got up close to 'Mallard'. This was a Class A4 4-6-2 Pacific locomotive (or Streak) and held the world speed record for steam locomotives at 126 mph. It was a beautiful thing. Even now watching old footage it gives me goose bumps. Sadly my trainspotting days came to an end when those wonderful old steam locomotives were sent to the scrapheap in favour of the rather dull and unromantic diesels. The end of an era, but I feel privileged to have experienced (albeit for a short time) the golden age of steam.

In the 1950s Mum's mother, who we called Nainy, still lived in the family home in Holyhead, the same house where Mum and her sister Maudie were bought up in the 20s and 30s. Nainy's husband John was killed at Dunkirk during the war. Nainy was tiny at barely 5ft tall softly spoken and with a bit of a twinkle in her eye. She died when I was 12 but I do remember her visiting us in Bletchley when I was quite small and again when we went up to Holyhead. The likeness between Nainy and Mum was uncanny. In fact after her first grandchild was born Mum was known as Nainy herself until the end of her life. Mum told us that hers was a close, loving, and caring family, she always spoke well of her parents and the sudden loss of her father in such awful circumstances must have been devastating.

We would go to Holyhead and visit every year and stay for most of the school summer holidays when we were quite young up until Nainy died. Auntie Maudie was looking after Nainy at the time and Mum took over during our visits to give her a bit of a break. For me and my sisters the trip to Holyhead was a huge event, we loved it up there and looked forward to it for weeks. We travelled by train and set off quite early as it took about 5 hours to get there.

The departure day would start with us eagerly looking up the road waiting for the taxi to take us to the station. Always on time the black cab would draw up outside the house and Mr. Purcell, with pipe in mouth and wearing his black peaked cap would knock on the door. We were more than ready. The inside of the taxi had a lovely aroma of worn leather mingled with pipe tobacco which hit us as we'd slide into the soft and comfortable back seat. As Mum squashed in beside us Dad and Mr. Purcell put the large brown cases in the boot, we were soon off on the short journey to the station. When we got there, we'd spot Bernard Brown in his booth ready to clip our tickets. (Bernard was the magician in the same concert party as Dad during the war; years later I got to know him quite well.) The train would arrive noisily in a cloud of steam and smoke amid the opening and slamming of doors. Once aboard and having found a compartment the cases were heaved up onto the netted luggage rack, the guard blew his whistle, waved his green flag and with clouds of smoke bellowing from the chimney the train would slowly pull out of the station. We were off! We travelled as far as Rugby or Crewe where we'd change trains and await 'The Irish Mail'. Sometimes we'd have to wait as long as an hour before it pulled in alongside us on the platform. Invariably it was full, and it was often difficult to find seats for us all and we'd have to sit on the cases in the corridor. There was one occasion when the guard took pity on us and insisted we sat in an empty First-Class compartment. (I'm sure we didn't look like typical First-Class passengers with our home-made sandwiches and flasks of tea.) By the time we got past Chester the scenery began to change, and we knew we were on the final stage of the journey. We'd listen and smile as we heard the railway announcers with that lovely Welsh lilt…

"Calling at Rhyl, Colwyn Bay, Llandudno Junction, Penmaenmawr, Llanfairfechan (my favourite), Bangor, and Holyhead."

That final part of the journey was magical as it ran parallel to the sea. We were happy to stand in the corridor by a door and pull the leather strap down a notch to open the window and get a whiff of the sea tainted by the smoke from the train as it puffed along towards Holyhead. When we got there, we found a porter with a trolley, loaded it up and joined the crowds of people making their way towards the station entrance. Many of the passengers were already joining a queue for the next stage of their journey which was the boat across the Irish Sea to Ireland. We headed for the taxi rank and clambered inside for the five-minute journey to 11 Armenia Street, a small Victorian mid terraced house with a green door and a black iron knocker. As Mum knocked on the door Dad paid the taxi driver and sorted out the cases and soon Nainy or Auntie Maudie would be there to meet us. As Mum and Dad talked about the journey, we sat down on a shiny old black leather settee in front of the window. One side of the room was taken up with a Victorian solid black cast iron range. There would be a kettle sitting majestically on the hob with steam starting to

*Me and Jean, on the steps of
11 Armenia Street*

emerge from its long spout in readiness for a welcome cup of tea. In front of the range was a hearth with a selection of brass tongs and pokers complete with a matching coal scuttle. The room at the rear of the house was the Parlour, 'to be used for special occasions'. (As we grew bigger though, it became a temporary bedroom.) On the walls throughout the house hung large photographic portraits of Victorian family members looking stern formal and sedate. To the rear of the house was the kitchen which was tiny. There was an old sink with a single tap fixed to the wall. Opposite that was a small table with a white Baby Belling oven sitting on top of it. There wasn't room for anything else. The kitchen door opened onto a small yard and housed in a small shed was the toilet. This was built from stone bricks and was only big enough for a WC… and there was no heating. The door was thin and not a particularly good fit. It was kept shut (not locked) on the inside with a hook and eye; 'basic' is a word that springs to mind. Nobody complained though, unless a spider made an appearance. There were two bedrooms upstairs in the house and no bathroom. There was however in each room a large Victorian bowl with a matching jug filled with cold water. The cast iron beds seemed huge and had brass fittings with a ball on each corner, and of course under the beds (which were high) sat chamber pots. When we were small, somehow we all managed to squeeze into the house, eventually though me and Dad stayed with family friends who lived close by.

Opposite the house was the local shop owned by Mr. Roche, a lovely man. Sometimes I would go with him in his battered old black van delivering groceries around the local villages. It took a while as he spent a lot of time chatting to his customers, mostly in Welsh. The fact that the shop was so close meant that a lot of our hard saved pocket money was spent in there, mostly on sweets and ice cream. Next to the shop was a lane which led to the sea front at the bottom of which was a white building, 'The Laundry'. You could almost smell it from the house, not unpleasant at all, steam, and detergent. Once past it and just round the corner were the alleyways at the backs of the houses, this was our short cut to the seafront. Often smelly with over filled dustbins by the back gates and the obvious presence of dogs, we weren't bothered. We were going to the beach!

The seafront and beaches of Holyhead remain unchanged to this day. The cast iron railings and small wall that ran along the front are still there. There is a photograph of Mum as a young girl standing in front of those same railings taken almost a hundred years ago.

Holyhead in the 1950s was not a typical seaside town. The beaches were never overly crowded and were mostly frequented by local people. A steep stepped path on a grassy slope led down to the beach from the road which attracted masses of grasshoppers. The beach was in sections divided by sea walls which ran out into the sea for some distance. On one of these a yellow boat was moored offering trips round the harbour. The 'Captain' was a tall man with a flat cap and one arm. We did the trip a few times over the years, and it was interesting to get up close to the Mail Boats in the harbour. We would spend hours on the beach and on arrival would head straight for a large rock formation which was great to play on and to hide behind to change in and out of swimming costumes. When the tide was in, we'd have a wonderful time. Me and Jean couldn't swim but we would have a go with a rubber ring, happy just to splash about. About 20 yards out from the shore there was a raft with a diving board attached which is where the strong swimmers tended to congregate. I often dreamed of being strong enough to join them one day but never did. There were also a group of local lads who dived and swam off McKenzie Pier which was adjacent to the beach. Often, we would go and watch them as they swam underwater barely visible and took turns to jump or dive from the pier walls. They challenged each other to greater heights and risks; on one occasion a young chap climbed up the lamppost (a feat in itself) and performed a beautiful swallow dive from the bar at the top, to much applause from the Hawes family. There was little commercially along the front apart from a large cafe which, in a former life, was the lifeboat house; today it's a small museum. Inside I remember a jukebox playing popular music of the day. A song has just popped into my head from that era, 'Goodbye Jimmy Goodbye', by Ruby Murray. I Googled it and as it's playing, I find myself transported back there to a sunny afternoon in 1959. I can see the counter with cake and sandwiches on display, rows of cups and saucers ready to be filled with tea from a large steel teapot. There's a small queue with mothers and irritable children, and another group of youngsters peering into the ice cream display cabinet. We'd have been there of course, three children with bottles of orange pop and straws, Mum and Auntie Maudie sipping their cups of tea, and Dad (hopelessly overdressed with his thick shirt and trousers and sports jacket and tie) anxiously peering at his cine camera. He was constantly worried about sand getting into the workings. As well as the music playing in the background, Welsh children were chatting and arguing in their lovely accents, and outside on the beach could be heard that distinctive call of the seagull

Me and Dad, hopelessly overdressed with the ever present camera

which for us will always be synonymous with Holyhead. When the sun shone and the tide was in, we were on the beach happily playing and splashing about in the water. If the tide was out, that was impossible. The sea went out for quite a distance and the shore would be covered with masses of seaweed. Then it would be a case of away with the rubber rings and bring on the buckets! - "Let's go crabbing!' Sometimes in the evenings depending on the tide and weather Auntie Maudie took us to a part of Holyhead called Salt Island to do a bit of shrimp and winkle fishing. The technique was simple. The bait was a limpet which was bashed off the rocks with a heavy stone. The resulting mush was dropped into a net and then into one of many large rock pools. Once the shrimp got the scent, they'd swim straight into the net which was quickly lifted and emptied into a bucket. Job done. Winkles could be found under rocks, and they joined the shrimp in the bucket. The sun would be setting as we trudged home tired out after a day in the sunshine. What better way to end it than a shrimp and winkle supper, with vinegar and toast of course.

Dad loved Holyhead as much as we did. Given the opportunity he would have moved up there I reckon. With his 9.5 cine camera always around his neck we would walk for miles. He had a thing about always being prepared, so on many of our walks he would insist on us carrying plastic macs, "In case it rains," even when there wasn't a cloud in the sky and a minimal chance of a few drops we'd still have to carry a plastic mac. Most of the walks took us around the rather lovely heather clad area called Rocky Coast which surrounds Holyhead Mountain. Sometimes we would go as far as the beginning of the breakwater, the Victorian built structure which dominates the front in Holyhead. One day Dad suggested that the two of us go for a walk along it and perhaps even get to the lighthouse at the end. I was up for that and off we went. It was hard work on the concrete in the sunshine and wearing a pair of plastic sandals (and carrying the plastic mac didn't help.) Heaven knows how Dad coped with his usual winter clothing. We did make it though, and as luck would have it there was a lighthouse keeper there pottering about. My Dad went up to him and said, "Excuse me brother, but the old boy has been pestering me all morning about having a look inside the lighthouse when we get to it, be a shame to disappoint him after walking all this way."

I hadn't said a word! What I had said was, "Are we nearly there yet? I'm thirsty, my feet hurt, and can we go back now?"

Anyway the keeper obviously took pity on me and in we went for a conducted tour which was fascinating. It was a bit of a slog for a little lad like me (1.7 miles) but definitely worth it. Dad always referred to me as boy, or the old boy, and called every stranger he met 'brother', even after the many times we asked him if those complete strangers really were his brothers.

Several times we walked to the top of the mountain from where the view is stunning. On a clear day you can see Ireland across the Irish Sea and in the other direction the peaks of Snowdonia. As well as the breath- taking view was the silence, the only sounds coming from the wind and seagulls as they hovered above us. If we had time and the weather was good, we'd walk over the mountain to the South Stack lighthouse. A spectacular sight with 365 steps (as we were reminded every year) leading down the cliff to a narrow suspension bridge and that distinctive white lighthouse. Every time we went there, Dad would film the same scene panning

On top of Holyhead Mountain

from the top to the bottom probably overawed by it and forgetting he had filmed exactly the same thing many times before. By the time we'd walked down and back up the steps we'd be too tired and irritable to walk back so we'd catch a bus back to the centre of Holyhead. We also used the bus to take us to Trearddur Bay or Porth Dafarch which were other popular beaches in the area.

Dad used his cine camera a lot in Wales and when he got home the film, which was inside a cartridge, was sent away to be developed. It came back in the post on a small plastic reel. He would eagerly unwind the first few feet, "*to make sure it came out,*" peering through a pair of Nainy's ill-fitting old glasses (he wouldn't admit he needed an Optician) and then, when he was in the mood, the projector would come out and we'd have a film show. It was never straight forward though. The projector would have to balance on a pile of books so that it would line up with the centre of the screen positioned on the opposite wall. Sometimes he'd get himself into a state when the film would uncoil and tumble off the over-filled reels and end up on the floor. He'd get annoyed too when the film would be backwards or upside down. When I was into my early teens, I offered to do it for him, and he did finally relent which enabled him to concentrate on his commentary which he loved to do particularly if we had the neighbours in. The only comment I got from him was, "I should have done this years ago!"

Over the years a lot of footage was taken, and the short films were joined up to fit a larger reel. They are lovely to look at today having been transferred to a DVD format. Even though Dad wasn't particularly imaginative with his film making (there is a lot of repetition) they are still a record of a bygone era as well as being a poignant reminder of some of the happiest days of my life.

By 1961 my sisters had become friendly with some local girls and Dad had to go back home for work reasons and Mum was busy looking after Nainy, so I was left pretty much to my own devices. Even at the age of eleven I had the freedom to go wherever I wanted. I went for a walk by the station one day and discovered a hole in the fence by the side of the engine sheds. I squeezed through and walked across some waste ground to a wall. I peered over the top and was delighted to see lines of steam locomotives with the unmistakable sounds and smells of those majestic machines. It was heaven for a trainspotter. I popped into town and bought a notebook and pen at Chadwick's newsagents, and I was in business. I'd go trainspotting for a couple of hours first thing in the mornings, then I'd go to an area of the beach I'd found by the Coastguard station called 'The Borth'. This was great because there were piles of blue slates all over the shore, perfect for skimmimg - I was having a great time. As I made my way home for lunch one day, I had to pass my sisters and their friends who were sitting on a doorstep. One of the Welsh girls called out to me and said, "You're very independent Ken." I didn't really understand what she was on about, I'd have to find out.

"What does independent mean, Mum?" I asked when I got in.

"Why do you want to know?" asked Mum.

"One of the Welsh girls told me that's what I am."

"It means that you like your own company."

"What does that mean?"

Mum thought for a moment and said,

"When you're on your own, are you happy?"

"Yes," I said.

"Then that's what being independent means."

That was typical of Mum, being happy was all that mattered.

CHAPTER 2

The Magic Bug Bites

In 1962 my Auntie Maudie gave me a small diary. She said that providing I'd write something in it every day then next year she would buy me another one. I had a look at the small green book which measured 4 inches by 2 inches, opened it up and noticed there were only 5 lines on which to write stuff. If I wrote big, I could probably get away with a just few words. I was up for the challenge. Somehow, I did it. The following year she bought me a five-year diary I completed that and that's when she decided enough was enough, which was fair enough. I bought another five year one after that and in the early 70s I started buying a more traditional desk diary each year. To cut a long 60-year story short I haven't missed a day since January 1st, 1962. As you can imagine having a written record of every day of your life can make interesting reading (and a Godsend when writing an autobiography.) The following is a selection of entries from that first diary of 1962 exactly how they were written, I was 12 years old.

January 2nd: *I bought myself a pack of cards I am thinking of being a conjurer.*
September 13th: *Mum had her hair done she looked beautiful, pretty, LOVELY, and lots of other things.*
October 23rd: *There is bad trouble in Cuba there is danger of WAR there hadn't better be one.*

November 1st: *I went to the dentist today I have lost my bookmark it's the best I've ever had.*

November 15th: *Maggs went to choir practice Mum burnt her hair this morning nothing serious it's freezing cold.*

December 15th: *The concert went ok my first public appearance as a magician was jolly good, I shall appear next in the school talent competition.*

As well as having a lot of affection for my Mum, it's also interesting to read of me thinking about being a conjurer in January, and actually being one and completing my first appearance in December. That first show which was organised by the Sunday School was originally going to be an all-music event featuring the choir and individual singers, then somebody suggested a comedy sketch or two, and one of my sister's said, "Ken could do his tricks!". Then I piped up with, "Dad could play his saw!"

It would seem that both me and Dad were volunteered. Anyway, Dad was up for it as the Guest Artiste and rehearsals began. As well as performing magic for the first time I was also making my debut as an actor. I had a walk on part as a paper boy in the short one act play which opened the second half. The first half finished and after a short interval the curtains noisily opened, and the play began. I stood at the side of the stage nervously waiting for my cue. The young actor (Roger Tarbox) said his line, "Ah! Here comes the paperboy!" and pointed dramatically to the left. With the eyes of the audience following his pointing finger, I walked on from the **right** to howls of laughter from the audience. I decided to stick to the magic.

I honestly don't remember the tricks I did that night, but I do recall how I felt. The buzz of excitement and nervous energy I derived from performing in front of a live audience was memorable.

Looking back, I'm pretty sure that little show was the moment when Dad decided to encourage me all the way. He did say to me afterwards there would be a report in the Bletchley Gazette and to go and buy a scrapbook to stick the cutting in, implying that this would be the first of many which indeed it was.

My first performance on December 15th, 1962, was the culmination of events that began in 1961. Dad gave me a magic book which he'd had for years. It was by Will Goldston and was really old even then. The unusual thing about it was that it opened from bottom to top. There was nothing in it for the beginner it was more of an explanation of old props and illusions. Soon after that though one of my school chums gave me a book called Magic Made Simple (or similar). This was more like it! It had tricks with coins, matches, handkerchiefs, and cards, and would account for me buying my first pack in January. A school friend of mine, 'Bonzo', was also showing an interest and he had some tricks for Christmas which (according to my diary) he sold to me. I was really getting into it, I ordered 'Paper Magic' by Robert Harbin from the library, and for my birthday Dad gave me a large box of second-hand tricks and books. I also had, 'The Eagle Book of Magic' which was a book of press-out cardboard tricks. My second performance as a magician at the school talent competition was due to be on February 21st. Better get practising!

By this time I had left Water Eaton Junior School which I loved and was now at the recently renamed Leon Secondary. Prior to that it had been known for years as Bletchley Road. It's an old building that remains a school to this day. The talent competition was part of an inter-house festival rather than something for individuals. A week-long programme of events and competitions was held, from spelling to woodwork. The Talent Show (as it was called) was one of the final events. There were four houses in the school - Hampden, Milton, Cowper, and Penn. I was in Cowper. Auditions were held and each House was given time to come up with, rehearse and perform a 20-minute show. I arrived at the audition along with the rest of the brave volunteers and after an anxious wait it was my turn. I carried my table onto the stage which was made from an old music stand and a piece of plywood. The tricks I had decided to do were - multiplying billiard balls (which were the size of marbles), colour-changing handkerchief (again very small), and fanning cards. These were the cards I bought in January from Woolworths, the backs were of a colourful Indian chief in full regalia; they looked nice when fanned out, and for my big finish, my newly invented floating ball trick! It utilised a two-inch plastic ball, one of Mum's scarves, a painted egg box, and a spoke from an old bicycle wheel.

"When you're ready then Kenneth," said the young producer.

I went for it!

When I'd finished my act which lasted about five minutes she said, "Very good, but aren't you going to say something; Don't they call it patter?"

"No, I usually perform to background music," I lied.

"That's ok," she said, "There's a record player linked to the sound system in the small room by the stage, we'll play something on that. Next."

I was in! Somehow a show was cobbled together. The rehearsals didn't go too well but we knew we had a good act to finish. Alan Richardson was going to mime to, 'Jack the Ripper' a popular record of the day by Screaming Lord Sutch. He had good make-up and a costume covered in fake blood and as he "sang" he danced spookily around a darkly painted cardboard coffin in the middle of the stage. It looked great! The big day arrived; I was on towards the end of the show. The act before me, two lads telling jokes, performed in front of the curtains, so I was able to put my table on the stage behind them. In no time at all they had finished, the curtains pulled back, and I was on. I squinted out towards the audience and could see nothing, totally blinded by the spotlight. I picked up my first prop and looked towards the small room by the side of the stage and nodded for my background music (quite professionally I thought) but all I could see were blank faces.

"Music," I mouthed.

"What?" They mouthed back.

"Music," I mouthed back louder.

Nothing - they'd forgotten! I did the whole act in total silence; I got through it ok and left the stage to a smattering of applause. As soon as I was off, Alan was on being Jack the Ripper bringing our show to a noisy and spectacular end. Backstage it was relief all round we'd pulled it off. Then somebody said,

"Who's won?"

The Headmaster was on the stage congratulating everybody for providing so much entertainment,

"Somebody has to win," he was saying, "And the winners are… Cowper!!"

The next day I was approached by the Headmaster, Mr. Bradshaw, asking me if I would like to take part in a school concert in April. I had obviously performed better than I thought. The real reason I suspect was that he was desperate for acts. I agreed to do it but soon realised I'd have to get some new tricks. I had a chat with Dad, and he went to see Bernard Brown (magician/railway ticket collector) to see if he had any for sale or failing that details of where we could buy some. Sadly he had already given away a lot of stuff, but he did have the address of the Davenport Magic Company in London. The catalogue was duly sent for and arrived within a few days. It was huge - 400 pages! Me and Dad went through it page by page. The drawings and descriptions of many of the tricks were inspiring, I could already see myself plucking cards from thin air or producing loads of silk handkerchiefs from a small square empty box. Dad did make the point that it would be a good idea to buy a trick the audience would remember, something different and unusual that they'd probably never seen before. Another thing that had to be considered was the expense. In the end Dad agreed to contribute something but I would have to make up the difference. We came to a decision and ordered two tricks; 'silk handkerchief to egg' (silk not provided) and the 'swallowing razor blades' trick.

March 15th, 1963: *Dad has offered to give me 10 shillings for a trick from Davenports I have got 6shillings and ninepence of my own.*
March 16th: *Dad got the postal order for Davenports I am getting 2 tricks they come to the value of £1.*
March 17th: *I posted the postal order for Davenports this afternoon it went by the 4-30 post.*
March 19th: *The tricks arrived from Davenports they are smashing I can do them a treat the egg got a bit cracked in the post.*

The razor blade trick worked really well, it was certainly different and wasn't difficult to do but did require a bit of nerve, after all razor blades are sharp. I had some trouble with the egg trick though. The fake yolk didn't look convincing as it was made of plastic, the fake plastic shell was cracked, and for the white of the yolk I had to go to the chemist and buy a bottle of glycerine which was more expense and embarrassing too as I had to explain to the chemist what it was for. It wouldn't be the last time I'd be disappointed with a mail order trick.

For the next few weeks I worked really hard to get the act in shape. I had a black cover for my table which came from Dad's living marionette booth, which was long enough to cover the rusty music stand. For a costume I'd bought a second hand flashy blue jacket from the market, and I now had background music on a small reel-to-reel tape recorder. The only way I could record music was to put the microphone up against the speaker of our new radiogram while a record was playing; I didn't have the time or money to buy a new record, so I had to make use of what we had in our rather meagre collection. I decided on 'The Magic of Mantovani and his Orchestra.' As you can tell I wasn't exactly spoiled for choice. One evening I put the record on standby and positioned the microphone and then had to make sure nobody came in while I was recording. A notice stuck to the door did the trick – 'Do not enter, recording in progress!!' It seemed to have worked ok until I played it back. Every so often there was a strange clanging noise. Mum had just set the fire and the noise came from bits of coke and clinker dropping into the metal tray underneath. I left it - nobody noticed. I cobbled the act together and rehearsed for weeks and finally it was as good as it was going to get.

The show was performed 4 times, a full afternoon dress rehearsal for the local Darby and Joan Club, two performances for the public on consecutive nights, and finally another afternoon show for the school. All went well, and the swallowing razor blade trick went really well.

April 5th, 1963: *My fifth public appearance also went very well indeed. DAVID PARRISS a member of the Magic Circle was in the audience.*

Following the shows Dad went to see David (a local magician) who still lived at home with his parents and brothers over the family sweet shop in Fenny Stratford. David was very kind and said that he enjoyed my performance and suggested that we go along and watch him perform at a show in a couple of weeks' time in Bletchley. The plan was for him to meet us and have a chat afterwards. On April 27th, 1963, me and Dad duly turned up at The Labour Hall on the Buckingham Road to watch a grand variety show. David did two spots, a stand-up routine in front of the curtains which involved a member of the audience having his head chopped off, and a silent act which I believe closed the show. He did card productions, card fans, a multiplying billiard ball routine and ended with the floating ball. Both me and Dad were really amazed and very impressed! We had a chat afterwards and I told him I was working on a new act.

"Ok", he said, "Good luck with that, when it's all together I'll come over and have a look, and don't forget, practise makes perfect."

"I didn't know you were working on a new act," said Dad on the way home.

"I am now," I replied, "I think I'll do card productions, multiplying billiard balls, and the floating ball, and I might do thimbles."

Now that we were on the Davenports mailing list, pamphlets and flyers often came in the post. In one of these was a book I just had to have. 'It's easier than you think' by Geoffrey Buckingham.

It cost 26 shillings which in today's money equates to about £18. I had no money, so I was reliant on Dad helping out. First of all I explained to him the books worth, how it describes in great detail how to perform the multiplying billiard ball trick, a 13-ball routine! And there are sections of coin and thimble manipulation, all with top quality photographs. He thought for a moment and said the only way he could afford it was to sell something. I got the book… we didn't use that old tent anyway.

By now the weather was improving, Spring was in the air, Summer was on the way, and I couldn't wait to get outside. Although magic was obviously a major part of my life, it never did become all-consuming. I did have other interests, I spent much of the Easter holidays with my pals, Roger Tarbox (the actor from my first show) and Ken Rainey, who lived next door. We went trainspotting, cycling, walking, fishing, and kicked a ball about for hours. Both Roger and Ken went on to play football for local teams and were very successful. I played for the school team once, I was probably picked as a last resort.

Me, 'Skinner' Rainey, Roger Tarbox and his family friend

September 20th, 1963: *I have been chosen for the school football team. Janice came up to see Maggs.*
September 21st: *We lost our football match 16 nil. I have got a new pair of shoes.*

Needless to say, that was my first and last appearance in the school football team. Team sport was still definitely not my thing. I was however still interested in athletics. When I was at Junior school I'd shone at the long jump and loved it. One day when Roger and Ken were elsewhere, I went to the library and after a futile search for magic books went over to the Sports section for a browse, eventually arriving at 'Athletics'. There were books on each discipline, and I finally found one that covered everything. I took it home and read up about different long jump techniques and was anxious to have another go at it. Due to the absence of a long jump pit, it was never going to be easy. I turned the page to the High Jump and read with interest the various techniques; Straddle, Scissors, and the Western Roll. Here was something I could do! I went to the shed and found a length of old washing line which Dad would keep for his allotment for his runner bean frames. I also found a couple of broken broom handles (obviously from the brush factory) and after some experimentation I rigged up a high jump set. I studied the book and decided to have a go at the Western Roll purely because it sounded better than the other two. I had a great time and raised the bar consistently during the day.

When I went back to school after the holidays, it was athletics season, and our first PE lesson was the High Jump. It took place in the playground with a set up made of a garden cane for the cross bar and thick pieces of wood set in small buckets of concrete for the uprights. If my memory serves me correctly the games teacher, Mr. Powney (who I really liked) taught us the Scissors technique. We formed a line, and each took a turn on leaping over the bar. When it came to my turn, I jumped over it quite easily and started to run round to rejoin the queue. Mr. Powney called me back.

"Hawes, do that again!"

I went back and leapt over the bar for a second time.

"Do you know what you did there, Hawes"?

"Yes sir, the Western Roll."

"How did you learn it?"

"From a library book sir."

"Good Heavens! Well done, Hawes. Have 5 House Marks."

I couldn't have done anything but the Western Roll having spent a complete day doing nothing else.

Further into the summer we'd have swimming lessons at the outdoor and unheated Queens Pool in Bletchley. At the time I couldn't swim so I was in the shallow end with one of those polystyrene floats. I was often tempted to bite into it for some reason probably to stop my teeth chattering. Mr. Powney would get in the water with us, but he'd be further up having a one-to-one lesson from an instructor. I have to give him credit here for being a non-swimmer prepared to be taught with the rest of us. During the following week or two, I would go to the pool quite regularly after school and at weekends with my pals. I was slowly gaining confidence. I remember one occasion when I walked up to the deep end by the diving board (I still couldn't swim) and stood at the side close to the end of the pool, *if I dived in across the diagonal, surely momentum would carry me to the handrail below the diving board.* There was only one way to find out. It took me a while to pluck up the courage but finally I dived. Success! That gave me the confidence to do almost anything, and I was soon swimming. I went along to the next lesson happily swimming across the width of the pool and I noticed Mr. Powney looking at me with some surprise.

"Been to the library again, Hawes?"

"No sir, been practising."

"Well done," he said, floundering to the poolside.

In spite of being laid up for a week or two with glandular fever and falling off the barn roof (no doubt showing off again), I had somehow managed to get the new act together. I'd worked hard with my new book and had acquired: A set of one and a half inch wooden balls sprayed brush factory red, a giant thimble made from the bottom of a bedside lamp (also sprayed brush factory red), some fanning powder (to make the now almost worn out "Indian" cards spread more easily), and Dad had the ball holders made by a lady at the brush factory in return for a bag of mixed veg from the allotment. I had the props but what to wear was the next problem. Anything brand new was out of the question so I was always on the lookout for anything that was either cheap or free. Much to Mum and Dad's amusement I came home one day with an old dinner jacket suit I'd bought in a jumble sale for Five Bob (25p). It was of a 1920s style with the huge lapels and of course was miles too big. My Dad immediately came up with idea of asking my Auntie Vera, who was a seamstress, to alter it for me. I duly went over to her house to be measured up and some weeks later it was ready, I have to say she did a brilliant job, and I was able to wear it for a couple of years before I grew out of it. I already had a white school shirt, and I bought a clip-on bow tie from Woolworths and, with an old top hat, bought from Sid's Junk Shop in Bletchley, I was ready to go. Before running the act passed David Parriss, I said to Dad that it would be a good idea to try it out somewhere first.

"Leave it with me," he said.

He got in touch with a local old people's club called The Evergreens and they were certainly up for any sort of entertainment.

To make a show of it my sisters sang solos and duets, and Dad played his saw. We had a great time, and the elderly audience loved it. I don't know if he was aware of the importance of it, but Dad never missed an opportunity to get me performing, I did little shows for neighbours, relatives, and friends, and even anybody who came to the door was an audience, whether they wanted to or not.

By now the act was ready and rehearsed and it was time to get in touch with David Parriss. Even though Dad cycled past the Parriss sweet shop every day on his way to work and could easily have dropped a note in for David or phoned him, for some reason he sent him a letter with a stamped addressed envelope enclosed, the reply came back with a nice letter from David (which I still have) - he would come and visit on the 24th of July 1963.

The act was set up in the front room. As the time approached, I looked nervously out of the window wondering what sort of car he'd have. I have to say I was slightly disappointed when he arrived on his Mum's bike. He came in and sat on the pre-arranged seat as I went through the act. When I'd finished, the first thing he said was,

"You have been watching me haven't you!"

He asked me to set it all up again and he would stop me and comment as I went along. I donned the top hat.

"That looks stupid for a start," he said.

I carried on (minus the top hat, which was never worn again) and he made some valid points as I went through it. He did like my thimble routine and the comments he made were very encouraging. He stayed for about an hour and gave us contact details of more magic dealers, and as he left, he said, "When you're a bit older, I'd recommend you join the Northamptonshire Magicians Club, I'll put a word in."

That night was the beginning of a close friendship that would last over 40 years.

One of the magic dealers recommended by David was Harry Stanley's Unique Magic Studio based in London. We sent off for the latest catalogue and between us made a list of tricks that I might be able to do, and Dad could afford. Although he wasn't earning a lot of money in the brush factory, Dad was well thought of and his boss, Mr. Cook, was very generous with his annual bonus. I'm assuming that's where the money would come from to pay for my next batch of tricks. Having said that though, Dad certainly wouldn't waste money (something he was known for). He also decided that, rather than take the risk of being disappointed when a trick by mail order didn't meet our expectations or indeed get damaged in the post, it made sense to see a trick demonstrated before buying. We would have a trip to London.

Early one morning we got on the train at Bletchley station bound for Euston. On the way I was eagerly having another read of the catalogue. The name Ken Brooke was on just about every page. He seemed to have a hand in the routines of most of the tricks in there. It took about an hour to get to Euston and another hour to get to the studio at 14 Frith Street. Dad would never use the tube or public transport.

"Why pay when you can walk?"

He also liked to look in the windows of the many radio shops along Tottenham Court Road. When we got to the end, we spotted a small shop with magic props in the window. I believe it was called 'The Magic Shop'. We had a quick browse, but it seemed to specialise in jokes and novelties rather than "proper" magic. We wandered down Oxford Street and then turned left into Soho. Frith Street was a short walk away. It may well have been a short walk but there was a lot for a 13-year-old to look at! We walked up and down trying in vain to find number 14. We finally came to the conclusion that it must be between two rather seedy looking shops and up a flight of stairs. Up we went and came to a door with a sign, 'Harry Stanley's Unique Magic Studio'. We pushed the door open and found ourselves in an airy well-lit room. There was a sofa underneath the window, and a small table with a couple of chairs in the middle of the room. To the left was a bar and a couple of stools and around the room were various props on display. The wall next to the door was covered with autographed photos of famous magicians. 'To Ken and Harry best wishes Fred Kapps', 'All the best from Johnny Hart' - It was like a Who's Who of world stars of magic. Suddenly a man popped out from the small room behind the bar. He had a friendly face and demeanour with a smart Brylcreemed haircut. He wore an open necked white shirt, grey trousers, and red braces.

"Hello, are you Mr. Stanley?" asked Dad.

"No, my name's Ken Brooke," he replied, with a pronounced Northern dialect.

We told him where we were from and what I'd been up to and soon got onto the subject of our list. Dad began to read it out and then Ken asked to see it. He looked at each item and as he read down the list he said,

"No. No. No. Fanning cards - Yes."

He told us to take a seat and said,

"You could spend a fortune in here, and I could sell you what's on your list. If I did that, you'd be wasting your money. At the lad's age you need to buy him something that will give him an education. Something that will give him not just a good start, but the right one."

He reached underneath the bar and came up with a book.

"Take my advice, and buy him this book, 'The Dai Vernon Book of Magic'. This book will give him his magical education for life. The first two chapters alone are worth the price of it. Those two chapters will tell him how and when to perform, the importance of being natural, what misdirection really means and how you apply it to suit yourself."

"This book son," he said, looking at me, "Is my Bible!!"

He was obviously very passionate, and he didn't stop there. He sat at the table, and we joined him. He showed us six coins and a ring and then one by one they appeared to be knocked clean through the table.

"That's just one of the tricks in the book," he said, "Here's another…"

We stood up as he went to the back of the shop and came back with a black leather cone about six inches high and a large white ball, he covered the ball with a cone, lifted it, the ball was gone! Still he went on, and bought out three copper cups, and three small balls. A ball was placed on top of each cup, he picked up a ball, then a wand, tapped his hand with the wand, the ball had gone, he did the same thing with the other two. The balls then appeared underneath the cups! To my 13-year-old eyes this was wonderful stuff, this was real magic.

"In this book," said Ken, riffling through it, "Are tricks with coins, cards, rope, linking rings and even thimbles, but nothing is more worthy than those first two chapters."

I looked at Dad as he asked the price.

"Forty-five shillings," came the reply.

Bearing in mind that's about £35 in today's money and probably more than he'd earn in a week, it was an awful lot of money to part with, especially for a book. I waited as Dad thought about it; he looked at me, and all I could come up with was, "There are a lot of good tricks in it."

"Ok," he said, "We'll have the book and the fanning cards."

I assumed Dad had spent all that he'd wanted to, or even all that he had. We went for a wander for some time walking round the big stores Selfridges and Hamleys and then made our way back to Euston. When we were on the train Dad asked to have a look at the book, he opened the front cover and asked me if I had a pencil, I handed one over to him and I noticed he was writing something,

"What are you doing?" I asked.

"I'm changing that 45 to a 25. If your Mum knew how much money I spent on a book, she'd never speak to me again."

The burning question is, of course, was it worth it? Yes, it was, although it did take me a few years to discover its true value. The first thing I did the next day was to make a start on learning 'coins through the table'. I did quickly glance through those first two chapters, but quite honestly, I was too young to take on board the subject matter, I was lacking not only in performing experience, but life experience too. At that age it was all about the trick and not the performance of it.

Years later of course I read and absorbed every word of those first two chapters. To this day I perform material from the book (having put my own stamp on it.) The ball transposition became my trick with hazel nuts, The four ace routine became a trick with four queens with an added coin production. Both of these helped me to win competitions over the years. The cups and balls routine gave me a good groundwork to eventually create my own. The cone trick, and thimble routine I did in a stage act. All of this material saved me (or my Dad) from buying tricks. In that sense the book was wonderful value.

Many years later when I was in my twenties, Dai Vernon came to London (he was a Canadian living in America). He was to receive an award from The Magic Circle. A dinner was given in his honour in a private room in a posh London hotel. I'm not sure how the guest list was compiled, but I was on it.

A self-conscious me standing behind Dai Vernon while he chats to Lewis Ganson

There were about 20 of us there all of whom sat around a large circular table. After a drink or two at the bar (which was in the room) we sat down for the meal. The food was memorable not for being overly grand, but for being quintessentially English. It was something like steak and kidney pie followed by Spotted Dick. It was lovely. After the meal the table was cleared, coffee was served, and cigars smoked. Next came the presentation and speeches. After that the table was cleared and two bottles of Port were placed on the table and glasses were distributed. The Magic Circle secretary John Salisse tapped the table and said,

"It is a great honour to have Dai Vernon as our special guest here this evening, I'm sure every member sat around this table will have something to say about his magic and philosophy and what it has meant to them over the years. Let's start over there."

He pointed to a chap on the other side of the table who had no choice but to stand up and speak. He spoke about how the Vernon books on card magic had had a huge influence on his technique. He sat down and after a nod from John the chap next to him stood. Now I'm starting to panic, *what the hell am I going to say?* There was no escape. Luckily, I had a while to think of something as my turn came ever nearer. Meanwhile the bottles of Port were being passed round and I was able to have a glass full before I got the nod. I stood up and spoke about the day Dad bought me the book and of the faith he had in me to appreciate it's value, and of Ken Brooke and the enthusiasm he had for it, how he went through some of the material, and how much I had learned from it about the art of close-up magic… how to perform, as well as what to perform. I told them about Dad changing the 45 to 25 which got a huge laugh. I ended by saying the words Ken Brooke said to me on that day… "This book son, is my Bible."

I ended by looking at Dai Vernon and saying, "I would like to say with much gratitude, that your wonderful and informative book became my Bible too."

I sat down with some relief.

Before the evening finished, I had a quick word with the great man.

"Nice speech son," he said, before I could say anything.

"Thank you! Could I ask you a question?"

"Go ahead."

"What is the correct way to pronounce your first name? Is it 'Day' or 'Dye', I hear both versions."

He looked at me, and with a twinkle in his eye said, "Eether or eyether."

CHAPTER 3

Growing Up

March 5th, 1963: *I got a magic book from the library. I had a picture of a NUDE given to me.*
March 6th, 1963: *I am coming to bed a bit earlier because I have got a headache.*

I never did have sex education, at home or school. Some of the local kids were given a book to read called *The Facts of Life*, which apparently would cover all they needed to know. Occasionally a copy would find its way outside and a bunch of us would look at it and giggle. I do remember overhearing a snippet of conversation between my Mum and Dad one day where Mum said something like, *you'll have to tell him something.*

This all came to a head one day. I was in the front room practising my magic, I was learning card productions at the time and the top hat was on the table ready to catch the cards and there were a few red balls next to it. Suddenly the door burst open, and Dad stood there looking a bit embarrassed and said, "One day, before you get much older, they'll drop!"

"What will? The cards?"

"No your balls!" And with that he left the room!

Of course I thought the obvious - *Better ditch the balls and concentrate on the cards then.*

Things happened in 1963 that would reverberate around the world for many years. This is how they were reported in my diary. I was 13 years old.

May 15th: *Not much has happened today. An American spaceman has gone up in space. The weather isn't too bad.*

August 8th: *There was a big train robbery today £1,000,000 stolen. I went to the rec.*

August 9th: *I have been fishing with Dad. I caught 11 altogether. £2,500,000 was stolen yesterday.*

November 22nd: *I went to see Alan. President Kennedy was assassinated. Jean went to the doctors (Glandular Fever).*

December 14th: *I made my tenth public appearance as a magician. It went very well. I've got earache bad. We had a fuse go.*

December 24th: *My first day as a paper boy went very well.*

Ahh, the innocence of youth.

Yes, I had got myself a job. At last my own money to spend on whatever I wanted. It was an early morning round from Brinklow's, the Newsagents in Fenny Stratford. There were about 30 papers and the round covered quite a large area. I had to work Monday to Saturday (when I had to do some collecting.) For all of this I was paid ten shillings and sixpence, (or a Ten Bob note and Half a Crown. Fifty-Two-and-a-half pence in today's money). I'd get to the shop at about six-thirty and Mr. Brinklow would mark the papers with the door numbers and put the batch on a large table at the back of the shop. I would then have to check them and make sure they were in the right order... 6, 8A,10, 1,3, 5, 21, 24, 26, 28, etc. (Who'd have thought, I still remember that sequence.)

One morning I was checking the papers as usual, and I noticed there was one missing.

"Number 21's missing," I said.

"He's dead, you'll have a long way to go if you want to give him a paper!"

Once checked, the bundle of papers was put into a large bag with a flap which went over my shoulders and off I'd go on my bike. There were two methods of carrying the bag, over your shoulder which meant you had to lean to the left to compensate, or if the load was light (it varied depending on magazines and comics) you could put the bag over the handlebars. If it was too heavy the bike wouldn't steer, as I found out to my cost the first time, I tried it. I coped with it all ok and in all weathers too; more to the point though, I was saving money.

In spite of being able to perform magic in front of a lot of people, I was still a quiet lad and quite shy. I didn't have much to say to Mr. Brinklow. It was best to avoid him anyway as he was always busy and a bit miserable. One day I went to the shop as usual and he picked up a copy of 'The Bletchley Gazette' and opened it up, and there was a photo of me looking very proud, displaying my new fanning cards in one hand and four balls in the other. I had just joined The Magic Club.

"Bloody hell," he said, "Is that you?"

"Yes, it is," I replied.

"Well done, Marvo!"

And that's what he called me until I left a couple of years later.

I was still enjoying my school days at Leon and loved the atmosphere of the old buildings. The Science room had old wooden benches that had small taps attached for a supply of gas.

There was little or no 'Health & Safety' in those days. A large bench was at the front which housed a sink big enough to allow pupils to gather round. The science teacher was Mr. Ripley who was a lovely man and clever too. He loved magic and always took an interest in what I was doing, and he dabbled himself doing a few card tricks. Occasionally when he had a rowdy class of pupils (which was often) he would stand in front of the blackboard and do 'back and front palming' with cards.

"Wow! Do that again, Sir."

"Only if you get on with your work!"

Years later after he'd left teaching, I did a magic show for his daughter's birthday party in a pub he'd bought near Aylesbury. It was nice to keep in touch.

Just down the corridor from the science room was Room 4, which was not only the school library but also the home of English teacher Eric "Buck" Jones - a real character. He was about 60 with thinning hair and a round ruddy face. He always dressed the same - tweed jacket with leather elbow patches, corduroy trousers, and thick brogue shoes. He spoke with a local accent and smoked a pipe and had been there for years. The first lesson I had with him (which was in Room 8) was memorable. For some reason our usual teacher Miss Smith was unavailable, so he filled in. We took our seats and waited. At exactly 2.00 o'clock he strode into the classroom. There was a lot of noise as he entered but all soon became quiet as he stood in front of the blackboard and glared at each of us. He began to speak…

"Charles Darwin once said that the only difference between a man and a monkey is the fact that a monkey cannot remember."

He turned to the blackboard and drew 3 columns with a word on top of each, Nouns, Verbs, and Adjectives.

"These are what are known as the parts of speech," he said, "I'm reliably informed that you already know that; let's find out if that is the case."

He asked the class for examples of each which he duly wrote in the appropriate columns. The class was for the most part well behaved apart from one lad who obviously wasn't paying attention. Buck went up to him and glared.

"What's your name son?" he asked quietly.

"Smith, Sir."

"Well Smith, you'd better buck your ideas up."

He raised his voice…

"Unless of course you really want to be bounced round the parish!!!"

Smith obviously didn't, he was well behaved after that, as indeed were the rest of us. The lesson continued. By now we were starting to warm to him, we were learning and having fun at the same time. Towards the end of the lesson he wrote a list of questions on the board and after we'd copied them into our exercise books, he spoke to us.

"I understand that next week I've got the pleasure of your company again. This means that you have a whole week to remember what the parts of speech are and complete the examples on the blackboard as homework, I expect them all to be correct. And don't forget… Charles Darwin once said that the only difference between a man and a monkey is the fact that a monkey cannot remember."

The moment he finished speaking, the bell went to mark the end of the lesson. It was exactly 3.00 o'clock. If ever there was a perfect lesson then that was it.

Thanks to Dad getting me all sorts of little shows I was gaining a fair amount of experience with the magic. Thanks also to David

Parriss, I now had more dealers to contact and, because of money earned from my paper round, I was buying more and more tricks. Inevitably word was getting round locally, and I was asked to do children's parties. This was a field in which I had little interest until David said to us one day,

"That's where the money is."

I had yet to make a penny out of magic as all the shows I was doing were voluntary and mostly for Old People's clubs. So, much encouraged by Dad, I sent off for tricks suitable for entertaining children… most of them bought from The Supreme Magic Company based in Devon. I worked out a little act and accepted my first engagement as a Children's Entertainer, it didn't go very well.

January 4th, 1964: *I made my first appearance in front of children today. It was murder.*

Things hadn't improved by the end of the year…

November 9th, 1964: *We got a letter asking for me to do a show, but we turned it down because the audience are kids.*

Some years later I did go back to doing kids' shows, performing traditional stuff like baking a 'magic' cake and 'Run Rabbit Run', and similar tricks. I never enjoyed them although they went down reasonably well. I certainly didn't make a lot of money.

Dad by now had really got the performing bug. Every time we did a show for the elderly we were asked back. That being the case we needed more material. I could now do two spots with the magic, silent to music, and a patter act (which was hard work with a quiet voice and no microphone). My sisters would do different songs and duets, and Dad would still play his saw and occasionally sing, 'Keep right on to the end of the road'. We needed something different. It was suggested that I do some impersonations. I did have an aptitude for mimicry which would usually surface at mealtimes. I was frequently asked to do the rather wicked one I did of our Sunday School teacher. Mum would giggle until she almost fell off her chair. All very well but hardly suitable for an audience of elderly people who wouldn't have known him anyway. I could however do The Steptoes from the popular TV show of the time and some of the Coronation Street characters too. I also did a pretty good Kenneth Williams based on his radio characters from the Kenneth Horne programmes. The voices I could do, but soon discovered that the entertainment had to come from what these characters actually said. How could I do that? I eventually had to bow to the inevitable.

When I came home from school at lunchtimes the radio would be tuned to 'Worker's Playtime' as usual. One of the regular performers was a young impressionist called Peter Goodwright. I would listen avidly with pencil and paper and write it all down. I tried it out a couple of times, but it wasn't very successful because the elderly audiences couldn't hear me. I had yet to learn the skill of voice projection. In the end I gave them up and Dad took over the comedy slot by telling a few jokes, even doing a routine dressed as a vicar!

I remember on one occasion after a show, the elderly club secretary stood up to give the usual vote of thanks. He thanked Dad, and my sisters for their musical contribution, and of course the conjurer who, with a bit more practice, could one day be very good. I took exception to his final comment. I was practising every bloody day!

In January of 1964, Dad got in touch with the Northamptonshire Magician's Club, (with the usual s.a.e). We had a nice letter back from the secretary, Geoff Hull (which I still have). It gave details of the time place and format of my forthcoming audition at 3.00 o'clock on February 1st. The date wasn't ideal as Dad would be in hospital having tests for his heart problem. He would have loved to have been there to give me moral support. I can only imagine his frustration of being stuck in a hospital bed wondering how it was all going. Transport was always a problem in those early days too as Dad didn't drive. Had he have been well; we would have gone on the train. Luckily a neighbour drove me and my props there and back door to door (no doubt for a bag of veg and a couple of brushes!). The venue was the Y.M.C.A in Cheyne Walk Northampton. The club hired a room there on the first Saturday afternoon of the month. They also had another meeting on the third Tuesday where they would meet up in members houses on a rota basis. When I got there, I was made to feel welcome and was given as much time as I needed to set up my table and props in a small alcove adjacent to the meeting room. As I was setting up, I could hear the first part of the meeting taking place which had a 'First time try out' theme. Members were encouraged to stand up and perform material they'd been working on, and this would be the first time in front of an audience. Comments were made, advice given, and there was a lot of laughter too. After about 20 minutes it was time for my audition. Geoff gave me a hand with my table and offered to turn on my tape recorder on the nod from me. I was introduced, I gave the nod, I was on! From what I remember I did card productions, multiplying billiard balls, colour changing silks, and a thimble routine finishing with a giant one. At the end of the act I received a nice round of applause, was thanked by Geoff, and then asked to leave the room while my fate was decided. After a few minutes I was called back and stood in front of the members.

"First of all, Ken, I would like to thank you once again for travelling all the way from Bletchley to audition for us this afternoon," said Geoff, "And I'm really sorry that our President Reg Gayton couldn't be here today to watch you perform and be unanimously accepted as a member of 'The Northamptonshire Magicians Club'. Congratulations!"

I've never forgotten how my heart sank when he said, 'I'm really sorry that...', and then rose seconds later when he said, '... Unanimously accepted.' The other thing he said was that I was the best thimble manipulator in the club! That was the icing on the cake. Geoff asked me if I wanted to say anything before I was introduced to the members.

"Yes, there is one thing I'd like to say, I know that you have to be 14 to become a member, well, I'm only 13."

"When will you be 14?" asked Geoff.

"March the 9th," I replied.

"Bearing in mind that's only about 6 weeks away, I'm sure we know how good you'll be by then!"

I was introduced to the members, many of whom became lifelong friends. So began a relationship with the club that continues to this day. Fifty-nine years and counting.

I owe so much to the club for the help and advice I was given during those early years. There was even a meeting dedicated to me. I still have the Newsletter dated September 1964...

My first membership card

Saturday 3rd October 1964
at Y.M.C.A, Cheyne Walk, Northampton at 3pm.
'KEN HAWES INSTRUCTION SESSION'
Our youngest member, Ken, will bring along his apparatus, show us his routines and we will endeavour to give him a little guidance and advice. He is very keen, but due to living a little out of reach of Northampton, he cannot get the more personal instruction that we ourselves obtain on our visits to each other's homes.

We went to visit Dad the next day at Stoke Mandeville hospital, and he was over the moon when I told him. He'd obviously told everybody there who would listen about the audition. Doctors and nurses, patients, and visitors, all asked how I got on. I recorded the news in my diary in my usual understated style.

February 1st, 1964: *I JOINED THE NORTHAMPTONSHIRE MAGICIAN'S CLUB. Auntie Maudie's coming on Monday.*

During those early years I would go along to all the Saturday meetings on the train and soon got to know the regular members. They were all very kind and invariably I would go home clutching a bag of magazines and the occasional book or trick. Meanwhile the Sixties were in full swing.

In 1963 'Ready, Steady, Go' had burst onto our TV screens, and in 1964 the first 'Top of the Pops' was broadcast. By this time Dad had to relent and at last we had a TV which sat on the sideboard in the front room. Like any other young teenager of that time, I loved it all. By the end of the year our old Bakelite wireless had gone from the kitchen to be replaced with a transistor radio.

The Radiogram was still in the front room, which is where we played our records (6s 8d for a single). Although Radio1 was yet to happen, we did manage to tune into Radio Luxembourg and one of the first Pirate stations, Radio London (Big L!).

I went to a church youth club every week where records were played, and I heard The Beatles for the first time ('Please Please Me') and countless other groups who were all great. The Rolling Stones, The Searchers, Gerry and the Pacemakers, The Hollies, the list went on. It wasn't just the music that made the Sixties so special, it was everything. The feelgood factor pervaded just about all aspects of our lives. School was great, there was plenty of work and opportunity, and people of all generations were happy.

During the Summer school term there were the inevitable exams, but on a brighter note it was athletics season. I did the long jump and triple jump… or hop, step, and jump as it was known then. (I had given up the high jump to the lads who had longer legs.) There were regular inter-school competitions and much of the time I came third or fourth. I did my best and Mr. Powney was always supportive. There was one time, however, when I had a real result as my diary proudly pointed out.

June 11th, 1964: *I came first in the triple jump at Linslade. I jumped 31ft 5". I cut the grass for Dad; he's buying me a new trick.*

Yes, the magic was always there hovering in the background. I went to the club regularly with Bernard Brown and David Parriss. I'd also become friendly with another young local magician, Alan Fraser, who was a couple of years younger than me, and he too went on to be a member of the club. I was constantly working on new material and would get the occasional little show, usually church related but all experience. Meanwhile of course I was continuing to grow…

June 25th, 1964: *I had my first shave. I had a bath. I've been revising. I'm looking forward to tomorrow.*

'Tomorrow' was the brush factory annual coach outing. It would be either Clacton or Great Yarmouth and they were great fun once we got there! It was a bit of a nightmare for Mum and Dad though as I was always sick on the coach. Dad would usually sit next to me with a magic catalogue pointing out various tricks and books in a desperate, and usually futile, hope of keeping me occupied. When he got to the final page, he would point out places of interest out of the window which wasn't easy as there's precious little to see between Bletchley and Clacton, so that would fail too, and out would come the plastic bag. The strange thing is I would be ok on the way home, tired out I suppose after a day at the fair or on the beach. It was still a worry for Mum and Dad though as I would insist on drinking a bottle of fizzy pop. I was OK though and happy to join in with the communal singing usually led by the ladies at the back… 'One man went to mow a meadow', swiftly followed by, 'There'll be ten green bottles hanging on the wall, and if one green bottle should accidentally fall, there'll be…'. Zzzzzzz - well it had been a long day!

The rest of the school summer holidays were spent with my friends Roger, Jonah, Birdie, and Ken who all lived close by. It was about this time that Ken was given his new nickname of 'Skinner' because he was so thin. For years he played amateur football as a goalkeeper and the fact that there wasn't much of him probably helped as he dramatically leapt and dived all over his goal area.

When he was quite young his hero was Lev Yashin the Russian Goalkeeper. There's a famous photo of Yashin diving full length across the goal mouth with a white number '1' on the back of his jersey. Having seen this iconic photo, and to be like his hero, Ken got his Mum to sew a number '1' on the back of his. I have this abiding memory of me kicking a ball towards Ken on the green patch of grass opposite our house, with him giving his usual BBC style commentary as he too dived full length between the posts (two spindly trees) thus saving Russia at the last minute from certain defeat! Bizarre really that he would choose to hero worship a Russian when there were perfectly good English goalkeepers around, then again none of those had a number '1' on their jersey. He wore it until it became so tight that the number '1' looked more like a squiggle.

Birdie and Jonah moved to the area when I was about 11 or 12, but Roger I'd known since we were in nursery school together. We also shared our Infant and Junior school days and Sunday School as well. We were always together sharing a love of fishing, cycling, trainspotting and walking. That was pretty much all we did through the summer of 1964 when the sun was shining. If it rained, we'd go to the cinema, 'The Great Escape' came out around this time and 'Zulu' as well, and not forgetting the latest of the 'Carry On' series, 'Carry On Spying'. The undoubted highlight though was the Beatles film, 'A Hard Day's Night'.

Prior to 1964, Saturday Morning Pictures ran for a while at The Studio cinema in Bletchley, sixpence at the front and ninepence at the back. With a bag of sweets bought from the sweetshop opposite, we had a great time for a reasonable amount of money. The films shown were usually from the Hollywood of the 1930's & 40's. 'The Little Rascals', 'The Three Stooges', 'The Bowery

Boys', etc. There were also some good British films which were especially made for children. The show would always end with the serial, 'Captain Africa', or 'The Green Archer', or some other strange character from 40s Hollywood. As is normal with a serial. it would end with a cliff-hanger to entice us back next week for more of the same. It was good value to see at least three films and all for a 'tanner' (sixpence, or two and a half pence.) If ever the children got a bit rowdy the manageress would stop the film and stride down to the front threatening to turf us all out. She never did.

In September Dad suggested another trip to London in search of yet more tricks. We called in to see Ken Brooke and then decided to visit 'Davenports' in Great Russell Street. This was the complete opposite to Ken's studio. Where his was bright and modern, Davenports was more traditional rather like something from a Dickens novel. The door and window frames were painted black and there was a selection of tricks and old props on display in the window. Above the entrance door swung an old sign of a rabbit and a top hat. Walking into the old and musty Victorian shop was like entering a bygone era. There were cabinets of tricks on display around the walls and there was even an old mysterious illusion standing proudly in a corner. A young friendly chap was behind the large counter serving a group of French schoolboys as we entered. The fact that the shop was situated dead opposite the British Museum made the influx of tourists inevitable. Practical jokes and novelties were on sale to cater for such people as well as more traditional magic tricks. As the tourists left, we approached the counter and Dad gave the chap a full history of my magic career so far (all two years of it!). We didn't have a list this time, instead we decided to ask for advice and recommendations based on my age and experience (or lack of it). He was more than happy to oblige. He went to the room at the back and came back with two tricks and spoke directly to me.

"These should be suitable, they're not self-working or difficult, but you'll have to put some work in, what we call handling practice."

He demonstrated the Edward Victor cut and restored rope beautifully.

"We'll have it," said Dad.

He went on to perform another really good trick with large cards called The Maverick Card Trick.

"We'll have that too," I said.

He went off to wrap them up and when he got back to the counter with the packages he said,

"Your Dad tells me you do card productions."

"Yes, I do," I replied.

"Could you show me?"

He gave me a few cards and I showed him what I could do.

"Very good," he said, "Try this. Instead of pulling the card over the second finger, push it down, then grab the corner with your thumb and forefinger and spring it up, like this…"

He then spent 15 minutes teaching me this new technique. What a star!

"Thanks very much, I said. I really appreciate your help."

"My pleasure," he said, "Let me give you some more advice, get out there and do as many shows as you can and try anything and everything and be prepared to die on your arse. When that happens, as it surely will bounce back and learn from it."

"I will, thanks again."

As we were leaving the shop, another man came out from the room at the back loaded up with parcels and packages.

"I'm off now Pat," he said to the salesman.

"Ok Wally, see you tomorrow."

"I think that was Wally Davenport," said Dad, as we got to the street.

"And the other chap was Patrick Page," I said, "And what a lovely man."

"He is, said Dad, we'll definitely come here again."

Years later when I was in my twenties, I'd go to the shop pretty much every Saturday morning. Several of us would meet up there and have a chat with Pat (if he wasn't too busy) and then go on to a local cafe to talk magic and do tricks for an hour or two. Regulars were Alan Alan, Jack Avis, Alex Elmsley, Stanton Carlisle (known as 'Ronnie') and Colin Martin. Occasionally somebody would turn up who I didn't know. (Bobby would, he knew everybody). One day an American chap came in and Bobby introduced us, it was Cy Endfield. Cy was a man of many talents. As well as being an inventor and good card magician, he was better known as a film director. A few years earlier he'd directed the hugely successful film 'Zulu'. Over a cup of tea and a bun in a nearby Lyons Corner House, he told us that during the Zulu shoot, he was suffering with a bad back and was frustrated because he was unable to climb a gantry to check out a high-level shot. He asked the crew to make up a hoist and lift him up using a block and tackle. Up he went, checked the shot and, when he got down and was lifted from the hoist, his bad back was cured! Those Saturday mornings in 'Davvies' were just great, I learned so much just by watching and listening.

In October of 1964 came the Tokyo Olympics! I watched loads of it on TV during the next couple of weeks. I loved it all. My diary was full of results, times, distances, and medals. One of the highlights happened on October 18th when my hero Lyn Davis won a Gold Medal in the long jump. A leap of over 25ft! And there were other British success stories, Mary Rand in the ladies' long jump, and others, as I wrote in my diary…

October 20th, 1964: *Ann Packer won a Gold Medal in the 800 metres. Mr. Culley from No.24 gave Ken a set of chest expanders.* (I think Bert Culley took pity on Ken and tried to beef him up a bit.)

Chapter 4

Work

I was now into my final year of school. I could have stayed on for an extra year and gone into 4th Technical, which could have taken me into engineering. It wasn't something I was particularly interested in, but it would have guaranteed me a job in one of the many small engineering companies that were prevalent in the town at the time. The other option was 4th Commercial, which was a course for office administration and the like (which most of the girls took) and may have led to journalism. There wasn't a great deal of choice regarding education in those days. University or college wasn't even an option, but evening classes, or 'Night School' as it was known, definitely was.

If Dad wasn't involved in important decisions, he could get quite stroppy. The problem was that because of his poor health both he and Mum missed the parents evening that would have explained in some detail the few options I had. I ended up in 4A1 which was a class full of kids who were either not academically bright or simply hated school and couldn't wait to get out. I didn't really fit into either of those categories. A shame really as I did really well in the end of term exams and came top in just about every subject. I'm sure I could have done pretty well academically had I taken a different route. Dad's take on it was for me to get an apprenticeship and learn a trade.

"Once you've got that boy you're set up for life, you could leave it and do other things and always come back to it."

It made sense to me, but what did I want to do? No idea. In those days the printing industry was where the big money was, which didn't go unnoticed. Dad was friendly with a chap up the road who worked for Bletchley Printers and after a chat with him which probably went along the lines of, "*My old boy is thinking of getting into the print trade, any chance of putting a word in?*"

We were invited to visit him at his work to see what was involved. On the pre-arranged evening we were met and led into the area where he worked. He sat down at a huge machine which had a small keyboard at the front with a clipboard attached and pinned to that was a handwritten page which he had to decipher and type into the machine. At the back was a container of molten metal. This was the machine that made the print (among other things). He went on to explain that it was important to be able to understand bad handwriting (he pointed to the page on display) and that a good knowledge of English and comprehension was essential. We watched him work for a while, thanked him for his time and made our way home. As we walked Dad said, "I don't think you could handle that do you?"

I was a bit annoyed that he had little faith in my abilities but had to agree with him. Time was marching on, and it was January. I had 7 months to figure out what I wanted to do, or more to the point, what Dad wanted me to do.

In my diary for the middle of January, I kept a running report on the declining health of Sir Winston Churchill. It was derived from the daily doctor's bulletin from the 15th to the 24th on consecutive days - *Gravely ill, weaker, losing ground, no bulletin, deteriorated, weaker, no change, slightly worse, deterioration more marked - died.*

There's no doubt that even with only four lines, I did write some stuff that smacks of desperation in those early diaries.

January 11th, 1965: *It is Dr. Albert Schweitzer's 90th birthday today. I went and got a loaf for Mum this evening.*

I'm sure you'll be fascinated to know that I also wrote of Dr. Schweitzer's demise on September 4th. Anyway, the magic was making a lot of progress during the early months of 1965. I had bought a 'Svengali' fake pack of cards and was having a lot of fun with that. I learned the Dai Vernon routine for the cups and balls (from the book), and I was also getting interested in coin magic using an Okito coin box. The stage act was evolving as well, I had recently bought a set of multiplying candles from Ken Brooke and was anxious to slot that into the act ready for the forthcoming magic club stage competition. I was doing shows with the school and still doing old people's homes and clubs with Dad and my sisters. It was all great experience. Some of these went better than others and I was learning all the time. The magic club competition arrived, and I came third. I was pleased with that as I did better than some of the more experienced performers. David Parriss won the cup which was great as well.

It was around this time that I got interested in table tennis. I was playing once a week at the youth club on a full-size table and practising a lot with Ken next door on his kitchen table. We had great fun. Years later we played in the same team together in the local league. Cycling was also a big interest and Roger was as keen as I was. We cycled for miles around the local villages. If we saw a nice-looking bike the conversation would go something like this.

"Wow! Rog Look at that Claud Butler frame, it's got Reynolds 531 butted tubes and stays!"

"Brilliant! And don't you just love the way the seat stays wrap round the seat tube."

"Look! It's got a Williams Chain Set, and a Brooks B17 Champion narrow saddle."

"And a Cinelli handlebar stem. Look how long it is!"

"GB Centre pull brakes, and Campagnolo gears, perfect!"

We would get more excited over a bike than a car, or even a girl. Dad always promised to buy me a new bike when I started work. It was just taken that I would need one. We did have some disagreement about which model I should have; he was paying for it so he reckoned he should have a say. I had to ride the bloody thing so I should have a bigger say! He was just so old fashioned. He hated dérailleur gears and cable brakes. *What do you do if the cable snaps*? was his only argument. Then he'd go on about it needing a dynamo on the wheel to save batteries, and a chain guard and mudguards! We had many arguments. In the end we compromised. I chose "The Viking Allrounder Model" with a couple of concessions; instead of dérailleur gears it had a 3-speed hub gear set, and reluctantly, a dynamo front wheel. It was ordered on March 13th and was delivered on May 5th. Dad took one look at it and said it wouldn't last five minutes. Over the years, I put a 5-speed set of dérailleur gears on it, alloy handlebars with a long stem and got rid of the dynamo front wheel. I cycled thousands of miles on that bike, and I rode it for over 30 years. It cost £26.

Meanwhile, there was a glimmer of hope for employment. Barclays Bank had just opened a new Stationery Department in Bletchley. It was a large building which consisted of a warehouse and a printing department. Although Dad had worked at the brush factory for many years, he was tempted to leave and get a job in the warehouse. He went for an interview and was shown round the place but never did work there. He was however quite taken with the printing department as a possible source of employment for me. In March of 1965 a recruitment drive took place, and I went along there for an interview. I didn't commit myself one way or the other, but they took my details anyway. According to my diary the wages "*were a bit low*". During that final school term I had a couple of interviews with the Youth Employment people and went along to a careers exhibition but with little success. It seemed increasingly likely I would go to Barclays. According to Dad, if I went there, I'd be taught a trade and getting paid good money as I learned. It wasn't an apprenticeship though and I had my doubts. Anyway, schooldays continued and once again I was volunteered for a football team.

April 13th, 1965: *I played football in the six a side inter-house football tournament, we lost 11-0, and 9-0.* (Luckily it was athletics season again, this would be my last.)
May 14th, 1965: *I beat both my long, and triple jump records today, 15ft-9", and 32ft-7". I bought a pair of swimming trunks, 14 shillings and 11 pence.*

After a chat with Mum and Dad and the Youth Employment lady I decided to go for the job at Barclays for the simple reason I couldn't think of anything else. An interview was arranged for

June10th. I arrived in plenty of time and was shown into the Personnel Manager's office. I was interviewed by a Mr. Wisdom who was obviously an ex-army man, silver haired with a moustache, and dark suited with a regimental tie. He asked the usual questions and talked about qualifications (I had none). I told him that I would be going to Night School to get a Royal Society of Arts Certificate in English. (R.S.A. was one down from G.C.E.) I don't know why I said that, anyway now I was committed. He asked me about hobbies and was fascinated by the magic. I found over the years in other job interviews that talking about it may well have made the difference between getting or not getting the job. It only worked against me on one occasion. I didn't like the bloke anyway, he was a bit snide,

"If all else fails you could always wave your magic wand to get the work done."

I was beginning to discover there are some people who just hate magic. Glad I didn't get the job really. Anyway, back to Barclays. I was offered the job as a trainee lithography printer. I would start on Monday August 9th, 1965. According to my diary I wasn't too excited about it.

June 10th, 1965: *I went swimming for most of the afternoon. I had another interview at Barclays I have got the job. I've been footballing and cricketing.*

The rest of that final summer term was spent doing more of the same along with a resurgence of my interest in fishing. The brush factory had formed a club and were now holding regular matches on Sunday mornings at the gravel pits and luckily, I now had a licence to fish there whenever I liked. I also spent a lot of time at the swimming pool (now diving off the board) and of course riding my new bike. School work was dominated by the end of term exams and sadly the sports day was one of the final events of my school career. I did well though and won both the long and triple jump and came third in the discus. I was runner up school athletics champion! I left school for the last time at three thirty on the afternoon of July 28th, 1965. I was aged 15 years and 4 months with no qualifications.

During my last week at school I was approached by the biology teacher, Mr. Rose. He asked me if I'd be interested in a part-time job as the school gardener. It would only be for a couple of hours a week and the work would be mostly hoeing and weeding with occasional planting and greenhouse work, the pay would be 18 shillings and five pence per week.

"Ok, I said, when shall I start"?

"How about August 9th"?

The irony wasn't lost on me. Seven months previously it was doubtful I would have a job at all, and here I was with two jobs both starting on the same day.

I was going to be quite wealthy by the middle of August. Two jobs, with two pay packets. I quickly worked it out, my take home pay from Barclays was £4.11shillings, add 18 shillings to that, over £5 per week!

August 9th soon came round. I cycled the short distance to Barclays Bank Stationery Department in Bilton Road, Bletchley at 8 o'clock. I parked my bike in the shed behind the warehouse and made my way to the front door clutching sandwiches my Mum made, wrapped in grease-proof paper. I waited in the reception area along with another new starter, a girl of about the same age as me. Mr. Wisdom came out to greet us and said,

"I see you've got your lunch."

He seemed fascinated by my well wrapped package, perhaps he'd never seen one before. He led us through the warehouse and after visiting the office where the girl was to work, I was taken to the printing area and introduced to the manager and foreman. This was the CT or Credit Transfer department. Next door was General Print, and next to that the Cheque Room where cheque books were printed. I was told that I would start working on credit transfers on a Multilith 1250 machine. There were several of these lined up in front of us. I was informed that I'd be here for a short while until there was enough work for the "Multi" in General Print. He pointed and said,

"That one over there."

I looked over, and amongst several large machines (including a beautiful Heidelberg) there stood the "Multi" which would soon be mine. I was led to the nearest unmanned machine and the principle of lithography was explained to me. (In a nutshell, oil and water don't mix). I was told all about the chemicals involved, the process of mixing the ink (which was semi solid), how to fit the thin metal plate onto the roller, and finally how to deal with the paper. Each pack had to be 'knocked up' to allow air between each sheet. It was like shuffling a large pack of cards, I soon got the hang of that. Once the reams of paper were loaded onto the back, it was ready to go. Levers were engaged, knobs turned, buttons pushed… I was a printer. One of the other operators stayed with me for the rest of the morning explaining and advising as we went. Soon it was lunchtime and a visit to the canteen. Unsurprisingly there were people there I knew. Pat, her Dad worked at the brush factory, Linda, her Mum went to the church, and there were a few lads there who went to my school. That's how Bletchley was in those days, everybody knew everybody. During the afternoon I was summoned to the front desk and told to go with the company van driver down to the local Co-op to be fitted for a white coat. When I got back it was tea break which is when I discovered some of the lads playing table tennis. There was a small room in the warehouse with a full-size table. That was great news, something to do at lunchtimes and tea breaks. The rest of the afternoon sped by, and it was soon 4.30 and the end of my first day in the printing trade. An interesting day. What a shame the rest of the days I spent there weren't. I knew from that first day this was never going to be a job for life. On the way home I called at the school and did some weeding then cycled home to face Mum and Dad. I didn't want to worry them, so I said all went well. I decided to sit tight for a while until something else came up.

Meanwhile, I was working hard on the act for an appearance with the magic club at Wilton Hall in Bletchley. This was advertised as a "Night of Magic" and tickets had to be sold. For this the onus was very much on the four Bletchley members - me, David Parris, Bernard Brown, and Alan Fraser. Thanks to David's talent as a commercial artist a poster was on display in the family sweet shop and various other places in the town. Mum and Dad and my sisters were going, and Dad had managed to sell a few tickets in the brush factory as well. I wondered if anybody from Barclays would like to go, I asked a few people and, in the end, sold two tickets to the foreman and his wife. The day of the show arrived on October 7th. The only trick I remember doing was a fanning cards routine. Whether I had to cut stuff out for time constraint reasons I don't know. What I do know is that it wasn't my usual act and because of that it didn't go very well, I left the stage feeling miserable to a smattering of applause. I was really disappointed. What a time for it to happen though, in front of family and friends and people from work! I was dreading going in the next day. The following morning the foreman was standing with a group of people. He was saying how much he and his wife had enjoyed the show and how good Alan Fraser was. Then somebody asked the inevitable question,

"How did Ken get on?"

There was a pause…

"He did ok."

It was kind of him to say that, but I knew it was a disaster.

This was the first time it had happened (and it certainly wouldn't be the last). It affected me quite badly. I was annoyed, humiliated, embarrassed, confused, and jealous of Alan Fraser! In a way though, it was a valuable lesson. I had to realise it goes with the territory. You have to be able to live with the highs and lows of being a performer. Looking back now I'm wondering if at the age of 15 I took it all a bit too seriously. I eventually did get over it of course and remembered the wise words of Pat Page…

"Bounce back and learn from it."

A couple of weeks later I did the act at Loughton village hall (near Bletchley) and tried out the Dai Vernon ball and cone trick. It went very well, particularly the vanish of the cone at the end. As an added bonus I spotted a local press photographer snapping away. The following week my photo was in the Bletchley Gazette! I had indeed bounced back.

I was attending most of the magic club meetings by now and had got friendly with Bill Middleton. Bill was a lovely man and after the Saturday meetings I would go along to his house for tea followed by a magic session. Bill was a good performer; he did a really good comedy stage act as a character called Willie Twistem.

Loughton village hall doing the Vernon cone trick and still wearing the 25p suit

Enhanced by his knowledge of stage craft gleaned from his experience in amateur dramatics he performed a lot. He knew his stuff when it came to close-up magic too. He won both the club Stage Competition and the Close-up trophy many times. Thanks to Bill, after seeing his sponge ball routine I was now getting more into close-up magic. I was still getting regular local shows with the stage act though, I did a memorable one at the Coronation Hall in Water Eaton for Bletchley Young (drunken) Farmers. I got paid £1 for that.

The job at Barclays wasn't going so well though. After a while I was transferred to the General Print department, but the machine I was given was old and difficult to use and kept breaking down. I made a few mistakes and more than once got told off by the foreman who wasn't a pleasant individual. It was so boring as well; the only good thing was the table tennis.

By the end of the year, after a chance encounter with an old school chum I was seriously thinking about leaving and going to Wolverton Railway Works Training School. I talked it over with Mum and Dad who were supportive and quite pleased as it would mean an apprenticeship and a trade at the end of it. I sent for an application form and eventually had an interview on November 24th 1965. I travelled over on the train, was made welcome by the secretary, Mrs. Cameron, and told to sit at a desk where I had to do a written aptitude test. This consisted of general knowledge, a couple of simple maths problems and also questions about British Railways trains (the trainspotting came in handy there). I then had a face-to-face interview with the Principal, Mr. Dunkley. He was a pleasant chap who looked you straight in the eye all the time. He asked general questions; Did I have a job at the time? Qualifications? (I had signed up for RSA English in September at night school.) Why Wolverton? And finally hobbies? Again he was fascinated with the magic. At the end of it all I was offered a place the following Spring, pending a medical on December 1st. I thought it best not to say anything at Barclays. I'd carry on plodding away until it was time to hand in my notice. A week later I went to the Works medical centre for my examination. It was like a mini hospital. With over 3,000 people employed there, many of whom were working on dangerous machinery, a fully equipped medical centre would have been essential. I was weighed and measured (10st 5lb and 5'10"), asked a few questions and that was it. I was in.

The next intake for the Training School wasn't until April of the following year. I'd have to hang on at Barclays until then, I could cope with that.

It was Christmas week and the Friday we broke up from work. I didn't know what to expect. A normal day or what? I went to my machine as usual and made a start on my first job. Meanwhile the Heidelberg operator was setting up a record player and a few minutes later a Ray Conniff Christmas album was blaring out. After morning tea break, I looked around and noticed there was little work being done by anybody and there was no sign of the foreman. I just carried on as normal until lunchtime. After that I noticed that wine was beginning to flow, and office girls were wandering about in groups holding bunches of mistletoe. I started to panic. I was a very shy 15-year-old, I couldn't cope with anything like that! Suddenly I had an idea. If I gave the machine a good clean, which involved chemicals, rags, bowls of soapy water, and up to the elbow rubber gloves, surely they would leave me alone. They didn't, as my diary points out.

December 23rd, 1965: *I broke up from work today. I got mobbed at work by girls!! I had a bath. Richard Dimbleby died yesterday.*

CHAPTER 5

A Proper Job

I certainly had something to look forward to at the end of April. I just carried on normally at work, hoping the few months I had left at Barclays would go by quickly. Meanwhile I had a pay rise with the school gardening job; as from January, I'd be earning 19s 2d a week, almost a pound!

The magic was still taking up a lot of my time and I entered the club Cup competition again. I came last. I kept changing the act, that was the problem. It had yet to evolve into an act 'as known'. At least I could say I wasn't afraid to experiment. I was getting there though, albeit slowly. Magic competitions can throw up all sorts of things. Having been both competitor and judge many times, I've experienced some strange moments over the years. The spanner thrown into the works usually comes from the lay judge (a member of the public chosen at random). There was one occasion when a competitor dropped virtually everything and 'died a terrible death'. As the marks were being checked (I was the Magician judge) I noticed that the little old lady plucked from the audience had given him top marks…

"Why?" I asked.

"I felt sorry for him," she replied.

One year the club was desperate for competitors for the close-up competition. Two competitors had dropped out at the last minute.

"If only we had one more," I muttered.

As the judges were being seated in the front row there was a whisper in my ear.

"I've got the act in the car from a job I did last night; I'll enter."

The judges were informed of the extra name and the competition started on time. The new competitor was Ric Ellam who I had seen perform many times with his stage act but never doing close-up. I was intrigued to see what he would do and was about to find out. He was the final competitor and I realised there might be a problem when he began to set out his cabaret act. There were tricks with silks and rope and rings, and his big finish was a comedy routine with giant cards. He performed it well I thought, despite the time limit. Suffice to say the lay judge gave him top marks and he won the competition. There was as you'd expect dismay from some of the competitors as, in their eyes, the winner of the close-up competition hadn't actually performed close-up magic. The lay judge would not be swayed.

"I have no idea how he did his tricks which he performed directly in front of me. He was entertaining and he made me laugh."

You can't really argue with that. The decision stood.

The shows that me and my sisters were doing with Dad in the old people's homes were still happening. By this time in 1966 we had been joined by the son of our regular pianist and a lady who played the accordion along with her two young daughters who sang novelty duets. As well as doing a couple of spots with the magic I took on the role of compere and told a few jokes. Dad was still playing his saw and also having a go at performing the old comedy 'Flea Circus' routine. It wasn't a bad little show, and the elderly audiences loved it, especially at the end when we all sang a medley of old songs from the 40s and 50s. Again It was all good experience for a young performer such as myself. The downside was that I was living in this strange bubble.

I wasn't associating with people of my own age and was still very much under the influence of my Dad. I looked and dressed like someone from the 1950s and was far removed from the exciting and vibrant culture of the 1960s. I was 16 and began to realise I was missing out. My friend Roger had been to the local Grammar school and was growing up fast. With his new friends, he embraced it all - the music, the clothes, and his appearance too. I seemed to be stuck in a time warp and always felt inferior to him and his mates as I had so little in common with any of them. Dad had a thing about long hair too which would go on to upset the whole family for years. I had it cut square at the back on one brave occasion, and he almost made me go back and have it cut again, "properly". Dad's health wasn't good either, so I was caught between a rock and a hard place. On the one hand I felt I had to do something to escape his control of my life and appearance, and on the other not to upset him too much and run the risk of giving him having a heart attack. Mum of course was caught in the middle of it all. I just hoped things would change when I started my new job.

I handed in my notice on April 15th. I don't think anybody was too surprised once I told them where I was going. Most of my workmates were ok about it, but there was one who implied that Wolverton Works was for the no hopers and was where the Youth Employment people sent you as a last resort. I certainly didn't see it that way, I was looking forward to it. I started on April 25th, 1966, I was aged 16 years and 1 month and was to earn £4.08p a week. So began one of the happiest and most rewarding times of my life.

The Training School was an ideal place for a young lad to work for a number of reasons - if you left school with no idea of what you wanted to do, it was ideal; if you left school with a hat full of qualifications and wanted to continue with your education, it was ideal; if you wanted a secure job for life it was ideal; if you wanted a good apprenticeship and be qualified as a craftsman with a worldwide reputation, it was ideal. In a nutshell, it was ideal!

I would be in the Training School for a year where I would decide what trade I would take up. After that I would spend the following 5 years as an apprentice inside the Works culminating as a fully qualified craftsman. I went there with a totally open mind still not knowing what I wanted to do and how it would all end up.

On that first morning we were spoken to by Mr. Dunkley. I found him inspirational. He spoke of how lucky we were to have the opportunity to take up an apprenticeship at Wolverton Works.

"The training you'll receive here has a reputation of being one of the best there is. To be Wolverton trained almost guarantees you employment anywhere in the world should you decide to leave at the end of your apprenticeship. The workforce here have had years of experience and if you work hard everybody in this room has the ability to be as fine a craftsman as they are. To be a craftsman is not just about learning techniques and skills, you have to be able to prove that you know the theory behind those skills; you will learn this by attending college and completing at the very least a City & Guilds Craft Certificate to Final level. There is also the opportunity to carry on your education to the level of Higher National Diploma. Every one of you is capable of one or indeed both. On behalf of all of the staff here I would like to welcome you to Wolverton Works, and I wish you all the very best. Good luck lads!"

It was the word "craftsman" that resonated with me, I would hear it a lot over the next 12 months.

The Training School was largely made up of an open workshop divided into 5 sections:

1) Electrical and Turning.
2) Carpentry, and Wood Machining.
3) Trimming (upholstery), Painting, Signwriting, and French Polishing.
4) Sheet Metalwork, Plating, and Welding.
5) Fitting (metalwork), and Blacksmith.

There were two classrooms upstairs where a variety of subjects were taught; Maths, Industrial History, Workshop Theory, English, Science, and First Aid. Some of the lessons were taken by training school staff and others by lecturers from the local college. We had to go to that same college once a week to do a General Foundation Course which covered Maths, English, and Science. That G1 course was the very beginning of what could have led to an Higher National Diploma. Mr. Dunkley was right, some lads did actually achieve that, and it's all the more remarkable when many of them began with no qualifications at all.

Fitness was a part of the training there too, with a gym attached to the training school where we would have a PE lesson once a week which ended with a six-a-side football tournament. The days were certainly full.

From the first day we were divided into groups of about eight and we'd spend the first six months in those groups moving from section to section in the Workshop. My first section was Electrical where we were taught how to use a micrometer, did a few cable joints, had a go on a lathe and finally made a fully working doorbell. I found it all really interesting. After that was Woodwork where we made a mahogany tea tray. Joints were cut, timber shaped, and a spindle moulder used, and I loved it all. Next up was the Trimming section where we had to trim an arm rest. Although the instructor made it look easy it certainly wasn't. Before we began, we were told we'd be using a magnetic hammer and the first thing to do was grab a handful of tacks and put them in our mouths; we looked at each other and just went for it. The tacks were then transferred from mouth to hammer to arm rest and it worked perfectly (once we'd had a bit of practice). On the same section was Painting, Signwriting, and French Polishing. All of these took a lot of skill and a definite knack; some of us got it and others didn't. It was all fascinating. The next section was Sheet Metalwork and Welding. Again the instructor made something really skilful look easy. From memory I think we made a pastry cutter. It involved all sorts of bends and techniques including soldering which was a first for me. The welding, using both gas and electric arc, was interesting and again a definite knack was required, with a very steady hand a distinct advantage. I was enjoying it all and having a go at things I simply couldn't have done anywhere else. The final section was Fitting and Blacksmithing. We made a pair of fitters' clamps on the benches, and a cold chisel on the forge and anvil. The clamps involved a lot of precision filing. Each side had to be perfectly square and checked by the instructor before we went onto the next. It is a skill that takes a lot of practice, and again it came easy to some lads while others struggled.

We were assessed on each section and given one of several grades ranging from below average to quite outstanding, a bonus was paid depending on the grade you got. I was "Well Above

Average" on most of the sections, so got a bonus of about 10s (50p). After six months and having visited each section, we could then decide which trade we would like to pursue as an apprentice in the Works. We gave Mr. Dunkley a choice of three in order of preference. Luckily, I was given my first choice of Coach Finisher (woodworker), so I would spend the final six months on the Carpentry section. I enjoyed it all and at last made friends of my own age. There were some who weren't particularly bright in the classroom but discovered natural skills in the workshop they didn't know they had. One discovered he had a natural aptitude for welding and on completing his apprenticeship went to the Middle East and made a fortune working on the pipelines. Another who was an Electrician worked hard at college to the highest level and eventually ran his own very successful engineering business. There must be others too who owe so much to the training they received at Wolverton Works. No hopers? - I don't think so. Meanwhile….

…We had a bit of a break from the shows throughout the summer, but I was continuing to work hard on the magic and was still going along to club meetings. I entered the Close-up competition and came third and was quite pleased with that. I had also bought from David Parriss yet another trick for the stage act. This one was quite unusual; it was a miniature floating-lady illusion… I had bought a floating doll! Although it was very effective, I felt a bit uncomfortable about having a doll in the act. I eventually sold it to club member Norman Woodger - Norman did a comedy act called 'Woodger believe it'.

At one of the early summer meetings we were told that the Committee and President Colin Hooton, had come up with an idea to get some publicity for the club in the local press. They had a plan. Why not invite a reporter and photographer along to one of our typical informal club meetings? The suggestion was put to the members and passed unanimously. The Chronicle & Echo were contacted. They were up for it and a date was arranged. Obviously, we had a lot of rehearsing to do to make it appear as typical and informal as possible. The big day arrived. We had come up with some strange ideas, but they worked. Luckily the venue was perfect for what was to follow. It was a lovely old oak panelled room in The Franklin's Garden Hotel. The reporter was blindfolded on arrival and then had to knock on the clubroom door three times. The President then said rather dramatically, "Enter", and once inside the reporter had to agree to an oath of secrecy before the blindfold could be removed. When that was done, he was told he would have to remain silent while the members held a ritual that was performed at every club meeting. The ceremony of 'passing the wand'. At this point, the club ceremonial wand was passed around the room from member to member and then placed back in its holder at the front. (That was the first and last time I'd ever seen that done!) Colin welcomed us to the meeting and spoke briefly about future events and went on to say that tonight's meeting would be entirely informal (bearing in mind the word 'informal' would in normal circumstances refer to showing a trick that you happen to have with you). On that night credibility was stretched to the limit.

"Who would like to show us a trick?" Asked the President.

"I will," came the well-rehearsed response from Ken Savage, "I just happen to have my head-chopper with me."

He then went into his comedy routine using the reporter as a victim. It was hilarious and the perfect way to open the show. As the reporter sat down rubbing his neck, Norman Woodger piped up,

"I'd like to show you something. It's a brand-new version of sawing the lady in half, utilising my new home-made table!"

A bit of a groan with some laughter arose from the members, as you never knew what you'd get from Norman - his woodworking skills left a lot to be desired. He glanced around the room unperturbed.

"As there are no ladies present, I'll have to improvise."

He reached under the table (which was beginning to wobble alarmingly!) and came up with a familiar-looking doll. He placed it carefully on the table and then picked up a huge saw. He was just about to make the first cut when the table collapsed, to roars of laughter from the audience, including the reporter (which was reassuring!). As he was picking up the remnants of the table, Norman did say that he'd have another go and bring it along to the next meeting.

"We'll look forward to that, it is after all what this meeting is all about," said Colin glancing at the reporter.

After Norman, it was my turn. I did the Dai Vernon cups and balls routine finishing with three tomatoes. It went well. Following me were a couple of others, after which the President came to the front and explained to the press about the many different branches of magic there are - Comedy, Close-up, Illusions etc., and also Magic of the Mind. He went on to say how lucky we were to have in the club one of the best in the country in this particular field, Reg Gayton. Reg was invited to the front and performed an amazing routine with ESP cards. Next came a short interval when Bill Middleton performed his own brand of close-up magic to the guests as the rest of us chatted while relaxing with a drink. The evening 'was going very well' was the general consensus. After the break came the next stage of a 'typical' meeting. Colin stood at the front and asked the members for ideas for future meetings.

"How about some films?" replied young Alan Fraser.

"Or a lecture on home-made props," said Norman, to more laughter from the audience.

A general discussion was then had about the type of lectures we would like to see at future meetings, and of course Colin and the Club Secretary, John Lee, wrote copious notes. At this point Colin thanked everybody for coming, particularly our special guest David Abbott from the Chronicle & Echo.

"Finally," he said, "Would anybody else like to show us something to finish the evening?"

"I will!" said 15-year-old Ray Mclellan, "Would you like to see my new strait jacket escape?"

"Absolutely!" we roared.

He was duly strapped in, and the buckles were checked by the reporter. He writhed around on the floor for a few minutes, and finally escaped! It was a great finish to a great evening. The reporter did a wonderful spread in the paper the following week along with a couple of photos. He called us a "group of wand wavers", which I'm sure he meant in the nicest possible way.

Wolverton Works (including the Training School) shut down for the middle two weeks of July for the annual summer holidays. Dad had decided on a family holiday to Clacton for a week. He'd booked accommodation for all of us at a small family-run Guest House. Me and my sisters had mixed feelings about this as by now we were all teenagers. Our view at the time was to make the best of it as it would more than likely be the last holiday we'd have as a family together. (It wasn't just me that was growing up.) The guest house was pleasant enough with good food and the week

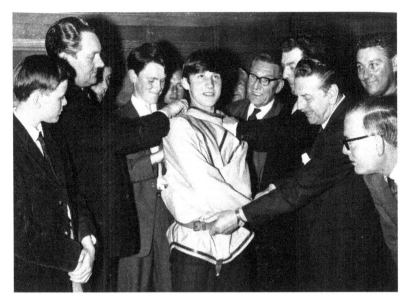

Press Night!!

started off pretty well. We went to see a variety show at the end of the pier featuring magician Alan Shaxon and we'd also been to the cinema. A swimming pool was close by, and we went there a couple of times. Needless to say Dad had made sure I'd bought a few tricks with me, so I had to do my party piece for the landlady and some of the guests. (As I got older there were times when I really didn't want to do it, but it made him happy and proud, so I put up with it.) Towards the end of the week he had been onto me about needing a haircut yet again. I'd get it every six weeks or so and he wouldn't let it go. I was 16 and more than capable of deciding if and when I needed a bloody haircut. It was starting to be irritating, especially when my work mates were growing theirs in all sorts of styles of the time. I was annoyed but I was with the family and his health wasn't great at the time and the last thing

I wanted to do was cause dramatics. I caved in yet again. I went in search of a barber shop and came across a 'Gents Hair Stylist'. In those days, photographs of different styles were on display in the front windows, most of them the often elaborate 'Mod' variety which were all the rage in the mid-sixties. I had a look and walked around the block a few times until I had the courage to go in. Luckily, by the time I returned it was almost empty. I was invited to sit in the chair and the young hairdresser asked me what I'd like.

"Could you do something with it?" was all I could think to say.

"Have a look through these books," he said, "And I'll see what I can do."

I flicked through a book of photos and pointed out a style that I thought would work.

"To be honest," he said, "It isn't really long enough for that, but what I can do is to start it off for you."

He went on to say that as it grows, I should dry it with a hair-drier and train it by brushing it upwards.

"Ok," I said, "I'll go for that."

I sat there thinking to myself, Hair-drier? Brush? It's never long enough to get a comb through! As he began to snip away, he started chatting, asking me where I was from and what I did. Inevitably the questions began to head in the direction I was dreading.

"What have you been up to since you've been here, been to any decent pubs?"

I didn't really want to tell him I'd never been in a pub in my life or tasted beer (both Mum and Dad were tee-total).

"I've been to the cinema," I replied.

"Ok, see anything good?"

"The Sound of Music," I answered, wishing I'd lied and said Alfie, or Blow up.

"Did you go with your girlfriend?" he probed.

"No, I went with my Mum and Dad and sisters."

By now I'm really embarrassed and finding this whole experience a bit of a nightmare. I can see it all in the mirror in front of me, bright red and sweating. And it's not over yet.

"Have you picked up any nice girls since you've been here?" he asked, already knowing the answer.

"No, I'm not a girls' man yet."

Then, thankfully it was over. I paid for the haircut which was twice as much as I'd normally pay and walked out of the shop wondering if shyness would be the death of me. Work and doing the magic was certainly a help but at times like that I felt as if I hadn't grown up. Up until then I'd had an idyllic childhood which had been so full, I never had the time or the inclination to even think about girls. Yet again though I felt a niggle at the back of my mind that I was missing out. How it would change or when I had no idea.

I wasn't particularly happy walking back to the Guest House. The haircut hadn't really worked, and I tried to avoid looking at my reflection in shop windows. When I got back Dad took one look at me and said,

"Call that a haircut?!!"

He would never know or be able to comprehend what I went through that afternoon, or that I went through it for his sake and not mine. At the age of 16 I wasn't ready or capable to stand up to him. I also knew that unless I did, I never would grow up. The hair problem would become almost obsessive for Dad for the next ten years.

Life of course went on and the second most important event of 1966 (the first was obviously my new job) took place on

Me looking decidedly uncomfortable with Mum and Maggs at Clacton

the Saturday after we returned from Clacton. The 25th of July. England won the World Cup! We watched it on our small black and white television in the front room. God it was exciting! When that last goal went in you could hear a roar from every house in the street. This was the culmination of what had been a great tournament. I didn't realise just what a colourful event the final was until the film of the tournament came out. It was called 'Goal' and went out on general release in cinemas throughout the country later on in the year. It was only then that I realised the England team wore a red strip. Up until then I thought it was a light shade of grey. The other thing that surprised me was how green the Wembley turf was. What a difference colour made. When I returned to work from the holidays, the World Cup was all we talked about, it made us proud to be British. As it happened, I had another reason to be proud on that first day back, I was made a Prefect. What this meant in real terms was I was given the job of Tea Boy. Why I had to be a Prefect to perform this menial task was a bit of a mystery. I was told to make myself known to the Caretaker who would train me up for the job. I went along to his small room which had the rather pleasant aroma of detergent and floor polish. Tom the caretaker was retired and worked part-time. He was a lovely old boy, as bright as a button and had a great sense of humour. He explained how the tea trolley was organised.

"The urn, which I fill with tea is on the left-hand side. The mugs, each containing the correct amount of milk are on the right."

"Why can't they put their own milk in?" I asked.

He peered over the top of his glasses and pushed his cap to the back of his head.

"Think about it," he said, "You have a limited time in which to give 20 lads a mug of tea. If they were to put their own milk in, it would take time which you don't have. The situation could also arise when some of them won't know how much to put in because their mothers have always done it for them. That being the case they might pour too much or not enough thereby making the tea undrinkable. This would be wasteful and cause extra expense, both of which as I'm sure you know are not tolerated by British Railways - that's why they're not allowed to pour their own milk. By the way, it's your job to make sure that each mug does in fact contain the correct amount. Mr. Dunkley obviously thinks that you're the one who can be trusted for this important and vital task."

"How do you know that?" I laughed.

"He's made you a Prefect." "Listen son," he said, "I'll give you one more piece of advice about doing this job."

"And what's that," I asked.

He looked around the room to make sure nobody was listening and whispered,

"Get your own first."

As well as being Tea Boy, I had been chosen to play for the Training School football team. Desperation on their part I suspect, as my diary confirms.

November 26ᵗʰ, 1966: *We had a football match against Leon School. We lost 13-1. I had a shocking game. I've been practising the act with my tape recorder.*

The magic was going well though. I took part in another Night of Magic with the club, and our little Concert Party was now doing village hall shows as well as the Old People's Homes. We were now known as "The Jollities" Concert Party. (Dad's choice.)

December 31ˢᵗ 1966: *Maggs and I did a show for Freeman Youth Club tonight. It went very well. I've done a total of 20 shows this year.*

Dad hadn't been feeling well for some time. One day in early January he decided to go for a short walk around the block. He barely made it. One of the neighbours found him fighting for breath holding on to a tree. The next day he was in hospital. He had various tests and stayed in for a couple of weeks.

At the beginning of February he went to see a specialist who told him he would need major heart surgery. That came as a bit of a shock. The operation could happen at any time during the next 12 months and would be at The National Heart Hospital in London. He was able to carry on as normal but not to lift anything and generally take things easy. He told me he'd be writing to the Training School to put them in the picture, and to ask if he could visit fairly soon in case he was in hospital when the forthcoming Open Day took place. After he'd told me that, he said, "I think you need a haircut."

Mum and Dad did visit the Training School a few weeks later. After a chat with Mr. Dunkley and his able deputy Mr. Whitlock, I showed them around and introduced them to the instructors.

They had a great time. It must have been a huge relief to know that I was doing well and in the right place, my future assured.

The magic continued to go well and yet again I entered the club Cup competition. I was anxious to win something this time and worked hard on the act and felt quite confident. It was still performed silently with music - multiplying lighted candles, multiplying billiard balls (producing eight), fanning cards, and thimbles etc. On the night I thought it went really well; obviously not well enough though, as I didn't come anywhere. The winner that year was young Alan Fraser who did a version of the cups and balls and some ventriloquism. Second was Ken Savage who performed his own brand of comedy magic. Both patter acts. I couldn't figure out where I went wrong. Still very much a naïve 16-year-old, I had the mindset of assuming that being clever, meant being good, the cleverer you were the better you were, and therefore the more points you scored. Well, I'd obviously got that wrong. Perhaps it was time to have a closer look at the judging system. In those days there were three judges - a member of the public, somebody with a theatrical background and a magician unconnected with the club. Judges marked up to 20 points for each of three headings: Appearance and Deportment, Entertainment Value, and Magical Content. The obvious route to winning is to score as many points as possible under each heading. In that case I needed to look smarter (I began saving up for a new dinner suit) and I definitely needed to make the act more entertaining and magical and with a bigger finish. I decided to have a fresh look at the stuff I was doing - multiplying candles, multiplying balls, and multiplying thimbles. It suddenly dawned on me that I was doing the same effect three times! It was time for a rethink.

I had recently become friendly with Archie Tear (a former Club President), and I went over to his house on a number of occasions to try and come up with some fresh ideas. Archie had a lot of experience and had performed an act similar to mine years before. His advice and help were very welcome. He gave me a number of tricks including the floating silver ball, more commonly known as the 'Zombie'. At last, I would have a good finish to the act.

Before the end of the year, I did buy an off-the-peg dinner suit - it cost me 17 guineas. The shows I did didn't always go to plan.

September 17ᵗʰ, 1967: *I did a show for St. Martins Youth Club. It was pretty grim, there were a lot of Germans in the audience.*
October 14ᵗʰ: *We did a Jollities show at Winslow I dropped the Zombie otherwise it went beautifully. I went to the pictures; I saw a James Bond film.*

Whenever I got a bit bogged down with the magic, I'd have a break for a while and go back to it later, often with fresh eyes. During one such break in 1967, I decided to pursue my love of table tennis and regularly cycled over to Shenley Brook End village hall to have a game with my cousin Geoff. There were a couple of other enthusiasts there Roy and Judith and we got a team together and bravely went into the Bletchley league, our first foray into competitive table tennis. We did quite well and really enjoyed it. During the year, I joined the AHW Table Tennis Club which was run by Bill Wooding. There were various coaching sessions throughout the week to suit age and ability. Bill would have been in his 50s in those days and was quite a character. He'd wear baggy shorts with about an inch of equally baggy underpants showing below. The girls would giggle, and point and he'd say, "At least you know I'm wearing something!"

I would be up there every Wednesday evening rain or shine. I was taught the backhand and forehand push, backhand and forehand drive, and backhand and forehand chop, and other shots in between. There were exercises where we'd have to knock matchboxes off the table positioned for us to get the correct range. There were mini tournaments as well, and I loved it all. As I improved, so did my love for the game, especially after buying a new 'Stiga' bat. It cost me 33s 6d, a lot of money in those days. The club was open to members pretty much all the time and often me and a couple of pals would go for a knock over a weekend. I was really enthusiastic, it kept me fit and it was good for me socially too as it gave me the opportunity to make friends of my own age, including girls. I played for several AHW league teams over the years and at my peak got as far as Division 1. The old clubroom was recently demolished; sad really. I spent many happy hours there and will always be grateful to Bill for his kindness and enthusiasm.

Meanwhile, I was on the final stage of my year in the Training School, permanently on the Carpentry section, under the instruction of Mr. Rutledge. We got on really well and he loved the magic. He lived in Northampton and would go along to the magic club shows and competitions. I would often see him beaming up at me from the front row as I was performing the act.

Those last 6 months sped by, and I was soon ready to make the move into the Works to begin my apprenticeship. Dad had bought all of my tools which were delivered to the Training School during my final week. They were really good quality. Yet again he had dipped his hand into his pocket for my benefit. My last day was on April 21st, 1967. What a year it had been! Definitely a good career move. I'd done well in the classroom too and had a glowing final report. I was ready and looking forward to moving on to the next stage.

CHAPTER 6

Into The Works

I started my apprenticeship as a Coach Finisher on April 24th, 1967, having just turned 17. The workforce was made up of gangs, each one specialising in a particular type of coach. Rolling stock was no longer made in the Works, it was purely a centre for repairs, conversions, and maintenance. As well as the internal woodwork fixtures and fittings that I would be involved with, other trades dealt with the undercarriage and electrical stuff, braking systems, wheels, upholstery, and French polishing. It was a huge place which at that time employed over three thousand people. My first job was working on 'suburban electrics' which were operational around London. My area of work was right at the top where the coaches first came in. From there they would progress all the way through from shop to shop ending up at the paint shop followed by a final inspection. My job involved stripping out all the woodwork, trimming, and metalwork and marking it all up before it was sent off to the polishers, trimming shop, and brass shop to be polished, cleaned, and re-upholstered. By the time the coach had travelled to the paint shop everything had been re-fixed, all as good as new.

The stripping out job wasn't what you'd call a skilled job, but it certainly got me used to the inside of different types of coaches and how the various components were fixed and repaired. I worked with a lovely chap called George who in a former life was a pianist in a dance band. He had a big allotment as well, so we had a lot in common. He explained the process of removing and marking up the various bits and pieces and also what they were called. Whatever was removed had to go back in the same place unless it was damaged and replaced with new. The system of marking was really clever. The Works were situated on the edge of Wolverton with Stony Stratford to the north and New Bradwell to the south. On the east side was the canal and on the west the houses and shops of Wolverton. The coaches would travel the length of the Works always facing the same way. George explained all of this and told me that everything removed on the canal side is marked "CS" and on the other side "WS" for Wolverton side. As for the ends of the coach they should be marked with either "SE" Stratford end, or "BE" Bradwell end. Simple! He pointed to a length of polished moulding just below the ceiling line.

"That is called cant rail," he said, "When you take it off, mark on the back of it 'number 1 Canal side cant rail' and be careful how you spell it!"

At lunch time on my first day I went to the huge two storey canteen or Mess Room as it was known to meet up with a few of my pals. We sat down at one of the tables which were set out in rows. Shortly after, a chap came in and said,

"You can't sit there, that's Bill's seat he's been sitting there for 40 years."

Why on earth would anybody want to sit in the same seat every day we wondered. He guided us to an area which wasn't claimed, and we sat and watched as the place filled up. Everybody did the same thing, we watched as they came in all making a beeline to 'their' seat. As it happened, we used the same seats when we went back the next day, and the next…

I settled into the job fairly quickly and soon picked it up. I was eagerly waiting for my first pay packet which duly arrived the following Friday. It contained £4 6s 8p - a drop from Barclays, but as Dad kept pointing out, "Don't forget the cheap rail travel and Free Passes, they're not to be sniffed at."

There was a bonus scheme in action there as well where each gang seemed to earn a different weekly amount. I never did figure it out. It varied from gang to gang which appeared to depend on how clever (or devious) the Chargehand was. Anyway I had enough money to live on and to give a bit to Mum for my keep. My rate of pay would rise each year, so I had no reason to worry. I didn't spend a lot and most of it went on the magic. My social life consisted of table tennis and a weekly visit to the Youth Club. Not what you'd call riotous living.

Each individual workshop in the Works had an office which was used by the Manager and a small team of clerical staff. Documents and mail that had to be transported from office to office were delivered by 'Circuit Girls'. They would either have a bag around their shoulders or push a small trolley. The girls were about my age and would come into our shop several times a week. There were three or four different ones, and I had a bit of a crush on one called Jill. She was a beautiful little thing with short brown hair and enormous brown eyes. The brake fitters, who would be working underneath the coaches, would always stop and have a chat with her. I couldn't even look at her without going bright red. I looked forward to catching a glimpse of her but at the same time dreading it in case she looked or (heaven forbid) spoke to me. I saw her many times but she never so much as acknowledged my existence (which didn't come as a surprise). There was another one, who one day made a point of saying hello to me. I had a chat with her and as it turned out her brother had been in the Training School at the same time as me. When I got to the canteen that day my pals were already there.

"Who was she then? Did you show her your magic wand?!"

Obviously, I'd been seen chatting to her. Needless to say I just coloured up again. I wasn't having any luck at all with the girls, as I wrote in my diary… "Too bloody Shy!"

Time sped by and it soon rolled round to the annual summer break which was very welcome. We were right about last year being our last family holiday together, my elder sister Maggs was now courting, another Ken. I had a good summer of fishing, cycling, swimming, playing table tennis, and helping out Dad on the allotment. Although he would still go on about my hair it was bearable, it was more important then to help out and make sure he didn't overdo things, bearing in mind his health problems.

Towards the end of the year the magic club had a lecture from Bobby Bernard which was really good and featured a lot of his coin stuff. He had stayed with my pal Ray Mclellan and I was invited over the next day to spend more time with them. During the day a visit to Eric Lewis was arranged. Eric was a clever magician who had written some well-received books and had a reputation for being a great ideas man. He had also been in business with club member Reg Gayton, manufacturing magic props. When we got to his house there were packing cases everywhere as he was in the process of emigrating to California. Sat on one of the cases was a young man about our age strumming a guitar. It was Eric's son Martin who really didn't want to go. Of course they did go and they both found fame and fortune - Eric as a builder of props and consultancy work, and Martin as a very successful performer.

It had been a good year with a few ups and downs. I now had a decent job which I was determined to stick at. I signed on at College and had made a start on a City & Guilds Cabinet Making course. The downside was Dad's health which hopefully would improve once he'd had his operation.

The year ended on a sad note as I wrote in my diary.

December 23rd, 1967: *Mrs Hall died during the night. Mr Fisher died a couple of days ago. Dad has had wind and he's got a cold. I did my Christmas shopping.*

Dad finally had his surgery on March 18th, 1968, at the National Heart Hospital in London. The hospital was quite famous around this time for carrying out some of the first heart transplants. He was certainly in the right place. In those days his procedure of a new plastic valve was a major operation which necessitated a long recovery time. After a spell in a convalescent home he came home on May 5th. It was a long job. He recovered well and I reckon it gave him another ten years.

I was doing a lot of shows at that time. Sometimes in strange places.

March 23rd, 1968: *I did a children's party at a farm at Bow Brickhill. It went very well; the chap gave me 30 eggs.*

We were still doing Jollities shows too.

April 20th: *We did a Jollities show at Winslow, it didn't go too badly. Mrs. Baker and I didn't feel all that well in the minibus. I bought a new pair of handlebars and fitted them. I've got a gum boil.*

The old 'baking the cake' routine was popular with children as was the 'funny funnel'. I was now doing both in the Jollities shows. I would get 3 children up to help, including the birthday child (if there was one). Milk was poured from a jug into the funnel apparently through the top of the child's head; it would then reappear from the elbow via the funnel and into the jug when another child pumped the opposite arm, like an old water pump. At the end I would give

Early Jollities show doing the cups and balls

two of the children a packet of sweets and send them back to their seats, leaving the birthday child. Sadly, I'd run out of sweets, but I could bake a magic cake instead! Then I (or the child) would don a chef's hat and apron, the recipe would be read, all sorts of stuff went into the pan and eventually a real cake (made by Mum) would be produced. Occasionally, if I did a kids show for somebody I knew, Mum would put icing on the cake and when it was produced, I'd put candles on it and we'd all sing Happy Birthday, a nice touch.

I was still doing the stage act both with the Jollities and other places as well - a lot of these were coming from connections at work, I even did one for Mr. Dunkley. Many of them were church-related - entertainment after a harvest supper was fairly typical. And of course the magic club stage competition had come around again. I was now becoming more creative, still doing a multiplying ball routine but had now added a couple of colour changes. As well as that, I did a penetrating block, a thimble routine, and finished with the Zombie. I came third. Oh well—one day…

My confidence was given a boost when I did the same act in a big Youth Club show at Wembley (sadly not the Arena or the Stadium, but a large church hall.) It went well, particularly the Zombie.

An early performance of the "Zombie" somewhat overshadowed by that poster. The rabbit image on the table cover was another one of Dad's ideas!

In the middle of the year I joined the IBM (International Brotherhood of Magicians). The local press was informed, and a nice article appeared a week later. Soon after I was contacted by the BR Newspaper 'The Rail News'. I was interviewed by a reporter; photographs were taken and there was a good spread in the following issue. From that I was asked to provide some entertainment at the Works Horticultural Show in August. This was a big event for the Works and all the stops were pulled out to make sure it was well supported. A huge banner was hung above the main gates featuring events that were happening throughout the day, including in very large letters, 'SHOW BY INTERNATIONAL MAGICIAN!'. I couldn't believe it - performing the Funny Funnel and baking a cake hardly matched the publicity! That was the first time I ever worried about doing a show. *What if hundreds of people came along expecting to see an*

International Illusionist? As it happened, I needn't have worried, only 20 people turned up and most of those were children.

In September, I went to my first IBM Convention which took place in Weymouth. I was able to go with Archie Tear as his wife couldn't make it. We stayed in a large posh hotel (Archie was quite a wealthy man) which was all very nice, but I did feel a bit out of my depth particularly in the dining room. I got over that by having whatever Archie had. The first event that afternoon was a show presented by renowned author and inventor, Peter Warlock, entitled "Magic of the Twenties." I don't remember much about it which says it all really. Following that I was about to see something that would change my life forever. It took place in a small theatre on the pier. It was entitled "Magic by Goshman." I knew very little about Albert Goshman apart from the fact that he was American and was a resident magician at an all-magic venue in Hollywood called The Magic Castle. I was looking forward to it. As the theatre was so small the show was performed twice; I was in the queue for the second audience and waiting for the first show to finish. Soon the doors opened, and people came out into the sunshine. The first person I saw was Lewis Ganson (author of the Dai Vernon book).

"That was one of the best things I have ever seen, absolutely amazing," he said to nobody in particular.

I knew then we were in for something special. I eagerly made my way inside. The theatre was small and intimate with raised circular seating. At the front was a table covered with a green cloth, lit by a spotlight, upon which were a pair of large salt and pepper shakers. There were three chairs at the table, one at the back for Albert and one each side for two spectators. The conditions were perfect. The lights dimmed, then an American voice,

"Ladies and gentlemen, The Magic Castle proudly present for your entertainment, Albert Goshman!"

The spotlight came on and a figure walked out, quite stout but smart in a dinner jacket and bow tie, a pleasant face with a large moustache. He walked to the front row and chose two ladies who took their places either side of him.

"Good evening, good evening," he says. He turns to the lady on his left and says, "My name's Albert, what's yours?"

"Jean," she answers.

"Jean, I'm going to magish for you." He turns to the other lady, "My name's Albert, what's yours?"

"Linda," she replies.

"Linda, I'm going to magish for you too."

Coins appear and disappear and end up underneath the shakers. He does a routine with large sponge balls. Another one with bottle tops. A signed card in purse routine. This is just brilliant stuff, some of it performed with music and beautifully timed and choreographed. I had never seen anything like it. If ever there was a defining moment in my magic career, that was it. Up until then, all I had seen of close-up magic was a few card or coin tricks performed by magicians who all looked and sounded the same. They just did tricks. Albert transcended all of that. He delivered a magical performance, a performance that affected me in many ways. I laughed and was amazed and thrilled and almost bought to tears by the artistry of magic and music combined. It was a privilege to watch.

After seeing Albert everything changed. That twenty-minute act on the Thursday afternoon of 26th of September 1968 was the moment I decided to be a Close-up magician.

1968 was eventful for something else as well… my first girlfriend! Yes, at last. She was a table tennis player and went to the AHW club regularly with her Dad who also played. We got friendly during the course of a few months and one day she invited me to her house for a game of table tennis on the table they had in their garage. I walked to her house and later that evening she gave me a lift home. After sitting

Pat Page and Albert Goshman, two of my all-time heroes

in the car outside the house in uncomfortable silence for a while, I finally had my first kiss! Although I was 18, I was incredibly naïve which was proved by what I did next. I wrote the shape of a heart on the steamed-up windscreen and wrote our initials in the middle of it. God knows what that poor girl must have felt, but I was in heaven. For the following 2 months or so we'd meet at the club or go to the cinema. I'd cycle the few miles to her house, and we'd walk the mile or so into Bletchley to watch the film, praying that it wouldn't rain. One night we went to her school dance which was another first for me. Sometimes I'd go and see her of an evening and watch TV with her family. Occasionally her brother would be there. He was a student with long hair and dressed as students do, jeans and T-shirt, and he played guitar as well. I didn't even own a pair of jeans and I still dressed like a 1950s youth. In his presence I felt awful, with my short un-styled hair and beige jumper, and shoes I'd bought from the market, I felt and must have looked ridiculous. I had no conversation to speak of either, I may as well have come from another planet.

Our relationship staggered on for a couple of months, and during that time I took her home for Sunday tea. Both Mum and Dad liked her, which was nice, in fact she was the only girl I took home that Dad ever did like. Soon things began to change. She stopped playing table tennis and I was getting excuses as to why she wasn't able to see me. It wasn't the same anymore and I was heartbroken. I called round to her house one evening and her Dad summoned me into the front room for a bit of a chat. He was really nice about it and told me that due to A levels and studying she wasn't able to see me anymore, there were other reasons or excuses as well that I can't bring to mind. As good a way as any I suppose to let me down gently.

Life went on, back to normal…

November 9th, 1968: *I went to the pictures and bought a back reflector for my bike. I've been practising card catching. I mended the coal scuttle.*

It was becoming obvious I would have to do something to drag myself into the 20th Century. How or when, I still had no idea. Meanwhile I buried myself in the magic. I was now really into close-up, particularly with coins. I had a couple of good books which I pored over and studied for hours. The first one was 'The new modern coin magic' by J.B. Bobo. This was a huge book packed with sleights, tricks, and routines, with contributions from many top magicians. The other book was 'Slydini Encores' by

Leon Nathanson which featured the magic of Tony Slydini - tricks with coins, cards, cigarettes, and rope as well. This book though was as much about a style of working as it was about the actual tricks; I loved it and spent hours absorbed with cards or coins in hand. The first thing I did on my return from the Convention was to grab the Bobo book and look down the index in search of the name of Albert Goshman. I devoured it all. A lot of it was technically demanding but I stuck at it and was also coming up with my own moves and ideas. What I needed next was an audience and somewhere to perform it.

The Jollities shows were still happening, and I'd try out some of the new coin stuff during the interval which went reasonably well - unlike at the club Close-up competition, when I came last. I didn't do very well in the stage competition either that year, probably due to lack of practise. Bill Middleton won it for the second or third year on the trot with his comedy act. He sent me a lovely letter saying that I shouldn't be downhearted and to persevere, it'll only be a matter of time before I'd win it. What a lovely man.

Work was going well. I was moving from gang to gang, learning all the time. The Works was a great place for characters. There was a huge amount of talent in there, not only fine craftsmen, but entertainers as well. There were some wonderful singers who sang as they worked – Bill Church and Bob Fielding were really good. Bob had a beautiful bass voice very similar to Paul Robeson and did a great version of 'The road to Mandalay', singing as he hammered and drilled the coach doors. Bob was also the funniest man I've ever known (and I've known a few). He was a well-built, muscular chap with wavy hair. His eyesight was terrible, and he wore a pair of thick pebble glasses. He was a bit like Tommy Cooper inasmuch as he didn't have to do anything to make you laugh, you fell about just looking at him. He'd tell me stories about characters he'd worked with over the years. There was one called Percy Beech who was a bit odd as he constantly talked to his tools. One day Percy caught his ankle on his toolbox as he walked past. He hopped up and down clutching his foot and glared at the box.

"That wasn't a very nice thing to do, was it toolbox?!! I'm going to walk up to the end of this coach to get my screwdriver, and if you're still here when I get back, you're in dead trouble!!"

Off Percy went to the end of the coach, picked up his screwdriver, walked back, and glared at the toolbox.

"You're still here!! Right!!" he said. He picked it up, raised it above his head and threw it out of the end of the coach with a loud cry of,

"BASTARD!!!"

There was one hilarious incident involving Bob himself. We were allowed to buy bits and pieces from the Works, as long as you had the ok from a manager and the necessary signed piece of paper. You could then take it out in plain view as long as it was checked out with the chap on the gate. Needless to say, there were countless ingenious ways of getting stuff out. Bob found a length of wood that would be ideal to repair his greenhouse, he put it to one side and arrived at work the next day wearing a very long raincoat. Just before going home time, he manoeuvred the timber across his back and by the side of his leg down his trousers. He was then helped on with the raincoat. If he leaned to his left, and walked with a stiff leg, you couldn't see the wood (well, that was the theory!). At going home time, everybody poured out of the gates across a zebra crossing. Bob's plan was to be in the middle of a bunch of men, thereby making himself less conspicuous. Me and a couple of mates watched from a distance as the tall figure of Bob Fielding strode through the gate with his right leg stuck out at an alarming angle and with the top 3 inches of the timber almost pushing through the material of his raincoat! One of the funniest things I've ever seen!

During that summer I had a spell of working in sleeping cars. Often difficult and uncomfortable as it meant working in a confined space. It was particularly unpleasant in the heat, especially if the Formica panels had to be replaced. This was my first experience of contact glue. Both the Formica and the wall had to be coated and you only had one chance, as the positioning had to be spot on, there was no wriggle room. Getting that right was hard enough, but the other thing was the powerful fumes. Assuming the gluing went ok, we'd walk out into the fresh air as high as kites. Unbeknown to us, we'd been glue sniffing! Luckily Wolverton open air swimming pool was close by and we'd often go there for a welcome lunchtime dip. I was more than ready for the annual break...

While many of my workmates were buying motor bikes and cars, I had bought myself a high-quality racing bike - I seemed to be a couple of years behind everybody else. Anyway, I'd bought the bike from 'Goz' Goodman, the local cycling champion, and spent my first week happily riding around the local countryside. For my second week I took the train up to Wales (with my first Railway Free Pass) to spend a week with my Aunt Maud in Caernarvon. I had a great time. As well as the

Me on my rather smart racing bike

spectacular scenery, it was lovely to visit Holyhead again and meet up with some of Mum's family. I was also introduced to a friend of Aunt Maud's, a local compere and magician called Ivor Parry whose stage name was Rovi. I spent a great evening with him in a large hotel in Caernarvon. He was a great entertainer with a pack of cards, and we went on to become good friends, often meeting up for a chat at Magic Conventions over the following years. Another event that made that week memorable was watching the first Moon landing. Although we watched it on a grainy old black and white TV, it was still fantastic to watch history being made.

Still the only social life I had apart from magic was table tennis. I went to the AHW Club as often as I could, playing regularly in the league and throughout the summer as well. I also went on a coaching course led by the former international player Jack Carrington. On the first session he talked about stance, positioning, and footwork. A young volunteer was at the end of the table with bat and ball ready to play. Jack asked to borrow a bat, as I was close by, I lent him mine. A ball came over which he hit straight into the net.

"Good heavens!" he said, "Whatever's this?"

He peered at my bat and looked at me.

"My advice to you young man is to buy another bat, this is like blotting paper! Send another ball over!"

It came over and Jack hit a hard textbook styled forehand smash with his bare hand. He looked at me, displayed his hand and said, "This is better than your bat!"

He did say it with a smile though, and after watching me play did recommend the type of bat I'd need. I bought my new one soon after which cost me almost two quid - a lot of money in those days! Not long after that, a few of us went over to Northampton to watch an International match between England and Sweden. Before the match started The Swedish team came up to the table and went through the usual ritual of choosing the match balls. They were tipped out of the boxes onto the table and given a spin to check for wobble. Duly chosen they were put to one side. Next came the England team with young Chester Barnes. He picked up a full box, gave it a spin on the table, tipped a ball out and said, "This'll do.", to the great delight of the crowd. Gamesmanship? Possibly, but I think it just showed the supreme confidence of a young man at the top of his game. England won 6-1.

One day one of my mates from work suggested going for an evening swim at the local pool which was now covered and heated. There were several of us and it soon became a regular event. After one such visit it was suggested we visit the pub next door, *The Bletchley Arms*. Not to be left out, I went along with it and tasted my first beer which was half a pint of Watney's Red Barrel. I was 19. My social life had begun. The following week there was a change of plan. It was decided to have a bite to eat as well as a drink. After a short discussion it was decided we go to *The Bridge* in Fenny Stratford for a couple of pints and a really tasty Ploughman's Lunch - thick wedges of crusty bread, a large slab of cheese, lettuce, tomatoes, and pickled onions. That certainly hit the spot after a swim. It was a lovely pub and a great evening. I got home around 10.30 pm and Dad was still up and sitting in his usual chair.

"Where have you been?" he asked.

"For a swim with my mates," I replied.

"What, for all this time?"

"No, we went to a pub for a bite to eat."

"A pub?!! How much did you drink?"

"Only a couple of pints."

"Two whole pints! That's more than I've had in 30 years!"

He was quite upset and must have wondered how it was all going to end - visiting pubs and drinking outrageous amounts of beer, and not only that, but I was also wearing 'work' trousers to go out in (my first pair of Levis!) and as for my hair, it was almost covering my ears!

During the following weeks and months he became quite despondent. I don't know if his poor health had anything to do with his attitude or whether he was just plain old-fashioned. Anyway, I may have left it rather late, but I'd grown up and he'd just have to live with it. After that night, a swim and pub grub became a regular outing. Soon I was getting out and about more and more, and enjoying myself with my pals, my new-found social life went on, gathering momentum.

One of the lads we went swimming with told me about a regular Friday night disco at 'The Swan' in Fenny Stratford. He told me how good it was and mentioned a few other regulars who I also knew. "So why not come and join us?" I did and had a great time. Who'd have thought me on a dance floor? By this time I had nurtured a taste for beer, which came in useful to dispel my inhibitions. Friday nights at The Swan soon became a regular thing. The music wasn't particularly important as long as I could have a bop or a smooch. I loved it there and soon fell into late sixties pop culture. I started to buy fashionable clothes and made new friends and was meeting and chatting to girls too - things were looking up! Often me and my pal Tom went out during the week as well, visiting the California Ballroom in Dunstable on a Saturday night. We went anywhere and everywhere for months; I just couldn't get enough of this new-found freedom. One day towards the end of September 1969, Tom suggested we go to a disco at Dunstable Civic Hall. I went along with it, little knowing that it would turn out to be another one of those life-changing moments, not dissimilar to my experience with Albert Goshman in Weymouth.

CHAPTER 7

Music

Tom did all the arrangements for our nights out. I'd give him a couple of quid for petrol, and he was happy enough. I asked him what sort of venue the Civic Hall was, and he knew as much about it as I did. Nothing. It did sound like a posh place though, so that being the case it was decided a suit and tie might be in order, after all we didn't want to travel all that way and be refused entry on account of a dress code. As we're driving over there, I wondered what the evening was likely to consist of. A bit of Soul perhaps, Tamla Motown, or maybe the new Reggae stuff. I asked him what was on the ticket. 'Blodwyn Pig,' he answered. Strange name for a disco I thought. We parked up and entered the building and made our way to the bar. It was packed full of long-haired students. Many of them wearing kaftans, patched up jeans and beads. We stopped dead in our tracks and looked at each other aghast. I felt ridiculous. Needless to say, the ties soon came off and after a couple of pints we felt a bit better and walked into the rapidly filling auditorium. Most of the people sat on the floor, pretty much covering it, while others stood in small groups round the perimeter. We made our way to the front, curious to know what was going to happen. On the stage was a drum kit and a stack of speakers and amplifiers. A chap came onto the stage, something was announced, and three long-haired young men walked out. Two of them carried guitars which they plugged in and the other sat behind the drum kit. They began to play; it was loud and wonderful.

"What is this stuff?" I asked Tom.

"I think it's the Blues," he answered.

I'd never heard anything like it. After about 45 minutes they did their last song and went off to a huge round of applause.

"Is that it?" I asked Tom.

"No there's more, Blodwyn Pig are on next."

"Who were the band we've just seen then?"

"No idea."

I never have been able to find out the name of that first band, which is a great shame. I do remember thinking to myself that surely Blodwyn Pig aren't going to be anywhere near as good. We went to the bar to grab another drink or two before joining the crowd to catch the headliners. We stepped through the crowd again and sat just in front of the stage. There was an expectant hum as we waited for the announcement.

"Ladies and gentlemen… Blodwyn Pig!"

The four members of the band walked on. Ron Berg sat behind his drum kit, Andy Pyle picked up his bass, Mick Abrahams his guitar, and Jack Lancaster stood directly in front of me with his saxophone. Seconds later he blew the first ten notes of 'The Modern Alchemist' and they were away! I had never heard music like it. Was it Jazz? Blues? Rock? Or what? I didn't care, I just knew it was wonderful stuff. They played for about an hour, and I was totally blown away. It was a great night and, with the often hilarious chat between numbers from Mick, it was entertaining too. The musicianship displayed from all of them was astounding, with Jack even playing two saxophones at the same time on a couple of songs. What a night! I'd experienced an evening of music that was *felt* as much as listened to, which for me was a completely new experience. Music was never the same after that. From then on discos and pop music went out the window.

Years later, I did the magic at Mick Abraham's 65th birthday party in Milton Keynes. It took the form of a concert featuring many of his musician friends and was compered by Whispering Bob Harris. On the bill was a performance from the original Blodwyn Pig line up. This would be the first time they'd played together for decades. The evening was packed full of good music, played by some great musicians, including Paul Jones the renowned harmonica player. As the music was playing in the hall, I was doing my stuff, in the room where a buffet was laid out, performing to family and friends of the musicians. An hour or two later, after the Blodwyn Pig set, I waited for an opportunity to say hello to those four young men (now pensioners) who gave me so much pleasure 40 years ago. I spotted Jack and Andy by an open door having a smoke, so I wandered over. Jack lives in Hollywood now, still playing and producing and looking and sounding very much like Keith Richards. Andy still lives in Bedfordshire and continues to do session and production work all over the place - both men still at the top of their game. I chatted for about ten minutes and left them to talk and have a catch up. I could have shown them a trick, but it wouldn't have worked - sometimes you just know. (Generally speaking, it hadn't been a particularly good night with the magic anyway.) I could have talked about the time I saw them in 1969 and the effect their music had on me like a regular fan, but I didn't even do that. It was enough just to say hello and chew the fat for a while and talk about Andy's bad back and Jack's forthcoming journey home. The honest truth? I was still awestruck.

On the way home from Dunstable I knew I had to see and listen to more of this new music, but where?

"Bletchley Youth Centre," said Tom, "I'm pretty sure they have bands playing there on Sunday evenings."

Sunday evenings it was then. Over the next three or four years I saw loads of great bands there. Me and a couple of mates would call at The White Hart first (which was the nearest pub) and then go on to the Youth Centre fairly tanked up. Often the hall was really crowded, depending on the popularity of the band. It had a great atmosphere which was enhanced by the always spectacular light show. My overriding memory of those days was the ringing in my ears at the end of another great evening of original music.

Soon I was buying albums. Blodwyn Pig's first, 'Ahead rings out' was top of the list, closely followed by their second, 'Getting to this'. I loved both of them, even when played on the only record player in the house, our 1950s mono radiogram.

I would often call at one particular record shop because I quite fancied the girl behind the counter. I did try and pluck up the courage to ask her out, but never did - I'd always end up buying a record instead. One Saturday morning as I was idly flicking through the albums and rehearsing a chat up line, music came through the shop speakers. It was somebody playing brilliant saxophone, as I listened goose bumps came up on my arms (yes, another one of those moments). Sod the chat up line,

"What is that music?" I asked. She picked up the album sleeve.

"It's called 'The Turning Point' and it's by John Mayall. Do you like it?"

"Like it? I love it! I'll have it!"

As I'm paying for it, and she's wrapping it up, I asked her if she liked this sort of music.

Surrounded by an early collection of albums

"No, not my cup of tea at all, I like Edison Lighthouse."

Strange how you can suddenly go off people.

I do love The Turning Point album and play it to this day. It was recorded live, which added so much to it. Later on that year (1970) I went to see the same band at The Royal Albert Hall. Although it was the original line-up, I was a bit disappointed. The problem with improvisational music is the fact that it's always different (obviously). I knew every note of the original recording and I suppose I was expecting the same from a live concert. I soon learned though and began to appreciate music for what it is on the night. Anyway, it was still a good night out and the RAH is such a great venue.

1970 was a good year for seeing quality bands. I saw Free at the Drill Hall in Northampton, and at the California ballroom (bizarrely) a few of us went to see Eric Clapton's band Derek and the Dominoes. I went to my first festival during the year as well, 'Blues at the Eyrie' in Bedford, with Deep Purple, Chicken Shack, and Tyrannosaurus Rex with a young Marc Bolan sitting on the stage for the complete set. 1970 was a great year for generating and cementing my interest in music, one of the highlights was spending 3 very happy hours in the Empire Cinema, Leicester Square, totally absorbed in the film Woodstock.

As it turned out it was a good year for the magic as well. I'd been working really hard on the coin stuff and tried it out in the club close-up competition. I won! A month or two later, I did the stage act in the Cup competition and won that as well, along with the award for the best trick of the evening with the multiplying billiard balls. Bill Middleton was right, bless him. It did seem strange though, having entered the competitions on so many occasions and coming nowhere and now winning everything in the same year – and it wasn't over yet! I went to the IBM Convention in Hastings and entered the close-up competition there. My performance did cause a bit of controversy. The usual format is to work from a table which is positioned in front of several rows of people with the judge seated in the centre directly opposite the performer. You can either sit at the table and have a couple of spectators join you on either side, or work standing up behind it. I ignored all of that, wanting to do something different. I put a felt covered board on the judge's lap and worked directly to him, literally under his nose. The only people who could see what I was doing was the judge and a couple of people sitting either side of him. I performed strong and clever coin magic, but with little in the way of humour and entertainment. I still came second though. Oddly, there were some who thought I should have been disqualified, but I didn't break any of the rules. As far as I was concerned the only person who mattered in that room was the judge and sod the rest of them (well, I was young with little experience). Those that could see, did compliment me on my performance, and those that couldn't weren't so kind. Peter Warlock told me that I didn't actually perform close-up magic, what I did do was close-quarter magic. Talk about splitting hairs. I replied that it was certainly close-up to the judge! He went on to tell me that he couldn't see what I was doing, and neither could most of the audience. My response to that was, why didn't he move so that he could see. People could have gathered around, as there are no rules to say that members of the audience have to stay rooted in their seats! Ah, the arrogance of youth. It occurs to me now, that in the real world, the public would have done that. Also in the real world you hardly ever perform from a table in front of rows of people.

Later on that year I entered the Magic Circle Close-up competition and did something more traditional (I thought I better had, bearing in mind where I was). I didn't come anywhere, but I was commended and didn't disgrace myself. It was good experience.

Things were looking up socially as well. I was getting more confident and less shy. It was all down to the magic. I went to the Bletchley Arms on my own one Friday night and there was a chap in there who I knew. He asked me if I still did the magic. I answered him by showing him a quick coin trick.

"Bloody hell!" he said, "Come and show that to my girlfriend."

I went over and spent the rest of the evening doing tricks. That was the start of it. I was in there every week doing stuff. One day a chap came in and watched me for a while and introduced himself as the manager of the Co-op store in Bletchley. He went on to say that a staff function was to be held on the 5th of March at Wilton Hall, would I be prepared to provide some magical entertainment? I would, and I did, as I noted in my diary.

March 5th, 1970: *I did Close up at the Co-op do at Wilton Hall. It went very well. I met a nice girl from Woburn Sands.*

Win, Win then! It was my first ever paid close-up show. I went out with that girl a few times as well.

I was flicking through the local paper one day in the spring of 1970 and something caught my eye. It was a small article with a photograph of a local weightlifter. This chap had been quite successful having won several national competitions. He ran a small weight training club in a local village hall and was now looking to increase the membership. An open evening was set up for anybody who might be interested in having a go. *Why not?* I thought, I'd been interested in body building since I was quite young. I'd even sent off for the Charles Atlas Body Building course when I was about 11. I was obviously too young but did get a nice letter back from 'Mr Atlas', who suggested I keep the application form and apply again in a couple of years' time when I'm older. When I was 14 or so and had a bit of spare cash from my paper round, I actually sent off for the course. My thinking was that perhaps having a muscle-bound body might go some way to helping me get over my shyness - girls would throw themselves at my feet and my pals would be jealous as hell. The course was divided into exercises that had to be completed in a particular order. They were delivered by post on a regular basis and each envelope was plain apart from having the letters CA stamped on the back. Dad's curiosity got the better of him, he could stand it no longer. What were these mysterious letters and who were they from? I was really annoyed when he opened one and I was confronted. Perhaps confronted was the wrong word, he was amused as much as anything else. He did have the grace to apologise for opening my mail though, which didn't really help. The burning question is of course, did it work? Obviously not. I did have a go in the small confines of my tiny bedroom, but every time I exerted myself, I had a nosebleed. A year later I had to go the surgery to have both nostrils cauterized - I gave it up.

In spite of having a weak nose, I did go along to that weightlifting open evening. Three of us showed up. One chap was older than me and was a bit overweight, and the other one was about my age and had the physique of a dipstick. I explained I wanted to use it for fitness as an aid to my table tennis. The elder chap wanted to lose a bit of weight, and the other one did admit to wanting to "beef up a bit". We did a few warmup and stretching exercises first before being shown various lifting techniques and how to do them safely. Small weights were then put onto a bar and given to the first chap to have a go at curling from his waist up to his chest and he did well, I had a go with slightly less weight and coped ok, and the other chap could only manage the bar and struggled. It lasted an hour, and I really enjoyed it. I went over there quite regularly for about a year before the club lost the use of the hall. I got friendly with another chap there called Mick. He was about my age, and we went out socially quite a lot. Mick was a good guitar player as well as a weightlifter. He did have a go at teaching me some stuff on my new acoustic (which I'd bought from Marshall's Music shop for three quid.) Mick was a natural self-taught musician, I obviously wasn't.

I'd shown Mick and his family a few tricks and he was quite intrigued. One day he asked me a question that I'm often asked,

"Where do magician's buy their tricks"?

I told him about Davenports, Ken Brooke, and the Unique Magic studio in London.

"Why don't we have a day in London and go and visit them"? I suggested.

Mick was up for it, so we got on the train one Saturday morning and headed for Euston. We visited Davenports first. I introduced him to Pat Page and Bobby Bernard (who I was quite friendly with by then) and then walked the short distance to Soho and visited the Unique Studio. From there we decided to explore the West End and see some sights. As we're walking through Soho Mick suddenly stops.

"Why don't we go to a club?" he asked.

"What sort of a club"? I replied.

"One of these," he answered, pointing to a rather tatty looking window with an assortment of photographs of naked women plastered all over it.

"A strip club!?"

"Yes," he said, "Could be a laugh."

"And expensive! Wouldn't you rather see Big Ben and Westminster Abbey?" I could tell by his face he'd made up his mind.

"Come on, let's go for it!"

I somewhat reluctantly followed him down some dark stairs. At the bottom sat at a table was Neanderthal Man.

"A fiver each," he growled.

We coughed up the money and went through a grubby door and found ourselves in a small and crowded room with a stage at one end with several rows of seats in front of it. We stood for a while before finding a seat near the front. I had a quick look round and there were men of all ages and types. Soon the lights dimmed, and music began to play. It was 'Lovely Rita' by The Beatles. Unsurprisingly a girl walked onto the stage dressed as a traffic warden. She walked up and down the stage looking out over the audience. She stopped directly in front of me, pointed to the old chap in the next seat, looked at me and said,

"Your Daddy?"

She did her routine which ended with her being pretty much naked. Then followed more of the same from other girls. I suppose we were in there for about an hour. I didn't find it particularly titillating but some of the girls were really funny with a ready wit.

I didn't see Mick for a while and when we did finally catch up, we chatted about that day. He told me he went back the following week to the same club.

"Did you go on your own?" I asked.

"No I went with my Dad, he loved it."

March 9th, 1971, was my 21st birthday. What could I do to mark this momentous occasion? A family party? - God no, I hate parties! Go to the pub and get hammered? I didn't fancy that either. I decided to go to The Royal Albert Hall with my pal Chris to see John Mayall again. He had a new band featuring Don "Sugarcane" Harris on electric violin. It was another great night.

The summer of 1971 was a great one for seeing bands; King Crimson at Hyde Park was a good one, although their set was a bit on the short side. Anyway, it was free, so I couldn't really complain. Another memorable one was Pink Floyd at The Crystal Palace Bowl supported by The Faces and Mountain. I went with Chris who is a huge Pink Floyd fan. They were the first live band he ever saw when he was quite young. In those days they were known as the Abdabs (or something similar) and Chris has been a fan ever since. It was with some excitement then that we found a place to sit on the edge of the lake in front of the stage. At one point in the middle of the afternoon, an announcement was made that a very special guest would be making an appearance. Rumour had it that it was Elvis Presley and sure enough The King of Rock and Roll was introduced and ambled on to the stage to a huge roar from the crowd. He was asked if he could give us a song but sadly had to decline because he didn't have his regular musicians with him. I would say that at least half the crowd were convinced that it really was him, including me and Chris. Sadly it wasn't Elvis from Memphis, but an impersonator called Raving Rupert from Scunthorpe. Obviously Pink Floyd topped the bill and as they were getting to the climax of their set there was a huge thunderstorm. How they arranged that God only knows.

Another great day out featured The Who at The Oval. The weather was perfect, as was the line up; The Who topped the bill supported by Lindisfarne, America, and The Faces (again). The DJ was Jeff Dexter who was dressed in cricket whites all day, including pads and bat. The whole event was billed as a fund-raiser for Bangladesh which was a popular cause at the time. After the Faces had finished their set, the organisers decided to have a collection. The idea was to put money and loose change into an array of plastic slotted containers, to be passed from the front to the back, filled up, and then passed back to the front again. That was the theory. It started off ok, but soon the containers started to rain over the crowd. Not too bad when they were empty and you could see them coming, but lethal when they were full and thrown back from behind. One poor bloke in front of us stood up at the wrong time, got clobbered on the back of the head and went down like a sack of spuds, not unlike Keith Moon's drum kit at the end of the show, along with the rest of The Who's equipment. It was a memorable day. We travelled home with our ears ringing, a touch sunburnt, and very happy.

I saw other great bands for the first time in 1971, often accompanied by my sister Jean - Wishbone Ash, Mungo Jerry (who did a great concert at Wilton Hall), Chicken Shack a couple of times, and Johnny Winter. There was one band we saw four or five times that year, a band I was starting to fall in love with. They were from Swansea and called Man.

My life was now falling into a regular pattern - a train to London every Saturday to meet up with pals in Davenports, The Magic Circle every Monday night, the club at Northampton every other Tuesday, league table tennis matches, helping out on the allotment, regular visits to the cinema, visits to The Bletchley Arms or The Bridge, and going to see bands whenever I could. It was a full life.

Work was going well. I had worked hard at college and passed my City & Guilds exams and was approaching the end of my apprenticeship. I was working in the sawmill by now on the benches, and one of the jobs I had there was to make the view frames for the pictures that were on display in first class compartments - obviously still popular in the early 70s as I was making batches of 50 at a time.

Another one of the regulars to visit Davenports on a Saturday morning was escapologist Alan Alan. In the summer of 1971 he invited me to spend the Bank Holiday weekend with him in Great Yarmouth where he was appearing at the Hippodrome Circus. His act was quite spectacular and included a straight-jacket escape from a hanging burning rope. A member of the audience is invited to inspect the jacket and then strap him securely into it, a rope is then tied to his feet and attached to a hoist and, when Alan's hands clear the floor, the rope is set alight and hoisted high into the air. As the rope rises and gets to the top of the tent, Alan turns twists and struggles to escape before the rope burns through. Needless to say, he does escape, the jacket is thrown down into the ring and he's lowered down to take a well-deserved round of applause. A week or two previously, the burning rope had burnt all the way through, and he'd landed on his shoulders. Luckily it wasn't from a great height, and he was soon back in action. As you'd expect that incident added a lot of interest to the act and from then on, the audience was convinced of how dangerous the feat actually was. I travelled there on the Saturday and was able to go with him to the evening performance. As he got ready in his dressing room, I couldn't help noticing several ropes prepared and hanging on the wall including the one that

Alan Alan showing burnt through rope

had burnt through. He told me he kept it as a reminder to take more care! After the show we went back to his rented flat for a meal and chatted magic for a couple of hours. Like me he was a huge fan of Tony Slydini, so we had a long chat about his style of performing and misdirection. I got my coins out and showed him some stuff and it turned out to be a late night. On the Sunday morning we went for a walk along the front and had a game of crazy golf which Alan was peeved about because I won. (I bought him an ice-cream to pacify him.) After that it was time to prepare for the matinee performance which I was able to watch from high "in the Gods."

That night, after Alan's spot, we rushed round to one of the other theatres in town to watch a performance from The Great Masoni and Shan. We sneaked in through the stage door and watched it from the wings. Their performance featured their well-known and very impressive double memory act. I loved it and so did the audience. Alan introduced us after the show, and they were just lovely. The Great Masoni (Eric Mason) wrote a book called, "Showmanship out of the hat," a best seller within the magic fraternity, full of sound advice that is as relevant now as it was when it was published 50 years ago.

It had been an enjoyable weekend and Alan had been glad of the company for a few days. During one of our chats he did tell me that Show Business can sometimes be a solitary and almost reclusive occupation, particularly if you work alone as he did. I got the impression he was a tad lonely, so hopefully he enjoyed our chats and stuff as much as I did. Alan worked all over the world and when he retired from performing, he opened a successful magic shop in London which sold tricks and novelties and was often a meeting place for his many magician friends. Alan was always good company with a host of stories, as you'd expect from many years in the business. He never did get over me beating him at Crazy Golf.

October 7th, 1971: *I went to the pictures to see Little Big Man, I've been working on lavatory seats all afternoon. Dad saw a bloke about some flowerpots.*

Yes, I was still writing my diary. I didn't have the time or the inclination to write more than a few scribbled lines in those days, but I always wrote something. I wrote in November that I had been awarded the degree of Associate of The Inner Magic Circle, almost as an afterthought.

In February of 1972 I went to my first Blackpool convention and loved it. In those days it was much smaller than the huge event it is now. I went with Bobby Bernard and Val Andrews (Val is a he) and stayed in the guest house that they had been staying in regularly for years which was run by Cyril and Shirley Critchlow.

There were other regulars too, who would also stay in the same room they always had over the years. It was such a great atmosphere, and the place was pretty much an open house for the duration. There were many characters there, including David Davies. David lived and worked in Blackpool as a bingo caller. He had one suit which he would wear all the time, day, and night. It was a dinner suit complete with black bow tie. He suffered from Alopecia and his cheap and ill-fitting wig sat on his head like a rug. David was of a slightly nervous disposition and would bite his nails and also scratch his head a lot - unfortunately he'd scratch in the same place which meant his wig was worn down to the canvas in one spot just above his right ear. The

Cyril Critchlow with an early design of "Critchlow's Magic Palace"

David Davies with a pal, taken at Cyril's B&B

one thing David was known for was his laugh. It's best described as a cackle, and it was loud. You could always tell where David was in a theatre! Due to his appearance and demeanour, sadly David was sometimes avoided and dismissed as being just another Northern eccentric. Nothing could have been further from the

Val Andrews, a mine of information on all things show biz

truth. He was very intelligent and knowledgeable, and an expert in comedy and all things showbiz. Our B&B landlord, Cyril, was also another great character. He was a founder member of The Blackpool Magician's Club and an avid collector of show business memorabilia. He eventually went on to open his own museum and theatre in the town. In those early days it was just a pipe dream, and he would show us drawings of what it would eventually look like. One evening he was talking enthusiastically about this obviously passionate project and one of us asked him what he was going to call it. It appeared to be something he hadn't thought of, so we offered a few suggestions. I came up with 'Critchlow's Magic Palace' which it was then known as (at least on paper). His remarkable collection can still be viewed in Blackpool and covers 230 volumes!

After the final show of the Convention, we all headed back to Cyril's and cups of tea and sandwiches were served. One by one everybody retired to bed apart from me, David, and Val Andrews. Val also knew his stuff and was the author of several books on bygone performers. Val was a lovely sweet, softly spoken man, in many ways the complete opposite of David. I sat up with them all night just listening. They talked about comedians they'd known and admired and discussed how and why they were funny. They traced the evolution of jokes and gags - who did it first and who did it better. They went through Max Miller's routines. They sang the songs of George Formby. They explained how to get an extra laugh from a gag by a pause or a look… and so it went on until breakfast at 8.30 in the morning. I don't think I've ever laughed (or learned) so much about comedy and entertainment as I did in those few hours. That evening was worth the price of the convention. It was a privilege too to spend it with those two wonderful and knowledgeable characters.

In September I went to the Llandudno IBM Convention. I entered the close-up competition again (without the felt covered board) but didn't come anywhere. Trevor Lewis from Holyhead won it, which was some consolation. While I was there, I was lucky enough to meet one of America's finest magicians, Larry Jennings. I was in the Headquarters hotel by the reception when I saw him. He was looking a bit lost, so I asked him if he was ok.

"A bit jet lagged, but I'm ok. Where's the bar, and where are the girls?"

"The bar's around the corner," I replied, "But you won't find too many girls!"

When I got back to my seat, he came to join us. There were about four of us sat around a small coffee table. After a while he went to his pocket and took out a couple of coins. He set them up in a way I was familiar with. Bobby gave me a nudge and we started to laugh.

"What's up? asked Larry.

"Ken does that," said Bobby.

"Show me," he said, handing over the coins.

I did the move and handed him back the coins.

"Son," he said, "You do it better than I do!"

He put the coins away. The move was a one-handed coin change, incredibly difficult but in that case very rewarding!

Working at Wolverton for British Railways did have the perk of cheap rail travel. I made the most of it with my regular trips to London. In those days you could get on any train, as long as it stopped at the destination on your ticket. I'd try and avoid the local trains coming home as they were often crowded and stopped at virtually every station. I'd aim for the 10.30 overnight sleeper to Scotland, as it only stopped at Watford and Bletchley before heading up to Glasgow.

On the night of the 1972 Magic Circle close-up competition (*"I didn't win anything, but people said nice things,"* according to my diary), I caught the train with plenty of time to spare. I climbed aboard one of the few corridor coaches which were tacked on to the back of several sleeping cars. I slid open the door of an almost empty compartment. There was one passenger, a rather attractive girl of about my age sitting next to the window. I asked her if it was ok to come in.

"Sure," she said, with a rather nice smile.

"Thanks very much, are you American?" I asked.

"I am, but don't let that stop you," she laughed.

I took my seat opposite and we began to chat. She told me she was travelling up to Scotland to spend Christmas and the New Year with her sister who was now living there. I explained that I lived in Bletchley, and I'd be getting off in about an hour's time. I went on to tell her what I did for a living and pointed out all of the woodwork in the compartment that I repaired or replaced. I did it in a self-deprecating way which made her laugh. She told me about her hometown and her plans for the future, college, and the rest of it. We chatted as if we'd known each other for years, an unusual occurrence for me. She asked me what I'd been doing in London. For a moment I wasn't too sure how to reply. At that time in the early 70s, magic was in the era of sparkly suits, glamorous assistants, boxes, tubes, cards, and doves, and it just wasn't cool. I would often smile through gritted teeth when asked if I had a dolly bird assistant, or could I saw the wife in half, or other equally banal stuff. Often it was better for people not to know. So that was the dilemma, should I tell this very attractive girl what I'd been up to that evening, or not…?

"I've been taking part in magic competition."

"Oh, wow, you're a magician!?"

"I'm afraid so."

"Could you show me something? I love magic!"

"Ok, why not?"

I retrieved my small case from the luggage rack, put a few things in my pockets and used the top of the case as a table. I glanced up and she was smiling in anticipation. A coin appeared at my fingertips, then it was gone, it reappeared behind my elbow, then it changed from silver to copper. Suddenly a thimble appeared which jumped from finger to finger then it was gone, and a giant one was suddenly there! She laughed out loud. I did other stuff as well for about half an hour before we pulled into Watford Junction station. Nobody came into the compartment. I carried on. We looked at each other, both of us smiling. What lovely eyes I thought.

"Have you had enough yet?" I asked.

"No! More, more!!" she laughed.

"Can I borrow your hands?"

"Sure," she said.

I took her hands in mine and looked at her, and my stomach did one of those flippy things.

"Are you sure you're up for this?" I asked.

"Definitely," she said.

I did the routine with small, coloured sponge balls which jumped from my hands into hers. It ended with me asking her to take my closed left fist into both of her hands.

"Let's see what's in there," I said.

She slowly released her hands, and I opened mine to reveal a huge 6" diameter ball. We both burst out laughing as the train slowed down and pulled into Bletchley station. Why is it that when you're anxious to travel somewhere it takes a lifetime, and when you want the journey to last forever it never does? I hurriedly re-packed my case. We looked at each other and I gave her a hug as the train came to a noisy stop. I left the compartment, then the train, and stood on the platform. She had her lips pressed against the window. I pressed mine against the glass to match hers until the train began to pull out of the station. I watched as it gathered speed, rounded the corner and was gone.

CHAPTER 8

A bit of a Hippie

When I look back at my life, I usually say that the years from 1971 to 1973 were probably the happiest - I had money in my pocket, enjoyed my work, loved my music, and was free. Free to go and do whatever I wanted. This was the era when I was engrossed in the underground music scene. It seems strange looking back now how there were two definite strands of music being played and listened to. On the one hand there were groups and bands doing rather mindless pop such as Chirpy Chirpy Cheep Cheep which catered to young teenagers and the singles market, and on the other hand there was a thriving underground scene with Rock, Blues, and Soul. This was popular with older teenagers and young people in their early twenties. Fans such as myself bought albums by the shed load. This was also the era when a good hi-fi became a 'must have'. I bought mine in separate parts and was lucky enough to have the skills to make my own cabinets, helped by future brother-in-law, Ken. The first album I played on it was of course, 'The Turning Point', and with the speakers either side of the room it felt as if I was actually there. I'd play my music as and when I could, and my new headphones were a Godsend. I'd often come home from the pub on a Friday night, put on an album, switch the button on the amplifier to remote, don my headphones and play along on my air guitar. On one memorable occasion I forgot to press the button and the sound was coming through my rather large Wharfedale speakers. I think I was being Peter Green at the time, but very soon became Ken Hawes again as I noticed Mum at the front room door with her nightie and curlers in, mouthing to me, "Turn it down!"

As is normal with popular culture, appearance and dress went hand in hand with the music. As far as I was concerned it meant long hair, denim shirts (had to be Wrangler), Levi jeans, and boots with big heels. I had a leather and suede patched jacket, as well as a selection of loon bell bottom trousers and T-shirts. Most of my clothes were bought from Kensington Market where I spent a fortune and many happy hours. I just loved it there particularly that distinctive smell of leather and joss sticks. My hair was long but never outrageously long. It was on my shoulders rather than down to my elbows. It was still a nightmare for Dad though, he hated it. On more than one occasion he'd refuse to even be in the same room as me. I tried to avoid him as often as I could to avoid a confrontation and upsetting the rest of the family. Inevitably there were unpleasant moments when he'd threaten to throw me out if I didn't get it cut, deadlines were set, (and broken), he told me I was obviously gay (but didn't use that word) and looked like a girl, and bizarrely he said I didn't have a mind of my own and was just doing what everybody else did. I tried to explain that he was trying to prevent me from doing exactly that. It didn't make any difference though and he never did accept it. Most of the time I kept my cool but there were times when I just lost it and said things I wish I hadn't. He was just bewildered by it all, the music ("It's got no tune in it."), the clothes, and pretty much everything else. He struggled to accept the fact that I wasn't a child anymore, but a 22-year-old adult trying to have a life.

I was still going along to the regular Sunday night concerts at the Youth Centre. It was there that I had my first taste of violence. That morning I'd been for a swim with a few of my mates. The seating was quite close to the edge of the pool so it was inevitable anybody sitting there might get splashed. Somehow, I'd accidentally sprayed a young teenage girl as I dived in. She made a bit of a song and dance about it and her boyfriend (a young skinhead) gave me some lip. I told him to sod off and it got a bit unpleasant for a few minutes. It was obviously all about him trying to look big and macho in front of his girlfriend. That night me and the same bunch of mates went to the Youth Centre to see the wonderful Champion Jack Dupree. As we were leaving, I noticed the same young skinhead hanging around by the door with a few of his pals. I was recognised and pointed out. They left the building before us and were waiting outside in the car park where there was no escape. I was soon surrounded (my mates nowhere to be seen). The young skinhead swaggered in front of me, pointing his finger and saying that I wasn't looking so big now that I didn't have my mates with me. The fact that he had a bunch of his cronies with him, and it was six or seven against one, wasn't lost on me. Just then he was pushed aside by another bigger lad who I assumed was the ringleader. I thought it best not to say anything. He glared at me and started to push and shove obviously enjoying the limelight. I soon began to find this young twat's arrogance and ignorance really annoying. I wasn't particularly scared; I was just angry. As his face came within an each of mine, I spat all over it. That's when they hit me from behind. I hit the deck, curled into a ball, and laid there while they put the boot in. All I thought about was protecting my hands. When I got to my feet, the ringleader, who I knew by reputation, gave me yet more verbal threats before they all strutted off into the distance. Although I wasn't hurt, it still shook me up. Years later I was doing the magic at a function in Bletchley and at one of the tables sat that same skinhead ringleader. He no longer looked slim, hard, and arrogant. He was obese. The years hadn't been kind to him, perhaps he was ill. I showed him a couple of tricks which made him smile.

I first saw Man (or the Manband as they're often known) in early1971 at the Youth Centre. For some reason it was an all-day event, and they did their set to a half empty hall in the middle of the afternoon. Like many bands at that time they were unique and didn't sound like anybody else. I loved what they were doing from the first note. The quality of the musicianship was outstanding. They began their set with a slow build up which led into the now familiar riff (for Man fans) of Spunk Rock. Several numbers in, they did something really unusual - a lovely haunting piece of music inspired by a storm at sea. You could almost feel the wind and rain as the storm erupts to a terrific climax and then disperses to a calm aftermath; all of this enhanced with sound of seagulls. I loved it. They ended their set with a 12-bar bluesy song which had everybody on their feet. The chat between songs was entertaining as well, the bass player being the perfect front man. I noticed the Welsh accent as well, which adhered me even more to the band. I saw them quite a lot throughout 1971, I'd buy the Melody Maker and scan the gig list, and if within easy reach of Bletchley (usually London), off I'd go often with my sister Jean. In 1972 my pal Chris became a fan as well. We saw them many times throughout the year, including twice on the same day, February 13th... in the afternoon at the Roundhouse where their set was recorded for the 'Greasy Truckers' album (that's Chris shouting, "More, more!" at the end of Spunk Rock), and in the evening at The Torrington, a pub in Finchley which came to be a regular haunt. Bearing in mind we were always at the front it was inevitable the band would recognise us. Soon we were invited backstage for a chat. From then on, we were on the guest list for future gigs and having a great time. Over the next year or so I began to do tricks for them before and after the gig which became as much a part of the evening as the music (well almost). This went on periodically for the following 30 years. I got friendly with them all, particularly Deke Leonard. Deke was a great guitar player and song writer, and later on became a bestselling author of a series of hilarious autobiographies. If it is true that this was the happiest time of my life, then Deke, Martin Ace, Clive John, Micky Jones, and Terry Williams, and all of the other musicians and roadies who played with the Manband over the following 50 years, were instrumental (pun intended) in making it so.

I spent a few days in Swansea with Deke and family in 1972. Much of it chatting and doing tricks and visiting a local pub. By this time I was used to performing in pubs so had no qualms about filling my pockets with bits and pieces and just going for it. In those days I was fearless and confident (perhaps overly so) all helped along after a couple of beers. There was a certain amount of danger here though, as once I'd had a few pints, I'd tend to do tricks to all and sundry whether they wanted to see them or not. Up until then I'd been lucky in the pubs in Bletchley as people had been generally positive and responsive. That night in "The Rhyddings" I was bought down to earth with a bump. I showed a trick to a young chap who happened to be sitting opposite. He watched with vague interest and when I'd finished, he explained exactly how I did it, and he was right. I did an Okito Coin Box routine, and he came up with the principle and explained that as well. So it went on. Whatever I did or tried he worked out and told me, and he was always right, I was getting despondent. I thought sod it, I'll do my thimble trick. This is novelty routine that I adapted from the stage act which I'd show to kids. By the time I'd got halfway through he was smiling and when I got to the big finish with the giant thimble he was laughing, as were the rest of the people there. He obviously enjoyed it but didn't tell me how I did it. He didn't tell me because it didn't matter. What *did* matter was that for those two minutes he was being entertained, while for the previous 18 he was trying to solve what to him were a series of puzzles. I learned a lot that night and soon began to rethink and adapt everything I did. Sleight of hand and being clever for its own sake isn't enough. You just cannot beat laughter to endear you to an audience however big or small it is.

Walking back to Hanover Street, I asked Deke if he'd ever had a bad night with the band.

"Too numerous to mention," he laughed, and told me a few stories as we walked.

"You should put those in a book," I said - and of course, he did.

I went to the Crystal Palace Bowl again, twice in fact. In June with Jean to see the Beach Boys (with Elton John), Melanie, Joe Cocker, Richie Havens, and Sha-Na-Na. The last three probably still cashing in on their appearance at the Woodstock Festival, and they all delivered. The Beach Boys were ok, but there were a lot of sound problems more than likely due to the horrendous weather. It just poured all day. Luckily, I had the foresight to check out the weather forecast beforehand and took a huge fishing umbrella which was big enough for the both of us. We took plenty of food as well which made the day bearable and cheaper. The weather was better for the second one in September. I went on my own this time although I was sort of seeing a girl based in London. It's a shame I didn't have a girlfriend at the time who shared my taste in music. I either went to see bands on my own or with our Jean or Chris, but then again, I was enjoying the freedom of having no ties. Anyway, on the bill were The Mahavishnu Orchestra with wonderful musicianship, but a bit too jazzy for my taste. Lindisfarne, who I loved with a set full of their own brand of Geordie sing along songs, and finally topping the bill, Yes. Having bought and played to death their two most recent albums, The 'Yes' album and 'Fragile', I was looking forward to seeing them. I wasn't disappointed. Not only did they perform music I was familiar with, but they also played, in its entirety, the brand-new album 'Close to the Edge'. Brilliant! My one memory of their set was the fact that the singer, Jon Anderson, had the words of the songs on huge boards in front of the stage (it was long before the days of iPads). It was a great and memorable day. There's nothing quite like sitting in the sunshine while listening to quality music.

I listened to the radio quite a lot in those days, John Peel mostly on Radio 1. One day I came across another Radio 1 programme on a Sunday evening. The DJ was Mike Raven who played mostly traditional American blues. I was hooked. Not just for the music, but also for the history of some of these remarkable musicians, many of whom were still playing. I did go and see a group of these traditional players when they visited England for a short tour. The gig was in a small lecture theatre in a college somewhere in London. It was a good night, and lovely to see these elderly gentlemen perform music that obviously meant so much to them, and indeed to the young audience - I'd always loved the blues and was getting back into it having recently bought a couple of early

Fleetwood Mac albums featuring the great Peter Green. There were other bands around playing authentic blues and Mike Raven would often feature them on his show. He played a track by a band based in London called The Nighthawks, I was really impressed. He went on to say they played regularly at a pub in Greenwich every Sunday evening. The next week I got on the train and the tube and went to see them. They were just great, and I regularly went every Sunday whenever I could. The guitarist's brother was on the door, and when he found out I travelled all the way from Bletchley every week, he'd let me in for nothing which was kind of him. I turned up one night and was told the singer/harmonica player was leaving the band. When I asked him why, he told me he'd put a lot into the music but was now getting little out of it. Make of that what you will. That's often the way in bands, differences of musical direction, personality clashes, boredom, disillusionment, the list goes on - ask the Manband, they made a career of it. Anyway I feel lucky and privileged to have seen The Nighthawks at their peak and still have happy memories of travelling down on the train, having a few pints, and absorbing the blues, often releasing emotions I didn't know I had. Nothing quite like it.

Meanwhile, the magic was going well. Thanks to my performance in the Magic Circle close-up competition, I was beginning to get a bit of a reputation. I was asked to take part in a, 'We teach you' session at one of the Circle meetings. I performed and taught some of my coin stuff. I suppose that was my first lecture. Soon after that I was asked to join the team of close-up performers involved in the 'Magic Circle At Home' events. These were evenings arranged especially for the public. Organised groups of people came in to see what The Magic Circle was all about. On arrival they were given wine and nibbles and then entertained by several close-up performers before going into the theatre. There they were given a lecture on the history of the Circle and magic in general. On completion of that they had a short break and the opportunity to buy Magic Circle packs of cards etc. Finally they'd go back to the theatre to see a stage show performed by the Circle's finest magicians. It was a good night out for both performers and the public. It also raised much needed revenue for the Circle coffers. For Magic Circle members who were not able to visit the club room regularly, a day of magic was organised especially for them. Members who live outside London are known as Country Members. The day of magic was called 'Country Members Day.' (Well, what else could you call it?) It was a similar format to the 'At Homes' inasmuch as both close-uppers (I was one) and stage magicians did their stuff. There were dealers as well displaying their latest miracles and all in all it was a good day. Later on in the year (1972) I was on the bill as a close-up performer at 'Ron Macmillan's International Magic Convention' in London. This was the first one of many organised by Ron and his family and became a regular and popular annual event. It soon became known affectionately as 'Ron's Day'.

Having finished my apprenticeship, I was by now a fully qualified Coach Finisher. At the time, I was working on restaurant cars, stripping out old counters and fitting new bars. It was a really interesting project and because I worked with a nice bunch of lads it was a good laugh as well. Over time I got friendly with the gas fitters who were sorting out the kitchens. They soon found out I did the magic and booked me as their 'After Dinner Christmas Entertainment'. The venue wasn't a fancy restaurant or pub, it was in one of the restaurant cars that had come in for repairs. The kitchen ovens were cleaned and lit, a turkey dinner cooked, and then served for all the blokes in the restaurant car. It all took place on the Friday we broke up for Christmas in a quiet area in one of the huge shops. God knows how they got away with it, apparently this happened every Christmas so I'm assuming a blind eye was turned. The day in question duly arrived. I found out the position of the coach and was told dinner would be served at two o'clock. I had some time to spare, so when I finished work at lunchtime, I thought I'd go over the road to the pub and have a quick pint beforehand. I think I had a bit more than a pint - by the time I got to the restaurant car I was swaying! I can only remember one trick, and that was the torn and restored bank note. I borrowed a pound note from a worried looking gas fitter and went for it. Luckily it went well, and I was re-booked for the following year.

It had been a good apprenticeship. I'd learned a lot and had been lucky to have experienced a wide variety of work. I'd really enjoyed a spell on the maintenance carpentry gang and learned a lot about work unconnected to a railway coach. I also enjoyed working on the benches in the sawmill. I was beginning to think about moving on to something else. Many of the men I worked with had been there for years, man and boy, all of their working lives. I wasn't sure that was anything to be proud of. I'd give it a year or so and then see how I felt.

In the summer of 1970 I went to Jersey for a week with a pal of mine from work. It was really nice, we hired a couple of bikes and cycled all over the island, we had a few beers and sunbathed etc., and I got quite friendly with the girl who worked at the B&B. I was quite taken with the island, so the following year I went back. This time with two other lads from work. It didn't quite work out as well as the previous year. On the first night the three of us went to a bar and had a few beers, and as we left a chap staggered past us and I said something like, "You look as good as I feel." He came up to me smiling and then nutted me in the nose! There was blood everywhere and I sobered up very quickly. The moral here is to avoid drunks, especially if they're Scottish as that bloke was.

Me in Jersey, loved it there

After that I preferred my own company, I wasn't on the same wavelength as the other two anyway. They'd prefer discos and clubs, and I'd rather go to a pub or a bar. There were other differences as well and, in the end, they went their own way and left me to it. I liked being on my own and having the freedom to do my own thing. The next year I sailed to Jersey for a third time on my own. I didn't book accommodation. I went to the tourism office on the quay and booked a place from there. As I wandered along the front, I bumped into a couple of lads I used to work with in the training school who were there for the summer working on a farm. I spent most of my evenings with them and a few others as they knew the best pubs and bars away from the usual tourist haunts. The days were spent visiting places of interest walking all over the island or lying in the sun. I was there for two weeks and had a great time.

When I got back, I thought it would be a good idea to book some driving lessons. There was a chap I knew quite well at work who came highly recommended. He had a small part- time business as a driving instructor and It seemed the sensible thing to do. I booked my first lesson which was about a week away. Somehow, I knew I'd struggle. We weren't a motoring family. Neither Dad nor Mum drove so I was never going to get any practise or experience and the father and son thing of tinkering with a car at the kerbside was never going to happen. I wasn't exactly desperate to drive or even own a car I just thought it would be useful and come in handy. Anyway, I still had my Railway Pass and a bike. During that week of waiting for my first lesson, I almost bottled it. Somehow, I persevered, and the big day arrived. The lesson was booked for after work at about 4.30. I assumed that the instructor would drive the car to a quiet country road somewhere or preferably a vast empty field. There he would explain the controls and then perhaps let me have a little go driving up and down in a straight line for an hour. Sadly that wasn't the case. I was very nervous as I walked out of the main gate and approached the car which was parked in a side street opposite the Works entrance. Autin (that was his name - I'll never forget it as it looks like a spelling mistake) was standing by the side of it. I went to get in the passenger side, "You're driving not me," he said. I got inside and he went through the controls for quite a while as we waited for the traffic to ease up. Eventually I turned the key, and we were off to Bletchley. I was terrified from start to finish. As we're driving down Bletchley Road where the shops are he told me to mirror, signal, and manoeuvre to the left and park outside Fosters menswear shop.

"Why?" I asked.

"Because I want to change a pair of trousers."

By the time we pulled up outside my house I was a wreck. I almost gave up there and then. I did go on to have over 30 lessons and passed my test on the second attempt over a year later. Even then I wasn't all that anxious to buy a car. It was about a year after that before I took that particular plunge. To this day I've never really taken to driving, and it was with considerable relief when in 2015 I got my bus pass!

I was still seeing bands regularly. The highlight of 1973 was going to see Carole King at the Rainbow in London, wonderful! I saw the Manband several times, mostly with Chris who was seeing them more than I was. He almost became a roadie at one point. Chris would often call round to see me to chat music and play records. It wasn't pleasant if Dad answered the door when he came to call. It was the hair thing again. With Chris it was down to his elbows. Dad got it into his head that I had long hair just because Chris did. I was then subject yet again to a predictable rant about not having a mind of my own. Things were getting uncomfortable, and it was affecting the whole family. My elder sister had moved out and married by this time. She wasn't shy about having a go at him for being so narrow-minded. My younger sister had a regular boyfriend and understandably kept out of the way. Mum was caught in the middle and getting fed up with it all. Her main concern was Dad's health. Something had to happen. Not only was I thinking of changing my job at this point, but I was also toying with the idea of moving out.

CHAPTER 9

Time for a Change

It was such a shame Dad was the way he was regarding the length of my hair. Because of his stubbornness and intransigence he missed out on seeing me perform. He could have come to the pub and sat with a glass of stout and would've loved it, especially in The Bridge where there were customers of his own age. I wouldn't have stood out as being outrageously different to anybody else of my age as we all looked pretty much the same. Oh well, I did ask, but he declined.

I was now actively looking around for a change of scenery regarding work. The way I saw it, I'd served my apprenticeship and got my City & Guilds qualifications and then spent some time gaining experience on the factory floor. Now it was time to move on and do something else. As Dad pointed out years ago regarding having a trade, "Once you've got it, you're set up for life. You could leave it and do other things and always come back to it." As I wasn't planning on leaving my trade but wanted to use my woodworking skills in other ways. I thought he'd be pleased. Predictably that wasn't the case when I told him of my plans.

"What! Why?!! You've got a job there for life, and what about the free rail travel?!!"

Never did the generation gap feel bigger.

There were two possible places of employment popular with ex-coach- finishers. One was Terrapin who built a type of Portakabin, and the other was Kemble's, better known as the piano factory. I made enquiries at both but with no luck. I finally found what I was looking for after spotting an advert in the local paper. A building company called Llewellyn Homes were setting up business in what by then were the early days of the new city of Milton Keynes. They'd booked an office in the Bletchley Job Centre and were having a mass recruitment drive for skilled, semi-skilled, and unskilled labour. It seemed perfect to me. I was a little concerned about lack of experience but as it said on the advert, "Full training will be given." I went for it. The interview went well, and I was offered the job. This time I didn't mention the magic, but they did eventually find out by default. After I'd been there for about a month, a photographer I knew (who had taken some of my early publicity photos) turned up for a shoot in the factory. After he'd gone the foreman came up to me and said, "Show us a trick"! It seemed Ray Lubbock, the photographer in question, had told all.

I started work there on May 7th, 1973. The company had a huge contract with the Milton Keynes Development Corporation for timber-framed houses to be erected locally and other contracts for sites all over the country, which was encouraging. Before we could begin churning out the panels though, the new factory had to be finished and prepared for production. For the first few months we built huge shop doors, benches, and racking for the stores, and also the production line where the panels were to be made. It was hard manual work, and I was knackered by the end of the day. Having spent the previous seven years in railway coaches I certainly noticed the difference. I had no regrets on leaving the Works though and soon settled in with my new workmates.

Work was going well, but my love life was all over the place. The relationship I was sort of having with the girl from London

The great Fred Kaps moments before I drunkenly showed him a coin trick

was sort of carrying on. Looking back now at my diaries of the time it was never going to come to anything. She lived 50 miles away for a start. I would go down to her place for the occasional weekend and she visited me a couple of times. During one of her visits to Bletchley (probably the final one) she told me of a conversation she'd had with my Dad. "He wants me to tell you to get a haircut, he obviously thinks I have some sort of influence over you, how strange." Strange indeed, it was getting beyond a joke. Anyway, life went on. We decided to book a few days away later on in the summer to a large magic Convention in Paris. There were a group of us going - Bobby Bernard, Ali Bongo, and his Mum Nellie (she was lovely), Geoff Ray, and a couple of others. I was looking forward to it. We booked well in advance as you do, but a lot can happen to a relationship in a few months. By the time we got there the throes of early passion had dissipated. We got to the hotel room and the first thing she said to me regarding 'us' was, "It's all over." Not the sort of thing you want to hear on the first day of a stay in Paris. It turned out to be a frustrating week. If that wasn't enough, two days later she was asked to be an assistant for one of the acts on the Gala show and ended up spending the night with him. Oh well, the magic was good. I met some of my heroes, Ricky Jay, Derek Dingle, and the great Fred Kaps which sort of made up for losing out on other things. The day after her night away, when I wasn't feeling very happy, I decided to sink a few beers at the bar. After about an hour I noticed Fred Kaps standing on his own flicking through a book. *Sod it*, I thought, *I'll show him a trick*. I went up to him and asked if he'd mind me taking a photograph. "Carry on," he said. I took the photo (which came out really well) and then I said (with some bravado fuelled by alcohol), "Do you mind if I show you a coin move I've been working on?"

"Not at all," he said.

I showed him the move where an English penny visibly changes to a Chinese coin.

"That's beautiful!" he said.

At that point (very much aware of outstaying my welcome), I glanced at my watch and said,

"I must go, thanks for the photo."

"My pleasure, thanks for showing me the move."

We shook hands and I weaved back to the bar where I spotted a grinning Bobby Bernard.

"I bet you couldn't have done that sober," he said.

"Probably not," I laughed.

There were other events that made Paris memorable - some great magic, a champagne breakfast up the Eiffel Tower, and there was a buffet lunch at the Palace of Versailles which was just wonderful. All in all it was ok and could have been a lot worse. We travelled home together as a group and said our goodbyes in London. With a quick peck on the cheek and a "No hard feelings," my ex-girlfriend went off to the nearest tube station, on the way no doubt to fall into the arms of her new boyfriend. I went home to Bletchley.

I was still going along to Magic Club meetings and was now on the Committee. I also did my first ever lecture at the club. A lot had happened in my 10 years of membership. Outside of the club things were looking up. As well as the Magic Circle 'At Homes', I was also on the close-up show at the Portsmouth Day of Magic. My reputation as a performer was growing. I was always striving to improve. Bobby Bernard was really helpful in the 70s. He kept me on the right track and was often brutal in his criticism, but it worked. I listened because he was right. I asked him once who he considered to be the best. "John Ramsay," he said without a moment's hesitation. Archie Tear had also said wonderful things about him. When I asked why, Bobby replied with a series of anecdotes. He told of when Ramsay was at a Convention banquet, the meal had finished, and everyone was waiting for the great man to perform. He asked somebody to collect his small case from his room. This was done and bought to him at the table. He asked for two small cardboard cups and a wand to be removed from the case and placed in front of him; that was done, and the case taken away. While all of this was going on he was drinking a cup of coffee and smoking a cigarette. When he was ready, he stubbed out his cigarette, picked up the wand and produced a small ball from the end of it and then went into the routine as known, producing yet more balls, then large ones, and finishing with paper streamers. Bobby went on to say that he'd watched it many times, but on this occasion was baffled as to when John had stolen the balls, as his hands had been in full view all the time. It turned out that John had eaten a 4-course meal, had a cup of coffee, and smoked a cigarette whilst four small balls were concealed in his hand! He knew he'd be asked to perform and, typical of John, was several moves ahead for over an hour. Ramsay's use of misdirection and psychology has never been equalled never mind surpassed. Sadly I didn't see him perform, but I did meet, and watch Andrew Galloway perform who was his one and only pupil. The phrase 'blown away' springs to mind. I suppose the greatest accolade received for the magic of John Ramsay came from Dai Vernon who, after watching John perform, went up to him and kissed his hands. Wow! That is the accolade to end all accolades.

After Paris it was back to a sometimes dreary normality so I decided to spice up my life by girl hunting.

There was a girl I'd fancied for quite a while, I'd often see her with her Mum and brother in The Bletchley Arms, and occasionally with a few of her friends in The Plough. The fact that we frequented the same pubs was encouraging. Somehow, I plucked up the courage to get in touch and we arranged to meet at the new Leisure Centre. As I went to the bar, I recognised the chap who was serving, he worked as a driver for one of the local timber merchants. I asked for a pint of bitter, a glass of white wine, a sheet of half-inch ply', a pot of glue, and a bag of 6" nails - he wasn't amused! Sometimes my sense of humour has that effect and has got me into trouble over the years. It's a risk I'm prepared to take though. Speaking of which. Should I take a risk with the girl waiting for her glass of white wine? - Yes, I decided, why not?

To begin with it was a bit of a struggle. There certainly wasn't an instant mutual attraction. She had recently had an acrimonious split from a long-term relationship, and as she was going through the emotional aftermath of that, her father died suddenly which really upset her. I certainly hadn't the life experience to advise or suggest very much to help. I wasn't equipped for it. All I could do was be there. There was a lot of emotion and strange moods which I took the brunt of. Over time and after one or two false starts, we eventually ended up as a couple in a relationship that would last for three years. I do have a lot to thank her for as she ignited my passion for reading and books. She also introduced me to the joys of live theatre and the songs of Leonard Cohen. We had some nice times together and one or two hairy moments regarding transport.

My mode of transport had graduated from on foot and bike to the internal combustion engine. I had bought my first car. To say that I bought it from a bloke in the pub should've possibly rung alarm bells, but in this case, Tony (the bloke in the pub) was great throughout the following year or two with motoring mishaps, and there were a few. He drove it over to the pub one evening for me to look at. Look at was all I could do as I knew sod all about cars. Luckily Tony did, as he ran his own car repair business. It was a 1966 Mark 1 Cortina and he wanted £150 for it. It looked ok to me, coloured white with the central panel a rather nice shade of red. I can remember the registration number OAR 216D (yet I can't remember the one presently sitting on the drive that I've had for two years.) I gave Tony the ok and arranged to pick it up from his garage which was close to Leighton Buzzard railway station. It was February 16th, 1974. I went over on the train and walked round the corner to where the car was parked, gleaming in the February sunshine. After Tony had pointed out various things I needed to know, I paid him the money and off I went on my first solo trip to Bletchley. I was terrified. I hadn't driven since I passed my test six months previously. I felt just as nervous as I was on my first driving lesson. It was a real white-knuckle ride speeding along at almost 40 miles an hour. By the time I got home I was so tense I could hardly move my neck. I parked outside the house and went inside. Dad hadn't said a word when I told him I was buying it and he didn't say anything when I walked in. I drove it round to show my girlfriend and later we drove to the table tennis club for a game with her young nephew. Parking there was easy enough, getting out wasn't. It took about a 10-point turn with my girlfriend out of the car giving me instructions from the back... and then the front ...and then the back. We got out eventually. (It was all good practice.) The next evening I took it round to show my sister, and on the way the windscreen wiper fell off. Was this an omen of things to come, I wondered? In a word, yes. The big test was to come the following day. My first long haul solo trip to Earls Barton in Northamptonshire, a distance of some 22 miles. It was the Magic Club Stage Competition. Although I hadn't performed the act for a couple of years, I managed to cobble something together after a couple of evenings of rehearsing. To be honest though I didn't really think about the Competition, it was all about the journey. The aim was to get there and back in one piece without incident. I allowed plenty of time, and after studying the map and writing down road numbers, off I went. After about 40 minutes of trouble-free driving, I managed to get to the general area of Earls Barton, inasmuch as I was in Northamptonshire. I knew I must be somewhere close, but I was starting to panic, and time was marching on. Suddenly I saw a sign on the left for Earls Barton. I spotted it as I drove past. I'd just have to turn around. I carried on along the quiet country road until I saw a field entrance by a gate. This'll do, I thought. I pulled up some way in front of it and reversed, turned the wheel, and drove straight into the ditch, missing the tarmacked entrance by a country mile. The car now had the rear wheels in the ditch with the headlights pointing skywards. *Oh shit*, I thought, Now what?! I'll have to try and get to Earls Barton and see if I can get some help there. But how? There's only one way, I'll have to hitch. I took my bag of props out of the car (God knows why.) and began to walk in the direction of the Earls Barton turning. Luckily a car soon came by, I stuck my thumb out and he stopped. I explained what had happened and he was kind enough to drop me off outside the hall. I rushed in and noticed the Competition had actually started. I found John Lee who lived in the village and straight away he phoned his mate who owned a tow truck.

"He'll be here in ten minutes," said John.

Sure enough the truck arrived, and he went back to the car and pulled it out (luckily undamaged). He left me by the side of the road with the car still pointing away from Earls Barton. Not to worry, I thought, If I drive up the road and take a left, then another left, that should lead me back to the village. That was the theory. I was soon totally lost in the middle of the Northamptonshire countryside. In an act of desperation, I stopped the car in another village (that wasn't Earls Barton) and knocked on the door of the nearest house and asked for directions. I finally got back to the hall just as the last act was on.

"Where have you been?" asked John, "Do you still want to enter?"

"I might as well, now I've got this far," I said.

I went to the car, picked up my bag of props and then realised I didn't have my suit with me. The suit with the ball-holders and special pockets was sitting at home! I'd have to perform the act wearing an old leather jacket and a pair of old faded cord trousers. I hurriedly put my tables on the stage, set up the props and tape recorder and was on. In nine minutes it was over, and what a relief. I packed everything away and was having a drink at the bar when they announced the competition result.

"Finally, the winner of the Northamptonshire Magician's Club Cup Competition of 1974 is… a young man who has had a few problems tonight, Mr. Ken Hawes!"

I went up to receive the cup and the President said to the audience,

"Would you like to hear him say something, just to prove that he can?"

"Yes!!" came the reply.

I approached the front of the stage and said,

"I'm sorry if I look as if I've been dragged through a hedge backwards, but I have! Thank you very much."

Winning! In spite of forgetting my suit!

Winning the competition hadn't entered my head, but what a lovely surprise. I soon came back to earth though when it dawned on me that I'd have to go through it all again and drive home. I made sure I knew the route and John gave me landmarks which were very useful. Off I went into the darkness and heaven knows what else. I actually did really well, I spotted the landmarks and knew I was on the right road. I got to the point where I knew exactly where I was, almost into Bletchley and I started to relax. Until I saw flashing blue lights behind me. A police car came along side and indicated for me to pull over. I wound down the window and was asked a few questions.

"Is the car yours, sir?"

"Sadly it is Officer."

While one Officer was asking the questions, the other was walking around the car with a torch.

"Why have you stopped me?" I asked.

"Because you were travelling so slow it looked suspicious."

I told them all that had happened, and they were really nice about it. I asked them if they had a Social Club at the local nick, when they said yes, I gave them a card. (Well, why not?) Off I went again. Almost home... only another couple of miles... then the engine coughed and spluttered and died! *For God's sake, now what?* I looked at the petrol gauge, out of bloody petrol. *Now what do I do?* I got my bag of props out of the car (to this day I don't know why I would put any value on a bag of old props) and walked about a mile along the road to a phone box. I had no change, so I dialled 999.

"Emergency, which service do you require?"

"I've broken down by the side of the road."

"I'm sorry caller but that isn't an emergency."

"It is if it's causing an obstruction."

"And is your car obstructing the highway?"

"Yes," I lied.

"I'm going to give you a number to call."

"I'm sorry but I don't have change."

"...Ok, where is the vehicle."

I gave the position and was told a breakdown truck would be there within the hour and to go back and wait by the car. By now it was raining which added to the misery. I picked up the bag of props and trudged back to the car. Sure enough a truck duly arrived. He checked out the car and said,

"You're out of petrol mate, not to worry I've got a can in the truck."

He reached for a can, lifted it up - empty. Then he went to the other side found another can and gave it a shake - empty.

"I'll put the car on the back and drop you off."

The car was hoisted on and dropped off outside the house at about 1.00 am. What a day! It turned out to be an expensive one as well, by the time I'd paid for two tow trucks. I did get some good publicity though. The local press came round to interview me about winning the cup and they used the whole saga as an angle. There was a photo of me with the cup and the car and the headline, 'Ken can't work magic with jinxed car'. Perhaps it would have been more honest had it have read, 'Ken won cup in spite of being a crap driver.'

My diary entry on the day after the competition was interesting.

February 20th, 1974: *Dad and I had a bit of a "barney" this morning about the car, hair, and appearance. It still upsets me to know that I'm hurting him - I Just don't know why.*

I think he was just worried from the night before when I got back really late. I'm sure many of us have experienced something similar when our offspring have taken the plunge into motoring, lying awake worrying, and waiting for the car to pull up outside the house and always fearing the worst. I was still baffled though as to why he had this thing about hair. Perhaps it was some sort of psychological quirk, who knows? What I did know was that if and when I had sons of my own, I wouldn't be anything like him. Judging by the tone of this piece in my diary it looked as if I was beginning to feel some sympathy. He was still my Dad.

The article in the local paper about the competition didn't come

The infamous car - and the cup

out until about a month later. I was quite surprised when the young reporter knocked at the door on April 16th. As we finished the interview, I asked him how he found out about that night.

"We had a letter from your Dad," he replied.

In spite of everything he was still a proud father.

By the end of the year he was back in hospital. He had various tests and had a more permanent Pacemaker fitted. I went to see him with Mum and was quite concerned by his appearance. He'd lost a lot of weight and didn't look well at all. He came home in time for Christmas and was soon back to his old self.

Unsurprisingly that night of the competition wasn't the only disaster of my first year of motoring. I drove to the pub one day and crunched the nearside wing on the car park wall. A few weeks later one of the battery terminals sheared off (new battery required), soon after that I drove to the pub again and crunched the offside wing (on the same wall). So much for not making the same mistake twice. The most spectacular thing happened on the M1. I was driving home after visiting my girlfriend who was at college in Derbyshire. I heard a bit of a clunk from under the bonnet and a red light came on the dashboard. I pulled onto the hard shoulder as soon as I could as smoke and steam began to emerge from under the bonnet. To cut a very long and painful story short, it cost me (among other things) a taxi fare from Leicester to Bletchley and a new engine. Finally it failed the MOT (of course) with rusty brake pipes. There was one plus though amongst the horror stories, I did manage to drive up to Dundee and back unscathed - 12 hours to get there and 9 to come back. So ended my first year as a driver. Eventful? - Yes, Expensive? - Yes, Enjoyable? - No, Regrets? - Yes and No.

It had been an eventful year. The car and driving dominated, but there was success with the magic. Winning the club Stage

Competition, and the Close-Up too, in spite of shooting a nail through my thumb at work during the day. Yet another Competition with mixed fortunes. Life carried on in its familiar and predictable way.

One Saturday morning in September, I went to London as usual and met up with Bobby Bernard in Davenports.

"I've got a surprise," he said, "How would you like to meet John Calvert?"

"Great! I said, how and when?"

John Calvert was a charismatic figure and one of the few magicians able to put on a lavish magic show. At the time he was travelling the world on a yacht and was visiting England to perform at the IBM Convention in Hastings followed by his, "Magicarama" show in London and finally an appearance at the Blackpool Convention. Bobby had arranged for the two of us to meet him on his yacht which was moored up at Rotherhithe. We arrived at the docks in the afternoon and found out where the boat was moored and soon discovered it was some distance away from the quay. John was on his deck, spotted us, and called out directions as to the best way to reach him between other moored boats, which wasn't straight forward. When we finally got to John's yacht there was one final obstacle. A plank. Bobby was the world's greatest hypochondriac, blind as a bat and one of the least physical people I've known.

"I don't think I can do this," he said.

"Yes, you can," said John, "I'll hold my hands out, look me in the eye don't look down and walk briskly towards me, I will catch you."

And that's exactly what happened. Quite remarkable really, as Bobby wasn't a small man, and John was in his 60s. I followed a relieved Bobby onto the deck. We went down a couple of steps into a small but cosy cabin where John's assistant, Tammy, was waiting to greet us. She was a beautiful woman, petite with very long black hair. Her face wasn't exactly Oriental, more Filipino. She was beautiful in temperament too and the perfect hostess. Tea was served by John's other assistant and crewman, Henry. Once we were settled, the conversation soon began with John telling us stories about his time in Hollywood and his adventures of travelling the world. After a while, as it became dark, John asked Bobby what the time was. Bobby looked at his wrist and with horror discovered his watch was missing - Bobby did love a bit of bling and heaven knows what it was worth. He mentally retraced his steps and said…

"I must have taken it off when I washed my hands in the cafe after Davenports."

His face was white. He looked around the cabin in the forlorn hope of it suddenly appearing. Meanwhile John began to grin, he reached into his pocket and produced the watch.

"I stole it when you came on board," he said, "It was easy as your mind was obviously elsewhere, you'd just walked the plank!"

Bobby laughed as he replaced his watch on his wrist with considerable relief. John carried on with tales of his remarkable life. I asked him if he thought people who were really bright and intelligent were harder to fool than those who weren't.

"Not at all, he said, anybody can be misdirected, I stole the watch of Albert Einstein - twice!"

The evening was drawing to a close and it was time to go. John went on deck with a torch, and we followed him over the plank, past the moored-up boats and back to the quay. We said our goodbyes and thanks, shook hands and with a shout of, "See you in Hastings!" he was gone, leaping from gangplank to gangplank like a 20year old.

A few months later I went to see him perform in London. It was a great show. Before I took my seat I popped down to the Gents and, as I was washing my hands, I heard a bit of a commotion from one of the cubicles behind me. I turned round to see a middle-aged man almost falling through the door, obviously the worse for drink. He stumbled back inside leaving the door half open.

"Are you ok?" I asked.

"I'm fine thank you, but I can't find the flush handle."

I reached over, pulled the toilet roll off the handle and pressed it.

"There you go, easy when you know how."

"Thank you very much, you're a very kind young man," he said, as he weaved towards the exit door.

I recognised him straight away as a former Minister in Harold Wilson's government. The rumours regarding his input of alcohol obviously true.

CHAPTER 10

Decisions, decisions

My love of music was continuing. I was still going to see the Manband regularly and had a memorable night at the Adelphi theatre in London. I didn't actually see them on stage. While they were playing, I was in the bar having a chat, a laugh and a few beers with Chris and Spiv, the roadie. At the end of the show we staggered into the dressing room where I did a few tricks for the band and guests. Happy days… well they were then. Some 6 months later I went to see them at the Roundhouse. I spoke to the chap on the door who told me the venue was full and they wouldn't be letting anyone else in. I could understand the rules and his position, but he was still a bit of a jobsworth. I asked him if he'd mind checking the guest list and look for 'Ken the magician'. He went inside the glass cubicle and looked down a list of names.

"Sorry mate you're not on it."

"Ok, could you get a message to the dressing room and tell them I'm at the door?"

Just then one of the Roundhouse staff walked by and the doorman asked him to pop down there and pass on the message. After a while he came back with the message, "Never heard of him." I went to the pub over the road for a couple of hours and had more than a few. People were coming out at the end of the gig as I went back to the front entrance.

"You're persistent I'll give you that," said the doorman, "Follow me." I was led to the dressing room which was full of people I'd never seen before. I saw Micky Jones the guitar player who introduced me to new band member John Cipollina. The atmosphere was different. The band were riding high after a recent successful tour in America. No wonder they were all excited and hardly surprising I'd been missed off the guest list. I didn't stay long as I felt I was in the way. It looked as if the days of chatting and doing tricks in college and pub dressing rooms were over. It would be some years before I'd see them again.

Anyway, I was still enjoying life in general, I had a girlfriend, the magic was going well, I was still playing table tennis in the local league, and I had a well-paid job – and finally, I was mobile… most of the time. I had every reason to be proud as well.

April 15th, 1975: *I'm President of the Northamptonshire Magician's Club as from today. It was the AGM. I don't think I handled it all that well, in fact I'm just beginning to realise what I'm letting myself in for. The venue for next year's dinner is a bit of a headache at the moment. However I might get a lot of work done at the committee meeting next week.*

(Some 47 years later I'm back on the committee and we still have the same problem!)

Dad was pleased with the news, of course he was. One of the reasons he was pleased was because he assumed it would mean me getting a haircut. We also had a disagreement about what form the photograph should take in the local press. He suggested it should be an almost Victorian pose of me standing proudly wearing the chain of office with the ceremonial wand displayed in front of me.

I wanted a photo of me doing something that might sell me as an entertainer. The photo appeared a week later with me smiling into the camera producing a large coin from a purse frame. I had my way and why not? After all, I was the President!

By this time I'd been friends with Bobby Bernard for about ten years. As well as being a good magician he was an experienced producer and actor. He knew his stuff and was able to instil in me not just the importance of personality, but also how vital it is to communicate to and with an audience. He put it like this (bearing in mind I was a teenager at the time) …

Mick Chardo and Bobby Bernard - I owe them both so much

"The audience must *want* to watch you; they'll want to watch you if they like you. You need to have the ability to communicate with as wide a range of people as possible. Mums and Dads should want you as a son, girls as a boyfriend, lads as a pal, and you have to be at the very least acceptable."

He went on to talk about tricks…

"The trick is a means to an end. The trick is the hook upon which you hang your personality. The trick and the performance of it should be as one. **You** are more important than the bloody trick!"

Bobby would often lose it and get frustrated when I didn't quite get it. A few years passed before the penny did finally drop. We were at a convention somewhere and he said there was somebody he wanted me to see.

"Watch him, and the audience and learn," said Bobby.

"Who is it?" I asked.

"Mick Chardo, from Manchester."

"Never heard of him."

It was a close up show and I watched with interest as the first performers did their stuff with cards and coins, most of it clever and very slick I thought. They performed for ten minutes and left to polite applause from the audience. Then Mick was announced. A small middle-aged man bounded out and walked to the front row and said, "Lady chose a card," in a broad Manchester dialect. I don't honestly remember what he did after that, but I do know it was hilarious. That makes the point, it didn't matter what he did. **He** was entertaining. He finished his spot and left with hearty applause and laughter ringing in his ears. After Mick there was one more act who did yet more card tricks in a similar style to the previous performers. The difference between Mick and the rest of them was like chalk and cheese. The other performers may well have been better magicians with impeccable technique, but none of them could hold a candle to Mick as an entertainer. That afternoon was a lightbulb moment and things were never quite the same after that. I spoke to Bobby afterwards and said,

"Now I get it."

"FINALLY!!" he shouted.

That night we spoke at length.

"Mick works for the public while most of the other performers this afternoon don't. That's the difference, and did you notice his entrance? He made an impact the moment he walked on."

"I did, and something else has occurred to me, if you have a strong personality with certain traits that are unique to that personality you can use them as misdirection."

"YES!" he shouted again, "Like John Ramsay, Slydini, Malini, and Vernon. At the very least you have to aspire to be as good as the best. Use their technique to suit YOU!"

These were wise words. Some years later when I was on the magic club lecture circuit, I would do my best to pass all of this on to other magicians, particularly youngsters. Invariably, during questions afterwards, I would only be asked technically based things. All they were interested in was the trick and the technique and not the performance of it. I had lecture notes full of useful information, but with no tricks. I didn't sell many and I gave up in the end. Bobby would often say to me that he had the same response.

"They don't realise that if they listened then it could open a door to something that would make them much better performers."

Bobby was also a great raconteur, with stories of when he met Cardini, Richard Himber, Vernon and Ramsay, the list went on. He was always very good company and spoke a lot of sense. He would constantly tell me to make the most of what talent I had and if I carried on improving both technically and personally then I could be a very successful professional close-up entertainer. All very well, but was it something I really wanted to do with my life? In all honesty, at the age of 25, I had my doubts. Right from the beginning, as much I loved the creative process and performing for people, I never really aspired to do it for a living. The difference between me and Bobby was that magic and show business was all he had. He was in his 40s, living alone, and magic, the theatre, and films dominated his life. Whereas I had other interests. There were times when I wanted and needed a break from magic. Bobby would often tell me of other young performers with potential he'd helped and tutored over the years, many of whom had stopped performing and sunk without trace once they'd gotten into a relationship. Now that I had a girlfriend myself, and judging by the stuff I was writing in my diary, I too would find it difficult to choose between a loving relationship or being a professional entertainer, if it ever came to that. It seemed obvious to me having thought about it, that if you work as a semi pro' you can have both. Then Bobby had an idea which made me change my mind again.

He came up with a plan of booking a cruise. He could see potential there as a possible outlet for close-up magic. With bars and restaurants and private dinner parties and all sorts of things happening they were perfect conditions for performers such as us. The idea was to book it as a holiday, do the stuff in the bars and get ourselves noticed and hopefully booked as entertainers for the entire cruise. After that who knows. Other cruises? I have to say the idea of sailing around the world performing magic and getting paid for it did have a certain attraction. We went ahead and booked a 9-day cruise with the Shaw Savill Line taking in Tangier, Gibraltar, and Lisbon. We agreed that at its worst it would be a good holiday, and so with the attitude of nothing ventured nothing gained, on June 7th we arrived at Southampton and boarded, 'Northern Star'.

The cabin was a 4-berth which for some reason we had to ourselves, but even so, it was a bit cramped. We unpacked and went to explore and found the

Northern Star - hardly comparable with modern day cruise liners, nonetheless a memorable holiday

167

restaurant where we'd be having all our meals. That evening we duly set off and sat at the table which we'd made a note of on our earlier visit. Other passengers turned up and there was some confusion as to the seating arrangements. It turned out that not only were we at the wrong table, but we were also in the wrong restaurant on the wrong deck. Bobby's sense of direction was as useless as mine. We got there in the end and found our table which we shared with the ship's doctor. By the end of the week I felt a bit sorry for him… surely there is nothing worse for a doctor than to be sat next to a raving hypochondriac such as Bobby. Also on our table was a father and his teenage son from Manchester and a rather plain single lady who goes on a cruise every year looking for a man (according to Bobby, although he didn't put it quite like that) - no chance with either of us. Further down the table was a group of teenage girls from South Wales. That was more like it!

The food was amazing, and you could eat as much as you wanted, which we did. After the meal we adjourned to the bar and Bobby went off to, "have a quiet word with the Purser." Meanwhile I went off to do something similar with the Welsh girls. It was at this point that I realised how odd it must have looked with me and Bobby sharing a cabin. I was a 25-year-old bloke and Bobby was 20 years older, bald, and very Jewish. I explained to the girls what the plan was regarding the magic etc. (to this day I reckon they assumed we were a gay couple). Anyway not much I could do about it apart from chatting them up and showing them a few tricks. Bobby returned from his quiet word and told me what had happened. He'd explained to the Purser that we were entertainers and was it ok if we worked in the bars? He was happy for us to do that, but then went on to explain the entertainment was bought in as a package which in this case was a group of

Australian singers and dancers plus one English comedian. The entertainment budget had gone, implying of course there would be no money for us. When Bobby asked about potential work on other cruises, the Purser continued with yet more bad news. This was the final passenger cruise that the Shaw Savill line would be doing. From mid-June it would be cargo only. Not the news we wanted, especially on the first day! The Purser did say that he'd like to see us perform and to take some stuff along to the captain's cocktail party the following evening. Although things weren't quite going to plan, we were philosophical and decided to make the best of it. I asked Bobby if he wanted a drink and he said,

"I'll have one when I get back."

"Where are you off to now?"

"I'm going to have a quiet word with ship's photographer."

When he got back some time later (he'd got lost) he told me what had transpired with the second quiet word of the evening. After buying him a drink and slipping him a fiver, the photographer agreed to take photos of us performing.

"We could get some really good publicity photos out of this," said Bobby (his enthusiasm undimmed).

"Ok," I said, "I'll do the bottle trick; if I do it for the Purser, hopefully the photographer can get a good reaction shot."

The bottle trick is the production of a full bottle of wine right under the spectator's nose. The following day I explained all to the photographer and made him aware of the best position to be when the bottle appeared. That evening we dressed up and made our way to the party. We had a drink and a chat and eventually I was introduced to the Purser. Everything was set and the photographer was in position to capture the moment. I did the preamble leading up to the production and then, under his nose, the bottle! To say that he was underwhelmed was an understatement. He barely blinked, there was a half-smile and that was it. I'd performed it hundreds of times always to a strong reaction, from screams to total open mouthed amazement; never before had I performed it to a mere half-smile! After that he was off to circulate and mix and mingle leaving me slightly bewildered, it was a strange moment. All was not lost though as some other passengers who had seen the bottle trick **were** impressed and we were in.

After about an hour of doing tricks, the passengers began to disperse and head back to their cabins. At this point the Purser had a **very** quiet word with us. He said that the guests had obviously enjoyed what we did and to feel free to do the stuff whenever we wanted. Sadly, as already implied, he wouldn't be able to pay us a fee. However, he suggested that we keep our eye on the Bingo game that runs throughout the week. Each day every passenger receives the day's events on a type-written sheet. In the top right-hand corner is a number (chosen at random of course) which you add to the supplied Bingo card.

"You never know you might WIN," he said with a wink and something more than a half-smile.

Believe it or not, at the end of the week, when we checked the numbers, we'd 'won' £40 which I went to collect.

"What a nice man," I said to Bobby as I handed him a £20 note.

We arrived at Tangier first and did the usual tourist stuff including visiting the markets where we were continually hassled by small children asking for money. Some of the stall holders had a limited knowledge of English; there was one who repeatedly spoke his one and only sentence with perfect pronunciation…

"Good morning! Marks and Spencer and British Home Stores here," which sounded really funny, and of course got him noticed.

We also went on a pre-arranged bus trip to another local town and visited a school. I watched with interest some young lads who couldn't have been more than ten, making copper cups using only a hammer and a lump of wood. Beautiful craftsmanship. The next day we berthed in Gibraltar; I wasn't impressed, as I wrote in my diary…

June 11th, 1975: *We berthed in Gibraltar early this morning. The day had a bad start when a woman spilt something over Bobby's suit. This upset him somewhat. We had a trip in a taxi. It's quite a pretty place, but apart from that it's a bit of a dump.*

Before we left the boat that morning, we were told the importance of being back on board at the correct time.

"The boat cannot and will not wait for latecomers. It has to sail with the tide."

With that in mind, and Bobby being a worrier, we were back on board with about an hour to spare. At the given time we decided to go on deck and watch as we pulled away from the quayside. We were a few hundred yards out and I noticed a bit of a commotion on the quay. There was a young couple waving and pointing at us along with a port official; obviously passengers, and obviously late. Soon after they were put on to a launch which came hurtling towards us. The question was, how on earth would they get on board? They came alongside bobbing about in the swell as a rope ladder was thrown over the side. They made a grab for it and hauled themselves on board. It was quite a height, I'm not sure I would have attempted it, Bobby certainly wouldn't.

Early the next morning, we berthed at Lisbon and got on a coach for a guided tour of the city. The guide was good and his commentary interesting. I was really impressed with the place. The huge statue of Jesus was undoubtedly the highlight. For the remaining few days on board we did bits of magic in the evenings and chatted to the passengers and generally had a nice time. By the time our last day arrived I'd just about had enough. I'd over-eaten, had too much to drink, and smoked too many cheroots. I did have a pleasant afternoon though sun-bathing on deck with the four bikini clad Welsh girls. That evening we made sure the photographer earned his fiver by using up a roll of film as we entertained a rather nice family from Worksop. We did get a load of photos which was about as much as we could have expected from our time on the boat. All in all we'd had a good time. Sadly, the week was to end on a sad note.

The next evening alarm bells sounded, and we made our way on deck to find out what had happened. We noticed our friend the doctor on board one of the lifeboats which was still in its harness and ready to be launched should it be required; he had his safety gear on, as did the few crew members with him. We discovered that a young 19-year-old crew member had thrown himself over the side. The ship circled for a while until it got dark and then set sail for Southampton. Sadly his body was never found.

The cruise was a good experience, we had some useful publicity photos, weren't out of pocket, and it did meet the worst of our expectations, it was a good holiday.

Things soon got back to normal at home. I was still with my girlfriend who by this time had finished college, had a job, and her own flat. I would get together with my pal Chris from time to time and he also had his own flat. I decided to start putting money away every week into a Building Society to save for a place of my own. I still had no real desire to pursue a career in magic, even after the cruise. I was also toying with the idea of changing my job. I fancied being a cabinet maker; after all, I was qualified to City & Guilds level. My interest in music was still as strong as ever. I listened to the radio a lot at the time and the Nicky Horne show on Capital Radio was one of my favourites. It was called, 'Your Mother Wouldn't Like It'. In my case though it was more a case of, 'Your mother might like it, but your father definitely wouldn't!' That was however bought into question on a Monday evening in September.

One day Nicky gave his listeners prior warning of a huge event that would be happening on the programme on the evening of September 8th 1975. He would be playing the brand-new Pink Floyd album entitled, 'Wish you were here', in its entirety. I'm fairly certain I wasn't the only Pink Floyd fan to set up a tape recorder on that Monday evening. This was a huge event. I tuned in as usual on the big night and made sure everything was plugged into my Grundig tape recorder correctly and waited for the moment. It was duly introduced, and I pressed the start button. A few minutes into the opening track my Dad walked in, he stopped in his tracks and listened to the opening sequence of 'Shine On You Crazy Diamond'. We were both mesmerised.

"That's really lovely," he said, "I've never heard anything quite like that."

Neither had I. To be honest I was surprised by his reaction. It was unexpected as at any other time he would have dismissed it as being yet more long-haired rubbish. Perhaps he was beginning to mellow or making an effort to get to know me again. Whatever the reason, it was a lovely moment.

"What's it called?" he asked.

"Wish you were here," I replied.

1976 was a year of mixed fortunes regarding the weather. It has gone down in history as one of the hottest on record. It didn't start too well though with almost hurricane force winds in January. A sad time for Dad as well. His health was deteriorating, and I think he was finding work difficult too. What happened in January may well have been a last straw moment for him.

January 2nd, 1976: *Tonight has been a disaster. The weather has been dreadful with gale force winds, and as a result Dad's greenhouse has been wrecked. Poor chap. I've never felt as sorry for anybody as I have for him tonight. He walked in and said, "It's gone," and cried like a baby.*

Dad in his new greenhouse

I helped him tidy the broken glass the next day and tried to cheer him up as best I could.

"We'll soon get another one," I said.

A drive over to a Northampton supplier cheered him up a bit. A couple of months later a new one was delivered, and with the help of family and friends it was erected and fixed firmly to its new base.

Car problems were still happening on an almost daily basis, and it was getting me down. It came to head early one Sunday morning. Whenever I visited my girlfriend, I'd park the car on the well-lit road opposite her flat. I thought it would be safer there than the secluded car park at the rear of the building. Although she lived on the top floor of her block, the car was plainly visible from her kitchen window. One cold January morning, it wasn't. Somebody had nicked it. I phoned the police to report it missing and then went over in my mind what I had foolishly left inside it. Logbook, driving licence, a good quality cassette tape recorder (which I used for the magic) and a box full of home-recorded tapes (including the Pink Floyd one). How stupid and naïve! It took months to make those tapes. I didn't hear anything from the police until the following Tuesday. The car had been found in Bedford some 20 miles away. It was drivable and I had to go and pick it up from the police station. I got a train over there and of course everything was indeed missing. I wasn't happy. The next day I had a visit from the police, who were a bit cagey and were reluctant to tell me anything; they were more interested in my insurance details. I suppose looking back they had to make sure I wasn't involved in anything devious. I had after all left both the logbook and my driving licence inside it. What sort of idiot would do something as crazy as that? Anyway I'd had enough of the bloody thing. Time for a change, I'd look for another one. As it happened, one of my workmates was selling his car, and would I be interested? It was another "D" reg Mark 1 Cortina, but this was a GT model. It had black leather bucket seats, a low suspension, a dashboard that looked like Concorde, and a twin choke Webber carburettor! It was two-tone in colour, orange and green. How could I refuse? There soon came a time when I wished I had. The main problem was the low suspension. Every time I went through a deep puddle the engine cut out. Lucky then that during the summer of 1976 it hardly rained at all. It was also lucky that I'd booked a two-week holiday in Cornwall with my girlfriend. I'd hired a privately owned cottage in the picturesque town of Lostwithiel, close to the river. We travelled over night to miss the bulk of the holiday traffic, stopping once in a layby as I began to nod off. That was a bit scary. There was a huge sign close by warning people to take a break, obviously an accident black spot. We got there ok, but car trouble started the next day when the lights refused to work, and when they did decide to come on again, the indicators packed up. Not a good start to the holiday. I booked the car into a local garage which got it sorted. Two days later the red warning light came on and water was dripping onto my feet from a leaking heater hose. Neither of us were very happy and I was also getting 'the silent treatment', which didn't help. Back into the garage and more expense.

At the beginning of the second week, I took a gamble and booked a trip to the Scilly Isles. This necessitated an early morning 50-mile drive to Penzance. Luckily the car behaved itself and we got there in time to catch the ferry. We were on the boat for almost 3 hours; not a pleasant trip as many of the passengers were struggling (and failing) to hang on to their breakfast. On arrival we decided to take a guided tour on a coach that was as ancient as the guide. It was good fun though as the battered old 1950s bus slowly made its way around the Island of St. Mary's. The guide pointed out places of interest and spoke about the history of the island as we chugged along. Suddenly the bus came to a grinding halt as he pointed out a small red roofed cottage.

"That", he said dramatically, "Is the holiday home of our former Prime Minister, Mr. Harold Wilson!"

Every head in the bus turned to have a look at the rather plain little house hoping to catch a glimpse of the man who was still in the news, having unexpectedly resigned from office some 6 months previously. We were disappointed as there was no sign of life. There was however a washing line upon which hung a solitary item, an enormous pair of men's underpants which were flapping majestically in the breeze. Many people could lay claim to having met or seen a national leader, but there can't be many who could say in all honesty that they've seen a pair of a former Prime Minister's underpants. It was a good day. In fact we had a nice time for much of the fortnight we were in Cornwall. By the end of the final week though, cracks began to appear. I was still getting the silent treatment, and she was really winding me up with her moodiness. One of the last events we'd planned was a visit to the small town of Fowey on the evening of the local carnival. At the last minute she decided she didn't want to go. Sod it, I went on my own. Off I went and luckily found a parking space and made my way to the main street. It had been yet another hot day and it was a beautiful warm evening. The carnival parade wound its way through the narrow streets led by a brass band playing the Cornish Floral Dance. As they were playing, local people in flowery costumes danced alongside collecting money for a children's charity. As they passed by, I popped into a pub for a pint and noticed there was a folk club in the room upstairs. I stayed there for about an hour listening to local performers sing traditional songs. At one point the young Carnival Queen and Princesses called in looking flushed and happy. They stayed for a while and left to warm applause and best wishes from everyone in the room. Soon it was over, and I drove back to our cottage. My girlfriend was asleep in bed. I was beginning to get a touch irritated. Perhaps it was time to change girlfriends as well as my job.

After the holiday I decided to look for another job hopefully in the furniture business. I was aware of a factory in Bletchley that looked promising. As far as I knew they weren't advertising, but I popped down there one evening and put a letter through the letterbox. A couple of days later I was asked to go for an interview and was offered a job. The money wasn't as good as Llewellyn, but with a bonus scheme there was the potential to earn more, depending of course on how fast you were. I decided to go for it. I handed in my notice at Llewellyn who were really kind and said I could go back there any time if things didn't work out.

I started work at 'Cleanline Furniture' on October 4th, 1976. The company manufactured reproduction antique furniture out of veneered mahogany, yew, and oak. Most of it was exported to Europe. It looked great when it was polished and finished. I soon settled in and enjoyed the work in spite of the dust which was everywhere. I was working less hours as well which was good. I did notice the drop in money though as my diary implied.

October 18th, 1976: *It's Mum and Dad's anniversary today, they seem to be happy with the present I bought them… an apple sauce holder.*

Chapter 11

Onwards and Upwards

The end of my Presidential year of office culminated with the magic club dinner. I was looking forward to it although slightly apprehensive as I had to give a speech. The last thing I wanted was to make a fool of myself as I'd invited some of the lads from work as well as family and friends. It had to be good! I didn't want a 'Thanks for your support' type of thing which was the usual format. I needed something different. I thought about it for a while and decided to relate the story of the night of the competition when everything went wrong. If it was good enough for the Bletchley Gazette, then it was good enough for the dinner. I rehearsed it a few times and wrote it in a self-deprecating humorous style which was pretty much how I delivered the magic anyway. I do remember a small part of it which was when I'd just been pulled out of the ditch and then had to drive the relatively short distance to the hall in Earls Barton...

"I got back into the car which was now facing in the opposite (wrong) direction. I had a plan though. I would turn left, then left again, which would take me into the centre of Earls Barton - simple. I drove off. Why is it you can never find a left-hand turn when you want one?! Loads of right turns, no lefts! Miles later, I found one. I turned left and then left again. Still no sign of it! To this day I'll swear that on that cold February night in1974, somebody moved Earls Barton."

It went down well, and I finished by thanking the members and committee for their huge support and I promised I'd wear it! It turned out to be a really good evening.

Things were going well with the magic too. I went to the IBM Convention in Brighton and was on the bill as a tutor in one of Bobby Bernard's Clinic sessions. The highlight of 1976 though was undoubtedly winning the Magic Circle close-up competition, or as it's now known, 'Close up Magician of the year.' I was chuffed to bits and the £10 prize money came in handy too. I got home quite late, but Dad was still up and waiting to find out how it all went. (We never did have a phone installed at home.) He'd had to retire from work due to his failing health a few weeks previously and wasn't at all well, he was however reasonably happy and philosophical about the future. He was delighted I'd won, and it was a proud moment for both of us.

A week later I took part in a 'We teach you' session at the Magic Circle, teaching coin moves and tips about creating routines. It was all very well doing this type of stuff, but I wanted to get out into the real world and earn some dosh to make up for the shortfall with the day job. I did get regular work for a while in the restaurant of a country club near Bedford. The venue was nice but the management there was all over the place, they seemed to spend most of their time propping up the bar. I was paid £10 per evening which wasn't bad for the mid-70s. I arrived as usual one Saturday night and said hello to the regular waitress and started working the tables. After about half an hour a suited arrogant chap came up to me, told me he was the new Manager and asked me what I was doing. I told him I was the regular magician and he said,

"News to me, how much do we pay you?"

"A tenner for a couple of hours."

"What?! A tenner, for a few magic tricks? I don't think so, on your way!"

I went off to find the main manager, who I found asleep at one of the bars. I explained what had happened and he reached into his pocket, gave me a tenner, and went back to sleep again. That was the end of that. I never went back. I was beginning to learn an important show business lesson. Nothing is forever.

I was still obviously short of money at the end of the year according to my diary…

November 30th, 1976: *It's my girlfriend's birthday today. I bought her a box of chocolates and a rolling pin.*

As I re-read my old diaries (often with some embarrassment) there are times when I realise just how fast time flies. This was made apparent at the end of the year. In spite of not working for them at the time, I did the magic at the Llewellyn staff Christmas party in December of 1976 (at Woburn Abbey, a lovely venue) from that I was asked by the Managing Director if I would go along to his house and entertain his family and friends on the evening of January 1st. Of course I would. He lived in a huge old rambling farmhouse just outside Buckingham. I arrived early (in case I had car trouble) and went up to the front door where there was a sign which said, 'Please do come in'. I entered and was greeted by the MD and his wife who took me into a huge lounge where I was offered a drink and introduced to some of the guests. I was then shown into a large kitchen where every surface was piled high with quality food.

"Do help yourself whenever you like," I was told.

People began to arrive, and I started to mix and mingle and do a few tricks. After a while I was approached by the MD and asked If I'd mind showing the children some magic before they went to bed.

"They're through here," he said.

I was led into yet another huge lounge where there were a group of children all in dressing gowns sitting in front of a large open log fire. I sat down with them on the carpet and entertained them for about 20 minutes, much to the delight of the parents who by now had gathered around. There is nothing quite like the expression on a child's face as they react to 'real' magic. Some 25 years later I had a phone call from the same MD asking, firstly if I still did the magic, and then if I was available to entertain at his daughter's wedding. Neither of them had forgotten that night in front of the log fire. I was delighted to be there on that special day. Time does indeed fly.

1977 was an eventful year in all sorts of ways. It was the Queen's Silver Jubilee and the advent of Punk. I was happy for the Queen but hated Punk. Compared to what I had been listening to for five years (quality and original music performed by quality musicians) Punk was the complete opposite. Although I could accept the fact that anybody and everybody could pick up a guitar, learn a few chords, and bang out their often angry songs, it was all too 'samey' for me. It did occur to me at the time that I might be turning into my Dad, especially when I found myself saying the very words that he said in the early 70s, "There's no tune in it."

It was during this year that I combined live magic with live music. There was a really good local band called Teaza, who I would often go and see play at local pubs. It was made up of local lads some of whom I'd grown up with, Eddie Mac was the front man and singer, Wicksey played guitar and keyboards, Paul Sanderman was on bass, Don Hollis on lead guitar and Paul Herbert (Bert) on drums - they were all great characters, and it was always a good night out. They performed mostly original songs, one of which was called, 'Ace of Wands'. It had sort of magical connotations, so we got together, had a rehearsal and I did a couple of gigs performing in front of the band as they played the song. I seem to remember doing a double bottle production, fanning cards, including the Bob Hummer spinning card thing, and a couple of other tricks that have disappeared into the mists of time. It was good fun both for me and the band and it also went down well with the audience. I loved it for another reason too, I'd always wanted to be on stage as part of a band and thanks to that lovely bunch of lads it was an ambition achieved.

I hadn't seen the Manband for some time, but I had read in Melody Maker that they'd changed personnel once again. Also that Martin Ace (former bass player) and his then wife, George, had formed a new band together called the Flying Aces. At the end of the year they came to play in Bletchley, and they were supported by Teaza. What a great night that was! I spent some time that night chatting to my pals and soon came to the conclusion that I didn't have the freedom that many of them enjoyed. That being the case I decided to pursue the idea of finding my own place once again - I was 27 and more than ready. I realised it wouldn't be easy for all sorts of reasons, expense for one thing. The money I had saved for a deposit on a house was gone and had been spent on a forthcoming trip to America, and of course my wages had dropped. I wondered if I could get something for rent from the newly formed Milton Keynes Development Corporation. I wrote to them and was told that priority for housing was given to the London Overspill, which

I found a bit annoying. The local council had a waiting list as long as your arm and I was running out of options. Then I heard of a new housing complex that was being built in the new area of Coffee Hall in Milton Keynes. It was specifically for single people and was run by a Housing Association based in London. I applied for a form and filled it in. It was quite lengthy and required a couple of references from 'professional people'. My local vicar and doctor were kind enough to do that and I duly sent off the application. I received a reply some four weeks later when I'd all but given up. I was offered a flat pending an interview. I was quite optimistic and excited too. I then had the problem of telling Mum and Dad. The next day I told them I had something important to tell them and to come and sit in the front room. They assumed it was something to do with my girlfriend.

"Are you getting married, is she pregnant?"

"No, nothing like that, I've been offered a flat."

"What! So you're going to leave home when we need you the most?!" said Dad, "Who's going to cut the grass, and dig the borders?"

He wasn't happy. Mum didn't say anything, I think she had seen it coming for a while. I explained to him that I wasn't leaving the country, the flat wasn't all that far away, and I'd still be able to cut the grass, dig the borders and anything else he needed me to do. I also told them that I needed some independence. Somewhere to invite my friends where they wouldn't be made to feel uncomfortable because they had long hair! Anyway I was 27 for God's sake! I left them to talk about it between themselves and called round to see my elder sister, Maggs.

"Of course you should take the flat, don't worry about Dad, I'll go round and sort him out tomorrow."

I also went to see my younger sister, Jean, and over a pint in the Bridge she more or less said the same thing, adding, "I'll make the curtains!" I was really grateful to both of them for their support. A week later I went along to the interview and was offered a single flat, pending my acceptance after viewing it. I went up to the site which was still being built but almost finished and spoke to the lady who would be running the place. I had a look at number 54 and accepted. Although it was quite small with a single bedroom and tiny kitchen it was certainly big enough for me. I wouldn't be able to move in until the middle of July which was another two months away. That would give me time to sort out a fridge, cooker, and all the other stuff I'd need for the next stage of my life. Meanwhile me and my girlfriend had gone our separate ways and I decided to leave Cleanline Furniture (purely for economic reasons) and go back to Llewellyn. Not only was the pay better, but my new flat was directly opposite the premises, and I could walk there in five minutes. I left Cleanline on good terms and was told I could go back at any time which was nice of them. Although I'd only been there for eight months, it was enough time for me to have learned enough about furniture construction and sowed the seeds of perhaps making my own stuff at some point in the future. I left home and moved into my new home in July...

July 10th, 1977: *I moved into my new place today. Steve and Jean helped me this morning. The actual leaving was a bit emotional. Poor Mum was in tears. However it's done now. Dad's last words were "get your hair cut."*

I can't recall whether he was being serious or not, perhaps he wasn't. I didn't want him to think that he'd driven me out. I'm sure Maggs had put him in the picture and hopefully he'd soon come round. I soon settled into my new home and discovered a love of cooking in my first week. I used cookbooks and just went for it. I certainly wasn't going down the road of chips and convenience food every day. The Complex had its own bar and clubroom, and a launderette. It was a really nice set up. I soon made friends with my neighbours and loved it all. I had been there for about three weeks and then it was time for a trip to America!

CHAPTER 12

America!!

We started to think about and organise the trip back in January. It was just the three of us - me, my sister Jean, and her husband Steve. The plan was to see as much of the country as possible in the four weeks we'd be there. Our only mode of travel would be on the Greyhound Bus network. We bought a book of 'Greyhound Ameripass' tickets, which gave us unlimited mileage. A ticket was removed after each separate journey and when the book was empty, we took it to the ticket office and were given another one. It was great value for money. We could also save on accommodation expenses by travelling overnight and sleeping on the bus. Other people we knew had done the same, so we had been given good advice before we set off at the end of July. We were prepared and excited, and just a touch apprehensive as we got on the train with our rucksacks, bound for the airport and the trip of a lifetime.

We flew from Gatwick Airport with Laker Airways and had a good flight, arriving in New York in the early evening. A short cab ride later we arrived at our pre-booked hotel, 'The Edison'. Our bags were taken up to our rooms by a porter, which is where we made our first mistake - judging by his reaction, we hadn't tipped him enough. Having said that though, we had to be very careful with what we spent. We went down to a very nice bar for a nightcap where I made my second mistake. The bartender seemed surprised when I asked for three beers and offered him some money…

"You're paying *now*?"

It hadn't taken long to realise we were in a foreign country. We slept well that night and soon after breakfast walked around the corner to our first Greyhound Bus depot, all of us looking forward to boarding our very first bus bound for Buffalo and eventually Niagara Falls. The plan was to meet up with Carole and Graham (from Bletchley) who lived in Canada not too far from the Falls. We had been in touch and were looking forward to seeing them again. We checked in and stored the luggage and took our seats. When the bus was ready to go, we heard our first (of many) driver messages…

"This is your Greyhound Bus travelling from New York to Buffalo City. There is a rest room situated at the back of the bus for your convenience. Keep the gangways clear, no smoking on the bus except the last two rows. No pipes, no cigars. Thanks for going Greyhound."

Occasionally there would be a driver with a sense of humour who'd say something different, but that was basically it on every trip. There were regular comfort stops every couple of hours or so which were handy for those of us not brave enough to use the on-board facilities, useful as well to stretch our legs for a while. The bus was comfortable, and air conditioned with the cold air emerging from vents at the bottom of the windows. That was fine, providing you didn't fall asleep with your ear directly on top of it, running the risk of earache. We each bought a small blow-up Greyhound cushion which was invaluable. The distance between New York and Niagara Falls is around 400 miles. We'd have to change buses at Buffalo for the final 30 miles or so, to take us on to the actual Falls. We pulled out of New York feeling excited. All went well for a couple of hours, but then the bus began to make a strange noise and shuddered to a halt. The driver got out to have a look and wearily shook his head. He got in touch with head office, and we were told we'd have to wait for a replacement bus. Who'd have thought? Our first one. We got out and sat by the side of the road and I had a chat with the driver.

"Oh well," he said, "At least you can say you've stayed in Pennsylvania."

We had to wait a while for the replacement and because of the delay it was almost dark as we pulled into Buffalo, in the middle of a spectacular electric storm. While Steve and Jean made enquiries about the next bus, I gave Carole a quick call to explain about the delay. By the time we got there it was dark. It wasn't quite what we had planned, but the floodlit Falls at night was an impressive sight, and of course it was lovely to see Carole and Graham again. We got the last bus (just about) from Niagara back to Buffalo where we had a bit of a wait until our next bus departed, bound for Cleveland, Ohio. We managed to have a bit of a sleep as we travelled the 200 miles along the length of Lake Eyrie. We soon began to realise just how vast this country was. We decided to spend all the next day travelling and perhaps do some sightseeing the following day. Looking out of the window was often sightseeing in itself. There wasn't time to see anything of Cleveland apart from the bus depot as we needed to get on another bus to Chicago. On arrival there we stopped off for a while to have a quick wash and change of clothes. It was here we met our first Bona Fide Americans. The conversation went something like this…

"Hey, are you guys Australian?"

"No we're from England."

"Oh wow! Do you know the Beatles?"

"I'm afraid not."

"Could you say something?"

"What would you like me to say?"

"Anything! We just love your accent, it's so cute."

We felt like celebrities.

From Chicago we got on a bus that would take us the 470 miles to Omaha, Nebraska. It took much of the day and once there we found a small and cheap motel from one of those 'Rough Guide' books. That book was to become invaluable as it not only pointed out cheap and recommended accommodation, but also places and areas that were best to avoid. The next day was spent entirely on exploring Omaha, a lovely town. We went to two huge museums (we had by now accepted that everything in America is huge, including a lot of the people). It was in Omaha that we experienced our first shopping mall which was a world and a half away from Bletchley High Street. I was interested in the furniture on display - too big and chunky for my taste, and again a world away from traditional English furniture. In the afternoon we boarded a local bus and headed for Boystown, the place immortalised by the 1938 film of the same name. It starred Spencer Tracy as Father Flanagan and gained him an Oscar for best actor (which was on display there). Boystown began life as a refuge for wayward boys who were cared for by Father John Flanagan and a team of volunteers. Over the years it grew into a self-contained community, a small town in fact. It had everything there including schools, a post office and even a farm. There's a lovely statue there of an obviously poor young boy with a smaller boy on his shoulders with the caption underneath, 'He ain't heavy, Father, he's m' brother.' There was something very special about the place, we all felt the love.

The next day was spent on the bus travelling the 935 miles to Salt Lake City in the state of Utah. This leg took us right across two states, Nebraska, and Wyoming. We were in cowboy country! I thought it was great passing through towns like Laramie and Cheyenne (where I spotted a 'Wrangler' shop). We arrived at Salt Lake City after a journey of some 12 hours at about six o'clock in the evening, our longest hop yet. We checked into a really nice hotel which was again recommended by the book. After a meal, we had an early night, too tired to do anything else. The next day we explored the city and found it a very clean place. It was surprisingly green, bearing in mind we were in desert country. There was an automatic sprinkler system that took us by surprise. Water suddenly spurting out from the rather lush, grassed areas adjacent to the sidewalks. We visited a couple of museums which were filled with interesting artefacts and information mostly from the era of the early pioneers. You can't avoid Mormon buildings as they're so synonymous with the city. We visited two, the Visitor Centre and the Temple. At the Visitor Centre we sat through a filmed history of the Mormon Faith, and by the time we'd experienced the very impressive Temple, we'd just about had enough of religion. It was all very slick and the story of how it all began was interesting, but compared with how we felt at Boystown, we came away feeling a bit cold. We ended the day with an enormous pizza meal, and were impressed once again with the huge, reasonably priced portions. We decided to spend the following day in the city, visiting places of interest unconnected with the Mormon Faith, including Trolley Square. Originally the home of the Utah Trolley Company, many of the shops (stores) and restaurants are converted trolley cars including, 'The Ice Cream Store'. Steve has got a vast appetite and if he says he's feeling a bit peckish you'd better believe it.

As well as ice cream, they served burgers with all the trimmings, including 'The Kitchen Sink'. Steve spotted it on the menu and went for it. It was a triple bun with two all-beef patties, bacon, a choice of dressing, slices of ham, a pile of grated cheese, tomatoes, and fries. It was served in a chrome replica kitchen sink and was huge! Even Steve was defeated. After that and with all of us feeling well and truly stuffed, we boarded a local bus to the Bingham Copper Mine, which was vast - a complete mountain had been mined away and was almost as deep now as it was high then. We looked down into it with a telescope and could just about make out the excavation trucks. We walked around the corner of the rim and there was a huge tyre from one of those same trucks on display. I took a photo of Jean sitting inside it, it was massive. After about an hour we caught the bus back to the Greyhound Bus Depot where me and Jean had a snack (Steve was still full) and soon after we climbed onto a Greyhound bus bound for our next destination of Portland in Oregon, a distance of 770 miles. We arrived there late in the morning after a scenic journey across the northern Rocky Mountains. We booked into a small hotel, which according to the sign outside was blessed with its own swimming pool. We deposited our bags in our rooms and went to explore. The pool turned out to be inside the hotel and was no bigger than a large bath. That was the only time we were disappointed about the small size of anything during the whole trip. We abandoned the swim idea, so I joined Steve and Jean in their room to watch a bit of tv before lunch. As Steve flicked through the many channels trying to find something watchable, Jean suddenly said,

"I can smell burning!"

Sure enough clouds of smoke were billowing from the back of the set. Steve quickly turned it off while I phoned down to reception.

"I'm sorry to bother you but we're having a bit of trouble with the tv."

"What's the matter with it," came the gruff reply.

"Well it sort of burnt out."

"What! What have you been doing with it?"

"Nothing, it just sort of happened."

"Don't touch anything, I'll send somebody up."

"Oh hell," I said to Jean and Steve, "he's not very happy."

Soon after there was a sharp knock on the door, and there stood a very big, angry looking man.

"What have you guys been doing with the tv?" he growled, striding towards the still smoking set.

"Well actually, nothing," I said.

"Hey, are you guys Australian?"

"No we're from England."

"Oh wow, whereabouts?"

"Near London."

"Gee, London, have you ever seen Queen Elizabeth?"

"We have actually, quite a few times," I lied.

"She's a beautiful woman," he said smiling all over his face, "Now listen guys, don't worry about the tv, it was old anyway. I'll give you new rooms. If you need anything else, don't hesitate to ask."

What a nice man.

We moved across the corridor to our new accommodation and by then it was lunchtime. Over a rather nice turkey dinner we wondered what to do next. The movies seemed like a good idea, and as the new James Bond film, 'The spy who loved me', was showing at the cinema round the corner, we went for that. We joined a small queue of excited people, all of us more than ready for a bit of escapist entertainment. The opening sequence featured a dramatic ski chase culminating with James Bond skiing off the edge of a high cliff and free falling for a while before gliding down to earth on a Union Jack parachute. As the chute opened the audience in the cinema were on their feet cheering! We'd never seen anything like it. We looked at each other rather bemused but feeling chuffed and proud to be British. After the cinema we had a drink in a local bar and discussed what to do next. We decided to pick up our bags and head off to the bus depot and travel down the coast to San Francisco, a journey of some 635 miles. Again it was a scenic route with the Pacific Ocean on one side and the spectacular giant Redwood trees on the other. I was lucky to find myself sitting next to a lovely elderly lady who pointed out places of interest as we travelled (before it got too dark, and we both nodded off). There were times throughout the trip where it was almost impossible to arrive at a destination at a reasonable time. San Francisco was one such occasion. The bus pulled into the depot at four o'clock in the morning. We sat down in the waiting room for a while until it was light enough to see and were surprised to see what appeared to be thick fog. We soon decided to go back into the waiting room to rest for an hour or two and have a quick wash. Once refreshed we deposited our bags and found somewhere for breakfast and then went to explore. By now the fog had started to lift and we had our first view of the impressive Golden Gate Bridge, the top of it poking through the mist. As the mist disappeared, the infamous Alcatraz Prison came into view, and we just stared in awe at those two iconic landmarks. There was another building too which caught our eye, some distance away. It was shaped like a long, pointed pyramid which we soon christened the Rocket building. As we stood gazing up at it by the side of the road a car suddenly pulled up with a sharp screech of brakes. The driver wound down the window and beckoned us over.

"Impressive building, right?"

"It most certainly is," I replied.

"Hey, are you guys from England?!"

(I almost replied, no we're from Australia.)

"Yes, we are, from near London."

"Welcome to San Francisco! Hey, did you know you can go inside that building? You get a great view from the top. Hop in I'll take you there!"

We looked at each other wondering whether to accept the offer. "Come on guys, you'll love it!" He wasn't going to take no for an answer.

"Ok, I said, thanks very much."

I got in the front and Jean and Steve got in the back; with a screech of burning tyres we tore off. He chatted as he drove, and it suddenly dawned on me that he was pissed. The clincher was when he told us that he always enjoyed a drink after work. We speeded along, not dissimilar to the car chase in the film 'Bullitt'. We held on for dear life and a few minutes later with another screech of brakes pulled up directly in front of the Rocket building. We got out and thanked him very much (feeling glad to still be alive). He stayed where he was until we'd actually got inside the building, and then with a cheery wave he pulled into heavy traffic to much honking of horns. We wandered over to the reception area where luckily, we were the first visitors of the day. We were directed to the lift (elevator), and we soon zoomed up to the top. That chap was right, the view was indeed spectacular. Luckily the fog had lifted by then and it was going to be a warm and sunny day. We spent all of it exploring as much as we could around the city of

San Francisco. Ambling through Chinatown, visiting the Cable Car Museum and even having a ride on one. It was fascinating to see how the system worked, I had no idea of the method until seeing it at first hand. Unsurprisingly, it was nothing like English trams and trolley buses. We had some lunch at Fisherman's Wharf and strolled around the shops just soaking up the atmosphere. We strolled around Nob Hill looking at the posh mansions and hotels, and walked down (or was it up?) Lombard street with its eight-hairpin bends. It was a long and tiring day, and we walked miles. After a final meal in this delightful city we headed back to the bus depot for a lengthy wait for a bus at midnight bound for Los Angeles. While we waited, we planned what we'd do when we got there. It was agreed our first port of call would be The Universal Film Studios. We boarded the bus and needless to say we slept pretty much all the way, arriving at 6.00 am after a journey of 380 miles. We had freshened up while we waited for a bus bound for Hollywood which soon arrived. It didn't take too long to get there and as I got off the bus at the small and rather rundown depot, I asked the driver if this was indeed Hollywood.

"This is it," he said, "Have a nice day."

Luckily, we got there early so missed the bulk of the queues at the Universal Film Studios. We spent all day there and had a great time. The highlight I suppose was the guided tour on one of the three-car open-trailer trips. We did have a few near misses which were a bit scary. The one at the front which was pulling the other two kept breaking down. Firstly the brakes failed as we trundled towards a lake.

"Oh no!" shouted the driver as we headed for certain death. Luckily the waters parted just like The Red Sea, and we drove all the way through back onto the road on the other side. What a relief! We carried on and a few minutes later we heard a rumbling noise. Looking up we noticed huge boulders rolling down the slope towards us! Again luck was on our side as they just missed us. Off we went again, and after a while we came upon a rather rickety looking bridge. The driver told us not to worry as he'd driven over it hundreds of times.

"It'll be ok as long as I drive slowly," he said.

As we got halfway across there was a terrific crash as the bridge gave way! All that was left was a narrow track just about wide enough to take the width of the trailer. Somehow, we managed to drive safely across to the opposite side. Surely nothing else could go wrong, I thought, as we approached a railway track. Suddenly everything stopped and we came to a halt right over the middle of the track. The driver couldn't get it going! Oh no! We could hear a train coming down the track, then we could see it with smoke pouring from its funnel, hurtling towards us. It's going to hit us! Hang on, it's slowing down! Will it stop in time?! Yes, but only just. We carried on with the journey with the driver pointing out the ominous looking house on the hill from the classic Hitchcock film, 'Psycho', then the perpetually burning house. The ride was almost over as we drove past a lake and noticed the unmistakable triangular shape of a shark dorsal fin emerging from the water. It sped towards us and just as it was about to hit the coach the head of the enormous shark leapt from the water, flashing its razor-sharp teeth before splashing back into the lake, spraying water everywhere. What a shock! It was a great day and we loved it all. At the end of it we got a bus back to LA and checked into a cheap motel in Santa Monica and then headed for 'Ye Olde Kings Head', an authentic British pub. We were more than ready for a few pints of genuine English Ale along with a meal of fish n' chips. It all went down a treat. The next day was spent either swimming in the Pacific or sunbathing around the motel pool. We also had a walk along the sand to Venice Beach where there was a group of heavily muscled body builders working out in what was actually a beach gym. (If only I'd stuck to the Charles Atlas course, I mused.) We ended the day back in the pub with Shepherd's Pie and chips, a few pints, and a game of darts - just like home, and a great end to a lovely day. We got up early (somehow) the next morning and got a bus to Disneyland.

What an incredible place! Certainly as good and exciting as the Universal Tour. It was the high quality of everything that was so impressive. From cleanliness and the politeness of the staff to the way the queuing system was organised. There was certainly nothing like it back home. It had been yet another memorable day. We got back to our motel in the evening and Jean and Steve picked up their bags and went off to catch the Greyhound to Las Vegas. I decided to stay in LA for an extra day to see if I could visit The Magic Castle, the renowned club and venue of quality magicians in Hollywood. As Jean and Steve sped towards Las Vegas, I spent the following morning exploring Santa Monica, an area of the city with a high proportion of English ex- pats in residence. At 11.00 O'clock I had tea and scones in 'Agatha's Tea room' (as you do) and had a chat with the young local waiter. He told me of another English pub situated on Pico Boulevard which was a couple of miles away.

"Ok, I said, I've got my map I'll take a walk and by the time I get there it'll be lunchtime."

"What?!! You mean you're actually going to walk over 2 miles?"

"I am, I said it'll be a pleasant stroll in the sunshine."

"I'll never understand you English," he laughed, "Have nice day, and a nice walk!"

It's true, they drive everywhere in LA. I wouldn't say it was a particularly pleasant walk pounding the pavements in the heat, but I did find the pub. It was called 'Sweeney Todd' and according to the sign outside it served "Excellent fish n' chips in our famous crispy beer batter." How could I resist that? It went down really well with a couple of pints. The English owners (from Blackpool) were very friendly and welcoming, the food and company certainly worth the walk. I stayed chatting for a while after the meal before walking back to the motel. I checked out and walked to the Greyhound depot ready to get on a bus, depending on what happened in the following 10 minutes. I found a pay phone and decided to give Jim a call. I'd met him a couple of months previously at the Dai Vernon dinner in London. He was one of a small group of magicians who had travelled over with the great man. We'd had a nice chat there and were about the same age and got on really well. He'd given me one of his cards and said, "Any time you're in LA give me a call." I took the card, convinced I'd never see him again and suddenly here I was. I entered the phone booth not really having much of a plan B if he wasn't in or available. I dialled the number and luckily, he was in, he'd pick me up in ten minutes. What a relief! When he arrived, I put my bags in the boot and then went to get in the car on the driver's side.

"I keep forgetting you drive on the wrong side over here," I said.

"I won't argue with that," he laughed, "I did the same thing in London."

"Where abouts in LA do you live?" I asked.

"Beverly Hills," he replied.

"Oh, that's nice," I said. What else could I say?

It didn't take too long to get to his house. Well actually it was an apartment, housed in a very impressive looking building. We

entered the lobby and made for the lift which I distinctly remember
because of the ankle-deep pile on the carpet inside of it. We sped
up several floors and walked across the corridor to his front door.
Once inside I was introduced to his family which consisted of his
Mum and Dad, (both retired) and a couple of elderly relatives.
(There may well have been siblings, the place was certainly big
enough). I dropped my bags in the hall and was able to make use
of one of the bathrooms to freshen up before joining Jim in his
room. It was huge (well of course it was). We had a chat for a while
and he showed me some card stuff he was working on, and I did
some coin moves, and then he said, "Do you smoke?"

"Yes, I said, cheroots mostly."

"No, I mean smoke-smoke, like this." He went to a drawer and
rummaged to the back of it and came out with a rather large joint.

"Ok, I said, why not?" He lit up and we carried on doing tricks
for a while as we shared it. By the time it had gone, I was pretty
much out of it. It had been a long morning.

"Let's go for a drive," said Jim suddenly.

"Ok," I said thinking that a bit of fresh air might do me good.
I stood up and almost fell over. I followed Jim out of the building
and into his car. We drove around Beverly Hills with Jim pointing
out homes of the stars and other beautiful houses, all of them (in
my stoned state) appearing to be beyond stunning. There was
one that looked like the sort of house that Hansel and Gretel may
have come upon in the forest, a log cabin with a long and bent
chimney emerging from the roof. Quite astounding. We stopped
outside a nice-looking bungalow with a red roof surrounded by
beautiful foliage.

"Guess who lives there?" he asked.

"No idea," I replied.

"Paul Newman."

"Wow! Shall we knock on the door and ask him if he wants to see a card trick?" I giggled.

"What a great idea!" said Jim, "But it's time for dinner, hope you're hungry."

As we drove back Jim pointed out various sites where films had been shot and where he and his family had taken part in crowd scenes. It had been a fascinating afternoon in every sense of the word. The shared meal with his family was really nice - it was the first time I'd ever eaten corn on the cob. The conversation was mostly about the Royal Family and the sites of London. I was beginning to realise just how much Her Majesty was loved and admired over there. Soon it was time for the ride over to the Magic Castle. Jim signed me in, and I was given a tie to wear from the lovely girl on reception. I didn't pack one as it didn't occur to me that I'd need one. The reception area was oak panelled and surrounded with bookcases, as you'd expect in a castle. I was told to approach the nearest one where there was a small wooden owl with blinking eyes and to say, "Open Sesame!" As I uttered the words a panel silently slid open, and I found myself in a beautifully styled club room (again just like a castle). We went to the bar and Jim held out his hand and said,

"It's been nice meeting you again, but I have to go."

I shook his hand and thanked him for his hospitality, and he was gone. That was a surprise, I assumed he'd be around all evening, and I was sort of counting on him to give me a lift to the bus depot later on. Oh well, I bought myself a drink and as I took my first sip a chap came up beside me and said,

"Hi, I understand you're a friend of Jim's."

"Yes, I am, sort of," I replied, and went on to explain how we'd met in London. He held out his hand and said,

"I'm from England as well, my name's Martin Lewis."

"Surely not the son of the famous Eric C!"

"The very same," he answered.

I went on to tell him that we'd met some ten years previously in Northampton, on the day before he'd left to begin his new life in America.

"I remember!" he said, "I was strumming a guitar, sitting on a packing case! What a coincidence."

We had a nice chat and then the two of us went to watch the close-up show, which was really good. After that it was back to the bar where I was introduced to other magicians. Tricks were shown, moves swapped, and stories told. It was great fun. Time was marching on though and I had a bus to catch. I asked around if anybody was driving home anywhere near the Greyhound bus depot as I could do with a lift. Nobody could. I got the impression that nobody wanted to, and I walked into the reception area at a bit of a loss. Then I saw a familiar face, Billy McComb. Billy was often at the Magic Circle where our paths had frequently crossed.

"What's up?" he asked.

"I need to get to the Greyhound depot; I've got a bus to catch."

"Not to worry," he said, "I'm sure this lovely young lady behind the desk will phone a cab for you, won't you?" he said smiling at the girl.

"For you Billy, anything."

Billy could charm the birds off the trees. Soon after, a cab drew up outside. I thanked Billy (who was now having a deep conversation with the girl), threw my bags into the boot, and with some relief, off we went. During the ride, the driver told me that the depot wasn't in a particularly good area and to take care. No wonder I struggled to get a lift! There were one or two odd looking characters around, but I had no trouble. Luckily, I had time to change from a suit into a pair of shorts. It was going to be hot where I was going. I boarded the bus bound for Flagstaff, Arizona, a journey of 465 miles. I slept like a log on the bus, and it was a job to keep track of the time, I wasn't even sure what day it was when I woke up. On this leg, the driver was a bit of a character. As the bus headed for Flagstaff and the Grand Canyon, he came onto the intercom and decided to tell the passengers a joke...

"There were three people looking over the rim of the Grand Canyon - a musician, an artist, and an old cowboy. The musician gazed out and said, 'This stupendous view inspires me to write the finest symphony that the world will ever have heard!' Then the artist gazed out and with tears in his eyes said, 'This remarkable and stunning vista inspires me to paint the finest work of art anybody, anywhere, has ever seen!' Then the old cowboy looks over the rim, hitches up his trousers, coughs, spits, and says, 'That's a helluva place to lose a cow!'"

It received much laughter and a well-deserved round of applause. I got to Flagstaff, picked up my bags and stepped out onto the pavement (sidewalk) and immediately stepped back inside. The difference in temperature was remarkable, like from a fridge to an oven. I'd arranged to meet Jean and Steve there at a certain time. Heaven knows how we coped without the use of a mobile phone. Half an hour later Steve arrived looking very sunburnt.

"Where's Jean?" I asked.

"She's in the motel recovering."

"What from?" I asked.

"Sunburn and mild heatstroke, she's burnt to a crisp!"

It seems they decided to do a spot of sunbathing by the side of the motel pool and had nodded off. They didn't realise they could get so burnt from a cloudy sky.

I booked into the motel, dumped my bags, and then went for a swim in the pool. Absolute heaven! That night we went out for a meal and a few beers followed by an earlyish night. The next day was going to be long, hot, and tiring. And indeed that was the case. The Grand Canyon! What a place! We looked over the rim of this remarkable natural phenomena which is bigger than Wales. Even with a telescope, pony trekkers at the bottom were tiny specks. It inspired me to come up with the best magic trick anybody has ever seen! (I'm still working on it.) That night after a meal, we got on a Greyhound bus bound for El Paso, Texas, a distance of 475 miles. We arrived mid-morning and soon discovered its definite Mexican flavour due to its close proximity to the border. We found a cheap and cheerful hotel, which is when Jean discovered that she'd left her jumpsuit back in Flagstaff. According to my diary, this 'created a scene for a minute or two'. A masterly under statement! Anyway, there was nothing we could do about it, going back wasn't an option due to lack of time. Once she realised this, she sulked for a while but was ok in the end and we spent all day sight-seeing and having a nice time in spite of the oppressive heat. We got up early the next morning and boarded a local bus to Carlsbad Caverns. We were looking forward to this as we read through a brochure we'd picked up in El Paso…

"In the foothills of the Guadalupe Mountains lies a wonder of nature unparalleled by any creation of man. A National Park 750 feet below the surface of the earth."

I have to say it exceeded all our expectations. In my view certainly as impressive as the Grand Canyon. It was here that some of the scenes in the 1959 film, 'Journey to the Centre of The Earth', were filmed. Words can't do justice to this place. If ever you find yourself in this part of the world, I highly recommend you give it a visit. The guided tour did take a while - hardly surprising when you consider it covered three miles. The scale of the place is quite astounding, and the undoubted highlight was, 'The Big Room', a vast area covering 13 acres, with a ceiling 250 feet high. It took over an hour to walk around it. We looked with awe at huge stalagmites and stalactites that over eons of time had formed into massive pillars. There was a small underground lake, hanging draperies of translucent limestone and onyx and an amazing array of rock formations, all of it well-lit and accessible and wonderful to look at. We were there below ground for several hours and even had a meal in the underground restaurant. We loved it all and had a great time down there.

Once back on the surface (and the heat) we had a short wait before catching the next bus to San Antonio. Much of the 450-mile journey was spent sleeping as we'd boarded the bus in the evening. The disadvantage of night travel meant we'd miss out on looking out at the scenery, not that there would have been too much to view across the vast Texas plains. We arrived early in the morning and decided to spend all day exploring the city. We were aware at this point of the danger of running out of money and we'd have to be careful. San Antonio is a lovely city and not at all what we expected. It's surprisingly green, particularly around the river that flows through the middle of it. We had a very welcome boat cruise for about an hour which allowed us to unwind after a night on the bus. After that we headed for the must see building in the city, The Alamo. It was fascinating to see what was left of this iconic landmark. The front of it still stands pretty much as it was in 1836 when the famous battle took place, and where Davy Crockett and Jim Bowie fought to the death. Inside there's a museum which explains all you need to know. There are also portraits of Crockett and Bowie hanging inside, which I have to say look nothing like John Wayne or Richard Widmark from the 1960 film of my childhood. Who'd have thought that, as a 10-year-old kid, wearing my 'Davy Crockett raccoon hat', and pretending to fight the Spanish with my pretend rifle (a broken broom handle from the brush factory), that I would one day stand in the spot where it happened for real? A surreal experience. From there we went to a building that dominated the skyline – 'The Tower of The Americas'. In those days it was one of the tallest in the world at 750ft. We went up to the top and took some photos of the spectacular view. Back on the ground again, I spotted a sign – 'Free Beer'. Actually, it was a part of a larger sign advertising the famous Lone Star Brewery which was open to the public. We decided to go along and have a look. What a place! Known as the 'World's most Beautiful Brewery', it sits in huge grounds, big enough for its own Olympic-sized swimming pool! This is available to employees when not in use for national competitions. As well as the actual brewery, there was an interesting traditional museum and also several halls of exhibits dedicated to hunting. It was bizarre really, as there were heads of hundreds of beautiful animals exhibited on the walls and immediately below them were display cabinets full of rifles and shot guns that were responsible for their deaths! Not the sort of place to visit if you're an animal lover. There was another strange room which featured the heads of animals, all of which were deformed in some way - a cow with two heads, or a sheep with three eyes - the room was full of them. For us it was rather off-putting, and it wasn't long before we got out of there and went for our free beer. That afternoon we had a change of plan in a bid to save money. Rather than look for a restaurant for a meal, we went to a supermarket and bought bread and cheese etc., and had a picnic in a local park, it was really nice by the river. Later on in the evening, we made our way to the depot and boarded a Greyhound bound for New Orleans, a distance of 540 miles. We arrived early in the morning, and it was very humid, even then. It took us a while to find accommodation, always frustrating, especially when hot and tired as we were. Finally, after an hour or two of searching, we found a cheap motel. It had no air-conditioning, but we still fell on the beds and slept for about 4 hours. We didn't do much else until the evening when we went for a stroll in the famous French Quarter. We strolled down Canal Street and Bourbon Street and watched countless jazz bands playing in the bars. There was one which featured several elderly musicians sitting down and playing a variety of old and battered instruments. In front of them was a collection box and next to that, a board with a list of song titles and the price next to each one. The more popular the tune, the more it would cost. Top of the list was of course, 'Oh when the saints…'. Luckily, we got there just as the box contained the right amount of money for them to play this great song. The trumpet player began the familiar tune and stood up and began to walk round the bar closely followed by the other musicians. After a circuit, he led them out of the door and into the street, still playing. As they walked away from the bar, they were joined by a group of people dancing, including us. The heat and tiredness swept away as we clapped and cheered and even sang along to the famous song which is synonymous with the music of New Orleans.

The next stage of the journey was an 863-mile hop to Miami. According to my diary, by this time we were bored and fed up with buses. Hardly surprising when you look at the number of miles we'd covered. Anyway, we'd had a great time so couldn't really complain. We boarded the bus, and a lot of hours later arrived in Miami on time in the middle of the afternoon. After collecting our bags we sat in the waiting room trying to get into the mindset of setting out once again to hunt for a cheap motel. As we were about to leave, we met another English traveller who warned us about how unsafe Miami could be, particularly in the area around the bus depot. He'd tried in vain to find accommodation close by and had found it a bit scary. He made the decision to travel the 30 miles further up the coast to Fort Lauderdale. We decided to do the same. It turned out to be a wise move. We got there in the late afternoon and luckily found a cheap motel fairly quickly. Yet again, rather grubby and no air conditioning… a case of getting what you pay for. The bed and room were comfortable enough, and then I looked inside the shower cubicle. It was the first time I'd ever seen cockroaches. I thought it best not to say anything to Jean and Steve. That evening we walked into town and as we strolled, we were joined by a couple of small lizards. It was certainly a popular place for wildlife. After a nice (cheap) Greek meal we headed back for an early night. After an uneventful night (thank God) we went off to explore Fort Lauderdale. First up was a river cruise on 'The Jungle Queen'. We had an interesting commentary as we chugged along on the massive two decked boat. We were informed of the history of the town and told a lot about local wildlife, including alligators. Then we went past the wealthy part of town and saw many beautiful riverside mansions. The guide told us that some of these were owned by rich celebrities, for example…

"That impressive one over there is owned by one of the Bee Gees!"

There were others that I just can't remember. Once off the boat and back into the oppressive heat, it was time for a swim in the sea. We spent an hour or two on the beach doing a bit of (careful) sunbathing and swimming. As the sand was so hot on our feet, we had to run into the surf which was wonderful! In the afternoon it was deemed a good idea to cool down a bit. What better way than to sit in an air-conditioned cinema for a couple of hours. At that time, 'Star Wars' had just been released to much acclaim (and hype), so we decided to join a lengthy queue and find out what the fuss was all about. Not a lot is the short answer to that. I hated it. Oh well, each to his own, but it did keep us cool for a couple of hours. After that we made our way back to the Greek restaurant of the previous night, stuffed ourselves, and then boarded a bus to take us 190 miles up the coast to the Kennedy Space Centre. We had a lot of hanging about to do once we got there, but it did mean we had an early start inside the complex. It's massive, and you do need a good few hours to get it all covered. I couldn't believe the size of some of those rockets, how on earth did they get off the ground? It was a fascinating and very full day. Needless to say, we slept pretty well on the next stage of the journey - 940 miles north to Cincinnati. It took all night and most of the following day to get there. At this point we were sort of on our way home. We'd agreed to visit a friend of Steve's (Zet Lewis) at a small town in Ohio called Defiance. We didn't have time to explore Cincinnati as our next bus was due to leave straight away. We did drive over the famous bridge though. It took about three hours to travel the 166 miles to Defiance. On arrival we phoned Zet, and he soon came to pick us up. We spent an enjoyable day with his family, culminating in me doing a little magic show. After a couple of drinks we fell into bed and didn't get up until 11.00 o'clock the following morning. During the day we did a bit of shopping and that night Zet treated us to an end of trip steak dinner. The steak was so big it had to go on a separate plate! The other plate was piled high with vegetables. It was a nice (and filling) end to our visit.

The next day we boarded our final Greyhound bus bound for New York City, a distance of about 600 miles. After a short stop at Toledo, we carried on via Pittsburgh and Philadelphia. The bus arrived on time and after locking up our baggage, we went off to do a bit of sightseeing around Times Square. Apart from the height of the buildings, loads of Yellow Cabs, and the many shops selling tourist tat, the other thing I remember was the manhole covers leaking great clouds of steam. We also went on a guided bus tour which took us on a round trip to The Bowery and Greenwich Village. I found that quite interesting and I soon found myself singing early Bob Dylan songs (to myself.) Soon it was time to head for the airport and home. We got there with plenty of time to spare, in fact we had loads of time thanks to a strike by British air traffic controllers. After spending an uncomfortable night on waiting room chairs, we finally took off 18 hours late.

I got back home to my flat around lunchtime on Bank Holiday Monday, 29th August 1977. I slept for much of the rest of that day and woke up with many memories still buzzing around my head. I'm now going to tot up the total mileage we travelled. This will be the first time I've actually done this since the trip, 45 years ago. Thanks to Google I've managed to keep a running and fairly accurate record as I've been typing (you've probably noticed). And the grand total is - 8,813 miles in four weeks! Wow! Amazing really that we achieved all that we did while doing that amount of travelling. The whole trip had been a wonderful experience, even if it did leave me broke.

Jean at Bingham Copper Mine

I don't know what's more impressive, the view or those shorts

The Alamo!

San Francisco, "The Rocket Building"

Steve and Jean somewhere in America

Impressing the ladies at Universal Studios

CHAPTER 13

Love and Loss

I'd been on the committee of the Table Tennis League for a couple of years and was still playing regularly. By the middle of 1977 I'd had enough of the backbiting and silly arguments, so I resigned. I still played in the league which is all I wanted to do anyway. I also had enough on my plate with my committee work in the magic club. In September of that year I was asked to join the Residents Committee at Chapter House (where I was living). Of course I said yes, at the same time wondering how on earth I kept getting lumbered with things I didn't really want to do. Nothing has changed. I always did have a problem saying no. Oh well, I was settling into my new flat and was now sharing my bedroom with my workbench. What more could a chap ask for? My social life was carrying on pretty much as normal, with the added attraction of being able to eat and drink what I wanted when I wanted.

September 16th, 1977: *I went on a pub crawl tonight. I got a bus down to the Bletchley Arms (a cracking new barmaid in there). Then on to The Plough, and from there down to The Bridge. Not a very exciting evening, and I'm feeling a bit rough. I've just had 6 pints of beer, a cup of black coffee, six fish fingers, and a tomato.*

Always willing to experiment with my cooking, a few days later I had Toad in the hole and Bubble and Squeak together. I called that gastronomic creation, a squeaky bubbly toad in the hole. It went down a treat.

Car problems continued with one thing after another. That car spent more time off the road than on it! I had a puncture one day, but luckily, I spotted it while it was still in the car park. I took the wheel off and then took the spare wheel out of the boot, and soon discovered that was flat too. Luckily, I was able to borrow a foot pump and get it to the right pressure and fit it to the car. The plan then was to take the punctured tyre to a garage to get repaired as soon as possible. Then I realised I'd locked the keys in the boot, including the one for my flat. Allen, from next door, suggested we try his key, his Marina? My Cortina? It worked! So much for mid 70s car security. I finally got it sorted and what a relief. The next problem arose a week later. The gear lever fell off. Time to look for a new car I thought.

We did our last show for the elderly in 1977. A familiar and friendly venue, the Coronation Hall in Bletchley, for the Evergreen Club. Although Dad's health wasn't good, he was still able to play his saw, accompanied on the piano by brother-in-law, Ken. I did the magic, and my sister Maggs sang. It went really well. About a week after that Mum and Dad came to visit my new home. I think they were impressed. I gave them some tea and cakes and Dad was able to use my phone to chat to Archie Tear for about half an hour. It would turn out to be his only visit.

For the first Christmas at Chapter House, a party was organised. My neighbour, Allen, and another friend, Anne, decided to provide some entertainment. The three of us would perform a ballet. Allen and I were about the same height and build, and Anne was, well, think Dawn French and you'd be near the mark. Anne made the costumes, including a tutu for herself. We all agreed that it had to be good and decided to do as much rehearsing as we could. We made use of a local church hall and began to get it together in October, rehearsing every weekend through to December. It was a choreographed routine to go with the music which was a familiar classical piece often used in ballet. We did a dress rehearsal for my Mum and sister, which went ok, and by that time it was as good as it was going to get. We were ready. The big night arrived, and the hours of rehearsals certainly paid off. It lasted for several minutes, beginning slowly, and working up to the grand climax with me and Allen carrying Anne around the room, 'struggling' to prevent our knees buckling. It was great fun to do, and it went down really well. In spite of its success, I decided not to pursue ballet as a career and to stick to the magic.

The girl I was going out with at the beginning of 1978 introduced me to a friend of hers by the name of Bill Billings. Bill was a great character. He became the voice of the early residents of the new city of Milton Keynes. He was a poet, raconteur, and a great artist and sculptor. He spent much of his time working with schools and local communities. I'm happy to say his work is still very much visible today. Only yesterday I walked past his sculpture at Peartree Bridge, the iconic Triceratops Dinosaur. Every time I see it, I think of Bill and the chats we'd have as he was building it.

The same girl introduced me to another friend of hers in January of 1978. Her name was Babs, who according to my diary I found *"really beautiful"* which she was. We eventually married in 1980 and set up home together with her two small children, Clare, and Jeff. We went on to have two boys Ben, born in1981, and Jay, 1983. Sadly, we divorced in the mid- 90s. It's a strange experience reading my diaries of those early days of being in love. It bought back a lot of very happy memories. Conversely, my diaries during the aftermath are really difficult to read to this day.

Meanwhile back in 1978…

I was getting fed up at work (again). In the Winter of 1978 I decided to leave Llewellyn and go back to Cleanline Furniture (again). Once more though, I left on good terms and with no hard feelings. I soon settled back into it and spent much of my time making davenport desks. I loved it there and certainly had a lot of job satisfaction, which was something I didn't have in the building trade. The other thing that came out of it was the realisation that I could easily make my own furniture. I had a workshop (a bench in my bedroom) and access to polishers from work. I started off making a sideboard and bookcase for my flat, then a bathroom cabinet and other stuff. As people came to visit, I'd be asked to make them something similar. It just took off from there. Looking back now, I wonder how I did it with hardly any machinery. It took longer, but it was all handmade and both me and the customer were pleased and satisfied with the end result. At this time I was living a very full life, Work, making furniture, league table tennis, magic, and I'd just acquired an allotment as well. That piece of news pleased Dad who was beginning to mellow by now. However his health wasn't good, and it declined quite rapidly in that February to the point where he was no longer able to get up and down the stairs. We then had to convert the front room into a bedroom for him. On the 17th February we took him to hospital in London for a check-up and they decided to keep him in, which was a relief. His condition deteriorated over the following weeks, and we were told his heart was failing. He looked dreadful. On March 3rd we went to see him, and as we talked it was obvious his grip on reality was failing as well. We spoke to the doctors who told us he was being allowed home the following day. I thought surely not in that condition, how could they?! I looked at Mum and my sisters and then the inevitable hit me.

"He wants to come home," said Mum.

They travelled home together in an ambulance the next day.

The following three weeks were difficult for all of us. We took it in turns to sleep on the sofa in the room with him, doing what we had to during the often long nights. One night, as I tried to make myself comfortable in the armchair in the corner, he became restless and said,

"I've been a silly old fool haven't I boy?"

"Of course you haven't, you always meant well, that's what's important."

"I dunno boy… I just want you to know I'm proud of you all."

"I know you are, we're proud of you too."

I went over to his bedside and looked down at him, a shadow of his former self. I held his hand. It was thin and bony. I recalled that many years ago I would bury my tiny hand in his, then it was big and soft and pillowy, comforting. When I was small, he would ask me to squeeze and pinch it as hard as I possibly could, he'd laugh as he said,

"You can't hurt me boy! You can't hurt me!"

If only that were true. I held it as he drifted off to sleep, thinking of how much I owed him. The encouragement he gave me with the magic, and the expense as well. Almost a week's wages for the Vernon book for God's sake! I thought of how he cared for us. Hours spent at the allotment, weeding, digging, and hoeing, all to keep us healthily fed. There were times when he was difficult to live with and now the whole hair thing drifted into insignificance.

In spite of his rather battered and weak heart, it was always in the right place. Dad would have given his life for his family, and in all honesty he probably did.

He passed away at 11.45 on the morning of March 25th, 1978. He was 65 years of age.

That night I went to the pub. On the way home my head was full of him. Happy memories, and above all gratitude.

I'm not ashamed to say, I cried all the way home.

It took a while to get back to normality and we supported Mum as best we could. As far as I was concerned I thought it best to carry on involving myself in the magic and the Club, which meant as much to him as it did to me.

CHAPTER 14

The end of the 70s & into the 80s

The magic club highlight of 1978 was an invite from Paul Daniels to visit him at his home near Buckingham. There was about ten of us and we had a great time. The house was huge and old with an impressive Inglenook fireplace in the lounge. Here's how I described the evening in my diary.

April 17th, 1978: *I drove over to Paul Daniel's house near Buckingham tonight along with several of the lads from the club and we had a great evening. His hospitality was really something else. The house is out of this world and has everything.*

'Everything' included a swimming pool, which was a waste of time, he told us, as he couldn't swim. It was lovely to see him and have a chat along with his obviously proud Mum and Dad. We were led into the lounge on arrival which was dominated by the beautiful fireplace. He told us that on the day he moved in he'd laid on his back on the carpet, waved his arms and legs in the air, and said "Yes!!" - He'd worked hard and had every reason to be chuffed and proud of his success. He spoke of his early years and some of his future plans, after which we were treated to a lovely buffet, it was a great evening.

While Paul was working on the club circuit, prior to the beginning of his long and successful tv series, I was doing a series of one-nighters myself, including - working the tables at the local athletics club dinner; providing entertainment after the presentation of trophies for the table tennis league; and also a job for Maxwell Printers & Publishers (owned by the infamous Robert). - I'm sure I was having as much fun as Paul and could certainly agree and identify with something else he said on that night.

"I love conjuring!"

In September, I went to the IBM Convention in Hastings and entered the close-up competition. I came second. I really should have won it that year, and perhaps would have had I not blown it on the first of the three tables. What made it worse was the fact it was self-inflicted and could have been so easily avoided. I had a stonking hangover, and that first table was just a haze. The other two went reasonably well after I'd sunk a pint or two of water. What a stupid thing to do. I'd never make that mistake again. With competitions you really do need to be on top of everything. When Bobby Bernard found out, he was scathing. Bring it on next year!

The final two years of the 70s were busy and quite eventful in all sorts of ways. The magic was taking off and I was getting a fair amount of work. I had a regular booking at the Westone Hotel in Northampton every Friday night and the occasional Saturday. Other jobs came in from a variety of organisations in all sorts of venues, from schools to fire stations. If I wanted to try out new material, me and my pal, Allen, would get in his car (daren't risk mine) and go off and find a pub somewhere. We'd have a drink and get the feel of the place and if it was ok, I'd show him a trick. Invariably somebody would notice, and I'd be invited to do some more and soon pulled a crowd. At this point, Allen or I would try and have a quiet word with the landlord to make sure he was ok with it. I did learn a valuable lesson early on. At one pub, when I was in full swing, I was asked to stop due to the lack of an entertainment licence. Anyway, it's courtesy to ask and it did put me on friendly terms from the start. Those pub gigs (which they soon turned into) were great fun to do. As well as the laughs and experience, I picked up a lot of work. In those days close-up was fairly new, and people had never seen magic performed under their noses before. Just about every business card I was asked for resulted in a gig - entertainment secretaries were always looking out for something different.

As time went on, it occurred to me that I could get some publicity in the local press. I gave them a call and explained what I did. They agreed it would make an interesting story. The paper contacted a local pub of their choosing, got the ok from the landlord, and an evening was arranged. We arrived early and I did a couple of tables before the reporter and photographer arrived. It was a great night and resulted in a half-page spread with the headline, 'Ken conjures up the crowds'. From that article I was asked to take part in a charity evening at The Bridge which was of course one of my favourite watering holes. It was a great night with the locals really entering into the spirit of it all. There was fancy dress, the raffle of a cake in the shape of a pack of cards (made by Babs) and other stuff as well. That too resulted in a nice photo and write-up in the local press, with the headline, 'Magic figure for charity'. It was a win win for everybody involved, great fun for the punters, good publicity for both me and the pub, and a considerable amount of money raised for local charities.

By the end of 1979 there were several pubs where I knew I would always have a guaranteed and receptive audience. It wasn't always plain sailing though, occasionally there were drunks to deal with, and 'know-it- alls' - and other things peculiar to the great British public. I was in the middle of doing my sponge ball routine one night and went to my pocket to pick one up, only to find it replaced with a lump of greasy cheese. From that night on, I always made sure I had a flannel and towel in my bag, as well as an assortment of spare sponge balls. Thankfully, most of the time it went well, and I was gaining invaluable experience. My diaries have been useful for looking up magic jobs I've done over the last 50 years or so. Many I can remember and some I have no recollection of at all. It's annoying when I can only half remember one…

May 26th, 1979: *I did a show at the new Post Office club tonight. It went very well indeed. I tried out a new watch gag which went great!!*

What was the gag? I have no idea. Obviously not as great as I thought it was.

In the spring of 1979, I was offered a job by a chap called Ronnie who was an acquaintance of mine from Blackpool. The job involved performing close-up magic in a small theatre on one of the piers for the Summer Season. At this point my life was fairly stable. I was in a relationship with two small children involved, I had an enjoyable job, and a nice flat – so should I, or shouldn't I? It was a dilemma that required some serious thinking. I thought the least I could do was go up and talk with Ronnie and have a look at the venue. I went on the train and arrived in Blackpool around lunchtime. The theatre was tiny and seated about 15 people. A card table was situated in front of several rows of chairs, and that was it. We talked money and accommodation and then it was suggested I give it a try. I'd had the foresight to take a few bits up with me, so I thought why not? There weren't many people about, so Ronnie (who had a lot of experience as a grafter) went onto the pier and managed to entice a local family to come in and watch a free magic show. Luckily it was raining which helped. They sat down and I went into my strongest material with a lot of gags and bits of business. Within three minutes one of the children whined, "Can we go now Mum?" I battled on and at the end as they left, I heard one of the parents say, "Not bad for free I suppose."

Ronnie told me that many northern families can be a world away from those found in the South. He went on to explain that many of them stay in the same guest house at the same time every year (often in the same rooms). They go to the same shows and eat the same food and play on same part of same beach. It's part of their DNA. They wouldn't go down south any more than they would fly to the moon – "You'll soon get used to them," he added. Well perhaps I would I thought, I also thought he was a touch unkind in blaming the audience, who were pleasant enough but, possibly because of the wet weather and having young and tired children, were just not in the mood to watch a magic show. In different circumstances it may well have gone better. Regarding his rather stereotypical view of northern families, back in the 50s and 60s it may well have been true, but the world had changed since then and people had changed with it, and anyway it wouldn't have been just northern families I'd have to entertain either. After they'd left, I glanced around the room, which had no windows or ventilation. It would be like an oven in the summer. I thanked him for his offer and politely declined. There were other reasons as well, which I pondered over as I travelled home. Magic wasn't my only interest and who'd look after my allotment? The most important reason though involved Babs and the children, I was still getting to know them, and they were becoming an important part of my life. I'd have missed them all.

I was still going to the magic club and doing the occasional lecture there, including one on my recent visit to America. Luckily, I'd picked up pamphlets and brochures which turned out to be really useful on the night. I was beginning to wonder if I could add lecturing to my magic career. I had the material and enough experience of performing, all I needed was a pile of lecture notes, definitely food for thought.

There were two other lectures at the club worth noting from 1979 - one from Des King, who was a working pro' and had recently moved to Northampton. It was great stuff. This was from somebody who had made a living in show business from quite an early age. I loved it, as I noted in my diary, "*The best lecture I've seen, all good advice.*" The other was from a couple of chaps from a drama society. They explained about deportment and how to move on stage, the correct make-up to use, the importance of voice projection and other advice invaluable to a performer. While it was nice to see a full house for the evening with Des, it was a disappointing turn-out of only four members for the actors - not the last time I would feel despair at a club meeting.

June 27th, 1979, was a very special day. Her Majesty Queen Elizabeth, accompanied by His Royal Highness Prince Philip, the Duke of Edinburgh, came to visit my home. To be honest, they didn't call in purely for my benefit, they came to have a look around Chapter House, to see how this complex for single people actually worked. One or two of the residents were carefully chosen to shake the royal hand and be introduced, while others were positioned towards the back. Hippie types, such as me and my pal 'Spud' Lubbock, who had hair down to his elbows, had no chance. We did, however, get to meet Prince Philip, who was great. He asked how we coped with cooking for ourselves and was really surprised to learn I had an allotment and grew my own veg. "Good heavens," he said. My one abiding memory of that day (apart from the remarkable colour of Her Majesty's eyes) was the incredible shine on the Duke's shoes. They were like mirrors; I couldn't help wondering if he gave them a final buff up himself or whether there's a man at the palace whose sole job (pun intended) is to do it for him. My one regret of that day was that I didn't ask him.

In the summer me and Babs decided to have a holiday with the children. We couldn't afford anything too lavish, so decided to have a go at camping in North Wales. We booked a pitch at a campsite near Llanberis and borrowed a tent, and a ground sheet and other stuff, and just about managed to cram it all in the car. In an effort to save money on food expenses, I bought a small gas hob and a wind break. The plan was to do all of the cooking ourselves, with ingredients we'd buy locally at a supermarket. As we hadn't done anything like this before, and assuming the campsite would be full of experienced campers, we went to a local park to practise putting up the tent and erecting the wind break. Just as well we did. We loaded everything into the car the night before and Clare (7) and Jeff (5) went to bed quite excited. We got up really early the following morning and after a big breakfast got them into the car and put sleeping bags and pillows all around them. Babs sat next to me with the Map Book as my navigator. We were ready and excited. It was Wednesday 1st August and we set off at a quarter to six. As we drove past Stony Stratford, Jeff asked if we were nearly there yet as he could see mountains! The journey went well, if a little slow. We arrived at the site at lunchtime, checked in and had the choice of five mostly empty fields (so much for being full of experienced campers). We drove the car up to the furthest one away and unloaded the tent. It went up ok, but because of the way the wind was blowing, we decided to move to the next field and use a hedge as a windbreak, which turned out to be a wise decision. After making sure the hob worked, with a welcome cup of tea we set off for a walk in the countryside around the campsite. We walked for miles, and I had to carry Jeff on the way back (I think we got a bit lost but didn't like to say anything apart from, "We're almost there now.") Eventually we arrived back at the tent tired and hungry. We had a meal of bits and pieces we'd taken with us to 'use up', played a few ball games and then fell into bed, knackered. For the following nine days we visited all sorts of places including a famous castle. We had a wonderful time...

August 10th, 1979: *We visited Caernarfon Castle this morning for an hour and then went to Dinas Beach a few miles down the coast from there. Although the weather wasn't too good, we still had a laugh catching crabs. From there we went to Pwllheli where we found a small funfair and drove back through the middle of the mountains. It was a beautiful evening and me and Babs played frisbee in the dusk.*

Looking back now, and reliving those few days, I reckon that was one of the best holidays I've ever had. It was probably due to the basic simplicity of it all, each of us happy to enjoy just what was there, the freedom to come and go as we pleased, have our meals whenever we wanted and experience the spectacular scenery. It was also an important one for me as it was the first time I'd spent any length of time with the children. In all honesty, I didn't know how or even if I'd be able to cope as it was all so new to me.

Apart from the occasional wobble when a tired Jeff had a tantrum, I thought I did ok.

September soon rolled around again and the IBM convention at Scarborough. This time I was much better prepared for the close-up competition and won it at last.

It was becoming apparent that I would have to make a decision regarding my future with Babs. At the time, I had the best of both worlds; I was in a relationship, and I had my own place. I wasn't too sure if I could give up my new-found freedom and then drop straight into family life. Love however is such a powerful emotion and in the end I succumbed. A decision I certainly don't regret.

I would've liked to have moved in with Babs and the youngsters, but I didn't like the area she lived in (any more than she did). The clincher came when my car was rammed overnight by a hit and run driver while it was parked outside her house. It was only an old Hillman Hunter, but it was still a shock. I made some enquiries about alternative housing to the Milton Keynes Development Corporation, to find out what the options were. Luckily, we were in the right place at the right time during the early days of the building of the new city. We began to look at a few show houses in various areas and were really impressed with Springfield. Unlike other estates we'd visited, it had a brand-new school in the centre, and it all looked perfect. We went through the inevitable process of form filling and wrote, as our choice of three, Springfield, Springfield, Springfield. We sent it off, were put on the list, and eagerly awaited the next stage which was an interview.

Meanwhile, I was making other more secret plans. It was Bab's birthday on October 30th, and I'd decided to propose (and had no doubt she'd say yes.) I'd met her family and she'd met mine and I felt the time was right. For the big night I'd arranged a meal at our favourite restaurant, Linford Lodge. I had also arranged a limo to pick us up, courtesy of my pal John from the pub, who was an undertaker. All went well, she said yes, and we toasted to the future with a glass of Champagne from a silver tray.

We had a reply from the MKDC and went for an interview and were offered a house in Springfield. We picked up the keys on February 7th and moved into our brand-new home on February 16th, 1980.

CHAPTER 15

Family Life

1980 was busy and eventful in all sorts of ways. Much of it was spent on doing jobs around the house. A lot of shelves went up, along with curtain track and even an extra internal door. I did some work in the garden and laid a patio and also erected Dad's old shed. Clare and Jeff had settled into their new school which was at the top of the road and were doing well. Both had chickenpox in the Spring which was really unpleasant but at least it got it over with.

I was still working at Cleanline and had a real shock when I arrived there one morning to find my tools missing. I was still using the toolbox I'd made when I was an apprentice. It was a huge wooden thing and housed planes, saws, hammers, and an assortment of other tools. It had two drawers where I kept my set of boxwood handled chisels among other things. All of the tools were of a high quality and worth a lot of money, and had sentimental value too, many of them bought by my Dad. The thief had broken in and walked off with the box. I was left with nothing. Many of those tools were irreplaceable, particularly some of the old planes which weren't made any more. The police were called but they were never found. My boss wasn't particularly helpful when he suggested I claim for them on my household insurance. He soon relented when I threatened legal action. He agreed to buy another basic set and I was taken up to the local hardware shop, 'Pollards', where the new ones were bought. It took a while to get over the whole sorry business. Needless to say, security was improved at the factory, but the words 'horse, stable door, and bolted' sprang to mind. I made myself a new toolbox along similar lines to the stolen one, this time with a substantial padlock.

In June, Babs discovered she was pregnant, which was great news! The whole family were delighted. We decided to get married before the end of the year, so we were in for a busy time. These days weddings are years in the planning; not so in our case. I phoned the Minister on June 5th, which was the first thing to do, as we wanted it to be in the family church in Bletchley. From then on it was a hectic time. During the following weeks we organised… the Hall for the reception, the caterers, and the rings. Babs had bought her dress; bridesmaids were chosen and dresses were sorted out. Invitations had been sent, and I'd bought a new pair of trousers. We were ready to go on August 16th. There was one slight hitch though, as I wrote in my diary on the day before the wedding.

August 15th, 1980: *It was panic stations today. We had a power cut from 3.00 o'clock this afternoon, as a result Babs and the rest of us couldn't wash, shave, press clothes, or anything. Annie came over and bought a bottle of Champagne which we consumed on the patio. I went to Mum's at around 10.00 o'clock.*

Happily all went well on the day. We were now Mr. and Mrs. Hawes.

We settled into family life in our new home. Clare and Jeff were happy and making friends and would regularly visit their Dad and Nanny and Granddad Holmes at Ascott House in Wing. They really enjoyed it over there, around the farm and the countryside. Clare loved the horses, and Jeff loved the tractors. They were both happy to help out at my allotment as well. I grew an assortment of vegetables, much of which Babs would freeze and deposit in the new freezer, a huge brown thing that stood in a corner of the kitchen. One day I arrived at the allotment to discover that somebody had pulled up a row of still growing swedes and just left them there. I was still grieving with the loss of my tools at the time and was beginning to despair of the human race. What is it with these people?

We went to the IBM Convention in Brighton in 1980 where I was on one of the late Close up shows. I was introduced by Jay Marshall which was a huge thrill.

I was still doing the occasional gig and having a go at the magic club competitions. I won the cup for the best trick in the stage magic with the bottle production. I was still finding time to keep my hand in and, after winning that one, I found myself in search of something to do for the forthcoming club Ingenuity competition. I decided to go back to the Vernon book and came up with an adaption of a trick from within its pages and won that as well. Things were looking up. In November I did a lecture at a magic club in Wolverhampton which I was pleased with, mainly because I got there, found the venue, and got home without a mishap with the car. From what I remember, the lecture went ok.

As well as the magic, allotment, and working in the house, I was still playing league table tennis - it was certainly a full life.

October 28th, 1980: *I've been playing with the kids for an hour or two, it's hard work being a horse for that amount of time.*

In January of 1981, my Mum was offered a small one-bedroom bungalow in Fenny Stratford. She'd been on the list for some time, as we'd thought it best for her to find somewhere smaller and warmer. There was a vast amount of stuff to sort out as you'd expect, moving from a large three-bedroom house. There wasn't a great deal of time to do it in either and it was the middle of winter. We all mucked in though and got both houses sorted out in about a week. Looking back, we've often wondered if we were a bit hasty in encouraging Mum to move so quickly. She wasn't elderly at 63, was reasonably healthy and I don't think she was unhappy. Perhaps we should have thought more about the emotional ties; after all, she'd bought up a family and had lived there for almost 30 years. Mum was never one to complain though and soon settled into her new home. Her bungalow was close to where both my sisters lived and a short bus ride away from us in Springfield. Her sister (my Auntie Maudie) had moved from Wales to a flat not too far from us also on Springfield, so really Mum was surrounded by loved ones, as she was for the rest of her life. She soon got to know her neighbours around the Close and was involving herself helping out with their shopping and all sorts of things, particularly with the housebound and elderly. Mum was an angel. There is no other word.

This is a rather bizarre entry to my diary…

February 9th, 1981: *I've had a bit of a horrible day at work today. Frank didn't turn up, so I was lumbered with finishing off some of his oak units. He came in later with a doctor's certificate and it seems his arse hole fell out on Friday night.*

Dave and I went out for a pint at 'The Springfield'.

On a lighter and happier note, Benjamin Peter was born on February 18th, 1981. The birth, which went well, was in a maternity unit in Bletchley. I was surprised how emotional the whole experience was (even though I was convinced he was going to be a she). What a beautiful baby! I was a very proud Dad. To mark the occasion I bought Babs a special present, a sewing machine. Clare and Jeff took to young Ben straight away which was lovely. The christening was some three months later in May which was another nice family affair.

Like most couples we did have the occasional row and disagreement. The following diary entry from the summer will I'm sure resonate with a few husbands and partners…

June 30th, 1981: *Babs and I had a silly row tonight. I wish she'd tell me to do things instead of expecting me to know and do whatever needs doing.*

I do remember saying to myself more than once, "I'm a magician, not a bloody mind reader!"

Car problems were continuing of course; in fact they would continue on and off for the next 30 years. Although I still had the Hillman Hunter on the drive (with the bashed in door), I had now bought a car from Bab's Dad. This was a huge Triumph. I can't recall the model, but it had double headlights and Overdrive (whatever that was). It was a nice-looking car but a rust bucket. I spent hours on it with filler and sandpaper and aerosol paint. The plan was to get rid of the Hillman as soon as I'd got the door sorted out. I'd saved some money and went to a breaker's yard and managed to find one. It was ok but would've been better had the colour been blue to match the car, rather than bright red. Anyway, I took it over to a chap to sort out, where he sprayed it blue - the wrong blue, but still blue. It was as good as it was going to get. I put an ad in the paper and had a phone call a couple of days later.

"I'll be over to look at it tomorrow," he said.

He didn't turn up. I put the ad in the following week. Somebody else phoned.

"I'll come over tomorrow at 3 O'clock."

At two O'clock that day, I thought it would be a good idea to drive it round the block a couple of times to warm the engine up ready for the prospective buyer. I'd got to the far end of the estate and the clutch went. I could have cried. A week later I'd had it fixed and eventually sold it for £250. What a relief.

Although things were going ok at Cleanline (in spite of the theft), I responded to an advert in the paper for cabinet makers required for a company called Indotraka based at Woburn. I had an interview and discovered that the company imported solid mahogany reproduction furniture from Indonesia. It was delivered to a factory unit in Elstow near Bedford where a team of cabinet makers and polishers would modify and prepare it for sale in the European market. I went over to Elstow to have a look and was quite impressed. It was about 18 miles away. The money was slightly better, overtime could be available and there was no bonus system. I accepted. I handed my notice in on the same day as two other lads. Dave was going to the piano factory, and John was going to the same place as me. That was good news, we'd share the driving. We started there on November 30th, 1981.

1982 began with yet more car trouble; It wouldn't start, the window seized up, the windscreen wiper motor packed up, and unsurprisingly it failed the MOT. It was suggested by the mechanic it was best to be shot of it - a familiar scenario. It did finally pass the MOT, but I had decided the days were numbered for that old Triumph.

The winter of 1982 was a hard one. On January 14th the temperature got as low as minus 20 degrees. Not many cars parked outside in the street could cope with that in those days, in fact John couldn't get his car going either. A day off work for both of us.

I settled into the new job reasonably well to begin with, but after a month or two began to struggle. I could do the work ok but was a bit on the slow side, or too fussy. The Foreman there was difficult and would often fly off the handle, which wasn't helpful. One day a new Manager turned up to oversee the work and the Foreman wasn't told. (That didn't go down too well.) It resulted in a lot of bad feeling between the two of them and unsurprisingly they'd have heated arguments all the time. At the end of February the Foreman was sacked. That came as a bit of a surprise and things generally went downhill from there. In April, the Manager had a quiet word with me, and I was asked to leave - sacked by any other word. To be honest I was glad to be out of it.

Luckily, I sold the car, but there were more pressing things on my mind. What to do next? I did toy with the idea of setting up for myself but decided it was too risky. With a growing family I needed something steady with a regular wage coming in. Back to Llewellyn then! I gave them a call and went for an interview and was told I could start the following Monday. There wasn't a great deal of work at the time but there was plenty in the pipeline. I was told that they could only guarantee me work for a month. I accepted anyway and it turned out to be considerably more than a month's employment. I would be there for the next 26 years.

I soon got back into the swing of things at Llewellyn and spent the first few weeks working in the timber yard with my pal Russ. It was nice to relax with little pressure for a change and have a laugh. We'd play our own version of Pop Quiz. I'd ask him to name a track from an obscure Man album, and he'd ask me to name the original Genesis guitarist. Great fun.

The magic was going well too, I was on the bill in the close up show at the Cambridge Convention in June. It was a good day with Geoffrey Durham as 'The Great Soprendo' on the gala show. I was also doing a few gigs and kid shows too. (I needed the money.) The magic club was going well, and I was voted as President Elect. Things were generally looking good until I had a bit of a health scare in July.

I peed blood one evening and it was all very scary. I phoned the doctor the following morning and he told me to call into the surgery as soon as I could. That alone set alarm bells ringing. When I got there, he put my mind at rest straight away.

"This is quite common and nothing to worry about. Sometimes when the bladder opens and closes, it can pinch a small blood vessel and release a small amount of blood which will then show up in the urine for a day or two."

"So I should be back to normal tomorrow then?"

"I would think so. Tell you what, I'll organise a few tests to make sure there are no underlying problems. After all it's the greatest feeling in the world to be told that there's nothing wrong with you."

I wasn't going to argue with that.

Sure enough it was all clear the next day, I got on with my life and didn't worry.

Work was going well, and I was now in the joiners shop in the factory. The carpenter who had recently left had decided to leave the building trade altogether and bought a chip shop in Olney (he went from being a chippy to being a chippy.)

Both home and family life were busy. We'd started to decorate at last. The entire house needed to be done as all the walls were plain white throughout. I'd made a start on designing and building some units for the front room in a mahogany reproduction style (which was all the rage at the time). We were getting there slowly. The family were keeping fit with a visit to the local pool at least once a week and I was cycling to work every day (I still couldn't afford a car so had little choice). Babs had started running regularly with some other girls and had completed the Milton Keynes Marathon. Clare was continuing with her ballet lessons which she'd started when she was really small. She was having health problems as well with an ongoing bladder problem, which was a bit worrying.

I went to the IBM convention in Hastings and on my return a letter was waiting for me from my doctor. I had an appointment with a specialist consultant at the Outpatients Department. I went along to that where I gave a urine sample, (which seemed ok.) I was poked and prodded and told I'd have to give a blood sample and have a kidney X-ray at a later date. Three days later I went back with another urine sample and had a blood test. According to my diary, *"I'm still not concerned."* Well, why should I be? After all it is only a pinched blood vessel. Life went on.

An Instruction night was organised at the magic club at the beginning of October so I thought it would be an idea to take young Jeff along. He was only 8 but it would be a night out for him, and you never know it may stimulate an interest in magic. It didn't quite go to plan;

October 5th, 1982: *Jeff and I went to a club meeting at Northampton. It was an instruction night. In spite of the low attendance he seemed to enjoy himself, particularly the new railway station, the bus and taxi rides, and a bag of chips on the way home.*

I didn't really think Jeff would take to the magic somehow. He was more interested in the great outdoors and the countryside, even at that young age.

On October 13th, 1982, I got on a series of buses and headed to Stoke Mandeville hospital to have a kidney X-ray. I'd had to starve myself for 24 hours and then drink regular glasses of water mixed up with a powder from a sachet. I didn't really know what the effects would be, but I soon found out. 'Through the eye of a needle' is a fair description - I was definitely empty! When I got there, I was given something unpleasant to drink and had to wait a while for it to get into my system. I had the X-ray, got dressed and was told to wait. After a while the door burst open and a stout doctor in a white coat strode in holding some large envelopes. He took out the X-ray photos and fixed them to a back-lit wall.

"I've looked at the results, and It's always been my policy to tell my patients exactly how it is. You have a tumour attached to your left kidney." He pointed to a circular shadow.

"Do you have any questions?"

Needless to say I was a bit shocked, the pinched blood vessel theory now firmly out of the window.

"How big is it?" I asked.

"About the size of a golf ball."

"Do you know what it is?"

"Not until you have a biopsy. That will probably be the next stage of your treatment which you will need to discuss with your consultant. If you have no further questions, I do have a busy day."

And he was gone. I wasn't impressed with his bedside manner but there can't be an easy way to tell a patient of potential bad news. I was left alone with my thoughts.

A week later I saw my consultant at the Outpatients Department. He told me that more tests needed to be carried out at Stoke Mandeville and I would be in for a couple of days. When I asked him when, he answered,

"Tomorrow."

The next day I travelled over to Aylesbury and got settled in. The ward sister spoke to me and asked if I'd mind if a group of students watched the procedure the following day.

"Not at all." I replied.

Early the next morning I was woken up for an antiseptic bath and then wheeled into a small operating theatre. I was stripped from the waist down and was told where a tube was going to be inserted (which made my eyes water) and then how far it would travel. A long way. I was given an injection (which made me feel sleepy) just before a group of very attractive nurses gathered round. The next thing I remember is waking up in a lot of pain. The end result was inconclusive.

At the end of November I went back to Stoke Mandeville for a couple of minor tests. From there I was taken in an ambulance to the Churchill Hospital in Oxford for the body scan and biopsy. The scan room was pleasant enough and the staff really friendly. I was told to lay on a table and to keep as motionless as I could. The table moved me slowly forward into the tube. I felt comfortable and there was even music playing inside it. A young nurse poked her head into the end and said,

"Is Mr. Hawes feeling ok?"

"No," I said, "Mr. Hawes is not feeling ok."

"What seems to be the trouble then?"

"It's the music. Haven't you got anything decent?"

(It was a light operatic thing.)

"What would Mr. Hawes like to listen to then?"

"Mr. Hawes would love to listen to the Pink Floyd album, 'Wish you were here'."

I only said it as a joke and got a bit worried when the music was turned off. There was a slight delay, a couple of clicks, and soon that memorable opening sequence of, 'Shine on you crazy diamond' was wafting down the tube.

"Are you ok now Mr. Hawes? We're about to start."

"Mr. Hawes is feeling great." (and a tad emotional, that music was synonymous with my Dad.)

"Thank you," I said.

That afternoon I went to another department, was told to lay on my stomach and was given a local anaesthetic. A tube was inserted into my back, and into that an instrument with a small pair of pincers on the end. I could feel it cutting out a piece of the tumour inside me, which was rather weird. The sample was placed in a test tube, and I asked to have a look at it. (I've always been interested in all things medical.) I asked the doctor what he thought.

"Looks ok to me," he said.

Well, what else could he say? - I had to wait.

In the middle of December I went to see my consultant to get the results. I was told it was a cancerous growth that needed to be removed. In fact it was decided to remove the whole kidney. I went into hospital on December 16th, had the operation the next day, and came home on Christmas eve. The prognosis was very good and there was no evidence of cancer cells or secondary tumours anywhere else in my body. I had regular check-ups for a year or two and that was it I've been fine ever since. The only advice I was given regarding living with one kidney was, "everything in moderation." What I wasn't told though was how it would affect my mental health and emotional wellbeing. I did struggle for quite a while trying to make sense of it all. I found that I couldn't tell anybody the reason for the operation or even mention the 'C' word, I told them that the kidney wasn't working properly and that was it. It all changed a few months later when a friend at work was diagnosed with testicular cancer and had to have one removed. I spoke to him and told him my story and how well I felt and did my best to reassure him - I think I did us both a favour. One other incident happened before I could put it all behind me, and that was when I went to donate my annual pint of blood. I was told they could no longer accept me as a donor because of the risk of cancer cells. It seems that once you have a history, no matter what the outcome, no chances are taken, which is fair enough. It was after that I put it all firmly behind me once and for all. Luckily, I had some of the Christmas break to recuperate but it was soon back to the grind on January 24th. My boss at work was kind enough to offer me an office job for a month before I started back into my workshop. I found that really interesting but couldn't wait to start back and do proper work. It finally happened on February 21st. I was tired for the first week or two but soon got back into the swing. All in all I thought I'd done well getting over a major operation in two months.

I soon got back into the magic as well. Me and Babs went to the Blackpool Convention where we heard the sad news of the death of Ken Brooke. He was such a lovely man, his kindness and advice when I was a lad was invaluable. Mum and Dad would call in and see him at his shop whenever they visited the hospital in London. Ken always treated them kindly even if he had a studio full if magicians.

I won the magic club close-up competition and was made President for the second time at the AGM. I also took on the secretary job. According to my diary I volunteered - probably because nobody else would. I was also in a close-up show at the IBM convention - "25 years of close-up competitions" - I enjoyed that.

My diary also had some great news!

April 26th, 1983: *Babs was sick this morning and is feeling generally pretty pregnant.*

It was confirmed on May 5th.

In the summer we all went on holiday to Butlins Pwllheli in North Wales. The journey was a bit of a struggle on the train, but once there we had a great time. The chalet was pretty basic, and we had our meals in a vast canteen. There was still a 'Hi De Hi' feel about the place which didn't bother us at all. There was plenty to do and Clare and Jeff went off to do their own thing for much of the time and soon made friends. There was an indoor pool and access to the beach via chair lifts. Shows were on every night and the resident kids' entertainer was Bob Wooding from Northampton. Bob had joined the club as a youngster and was really good at what he did. He is now recognised as one of the best balloon entertainers in the country. There were a lot of different bars which catered for every age and taste. Clare and Jeff took part in various competitions and did really well. Babs entered one for disco dancing, and I had a go at the table tennis and knobbly knees! It was tiring but a welcome break.

I stood on the patio in the back garden one day and came up with the idea of making a picnic table. The timber we used at work was ideal. I did a drawing and came up with a design and soon knocked one up in a kit form during my lunch hours in just a few days. I was able to buy the timber from the company at a reasonable price and it was soon on the patio. The next day I was asked by my neighbour if I could make one for him. To cut a long story short I made loads of them throughout the summer and the following year as well. I'm pretty sure my boss knew I had a thriving mini business going on, but nobody said anything, until one Friday lunchtime when I had a visit from the CEO. He said,

"I understand you've been making picnic tables, is that correct?"

I decided it best to come clean and said that I had - in fact I showed him one that I was planning on taking home that day.

"Mmm, how big is it when it's assembled?"

I thought I'd better show him - honesty is the best policy and all that - so I assembled it. He looked at it and said (surprisingly),

"Could you make me one?"

"Of course," I said, somewhat relieved.

"It will need to be a bit longer than that though as I have a rather long terrace, can you do that?"

"Of course I can. Tell me what you want and I'll do it."

He borrowed my tape measure and decided on a size, and then (even more surprisingly) asked me how much it would cost! I would have been happy to have made it for nothing, after all it was his wood, in fact I was expecting to. I charged him double the normal price which he was happy to pay – well, there was extra wood.

Earlier in the year I'd borrowed some money from Mum and bought another second-hand car. It isn't even noted in my diary what model it was, probably because I didn't care and it wouldn't matter. From memory it was a white Marina estate. It turned out to be useful that summer to deliver the many picnic tables I'd made, and also vegetables from the allotment. It ran reasonably well until winter arrived and there were the usual starting problems.

Speaking of arrivals, Jay Kenneth was born in the early hours of December 16th, 1983. It wasn't an easy birth as he corkscrewed during the delivery and there were a worrying few moments when the midwife had problems getting him to breathe. All was ok in the end though, and mother and son came home to Springfield two days later.

1984 was chaotic. No other word for it really. Both Clare and Jeff were at the age when they wanted to try things and join various clubs. Nothing wrong with that of course, in fact it was encouraged. Jeff showed an interest in table tennis, so I took him to Bill Wooding's every week. Later on, Clare too went on a course, playing weekly at the local campus (which was connected to a coaching course I was on.) Her ballet lessons were continuing sometimes twice weekly, and she was disco dancing as well. Babs was doing Keep Fit and aerobics and child minding (as well as looking after our four). Then there was the weekly Youth Club, and not forgetting Jeff"s brief interest with The Cubs!

It was busy for me too as I was dealing with the bulk of the transport. I'd often get frustrated as I had so little time for myself in the evenings. Somehow, we managed, in spite of me grumbling along the lines of, "All I am in this house is a bloody taxi!"

Something else arose from all of this activity - for every competition or course completed, there was a certificate.

"Wouldn't it be nice," said Babs one day, "If we could get them framed and hung on the wall?"

"I could do that," I said, "Leave it with me, get them all together and I'll have a go."

February 19th, 1984: *Babs found another two certificates today which brings the total to 27.*

By the middle of the year Dad's old shed had been replaced with a self-designed and self-built workshop. Although it was always known to the family as, 'The Shed', to me it was my escape. It was twice the size of the other one and the plan was to buy machinery and do some furniture making. For much of the 80s though, it was more of a bike shed with four or five crammed in there. But I still managed to get some use out of it and built just about every piece of furniture in the house, and of course loads of picture frames. I was working hard at work too, ten-hour days, plus Saturday mornings, and I was doing a lot of private work as well. Both me and Babs were exhausted and often at a low ebb.

The magic was still going ok (somehow), I did a lecture at the Leamington and Warwick Magic Society and won the stage competition at the magic Club with yet another act I'd thrown together!

Jeff, Ben, Clare and Jay 1984

CHAPTER 16

The Mid Eighties

Bringing up a family of four children was as full as it was rewarding. Expensive too. By the end of the year I had £3-12p to my name. The bulk of my wages of course went on household and family expenses. The car as well was a continuous drain.

I had talked about my decreasing finances to Richard Stupple who was a friend of mine in the magic club. Richard was also involved with The Magic Circle and said he might be able to help me out. In December 1985 I had a lovely letter from the Secretary of the Magic Circle Benevolent Fund along with a cheque. The letter ended with - "We hope the enclosed cheque may bring a little cheer into your home over the festive season, and that financial matters may soon improve."

What a lovely gesture from both The Circle and Richard. It also gave me impetus to try and raise some much-needed cash off my own bat. I felt I was failing my family by struggling to make ends meet. I could have pushed the furniture making, but that would have been too time consuming, the only other option was the magic. My track record was pretty good having won the two top Close-Up competitions in the country, and with a few lectures under my belt coupled with ten years of experience working for the public, it was time to hustle for some work. I sent publicity material to agents both locally and in London and the Midlands. I contacted The Stables in Milton Keynes and visited just about every social club in the area. I went to Working Men's Clubs in Wolverton and delivered stuff to local businesses and restaurants. Finally I gave Deke Leonard a call (who told me he had now taken up juggling!) I asked him if he thought the magic would "go" at record company shindigs. He thought it was a great idea and sent me addresses of 15 record companies. I wrote to them all and got a reply from two, EMI and A&M Records which resulted in several gigs, over a three-year period, which were all memorable. I did the first one in the summer of 1985 for the A&M company annual dinner at a rather nice venue, Pennyhill Park in Surrey. A country club, hotel, and three classy restaurants all standing in 112 acres of magnificent gardens and parkland. I got there an hour early so had a chance to explore and take it all in. I worked the tables for 45 minutes and got a really good fee. Although I was "suited and booted" most of the people there weren't, in fact jeans and T shirts seemed to be the most popular mode of dress. It went ok and nobody took it too seriously and neither did I. After years of hanging out with musicians I wasn't too surprised when it all ended in a food fight.

The lecturing at magic clubs was going pretty well too. I actually did two in one night at my own club, the first at seven o'clock for the junior section and then a repeat at eight for the rest of the members, both went well. I was by now well and truly on the lecture circuit. In 1985 I lectured at The Ace Magic Club at Hitchin, The Zodiac in London, and a really good one at The Order of the Magi in Manchester. Gigs were coming in too and I didn't turn anything down. One night I had a call from a friend of mine in London. He asked me if I'd step in and do one of his regular jobs the following night as he couldn't make it. I said, "Yes" before he'd told me the full details. It was a pasta house in Old Compton Street in Soho.

"It's only for an hour, it's an easy place to work, and you'll get £30 cash on the night, and you'll get tips as well."

"Ok, I said, what time?"

"Between midnight and one o'clock."

March 15th, 1985: *I caught the 9.25 express train from Milton Keynes Central and got to the Pasta House at about 11.00 o'clock. I did 4 tables and picked up £3 in tips. I really enjoyed myself and caught a train back at 2.30!*

The next day was a Saturday, but I still got up to go to work for a couple of hours.

In the eighties the entertainment industry was going through a bit of a transformation. What had been popular and mainstream during the previous 20 years or so, just wasn't any more. For me it all started with the TV series, 'The Young Ones' and various spin-offs featuring the same group of writers and performers. The umbrella name for this new wave of comedy was called 'Alternative'. I loved and embraced it all. Out of the blue one night I had a call from Alan Fraser. I hadn't heard from him since we were magic club juniors together in the 60s. He was involved with a group of performers called 'The Binliners Ensemble'. They were doing the rounds of pubs and venues in the area and he asked me if I'd like to join. Definitely! My role was working the tables during the interval. The first gig we did was at a pub in Wolverton called The Queen Victoria (known locally as "The Vic.") Also on the bill were John Sparkes from Swansea, and a young and unknown comedian called Paul Merton. It was a great evening. We went on to do a couple of other local gigs before stretching our wings and venturing into London. We travelled down in Alan's car to a pub in Kings Cross called The Water Rats. Weekly shows were put on there and we did that regularly for a while sharing the bill with Jeremy Hardy on a couple of occasions. They were great fun to do but for little financial reward. The most we got was £12 each. It was all great experience though and I soon found out what would and wouldn't work for that particular type of audience. Other venues were also beginning to catch on and tap into this new and fresh form of comedy. I did an evening at an event at the Open University which was another great night.

I was still doing more run of the mill gigs which I was happy to do. I did a nice one in the summer at the headquarters of a large organisation that was situated in rather lovely grounds. It was a barbecue but with other things going on as well including a Trad Jazz band. As I was having a break, I had a chat with one of the musicians. He was in the bar along with his instrument case (a banjo). I asked what time he was on, and he told me anytime in the next half an hour, as and when the others turned up. Just then another chap arrived carrying a double bass, the two musicians shook hands and introduced themselves and had a drink, meanwhile another one had arrived with his clarinet case and the same thing happened. Introductions were made and drinks consumed. I asked them if they'd met before or even played together.

"Some of them look familiar," said the banjo player with a grin.

By now there were five of them. They finished their drinks and made their way outside to a small platform. I followed them out and wondered how, and indeed if, this was going to work. Five strangers? The clarinettist looked at the others and said,

"Oh when the saints?"

The others nodded, and with a 1, 2, 3, 4, off they went. It was just wonderful, the hairs stood up on the back of my neck.

It sounded as if they'd been playing together for years, true musicianship.

I had started, and run, the junior section of the magic club in the early eighties. The original membership was half a dozen or so lads (and not forgetting Caroline, the daughter of David Parriss). At the time we held the meetings in a large upstairs room of a social club in Northampton. As I was chatting to a group of youngsters one night, I could hear the unmistakable sound of somebody struggling up the stairs. All of a sudden, two lads almost fell into the room pulling behind them two huge rather battered cardboard boxes.

"Come in boys," I said, "Oh you are in! Come and join us."

As they approached, I asked for their names and one of them said,

"My name's David Pennington and I've just moved to Northampton from Sheffield."

"Hello David, I'm Ken, nice to meet you, and what have you got there"?

"It's a brand-new illusion I'm working on," he said, rather proudly.

"That's great," I said, "And what is it?"

He looked at me as if it was obvious what the two boxes were and said, "It's a substitution trunk!"

"Ok," I said, trying not to smile and thinking to myself, sub trunk? Standing on top of it? How's that going to work? Rather intrigued I asked him where he'd got the idea from.

"I saw a picture of it in a book I got from the library," he said, and quickly added, "I'm having a few teething problems, but I'll get them sorted."

Here was a lad after my own heart. David was so enthusiastic in those early days. If he couldn't afford to buy a trick, he'd make it out of whatever material was to hand. This was in the days before video cassettes, so books were pretty much the only option. As he grew up, David's enthusiasm never dimmed. Over the years (with his new name David Penn) he became president of the club, a very successful close-upper, illusionist, and children's entertainer. There were countless TV performances and, with lecturing and dealing as well, he has certainly lived and fulfilled the dream he had as an eight-year-old. David has never forgotten his roots and is now the Club Patron. A worthy honour.

Around the same time I had a call from a chap called Vic from Wolverton who told me that his young son was really interested in magic, and could I take him along to the magic club? I drove over there and met Vic, who was also a carpenter. We had a chat about door types (as carpenters do) while we waited for his lad to make an appearance. Soon a slight, bespectacled figure came down the stairs and we were introduced. His name was Anthony Owen. He got into the car next to me and as he fastened the seatbelt and we pulled away he said,

"Did you know that today would have been Chung Ling Soo's birthday?"

I had to admit I didn't. By the time we got to the club room, I realised that here was a young lad totally immersed in all aspects of magic to the point of obsession. Anthony too went on to become President of the club. He was involved with the Magic Circle in a big way and his magic career took off in all sorts of directions. He was an inventor, dealer, performer, writer,

On stage at the Magic Circle and finally found his true vocation as a TV producer within his own production company, which was involved with the Paul Daniels series among other things. Sadly and tragically Anthony passed away in 2019 at the height of his career.

To be honest both Anthony and David would have been successful with or without my input due to their own personal drive and enthusiasm. I still feel proud and pleased that they never forgot the many happy times they spent with the club when they were youngsters.

The club was going well in the eighties and luckily, we had enough performers to put on a rather prestigious show. In October seven of us went along to The Magic Circle to entertain the members at their headquarters in London. It was a great night and a club highlight I reckon.

It was all change at work in the summer of 1985. My job as a joiner became redundant and I was transferred to Llewellyn General Works. This was a department that took on small refurbishment projects in public buildings such as schools, hospitals, and pubs. To begin with I felt like a fish out of water as this was something I had little experience of. Luckily the lads and supervisors were a friendly bunch and I soon got into the swing. One of the first jobs I worked on was in a large factory unit which involved replacing wall panels. We had to work off a tower scaffold which was another first for me. On site with us was a gang of roofers who were working high up on the internal apex. One morning we watched as they came in with a long wooden pole ladder. It just about reached the point where they were working. The empty building had a concrete floor which, due to the weather conditions, was damp. One of the roofers put a pile of tiles on his shoulder which he held onto with his arm over the top. Using his remaining free arm he grabbed the ladder and slowly went up. As he got near the top, the bottom of the ladder slid away on the damp concrete, and because it wasn't fixed at the top, the ladder came crashing down along with the roofer. The tiles had fallen from his shoulder, and he'd grabbed the ladder with both hands. It hit the concrete with his fingers still around the ladder and his face between the rungs. As you'd expect, it made a terrible mess of his hands and face. I hope I never see anything like that again. An ambulance was called and a First Aider from an adjacent unit came and did what he could before it arrived. The roofer was in hospital for about a week - it could have been much worse. This happened in the days before Risk Assessments, hard hats, and method statements were mandatory and wooden ladders were banned. It shook us all up for a while and the repercussions for the company involved were quite severe.

1985 was a busy year for Clare and table tennis. She'd been having regular coaching and had been to a couple of tournaments, including the England Junior Open. She played in the league with a couple of other girls for a season or two, but eventually gave it up due to pressure of schoolwork. She always kept up with her dancing though, and this was the year of her first pair of "blocked" ballet shoes. She was now, in our eyes, a ballerina!

1986 began with enthusiasm for woodwork and furniture-making. I was conscious that my new, "shed/workshop/cycle-shed/escape", wasn't getting the use I had hoped for. In January I bought a woodworking magazine and was pleasantly surprised to discover that plans and drawings for a davenport desk were available. I'd made a lot of them when I was in the furniture trade and had always liked them and planned one day to go into production at home. Here was my chance. The plans duly arrived and soon after I went along to the Practical Woodworker's Exhibition in London to check out machinery and materials. I arrived home with a pile of pamphlets and price lists, but soon reality kicked in. There just wasn't the time or the money. Any spare time I had was spent in the house either decorating or making more practical stuff. My furniture-making at this point consisted of making bunk beds and chests of drawers for the ever-growing family. I kept the drawings, but the davenport would have to wait. The magic was continuing to go well thanks to a good response I had from the agents I'd contacted. I was now getting work further afield; this was fine but always a worry with an unreliable car. The one I had then had gearbox trouble among other things, but I wasn't in a financial position to buy another one as I still owed Mum £500. She had just retired from the little job she had with a local nursery school so didn't have too much coming in herself. If ever I travelled any distance, I'd hire one; I just couldn't take a chance. Luckily though I was still getting some local work, including at a club in The Point (the iconic Milton Keynes landmark building). I also did my first car launch gig in a local garage. That's the beauty of close-up magic, it can be done just about anywhere, "Wherever small groups of people meet formally or informally," as I had printed on my publicity material.

The last big journey I did with that particular car was down to Butlins in Minehead. I checked it over before we set off, but still had to stop halfway to put oil in when the warning light came on. Luckily, I had the foresight to carry a couple of bottles with me, just in case. It was quite stressful driving along in a knackered car with the family, not really knowing what to expect. Anyway, we got there eventually and had a great time. Jeff signed up for a cricket course which went on all week, Clare won a fancy-dress competition and the table tennis, and the little ones had a great time too. It was pretty much our last family holiday together as the children were growing up and we could barely all fit in the car (which obviously was coming to the end of its life anyway).

I decided to take a chance and drive the car down to a gig in Surrey on the day before the MOT. It was another one for A&M Records for their European Convention. (The "bun fight" the previous year had obviously gone well.) It was held at the Anugraha Hotel & Conference Centre near Egham. It was on July 4th and took the form of an American Independence Day party. I travelled down there in the early evening sunshine, arriving at about 7-30 to another impressive venue. A beautiful building situated in 22 acres of parkland on the edge of Windsor Great Park. The first thing I noticed was the fun fair. Lots of rides and attractions, dominated by a large helter-skelter. I strolled through it and then into the venue which was just stunning. It was originally a family country home back in the 19th century and many of the rooms still had the original oak panelling and furniture on display. I did wonder if there might be a davenport desk there, no luck though. I made myself known to the organiser and was told that I had the run of the building and grounds.

"You know what you're doing, just wander around and do your stuff as and when."

I was ticked off on her clipboard as "Arrived" and left to my own devices. After exploring several large rooms to check out potential customers, I made a start. To begin with I did the usual mix and mingle stuff as people were standing around in the bar area; then, as the place began to fill up, I was able to sit with other groups and entertain that way, often using a coffee table to work off. It was a case really of improvising and making use of whatever was there and available. I tried to cover as many people as I could before they got too drunk and the rooms too noisy (based on my experience of the previous year). Most of the people there were great and up for having a laugh, but as always there were one or two exceptions. I was doing the sponge ball trick for a couple of ladies and had got to the point when I said that I had one ball in my left hand.

"No you haven't!" one of them said, "You've got two"!

She grabbed my hand and forced it open to prove she was right, and she wasn't finished yet as she said,

"And the other black one must be in your pocket!"

Then she reached into my pocket and pulled everything out and dropped them on the floor.

"Aha!" she said and then walked off.

That lady turned out to be the singer, Joan Armatrading. Oh well, another case of taking the rough with the smooth and confirmation that magic isn't everyone's cup of tea. After almost 3 hours it was time to call it a night anyway. I packed my bag and collected my cash and thought I'd have a quick drink in the bar before setting off home. I was in the middle of my pint when I heard people whispering, "Sting's here!" I wandered out into the funfair just in time to see him and his wife, Trudie, coming down the helter-skelter, finishing up in a heap at the base of it. They picked themselves up and headed towards the bar. I got there just before they did. Sting stood next to me and asked the rather star struck barmaid for a pint of lager. As she placed it on the bar, he patted his pockets and said,

"Oh no I haven't got any cash!"

"That's quite alright do have it on the house, and could you sign this beermat please?"

I thought to myself *tight bastard*. At this point I turned to him and said,

"Have you seen this?"

I showed him the trick and he said,

"Wow! Hey Trudie, come and have a look at this! Do you mind doing that again?"

"Not at all," I said.

By now Trudie was draped all over him and laughing along, as were the rest of the people around the bar, who had now come to the conclusion that magic was indeed a truly wonderful form of entertainment. Then Sting asked if I had any more.

"I have," I said, "Let's find a table."

Somehow a table appeared, and I spent half an hour going through my complete repertoire just for him and Trudie. They watched with interest and good humour. Occasionally his manager would bend over to him and speak into his ear, which he dismissed with a wave of his hand and a, "Sod off I'm watching the magic!"

It was a good night, and it's always interesting to perform for the famous, just to see how they react and what they're really like as people. That night I experienced both ends of the spectrum. It was also fascinating to see how other people reacted to their presence. Most of them just stared. I treated the whole thing as just another gig. I did have a feeling of satisfaction though, that for half an hour I had provided an escape for both Sting and his wife from the goldfish bowl that is celebrity and fame. I treated them exactly the same as I would anybody else. They appreciated that.

A couple of weeks later, I did the A&M annual "bash" which was back at Pennyhill Park, this time with the wonderful Graham Jolley. Needless to say, another memorable night. I did another music business gig around that time. It was at Fulham Town Hall and was for the 40th birthday party of a music publisher by the name of Bob Grace. Sadly I can't remember anything about it, all

I have is the confirmation letter and a line in my diary which says, "*It was a good night once I'd got started.*"

Over the following year or so I continued to get regular music biz jobs. One of them was yet again at Pennyhill Park; this time it was memorable because the audience were even more unruly than they normally are. I got through it ok and was curious to see how the cabaret would fare.

All the entertainers were given a large room to share overlooking the cabaret floor. When I got back there after doing my stuff, I noticed there was a large mixing desk positioned at the front, facing the performing area, which was visible via the windows. Sitting in front of it was a sound engineer complete with headphones, checking the equipment. At that point I assumed he was the DJ for the final part of the evening. Also in the room was a very smart middle-aged man easily recognisable as the star of the show, Peter Casson, the hypnotist. We had a brief chat and I wished him well and went out the front to watch. By now the room was really noisy and it took the MC some time to quieten them down and make himself heard to do the introduction. Peter was finally announced, the lights were dimmed, and music began to play. Soon the sound and mood of the audience began to change to an expectant buzz. The music was reduced to playing quietly in the background to suit the atmosphere and Peter strode out, went to the nearest table, and said to a young couple, "Good evening, I'd like you to assist me this evening would you please take a seat on the chairs provided."

He went on around the room, choosing (or volunteering) people until the chairs had all been filled. For an hour he made them do silly things to much laughter from the rest of the audience. The whole thing was choreographed with music provided from the sound engineer. To me it was a masterclass on how to handle an audience. Needless to say, he finished his performance with a huge round of applause from what turned out to be a very appreciative audience. What a great performer, a privilege to watch.

I did an interesting job at Christmas for EMI at their offices in London. This one certainly didn't turn out as planned. It was an annual event that the company organised for the Radio One secretaries. It took the form of a dinner followed by entertainment which in this case was me. I was asked to arrive at about 9 o'clock to coincide with the end of the meal. I walked into the room which was full of young ladies sitting around the boardroom table. I made a start, anxious to cover as much time as possible before they hit the bar (which I'd noticed as I entered). After a while it was obvious to me it wasn't working. One single table is never easy, but more to the point most of them weren't up for watching close-up magic anyway. I persevered for a while, but rather than flog an obviously dying horse, I was more than happy to write it off whether I got paid or not. I had a word with the DJ (whose name escapes me, but he was Scottish) who came up with a brainwave. He managed to make himself heard and said to the girls,

"Who's up for a Pop Quiz?"

"Yeahh!" they cried.

So that's what we did. Prizes were decided (a mixture of bottles), teams were organised (one of which I was a member of), and an enjoyable hour ensued. I have to say I wasn't much good, as I had little knowledge of eighties pop music (and there were no questions on prog' rock of the early seventies). It turned out to be a really good night, and I got paid.

Later on that year I was contacted by the same chap who gave me the Soho Pasta House gig. He offered me another unusual job which luckily was local. It was in the Dickens & Jones store in Milton Keynes City Centre. This was to be one of my early ventures into the corporate world. The brief was to do a regular presentation from 10.00 am to 4.30 pm (with appropriate breaks) featuring magic, incorporating a brand-new concept in watch design called, 'Le Clip'. This was a small-faced inter-changeable watch which was fixed to a small clip. The idea being to attach the watch to a tie or lapel or dress rather than on the traditional wrist. There was a wide variety of faces which meant you could match it to your clothes or event etc. I worked out a few things utilising the watches themselves along with the publicity material I was sent. As well as doing the demo, I was expected to sell them too. It was a long day, but it went reasonably well, and I sold two watches. Hardly surprising I didn't sell any more as they were vastly overpriced at £20. When I got home that evening, I had time for a quick bite to eat and then had to travel to Cambridge for a silver wedding party. It was all go.

In September, I had a phone call from Sir Hereward Wake who lived fairly locally at Courteenhall Estate just outside Northampton. He'd been informed by somebody from the magic club that I was the chap to contact regarding all things magic (heaven knows why). He went on to say that he was holding a party at the Hall in October for his birthday and would I, could I, teach him some tricks to perform. As soon as he mentioned party, I thought gig. I was quite surprised when it wasn't. I told him I'd sort some stuff out and get back to him. A few days later he came over to see me. (The first and last visit to my house, at the time of writing, of a genuine 'Sir'.) He was everything you'd expect from a member of the aristocracy - ex-Army, extremely polite, well spoken, and slightly eccentric. I spent an hour with him teaching him a few easy but effective self-working tricks I'd found in the loft. He coped with them fairly well, but I did tell him he needed to rehearse them a bit more.

"Of course," he said, "Practise makes perfect and all that!"

Off he went with the props in a carrier bag, and I thought that was the end of it. A few days later I had another call. Although he was very happy with the tricks I'd given him, he wondered if I had something bigger.

"How about sawing somebody in half?" he asked.

I told him I had nothing like that but would look for something else. A couple of days later, me and brother-in-law, Steve, went over to the Hall. We spent an hour in a beautiful, panelled room in front of a huge open fire. I went through the new tricks with him and made sure he could do the other ones and had a run through of the 'act'. I told him all would be fine as long he rehearsed it a few times before the big night. (Any doubts I had, I kept to myself.) A week later he called me again to thank me for my hard work.

"It all went wonderfully well!" he said.

I didn't get a penny. The experience, though, was priceless.

October 15th, 1986: *What a busy evening! First of all Richard Stupple called about my letter headings, then young David Barrs called, and soon after that Dan Johnson phoned about a show for the Operatic Society next year. A few minutes later Deke Leonard called seeking information about the Magic Circle, so we had a nice chat. Next was a call from "Plants" in Newport Pagnell about a gig in November and a meeting was arranged for Sunday. I was about to have a shower when Ian came over to sort out the Brighton trip. We'd just sat down in the front room when Ben was sick all over his bed. It looks as if we're in for a night of it.*

Life was hectic as you can see from the diary entry.

'Plants' was a lovely little restaurant/bistro, owned and run by magician Mike Miles and his girlfriend (now wife) Lorraine. The plan was to have a magic night with me working the tables on a regular basis. A press night was organised which generated a lot of local publicity. It worked well for about a year, and we had some really good nights there. The trip to Brighton referred to a weekend away with the company to a large hotel at Saltdean near Brighton. We had a great time, particularly in the pool, and it was a much-needed break for both me and Babs. We had an unexpected surprise on the Saturday night, as the cabaret was Des King from the magic club who did a great job. Speaking of which, the club was going through mixed fortunes at the time. Although I won the stage competition again there were only two competitors, but there were five juniors who stepped up and entered at the last minute. At least we had a show for the audience and obviously a bunch of very enthusiastic and committed youngsters.

We went up to the school just before Christmas to watch five-year-old Ben take part in a Nativity performance as a shepherd. It was lovely, especially when he dramatically pointed to the dangling yellow shaped piece of cardboard and said,

"We have seen the star!"

At the end of the year I was still without a car. In fact for my New Year's Eve gig in Bedford, I borrowed the neighbour's little VW Beetle. We were all getting fed up, both with the inconvenience and the weather.

December 30th, 1986: *I cycled down to Bletchley Timber this morning and got soaked, when I cycled back, I got soaked again. Then me and Babs and the boys waited half an hour for a bus to Sainsburys*

and got soaked yet again. Tonight we watched Blazing Saddles and then had an earlyish night, knackered.

Looking back, it seemed we were always either knackered or ill. If it wasn't coughs and colds it was some sort of sickness bug. We were all working hard, and it took its toll. Clare was still dancing and had been rehearsing for months for her performance in a local pantomime.

January 1st, 1987: *Twenty-five of us family and friends went to see Clare in the panto' this afternoon. She was marvellous! She impressed us all, particularly Grandad Holmes who was quite overcome at the end of it.*

Clare was one of the principal dancers and therefore one of the stars of the final scene. It was just magnificent. Even though it was an amateur production, the quality of it all was exceptional. Like

Clare the dancer

Grandad Holmes, I was affected by it too, in a way not dissimilar to the father at the end of the Billy Elliot film, emotional and proud. At the end there was an immediate standing ovation from all 25 of us and the rest of the audience too. As I watched I forgot about the endless trips to and from the many rehearsals I took her to and realised their worth. After that I did make the effort not to complain about being the family taxi.

Meanwhile, Jeff was now involved in local cricket and was going along to indoor training at the local campus. He was really into it for a month or two and even got up at 4.30 one morning to watch the Test match from Australia.

It was increasingly obvious that I needed a car that was reliable and of a better quality than previous ones. Although I had access to a van for work during the day I still had to get to and from the premises. I had my bike, which was fine in the summer but a real pain in the winter, and there was the endless running about I had to do for the family. Another reason was that I'd been offered regular work at a restaurant in Bedford called Leila's. I was booked for the big opening in December (1986) which went really well, and it took off from there. For a while I managed with taxi, bus, and train, and the kindness of the staff to give me a lift home. But that was never going to work; I had to have a car and it had to be a better quality one than I'd had before. Although the money owed to Mum had been paid back, I could do with another loan! I applied to my Building Society which was refused. Then I hired a car on a couple of occasions, but that didn't work out economically. Then, as I was having yet another look through the paper, I spotted an advert for what seemed like a good deal. A brand-new Mini Metro for £300 deposit and then 36 payments of £122 per month. Surely, I could afford that. The magic would pay for it. I was getting regular work at both Leila's and Plants at the time which should be more than enough. I talked it over with Babs and decided to go for it. I went down to the dealers for a chat and filled in the forms. All was going well until it came to choose the colour, which was something I hadn't really thought about. In the end I told him I didn't really care, and he could decide. Some weeks later, on March 4th, 1987, I drove my brand new (white) car home to show the family thinking to myself that at last my car problems were over.

I worked regularly at Leila's pretty much every Friday and Saturday evening, and the occasional midweek and Sunday lunchtime too. Most of the time things went well, but there were a couple of occasions when odd things happened. I arrived one evening as usual to find another close-up magician already there working the tables. That was a bit of a shock. When I asked him what was going on he said he'd answered an ad' in the local paper asking for magicians! That happened twice, and both times I wasn't told anything. All I got from the manager was that my role there was safe. It was very strange. Other times I'd arrive to find more entertainers there, a "Gypsy" violinist, and a couple of singer/pianists. On my final night, John Bouchier, the ventriloquist performed. I often wondered why the manager bothered with entertainers at all as the quality of the food was exceptional and would have been enough. Anyway, I enjoyed my time there and the few one-nighters I picked up from customers were handy as well, including a very lucrative one in Birmingham. Needless to say, I also came across a few characters. One night I did the cups and balls ending up with 3 apples. The man I was showing it to would not have it they were real. He picked one up and took a huge bite out of it! Apparently, this isn't an unusual occurrence as exactly the same thing happened to a friend of mine, Geoff Ray. I wonder what the reaction would have been had I used onions?

In 1987 the BBC aired, 'Bob says Opportunity Knocks', presented by Bob Monkhouse. Friends and family had often said that I should have a go at it and in the end, I relented and sent off for an application form (which was more like a contract). I filled it in and sent it off and sometime later received a reply and was offered an audition. Off I went to London not really knowing what to expect. I decided to play it by ear and do what I thought would work when I got there. I was given a table and the assistance of a rather attractive researcher to work to (who was great) and I worked through my best tried and tested stuff that got the most laughs. I thought it went really well, especially when the cameraman gave me a huge smile and the thumbs up. A few weeks later I received the standard rejection letter. Understandably, I was a bit disappointed but nonetheless had enjoyed the experience. No reasons were given, I can only assume that at the time close-up magic was deemed unsuitable for a talent show, or perhaps they thought I was crap. Who knows? Anyway, life went on.

So much for thinking that my car problems were over. Due to a lack of vans, I had to drive my new Metro onto a site one day where we were working on some factory units. I parked up on the edge of a small car park which was set aside for the purpose. I was rather annoyed (to say the least) when I was told that a JCB had reversed into the back of it. I'd had the car for five days. Luckily though it was sorted out quickly. A new bumper with light fittings was replaced during the same week. The boss of the guilty sub-contractor paid up straight away once I'd given him the bill. He was really nice and apologetic and when I asked what had happened to the JCB driver he said, "Sacked him."

Things were busy and as chaotic as ever at home. I was now making picture frames for certificates for a local karate club as well as the usual family and school stuff. I'd also carried on making the final part of the mahogany units for our front room - this one was for the corner which gave me a few 'angle' problems. Babs was busy painting garden gnomes which her cousin was churning out on a regular basis. She also had an early morning cleaning job at a local pub. I still had my allotment which produced an assortment of vegetables, but I had to keep on top of it. It was a full life. Somehow, we also found the time and energy to go for regular swims at the local pool and the odd game of table tennis. No wonder we were always knackered.

The children were growing up fast, Clare who was now 15 went to work at a local Prep school for a couple of weeks on a "Trident" course where she did really well. Jeff was a typical 13-year-old and got into a spot of bother when his birthday party ended up with a cushion fight, resulting in broken light fitting, oops!

There was a sad event in October of 1987. My Mum's sister, Auntie Maudie, passed away. She was such an important part of our childhood, particularly when we visited Holyhead. The times we spent with her are memorable and some of the happiest of my life. She was very bright and spent her entire life in the nursing profession rising through the ranks to become a matron by the time she retired. She put her whole career on hold to look after her mother for the final years of her life. Only now have we realised just what a commitment that was and just what she sacrificed. She eventually moved to Bletchley to be close to us, her only remaining family. Always brave and spontaneous and caring too. A remarkable lady.

In December Babs and I were invited to the annual Christmas dinner of a local angling club where her Dad was a member. It was based at a trout farm in a small village just outside Milton Keynes. The dinner took place in the village hall and the whole thing was set up beautifully with a lovely meal, a large raffle, and a bit of dancing afterwards. I love village halls, it's like going back to a bygone era. The owners of the trout farm were an elderly gay couple who had been together for years. They were quite flamboyant and definitely up for having a laugh. After the meal, (just before the raffle) I made a start on working the tables with the magic. I eventually got round to one of them and showed him the sponge ball trick. He positively squealed in delight when they appeared in his hands.

"You've got to show that to my partner!" he said.

He looked around and spotted him at the far side of the hall and called out to him,

"Eric! Come and have a look at this man's balls!"

"Coming dear!" came the reply.

Soon, he was there and holding his hand out.

"Watch carefully," I said, "I've got the small ones and you've got the big ones."

I then (apparently) place them in his hand. He gave his hand a squeeze, looked at me and said,

"Mmm, I've had bigger."

At that point we all fell about laughing. He then opens his hand to find a large one and screams,

"Oh, aren't you clever?!!"

By the time that happened we were just about on our knees. What a couple of stars!

I did another village hall job a couple of weeks after that at Swaffham Prior near Newmarket. It was for the local 'Over 60s Club' and was organised by the Women's Institute. I had a 3-page confirmation letter from the secretary with a handwritten map on how to get there, what and when they'd be eating, and even a small sketch of the table they'd be using with a small cross for each person sitting around it. (The more detail the better I reckon.) It was suggested that I do five to ten minutes at each table and… "You could do the same tricks at each table if you like."

I couldn't wait to get there! I woke up that morning feeling a bit rough. I had some breakfast but couldn't face any lunch at all. When it was time to set off (I had to arrive at "4.00 pm prompt"), I was feeling decidedly queasy and as I travelled there it got steadily worse. I found the hall without too much trouble and opened the door to be greeted by the rather strong odour of sprouts. I made myself known and just about made it to the Gents where I bought up my breakfast. I didn't feel too bad after that and managed to do a couple of tables before I had to rush back and stick my head down the toilet again. How I got through it and covered all the tables God only knows. The ladies knew I was having trouble and were really sympathetic. At the end of it they said,

"I don't suppose you'd like any food, how about a cup of tea?"

"No thanks," I said, "But a glass or two of cold water will go down a treat." (I was desperately thirsty.)

With a sickness bug though, it's the worst thing you can do, as I discovered on the way home. I had to stop at the side of the A428 and projectile vomit a stomach full of water into the undergrowth. I did feel better after that though and got home feeling relieved and knackered. I opened the front door to find Babs being ill in the downstairs loo, and Jeff as well in the bathroom. According to the last line in my diary, *"We all had an early night."*

One night close to Christmas 1987, I had a call from an agent who although realising it was short notice asked me if I was available for a gig at the end of that week. I told him I was, and he went on to tell me that as the job was rather special it was important that I wear a smart dinner jacket. He went on to explain that I had to do everything to the letter that was written into the contract. He gave me a quick run through as stipulated by the client. "The job is at the Mayfair Hotel in London for the management staff of a company of merchant bankers. You will arrive at 8.00pm and make yourself known at reception. From there you will be taken to a private room where you can prepare and get ready for a close-up performance of half-an-hour only, that's important. You will be notified when they're ready for you and you'll be invited into a private dining room at around 9.30, prepared and ready to perform. Payment will be made by cheque at the end of your performance to the value of £150."

I was up for that. Not bad for half an hour's work. (In today's money it equates to about £350.)

On the evening of the show I got on the train and tube and arrived at the rather beautiful hotel with plenty of time to spare. The door was opened for me by a top-hatted, uniformed doorman, with a greeting of,

"Good evening, sir."

I walked through the lobby to reception and made myself known.

"Ah yes Mr. Hawes, you are expected, just a moment."

She spoke into a phone and soon after a smartly dressed young man came down a flight of stairs and up to the desk.

"Mr. Hawes, lovely to meet you, a room has been made available for your convenience, please follow me."

I followed him up the stairs and was led into a rather plush room with a three-piece suite, a fully equipped bar, and a bathroom as well.

"Very nice," I said, "Thank you very much."

"My pleasure, I'll come and tell you when we're ready, is there anything else you need?"

"Yes, there is actually. Could I have a look at the room please?"

"Of course, follow me."

We walked down a corridor and entered a beautiful oak-panelled room. There was one long table in the centre with about 15 people (all wearing paper hats) sitting down and tucking into a Christmas dinner. They all looked up as we entered, I smiled and said,

"Good evening, see you all later."

They all replied and smiled back. So far so good. I went back to my room a touch apprehensive, but the hour I had available was more than enough to decide how and what I was going to do. One long table isn't ideal, but I had to make the best of it. I decided to introduce myself first and do one trick at the head of the table where they would all be able to see, and then go round the table doing the really close-up stuff for a small group at a time. Once I'd decided on the format, I began to relax and had plenty of time to rehearse all that I was going to do and in what order. Adrenaline began to flow, and I was looking forward to it. After loading my pockets and double checking everything, I helped myself to a soft drink from the bar and relaxed on the sofa for a while until the knock on the door came. I was led back into the dining room, prepared and ready. I stood at the head of the table and explained the format which they were happy with and then went straight into the bottle of wine production which went really well. I then followed it up with my usual tried and tested stuff, moving round from group to group. The people were lovely and relaxed, and it was a great laugh. There was a beautiful blonde lady there who turned out to be Tessa Wyatt, the actress. I spoke to another chap who asked me where I came from, when I said Milton Keynes he said,

"Good heavens, my father was your MP!"

I looked at him and said,

"You're obviously not a Maxwell, (which made him laugh), you must be Bill Benyon's son."

"I am," he said, "What a small world!"

Soon my half-an-hour was up, and it was time to leave - a shame really, I'd have been happy to have done another hour, but needs must, and I thanked them for being a lovely audience and wished them all a Happy Christmas. Then with a warm round of applause ringing in my ears, I left the room and headed back to my sofa and bar (for something a bit stronger). A few minutes later, I was joined by the chap who had met me earlier. He thanked me very much and gave me a white envelope containing my cheque. I expressed my gratitude to him, and after a brief chat said goodnight and walked down the stairs to reception. I said goodnight to the lady there, and also to the doorman as he directed me out into the street. I made my way to back to Euston, happy and content and better off the tune of 150 quid.

As I sat on the train going home, I pondered the gig. It suddenly occurred to me that far from being a short one of half-an-hour, it was considerably more. I worked it out at:

Two hours of rehearsal in the afternoon, one hour to get ready, an hour-and-a-half to get there, another one-and-a-half hours to wait and perform, and about two hours to get home. That's a grand total of 8 hours! All for £150! - Cheap bastards.

I spent much of 1988 designing and making furniture for the house. I finally finished off the made-to-measure mahogany units for the front room and also made bunkbeds, desks, and chests of drawers for the bedrooms. The three boys were sharing a room, so it did require some careful planning. And it was all painted, which I was able to do in my shed (after taking all the bikes out). I had an electric supply fitted in there by now which was a

Godsend as I could carry on working into the evenings. We were also doing a lot of decorating, wallpapering mostly, which I was to regret years later.

Work was going ok, and I'd settled into hanging doors, fitting plastic fascia and barge boards, and bits of roofing etc. All sorts of general carpentry and other stuff as well. There was one job, however, that dominated most of the year, and that was at a leisure centre in High Wycombe. We were there for months, and it was really hard work. Most of the carpentry was done by sub-contractors and I spent most of the time helping out as a labourer and towards the end of it putting right the "subby's" cock ups.

We arrived on the first day (two of us - me and Mick the builder) and entered the building through a rather dismal corridor. The first thing we noticed was the noise. It was a series of clicks and squeaks which were really unusual. We introduced ourselves to Dave, the site agent, who told us what was causing the unusual noise. I thought he was joking when he said crickets. He wasn't - the whole place was infested with them. They couldn't be destroyed because, apparently, they were a protected species. We would often see them hopping about. I wonder if they're still there. In those early weeks the place was like 'the black hole of Calcutta'. A Jacuzzi had to be installed in each of the two rooms which necessitated digging out huge holes for them to sit in. Tons of concrete was required to make up ramps and bases for lockers which had to be wheeled in by wheelbarrow. The ready mixed concrete was dumped in a large heap in the car park on a hot day which meant it had to be taken in and positioned before it went off. At one point we were adding buckets of water (which also had to be carried) to stop it happening. I don't think I've ever worked so hard in my life as I did at that place. It was an early start as well and by the time I got home I was fit for nothing. Me and Mick got on well and shared the same sense of humour - to make the daily 60-mile round-trip interesting, we'd play Pop quiz and a rather bizarre game called Animal Noises. If we saw a field of sheep, we'd make sheep noises until they were out of sight, and it was the same for cows and horses too. Occasionally a couple of donkeys would be spotted in a field which was great fun. I did get the better of Mick one day - as we passed through a village, I suddenly let rip with a loud bovine roar. Mick looked at me in surprise and I had to explain to him that we'd just driven past a pub called 'The Bull'. Well I did say it was bizarre.

By this time both Clare and Jeff were working with part-time jobs. Clare was at the local garden centre and Jeff had a paper round delivering locally around Springfield. They were both into swimming in quite a big way at this time too, going along to weekly lessons and qualifying in varying degrees of lifesaving. The pool was some distance away and connected to a school where we were friends with a couple of teachers there. Luckily, we had the opportunity to use it on a Sunday afternoon where we had it to ourselves. Occasionally Doreen (Clare and Jeff's swimming coach) would be there and give the little ones a few tips. Years later she deservedly won a BBC Sports award for a lifetime of dedication to swimming. I could never take to that particular the pool because the water was too warm. It was like getting into a bath! Both boys learned to swim in that pool and there was a defining moment in March of that year.

March 13th, 1988: *We went for a swim at Leon pool this afternoon. Jay went in without his arm bands for the first time - because we forgot to take them.*

We were able to have a couple of holidays this year. Due to the size of the car (or the children) we took Clare along with the little ones on the first one, and Jeff came with us on the second. The first was in late May when we travelled down to Looe in Cornwall to a hired caravan for a week. We had a nice time there despite the rainy weather. There was a lot to do on the site including a swimming pool, a club with a bar, and also entertainment for the children. We did some touring in the car to a monkey sanctuary (we loved that) and also a working open farm where I had a go at milking a goat. As luck would have it, a friend of ours, Ken Savage from the magic club, was working close by for the season, and we were able to spend some time with him. It seems I can't go anywhere without bumping into somebody I know. Even during our trip to America. I heard somebody calling out my name in New York - it was a chap I knew from my days of cabinet making. Ah! What it is to be well known and popular. At the end of August we had the other week away (where I didn't see anyone I knew) to a caravan on the west coast of Wales. Yet again the weather wasn't all that good, but we still had a lovely time. There wasn't much on the site in the way of entertainment but that didn't bother us. The beach, which was deserted for most of the time, was only a five-minute walk away, and the two beautiful, small coastal towns of Aberaeron and Newquay were close by. The larger town of Aberystwyth was just a few miles further up the coast in the other direction. The boys loved crabbing in the many rock pools and Jeff even had a go at fishing off the beach.

August 29th, 1988: *What a great day! We gave the beach a miss as the weather forecast wasn't too good. Instead we went to Aberaeron just up the road. We had a walk round the town, the front, and the harbour,* *looked round an aquarium and museum, and had some lunch. After that we walked up to the playing field for the local carnival festivities. It was great with a parade of floats, jazz band, and a funfair. From there we went for a ride up the coast ending up at Devil's Bridge which was quite spectacular. (Babs was quite astounded.) we didn't get back until late and our dinner of corned beef in batter went down very well.*

Another short weekend break to Jersey didn't go quite as well - at the time, 'Bergerac' the detective series, was on TV. Both me and Babs were huge fans. In fact, Babs had been to a local book shop to have a photograph taken with its star, John Nettles, when his book about Jersey came out. I'd promised her that one day I'd take her there. In November it was all booked. We caught a train to Gatwick and got on the plane on time at about 8.45am. Babs was a bit apprehensive as it was her first flight. We buckled up and anxiously waited. Some ten minutes later we heard the voice of the pilot telling us that due to a computer breakdown there would be a slight delay. There was nothing we could do apart from wait. After an hour, tea and coffee was served, and an hour after that, with considerable relief, we finally took to the air. The flight, which was about an hour, was smooth enough, and we were getting excited as we approached Jersey. Then we heard the voice of the pilot again. This time telling us that due to adverse weather conditions (fog) over the island, it was impossible to land. We'd have to head back to Gatwick. So annoying! When we got off the plane at around 1.30, we were told that we could either have a refund or risk waiting for another flight later on. The weather forecast was good and predicted that the fog would lift. We decided to risk it and wait. We finally took off at 5.15 in the evening and got there without incident at about 6.30. We should have been there at 10 o'clock that morning. We made up for it the next day though. We got up early and explored St Helier and did our present buying, then I hired a car, and we spent all day driving round the Island. We had a lovely Ploughman's lunch in a beautiful pub overlooking Bouley Bay and after some more sight-seeing, we dropped the car back in St Helier having driven some 75 miles. We ended the day with a huge steak dinner at the hotel with a couple of pints. We had a lovely time. We flew back the following morning into a beautiful cloudless sky.

The children were growing up fast and things were often hectic as you'd expect with six of us living in a three-bedroomed house. Clare and Jeff were teenagers by now and I was turning into my Dad. Who'd have thought? With him it was all about long hair, with me it was all about pretty much everything. Often it was a struggle. Arguments about something trivial would turn into full blown rows with doors slamming, the silent treatment, and everything else that goes with the inevitability of the generation gap. I have to say looking back now at those often-stressful days, I was a twat. Years later, me and Clare would reminisce (if that's the right word) about those days, and she would agree with me with a laugh that I was indeed a twat.

Clare left school and signed on at the local college and was doing well there. Like most teenagers she was into pop music in a big way. It started off with Adam & the Ants posters on her bedroom wall, but they were soon confined to the bin when Wet Wet Wet came along. She was lucky enough to go and see them along with Babs for her birthday treat at Alexandra Palace and had a great time. In September, on Jeff's birthday, after dropping the little ones at my sisters, the rest of us went to The Bowl to see Michael Jackson. What a great night that was, in spite of the crowds. One of the best song and dance men ever in my view.

CHAPTER 17

The late 80's & into the 90's

Mum had settled into her new bungalow, but all wasn't well. She was wearing herself out by getting herself too involved with her neighbours. She was shopping and cleaning and God knows what else. It got to the point when we had to get in touch with Social Services and put them in the picture and explain to them that there were people in The Close that needed help. The situation resolved itself over time as the really elderly and infirm either died or were moved into care homes. Nothing would ever stop Mum from helping other people. She would come and visit us once a week without fail. Bringing gifts of biscuits and crisps and cakes. She would travel the four miles from Bletchley on the bus, arriving in the afternoon and when she got too frail for that, she'd come by taxi. She had her own key and if nobody was in, she'd make a start on preparing the dinner or get stuck into a pile of ironing and after dinner she'd insist on doing the washing up. I would take her home at about 9 o'clock despite her protests of, "I'll be ok on the bus." For us she'd visit on a Wednesday. For Jean and her family it was Tuesday, and for Maggs and her family a Thursday. Needless to say the family gave her a lovely surprise party on April 24th, 1988, her 70th.

I was going along to the magic club and still serving on the committee, as well as organising the Juniors. I would meet with them at 7 o'clock before the main meeting at 8.00. Often it was a struggle to get there on time, but I did what I could. They (the juniors) put on a show for the rest of the members in 1988, imaginatively called "The Juniors entertain." It was a good night and featured Anthony Owen and David Penn, and also young David Barrs among others. I was still lecturing at various magic clubs up and down the country and in April of 1988 travelled up to Leeds. Somehow, I got there and back in an evening and still got up for work the following day.

I had regular gigs coming in and was really busy at Christmas time doing all sorts of things - private parties, corporate jobs, restaurants, etc. My job was also secure, and we were getting by reasonably well financially. We did look into the possibility of buying the house from the Corporation and got as far as visiting our Building Society but were told there wasn't enough money coming in for them to give us a mortgage anyway. Oh well, perhaps another time. Meanwhile I was increasing the value of the house by fitting extra internal doors and even a false ceiling above the stairs.

An advantage of keeping a diary is that it captures moments that are easily forgotten, particularly when the children were small. Luckily, I was able take Jay to school on his first day.

January 4th, 1989: *Jay started school today. It was lovely to be here and walk with him as he carried his little PE bag and big lunch box. He seems to have had a nice time although he looks pale and tired.*

We were aware that the little ones were missing out a bit. It was out of our hands up to a point as they were a bit too young to have gone to the Bowl to see Michael Jackson, but Ben was a bit peeved to have missed Wet Wet Wet. I don't recall hearing too much of the familiar childhood whinge of, "It's not fair", but we decided to take them on a trip to Jersey for Ben's birthday in February to make it up to them. We didn't say anything, it was going to be a total surprise. It was just as well we kept quiet as in early January there was an air crash that dominated the news for a day or two. It was when the 737 crashed onto the M1 near Birmingham. Jay watched it on the news the following day and it upset him quite a bit. It took him a long time to settle in his bed that night. He told Babs that he would, "Never, never, ever, go up in an aeroplane!" This was 5 weeks before we were due to fly out from Gatwick. Luckily, he appeared to have gotten over it by the time we were due to fly on the day before Ben's birthday.

We got them up at 4.30 am on the big day. We gave them some breakfast and told them they were going to have a big surprise. We'd booked a cab to take us to the station (which was late) and got on a train to Euston. From there it was the first ride for the boys on a tube train to Victoria and finally a train to Gatwick. At this point we decided to tell them what was going on. When we said we'd be going on an aeroplane, Jay cried, and Ben smiled. When we told them we'd be going to Jersey, Ben cried, and Jay smiled. With young children, there are times when you just can't win. We got on the plane ok with no problems; by now both boys were really excited. We buckled up, then yet again an hour-and-a-half delay due to computer problems. We kept them amused as best we could until finally, we were off, thundering down the runway and into the air! I'll never forget Ben's face at that moment. We finally arrived and got to the hotel at lunchtime and then spent the afternoon at Fort Regent, which the boys really enjoyed. We had a nice dinner at the hotel and went to bed at 9.00 o'clock - knackered.

The following day, I hired a car, and we visited a few places of interest, including the zoo. The boys loved the gorillas. That evening the hotel presented Ben with a birthday cake - a lovely surprise. We ended the day watching TV in our room - an episode of Bergerac! The next day we visited the Corbiere lighthouse and the zoo again and that was about it. The plane and trains all connected, and we got home at 10 o'clock that night, tired but happy. A great adventure for the boys, and a welcome break for us. what a great weekend!

It was a bit depressing having to go to work the next day, but I did have something interesting to do that I could get my teeth into. At the time we had a run of bathroom conversion jobs in occupied houses. We had to rip out the bath and replace it with a shower and then make good all the tiling. This was done for elderly people who had difficulty using a bath. There were distinct advantages in doing this sort of work, particularly in the winter - we were inside a nice warm house (often too warm), and elderly people were always generous with regular cups of tea and cake. I was working with Dave the plumber who was a bit of a character, and we got on really well. One day we arrived at a house to measure up and then went off in the van to pick up materials. The tenant, who was an elderly lady, told us that she'd leave the front door on the latch and to walk straight in when we got back. Off we went for about an hour and arrived back at the house. We unloaded the van, and Dave carried some lengths of copper pipe and his tool kit (whistling as he went); I followed him up the garden path with a box of tiles and a tub of adhesive. Dave opened the front door and turned immediately left into the bathroom. Just then, a chap came out of the lounge carrying a newspaper with his glasses at the end of his nose, closely followed by a lady with a puzzled look on her face.

"Who are you?" said the man.

It was only then that we realised we were in the wrong house! All four of us just fell about laughing, I don't think I'll ever forget the look on that chap's face.

Although I was doing ok at work, I would still apply for cabinet making jobs whenever they came up. The money was rarely as good as I was getting, and often I wouldn't get a response anyway. I'd also respond to adverts for entertainers. There was one in The Stage newspaper in March of 1989, asking for close-up magicians to work on a cruise ship in the Caribbean. I talked it over with Babs and she gave the ok and off I went to the Pineapple Studios in London to audition. I thought I might be in with a chance having had all that "experience" on my holiday cruise a few years earlier. I took the photos I had taken on board, including the one with me producing the bottle of wine for the ship's purser. Not a great photo I have to admit but beggars can't be choosers. I got there to find a queue of familiar faces, including Gary Smith (now Cassidy) from the magic club. I decided that for my audition trick I would do the bottle production and the sponge ball routine - the bottle because it's impressive (most of the time), and the sponge balls because it's funny, with a lot of gags. I was called into the room and there were two men leaning against a bar. One was an Entertainment Officer, and the other a Cruise Director. I went straight into the coin routine that leads up to the production of the bottle. Just before I got to that point, the Cruise Director was called away, so I now had an audience of one. I produced the bottle right under his nose and he nearly fell over. It was a great reaction. Just then the other chap returned so it had to be explained to him what had just happened -too late. I did manage to show them both the sponge ball trick, which was well received.

"We love it!" they said, "Now what illusions do you do?"

I really should have guessed. Why advertise for a close-up magician when they wanted an all-rounder to do several different acts, as is normal in the cruise industry? A disappointing afternoon.

I was still doing the occasional lecture at the magic club at Northampton, but I was running out of ideas. By now the members were familiar with all of my material, so in early 1989 I thought I'd better do something different. According to my diary I did a "Biographical Lecture" (whatever that was). It smacks at desperation to me. Luckily, we had other lecturers from outside the club, including Claude Perry from Cambridge. Claude was a fast-talking and very witty entertainer. On the evening of his lecture, we arrived more or less at the same time. As he was going up the stairs (I was just behind him), he was chatting to one of our members and I couldn't help overhearing the conversation.

"Do you do much close-up Claude?"

"Not a lot, but I am interested and love to watch it."

"Have you seen Ken Hawes' cups and balls?"

"Well I've seen his cups!"

At this point I burst out laughing. He turned around with his hand out and said,

"Hello, Ken, didn't know you were there."

Of course he did.

I lectured at the Watford Association of Magicians later in the year and from what I can remember, it went well. Lecturing for me at the time was still a bit of a novelty and I didn't take it too seriously. I had no tricks for sale, not even lecture notes.

The way I did it was to demonstrate my tried and tested material as the audience would see it, then I'd break each routine down move by move and explain all about the timing and how I use the trick to sell me to an audience. What I was beginning to notice was that the tricks themselves, and various sleights and moves, were of more interest than the more important areas of timing, misdirection, and communicating with an audience. I explained (or tried to) that they shouldn't do my tricks, but do their own, and apply my ideas and philosophy to their own material and style of performance. As Ken Brooke used to say, "Always be yourself." I carried on lecturing for a few years as I needed the money.

My shed by now was now coming into its own. I still made one off pieces of furniture and was knocking up picnic tables regularly. I did have to change the design though, following a call from the landlord of a local pub where I'd recently delivered six. He told me there had been an "incident." He said that six people were sitting on the bench, three on each side. One group stood up all at the same time and then the table tipped over with the other three still seated. Oops. He was ok about it and the customers involved thought it was hilarious. It was easy enough to sort out and I adapted the six tables to make sure it wouldn't happen again. I contacted as many people as I could that had bought them, and most said they were happy with them as they were, which was a relief.

I was also busy at home, sorting out the bathroom with pine boards and tiling - we'd had a new suite installed and it took forever to get finished. I was always busy doing something and I honestly don't know how I did it. A full day's work and then into the shed in the evenings and the allotment at weekends too. I certainly wasn't hindered in any way by the loss of a kidney.

By now, in the middle of 1989, Clare and Jeff were doing their own thing so we'd often take Ben and Jay out for the day.

May 1st, 1989: *We made the most of the lovely weather by going out and about. Clare had to stay at home to revise for her forthcoming exams, Jeff went to Santa Pod with Steve, and we took the little ones to Guilsborough Wildlife Park. It was really nice there and we had a bit of a picnic as well. From there we went to Naseby and had a look around the museum and then on to the actual battlefield. We ended up by visiting Market Harborough and then back home via Northampton. A really nice day.*

My memory of that day was when the boys ran down the slope of the battlefield with arms outstretched pretending to be aeroplanes - I wonder what Oliver Cromwell would have made of that.

Babs and I had some good nights out too. One of the highlights was going to see Pink Floyd at the London Arena. This was their first tour without original bassist Roger Waters and the gig was to support the album "Momentary lapse of reason." Nobody puts a show on quite like the Floyd. It was all there that night - filmed sequences, flying pigs, and even a crashing aeroplane. As we took our seats, the majority of the audience were rolling joints and by the time the band came on there was a cloud of dope smoke floating all around the auditorium - you could get stoned by the simple process of breathing! The show opened with the familiar and moving opening sequence of 'Shine on you crazy diamond' and went on from there, it was a great show. The place was packed with people of all ages singing along when the band performed some of their classic and well-loved songs. It was a great night.

Having had about 25 years' experience in show business by then, I knew that there were lows as well as highs. I had a call from an agent in early October asking me to keep every Friday and Saturday evening free for the whole of December. It was for regular work at a hotel in Aylesbury. A week later he called again to say they were all cancelled. It was disappointing both for me and the agent. Luckily, I still managed to earn enough over the Christmas period to pay for a few days away for us and the little ones to the Isle of Wight. We stayed at a hotel owned by Graham and Pam Wilson, formerly from the magic club. We had a lovely time. While we were there, Clare and Jeff were sunning themselves in Tenerife on holiday with their Dad. It all worked out pretty well in the end. Our little break was pretty much paid for from one gig. It was for a well-known Japanese banking corporation for their Christmas party held at Les Ambassadeurs Club in Park Lane. I was sent a confirmation letter along with a three-page party schedule. I just hate to be organised. The perfect gig for me is to turn up and be left alone to get on with it. Anyway, they were paying a lot of money, so I had to go along with the plans. I could see where I could do the mix and mingle stuff before the meal, then I noticed it was a buffet. I could cope with that, assuming there were tables. So far, so good. Then I had a bit of a shock when I read what was to happen at 9.15 pm - "After speeches, Ken does final illusion to everybody while Mr Yakamoto changes into Father Christmas costume in nearby office. As Ken finishes illusion, Mr Yakamoto returns, dressed as Father Christmas, to present raffle prizes. He then reveals himself from disguise!!" I read it again - Illusion? To everybody? What's difficult to understand about "Close-Up Magician?" I don't do illusions! Obviously, I'd have to do something. Mr Yakamoto was the boss and clearly it was something he wanted to do. The only thing I had, which meant the only thing I could do, was the bottle trick, yet again. As usual I'd worry about it on the night and play it by ear.

The close-up went really well, and as it got near to 9.15, I said to Mr. Yakamoto that it would be helpful if he got into his costume as quickly as possible. The bottle production is essentially a close-up trick that only takes a couple of minutes to perform.

"Ok," he said as he sneaked off to a nearby office to prepare.

I was duly announced and walked onto the floor which was surrounded by 100 people all looking at me wondering what was about to happen (as I was.) The bottle trick begins with the production of four coins which, under normal close-up conditions, I'd produce from my elbow or behind my knee; these however were not normal conditions. I wandered around the room, finding each coin from a different member of the audience. As the final one was produced, I asked the lady to help me. She joined me on the centre of the floor where the coins were dropped into her hand, she handed me the silk scarf, I reached underneath its folds and produced the bottle of wine and presented it to her. Her reaction was priceless. She took her seat to a warm round of applause. Seconds later Father Christmas emerged and walked into the room to cheers and laughter. What a relief! The hardest thing the audience had to do next was to pretend that they didn't know it was Mr. Yakamoto under the disguise. All in all it turned out to be a good night at a lovely venue.

I did a couple of weddings in 1989, one in a Community Centre which was a beautiful old, converted church, and the other at the Open University. I was certainly working in a variety of places. Weddings going into the 90s and beyond would turn out to be a good outlet for close up magic.

My first gig of 1990 was at another beautiful venue, The Monkey Island Hotel at Bray. Whenever I worked at a particularly nice hotel or restaurant, I'd pick up a brochure or postcard as a memento. I compiled quite a collection over the years. Sadly when I Google some of them now, they're not there anymore, thankfully The Monkey Island venue isn't one of them.

A few weeks before that, the magic club organised a trip to London to see The Paul Daniels Magic Show. We took Ben and Jay along and had a great time. The highlight for the boys was going backstage after the show to meet the great man.

I was living a strange life, working in posh places, and associating with the wealthy in the evenings, while during the days I could be working in a rundown and filthy house, often with tenants to suit. Council House repairs were something new for the company and they decided to give us price-work. Each job was given a sum and that's what you were paid. All very well if the money was good but more often than not, it wasn't. There's an example in my diary where I had to ease and adjust ten internal doors, which included going off to a supplier to find a door closer (which took an hour), all for £7.65. Often it was stressful going from job to job, trying to earn a crust. Thankfully though, most of the work involved small jobs such as replacing window handles or fitting draught excluders. This was in the days before all the wooden windows and doors were replaced with double glazing. Most of the tenants (especially the elderly) were ok and pleasant enough and kept their houses clean and tidy. Some didn't. After a while I got to know the bad areas and would dread going there. If I heard a dog barking when I knocked the door it usually meant trouble. On more than one occasion there was dog poo on the floor. When I complained they'd blame the dog, give it a whack, and scrape it up. The scrape marks would be all over the house. I'd do the work and get out as soon as I could, often with no thanks. How can people live like that, especially when there are toddlers around? In those days I met the great British Public on all possible levels.

It wasn't all bad though. I did meet some lovely people, including a blind pianist one day who'd play while I did my work. The irony being he kept his house immaculate.

One day I had a ticket to do some work in a house which wasn't in a good area. There was a long list of work which would take over a day. I arrived quite early in the morning and knocked the door (no barking dog which was encouraging). It was opened by a middle-aged lady who seemed pleasant enough and I was invited in. There was a shifty looking man sitting at the kitchen table who merely grunted when I said hello. The work was pretty basic with new door handles and catches and one or two adjustments to the windows etc. My final job of the day was refitting a bath panel which I could see had been taken off and replaced in the wrong position. I took the screws out and removed it, exposing the area under the bath. In a gap between the floorboards and in plain view was the unmistakable handle of a revolver. I didn't touch it and had no idea if it was real. It certainly looked genuine. Now I had a bit of a dilemma with all sorts of questions buzzing around my head. Do I pretend I haven't seen it? If it's a toy, why hide it behind a bath panel? Do I report it to the police, or what? I thought it best not to say anything to the tenants, so I refixed the panel and told them I'd be back in the morning. I headed back to the yard. As I drove, I thought of another question. What if it is real and it's used on a robbery and somebody got hurt, how could I live with myself? I parked the van got in the car and drove home. After a bit of a restless night, the next morning I went to see my boss and told him everything. He said he'd deal with it and off I went back to the house. The lady was ok, and her husband still looked shifty and neither of them said anything. I went up to the front bedroom and set about adjusting the window. Half an hour later my foreman turned up and knocked at the door. He told the tenant that I was being pulled off the job as I had to go and help out with something urgent that had just cropped up. He gave me a hand with my tools which I threw in the van, and he said, "Follow me." I followed him up to the Police Station. This was getting serious. I asked him what was going on and he said,

"They're going to raid the house, and they want to have a word, that chap in the house has got a bit of form."

"I thought he looked a bit shifty," I said.

I was shown into a small room where I was asked a few questions by a Sergeant. I told him where the bathroom was and a brief description of the gun. A week later there were banner headlines in the local press:

"House raided by Police; toy gun found!"

There was a photo of the lady holding the gun and generally slagging off the workman who reported it.

Pleased to say I didn't get into trouble with that little incident. In fact I was commended for doing the right thing.

I was kept busy throughout the year in the shed with other bits of woodwork. I did quite a lot of work for the local pub (now demolished). I made a glass fronted mahogany cabinet to house a single golf club. I know there was a story involved with it, but I can't remember what it was. Perhaps it had scored a hole in one? Anyway it looked nice on display above the bar. There was another bigger job which involved fixing a shelf all the way around a square pillar. It was only about a foot wide as it was only meant to take

289

glasses. It was still a lot of work though and involved mitres and fancy beading and brass fittings. The landlord was anxious to get it done as soon as possible, so I made it in sections in the shed and fixed it all together after the pub had closed one night. I got to bed at 3 am and somehow still got up for work the following day. I built yet more bunk beds for the boys as they had outgrown the last ones and later on in the year, I made a pine Welsh dresser for Dave the plumber. By this time the shed had more than paid for itself.

Babs was busy too, working at a newly opened fitness studio and was still involved with the local play group. There were often problems there with the committee, personality clashes and sudden resignations. What is it about clubs and committees? I've been involved with all sorts over the years; table tennis, magic club, schools, and even a church. There has been trouble and bad feelings with all of them. Why can't people just get on?!

I did another car launch job in May 1990 at a garage in Bedford. The car in question was the Rover Metro. (I was really impressed with it and bought one myself later in the year.) This sort of event seems to attract a wide range of people, including company reps who buy fleets of cars, little old (wealthy) ladies who change their car every year, even if it is only used for the weekly visit to the supermarket, and in between are regular family motorists and car enthusiasts. A mixed bag of people from all walks of life, and I was looking forward to it. I had a word with the manager when I got there, and the brief was simple - mix and mingle throughout the evening preferably before the big launch. I could carry on afterwards, but to bear in mind that the car is the star of the show, and the salesmen will be busy answering questions and hopefully taking orders. All fair enough to me. I made a start, moving around and doing my usual stuff and it was going well. I couldn't help noticing that I was being followed. There was a young chap who seemed to be always there hovering and watching at every group. As I was having a break, he came up to me and told me his name was Mike and was one of the team who travel the country building the launch sets. He said he'd enjoyed the magic and asked if I would do him an enormous favour. He went on to tell me that he was with his girlfriend that night and was going to propose, and could I, would I, "magic up the ring?"

"Wow," I said, "That's a great idea. I'm up for that."

I asked to have a look at the ring and although it was small it was still palmable (a technical term known only to members of the magic fraternity.) He let me borrow it for a while so I could find a quiet corner somewhere and figure out a method. It was simple enough using the same technique I use for coins. The important part was the setting up and presentation. This had to be right. I gave the ring back to Mike and explained the plan. Firstly, it would have to happen at the end of the evening when things began to quieten down a bit. He was ok with that as he'd be busy anyway. I also needed to know where his girlfriend was and who she was with. He pointed her out and I could see she was sitting with a group of friends. I said I'd go over and show her a trick so I could get to know her and see how she reacts.

"Ok," he said, "I'll leave it to you come and find me when you're ready." Off he went.

During the following couple of hours I visited her table several times and luckily, she loved the magic and her reaction got better and better at each visit - so far so good. As the evening was starting to wind down, I felt the time was right. I found Mike who, as he gave me the ring, said,

"What if she says no?!"

"She won't," I said, expressing more confidence than I felt.

I told him to make sure that everybody that needed to be there was there and when he was happy with that, go and join her at the table and sit on her right. When he was ready, and only then, give me the nod.

"It'll be fine."

"Ok," he said, "I'll get it sorted."

It took about 20 minutes to set up - I finally got the signal and walked over.

"It's the magic man!" she said, "Have you got any more?"

"I have," I said, "But this will have to be the last one."

I positioned myself between the happy couple.

"This is a trick with two coins, a 50p and this genuine antique Chinese washer."

I tossed the 50p into my left hand and picked up the Chinese coin with my right. I closed both hands and said,

"The 50p is on my left hand and the genuine antique Chinese washer is in my right." I looked at the audience and said, "Watch."

I slowly opened my right hand to reveal the 50p. I turned to the girlfriend,

"If the 50p is now in my right hand, what should be in my left?"

"The genuine antique Chinese washer," she laughed.

I looked at the audience, and looked at her and slowly opened my hand to reveal the ring. She looked puzzled for a second or two and then smiled. I said,

"This is from Mike for you. Congratulations!"

I gave her a kiss on the cheek and left the table as they tearfully embraced, and their friends erupted. What a lovely moment!

As usual, on my way home I pondered the gig. The ring was definitely the highlight, and luckily it all came together. The performance of the trick took less than a minute, but the setting up took 2 hours. I had to make sure the girlfriend wanted to watch me otherwise it wouldn't have worked. It had to be right, not for me particularly, but for the couple and their friends. The mechanics of the trick was of no importance, the effect though was paramount because the effect is all the audience will remember - the ring and the moment. There you have it in a nutshell the Ken Hawes philosophy on entertaining with close-up magic. The trick is only a means to an end. It's all about the people and the connection we have and what happens between us. That's the real magic!

Always willing to help out at the local school (I'd done a fair amount of carpentry over the years), I volunteered for something different. I was off to Bude in Cornwall for a week's holiday with a large group of children, including David who had cerebral palsy and his wheelchair. I had no idea what I was letting myself in for. It took all day to get there on the coach, arriving at about 5 o'clock in the evening. It was only then that I discovered I'd be sharing a six-berth caravan with eight ten-year-old lads (including Ben). I also found out that most of the others only had five or six. I mentioned it to Paul, the head teacher, who had little sympathy –

"Consider it an honour," he said, smiling.

Generally speaking the lads were as well behaved as ten-year-olds can be. I only lost my rag on one occasion. It was towards the middle of the week and the strain was beginning to tell anyway. I was doing some cooking and I could hear an argument going on which turned into a bit of a fight. It was the same lad who had continually provoked some of the others since we'd been there. I grabbed hold of him and shouted into his face.

"I will not have fighting in my caravan!! Do you understand?"
Everybody went quiet.

"Do you understand!?" I repeated.

"Yes," he whimpered.

The next day was spent out and about in Bude. From the moment we got there, I felt a small hand reach out into mine - it was the same lad. He stuck to me like glue for the rest of the week. Paul noticed and I told him what had happened the previous night, as I thought I might be in trouble. He told me not to worry as it had obviously had a positive outcome. He went on to tell me that the lad's home life was rather unstable with all sorts of stuff going on and as a result there had been some behavioural problems.

"Don't worry, you're doing a good job," he said, "He just wants a Dad for a week."

Our time there was fairly straight forward with daily organised events with bits of free time thrown in - a visit to Clovelly, a rather lovely harbour town; a couple of open farms; horse riding; museums; a lifeboat house; There was a lifesaving display on the beach and also a chance to swim in Bude's very own swimming rock pool. It was a full and enjoyable week, and occasionally stressful when after the umpteenth head count of eight I would only have seven. Needless to say, the odd missing lad would always make an appearance. One night, soon after I'd got the lads more or less settled, there was a tap on the door. It was Paul, who offered to stay in the caravan for an hour so that I could pop out for a pint or two in the bar. Paul looked after and cared for his staff and volunteers just as much as he did the children.

I have an image of our time there that I'll never forget. At one point during the week there was an opportunity for the children to walk/climb to the top of a fairly high tor. It wasn't easy. I had just brought my group down and were having a well-deserved drink when one of the lads pointed and said,

"Look."

We all turned round to see. Silhouetted on the skyline and nearing the top was Paul and his wife Chris, struggling and pushing young David in his wheelchair. They got to the top to huge cheers from everybody, especially David. It was an emotional moment. Paul was his usual modest self when I spoke to him later.

"David has the right to experience everything that the other children do. I wasn't prepared to allow him to miss out on anything. Why should he?"

I wasn't going to argue with that - Paul Freedland, a star.

Clare and Jeff were growing up and by now and into their late teens. Clare had signed onto Nene College in Northampton on an art and design course. Jeff was also coming to the end of his school life and was on a Trident course at a garage in Bletchley and working part time at a local McDonald's. Things weren't too well between us for a while and as a result they were both anxious to leave home and find some independence. Babs and I had some heated rows and things were said that shouldn't have been, and things were written in my diary as well that definitely shouldn't have been. It wasn't easy for any of us at that time. We were all under a lot of strain and sadly it was inevitable that things would come to a head, as indeed they did in 1991.

CHAPTER 18

Not a good year

1991 was a year of two distinct halves. Up until the summer, things were pretty much normal. It was after that when it all went pear shaped. In January there were the usual teenage angst problems. We all went for our annual check-up at the dentist and Clare was bemoaning the fact that she was struggling to remove staining from her front teeth. The dentist asked her if she smoked (which she did) and then gave her a telling off involving a list of the many other serious health consequences involved in smoking. She said, "Whatever," and then strode out into the street to light up! There were one or two boyfriend issues as well, all irritating, but normal stuff for an 18-year-old. I remember when my Dad discovered that I smoked. I was about 22, at the height of my hippie era, and was smoking 'San Toy' Cheroots. I was rehearsing some magic at the kitchen table one day and I'd emptied my pockets so I could work on a coin routine. The pack of ten and a lighter were on a nearby chair. Dad came in, spotted the cheroots, and said, "Do you smoke these now then?

"Yes, I do. Do you want one?"

"No thanks," he said, and off he went back to the front room to no doubt say to my Mum, "I wish he'd get his hair cut."

Thanks to Anthony Owen I now had a set of lecture notes. It was his idea and he offered to print a few copies on his new-fangled word processor. Mick Hanzlik from the magic club knew a cartoonist/

caricaturist in Northampton who drew the cover and, "Ken Hawes, Table Hopper" was born. It contained no tricks and was all sound advice on how to entertain with close-up magic. I sold them for a fiver each whenever I did a lecture. Many years later, Anthony came up with the notion of me doing a lecture tour in America. He did some groundwork, but the Americans wouldn't accept the fact that not only wouldn't I be selling any tricks, but there were also none in the lecture notes either. My attitude of, *don't do my material, do your own*, didn't cut it. Anyway, by this point I knew that my primary aim as a magician was to entertain the public. I had little interest in what other magicians were doing – however...

In February I was asked to do a lecture in Glasgow. It was a long way to travel but the rail fare and accommodation for the weekend was part of the deal so why not? Anyway, it would be nice to meet up with 'the Scottish lads. I'd had many sessions with them over the years and we got on really well. Their expertise and originality, particularly with card magic, was legendary. Even without the magic they were always such good company. The lecture went well (in spite of hardly any card stuff) and I sold a few lecture notes too. It was lovely to catch up with Dave Robertson, Roy Walton, Gordon Bruce, Peter Duffie, and Steve Hamilton and the other lads. A good weekend.

The Junior section was still going strong at the magic club and even Ben was showing a bit of interest. By the end of the year I took Jay as well. It turned out though, they were more interested in the crisps and cans of coke that were on offer rather than the magic. Ben would always collect up the used cans after each meeting to help tidy up, which didn't go unnoticed by the committee. At the presentation evening he was presented with a special trophy of a can on a very nice plinth!

We were lucky enough to have our own clubroom in Earls Barton at this time thanks to club member John Lee. It was a large room connected to his butcher's shop in the village square. It had a curtained platform at one end and also a small bar. It was perfect. Anthony Owen and David Penn were now of an age where they could help out with the juniors, and they often did. Occasionally I would receive letters from youngsters who had a magical interest. The following came via the Magic Circle. It reminded me of a young David Penn.

"Dear Sir/Madam
I am aged ten. I am a keen magician and was reading a library book when I came upon an address for the Magic Circle. So being a keen magician decided to write and ask if I could be a member (by post) or if I could be sent some things about your society. I would love to be a member, but I know with some groups there are limits. My standard is the sword box which we (me and my brother) went around the shops to get a very large cardboard box and use odds and ends as swords. We have now made a wooden sword box and are very pleased. I hope you can fulfil my dreams.

Yours in hope.
John Smith (age 10)

The letter was also sent to the newly formed Milton Keynes Magic Club which I believe he joined. Hopefully his dreams were fulfilled.

Ben eventually lost interest in magic and was now immersing himself in music. He was lucky enough to have inherited a keyboard from Auntie Maudie. Although it was quite old, Ben really took to it and was soon playing recognisable tunes. We decided for his tenth birthday in 1991 to buy him a more up-to-date Yamaha. He loved it, and a seed was sown. Jay was never really into magic, he was more sporty and loved playing football. We spent hours on the play area behind the house kicking a ball about. Jeff was a football fan too and soon convinced his younger brothers that Manchester United were the bees knees! All three boys are fans to this day. Jeff, ever the outdoor man, was now hooked (pun intended) on fishing. Babs was still working at the gym which had now expanded from being women only to catering for men as well. I was happy to join to keep fit, having retired (more or less) from table tennis. My dream of having a Charles Atlas body reignited (but never fulfilled). Clare had settled into student life at Northampton and was living there and coming home at weekends.

Babs and I went to the Blackpool Convention at the end of February and had a nice relaxing weekend. Ben and Jay were staying with my sister Jean and her two youngsters while we were there. We travelled up on the Saturday morning, found a cheap hotel and spent the afternoon wandering round the shops before driving to Lytham for a bite to eat. That evening we met up with Mike and Lorraine from the Plants Restaurant in Newport Pagnell. I tried teaching Mike some coin tricks - I think he decided to stick to his illusions! The next day was the convention proper, and although it was great to see such well-organised events, the whole thing was beginning to become a victim of its own success. Too big and too crowded. Anyway, I was more interested in catching up with friends I rarely see. Bob Read for one. We'd known each other since the 70s. He told me some bad news, Albert Goshman had died the previous week. What a shame, another hero gone.

On December 16th, 1990, we took Jay to Whipsnade Zoo for his birthday treat. There had been an advert in the local paper inviting families to go along and see Santa in his grotto, among other things. Perfect! We looked forward to it. It all went well in the morning, and we got in the queue to see Santa at about one o'clock. The queue moved really slowly and at half past two we gave up and spent the rest of the day just driving around the zoo. It was all very disappointing. When we got back, Babs wrote a letter of complaint, thinking we'd heard the last of it. Sometime later we received a very nice letter from the zoo inviting us back there along with complimentary tickets for some of Jay's friends. This is what happened - it turned out to be a good day from start to finish.

March 3rd, 1991: *What a day it's been today. It was our return visit to Whipsnade, it was great, they really did look after us. We were driven round in a Landrover and Jay was allowed to feed the penguins. Then we visited the elephants where we fed them with buns, and finally it was off to see a new baby wallaby. The manager was great and apologised again for the previous visit. After some lunch we were left to wander on our own for an hour or two, a really lovely day. Tonight we went to see Man at Woughton Campus, it was great to see them again after such a long time. A great end to the day.*

Woughton Campus was a good venue for bands for much of the 90s, thanks to Chris Kemp the promoter. I approached him about the Man gig and was able to put him in touch with the band's management via Mickey Jones. I got them the gig! I was really proud of that. The previous year we'd seen Wishbone Ash and later in 1991 Manfred Mann's Earth Band. Mostly local bands played there every Sunday lunchtime. It was a thriving venue for live music which over the years attracted some big names, including John Martyn and Robert Plant. It was always great to see live original music there, and indeed anywhere, before the advent of endless tribute bands. At this time I was learning the guitar myself, helped and assisted by my pal Don. I'd go over to his house, and he'd teach me an assortment of chords and bits of finger picking as well. Like everyone else I suspect who has picked up a guitar, the must learn sequence was Stairway to Heaven. It was all good fun.

Work wasn't going too well. There was little coming in and things were looking bleak. Men were laid off in March including Dave the plumber. Luckily, I was still in touch with him and did more work for him in his house throughout the year. I was still doing the certificate framing for the karate club and one day Glen the coach suggested I take Ben and Jay along to one of his sessions with a view to joining. I put it to the boys who immediately began to leap about doing a few "moves." They were up for it. We duly turned up one evening and watched with interest the discipline of several rows of youngsters being put through their paces by Glen. The boys however weren't keen. Ben was never a team player, too much of an individual (like me). It may have been different had he seen some one-to-one stuff, but based on what we did see he was having none of it. He suffered with asthma as well which he would have struggled with. Jay wouldn't have minded having a go, but I had to give him a choice for economic reasons, karate, or football. He chose football, and as it turned out that was the right decision.

I was still doing the council house tickets and, as we were competing with other contractors, the prices were lower than ever.

March 5th, 1991: *Another frustrating day. I had to replace a couple of unusual hinges on a kitchen cupboard door this afternoon, it took an hour to pick up the hinges, and half an hour to do the job, all for £1.37!*

Council house repairs were still more often than not in bad areas of the city. I had to replace a lock one day on the communal door of a block of flats. The door looked familiar, so I asked one of the tenants if it had been replaced before.

"Oh yes," he said, "The police are always breaking the door down."

In the same area I had to do some work in a flat where the tenant had been murdered. That was a bit spooky. Work wasn't what you might call a laugh a minute. Even areas of a reasonable quality weren't exempt from a criminal element. One day I had a ticket to replace a lock and carry out a door repair. When I turned up the elderly lady was quite distraught. She'd been burgled while out of the house attending her husband's funeral - you can't get much lower than that. Luckily, it wasn't all doom and gloom. I had to hang a pair of doors at Barclays Bank Stationery Department (the place of my first employment back in 1965). It was nice to catch up with a couple of people who remembered me and were still there. They were still doing the same type of work, feeding paper into a machine, and watching it come out the other end. As much as I'd moan about my own job, at least I was doing something different every day. Oh well, each to their own.

With work we never really knew what was in store for us until we got into the yard in the morning. It was getting to the point when we were glad of anything, including the council house tickets. Our concern about lack of work was reinforced when at the end of April our boss suddenly resigned. Because of the work situation, I daren't refuse private work. I made a floor to ceiling cupboard unit for Clare's dance teacher that required 12 framed tongue & groove doors, all handmade. That was a labour of love in my shed, and time-consuming.

I couldn't refuse lectures either. I did one for the Milton Keynes Magic Club which went well, but I never did join. My loyalties were still very much for my own club at Northampton, and I just didn't have the time. I also lectured at the Bexleyheath Society of Magicians. It seemed to have gone ok, although I did write in my diary that I had the impression they weren't really a close-up club. Perhaps they were mostly children's entertainers, who knows? I didn't sell many lecture notes either. Some lectures went better than others depending on the standard and interests of the membership. Often it is difficult to know just what a bunch of magicians are thinking. We do tend to tell each other how marvellous we all are and some of us don't take criticism too kindly. It can be dressed up as being 'constructive' but, it seems to me, the best policy is to keep quiet and to only give advice if it's asked for. Anyway, regarding that night, I seemed to have enjoyed myself and I did my usual stuff in my usual way. It was up to them if they chose to listen or not, I hope at least some of them did. At worse, it was a night out for which I was paid, and it was fascinating driving through the Dartford Tunnel for the first time. In April of 1991 I did another unusual gig. This was a corporate job for 'Rowenta', the company famous for the manufacture of steam irons. There were three of us working, and from what I can remember the deal was to do the Three Card Trick (Find the Lady) and to give away badges, mugs, and T-shirts featuring the company logo. I have to say it seemed bizarre to find a connection with an iron and a magic trick. The other unusual aspect to this was the venue - Waterloo railway station. We had to be there at 7.00 in the morning to set up in time for the rush hour. It seemed obvious to us that nobody in their right mind hurrying to work would have the inclination to stop and watch a magic trick, but they knew best, and we had to abide by the contract. We set up on the concourse. The other lads had to work from behind the main Rowena stand, but I was lucky and was able to work from inside my own booth. I got myself organised and was soon approached by a group of French tourists. I did a four-ace routine from the Vernon book which I adapted for the day. Instead of aces I used queens. The idea being to follow the whereabouts of the red ones. It had a kicker in the end whereby whichever cards were chosen there was a coin underneath all four. It went really well. I started work at about 7.30 am and finished at 5.00 pm - I stopped once for a tea break. I certainly earned my money that day. I loved it and just kept going. Most of the people were tourists, but there were others who had time to kill, and a few who just wanted a free T-shirt or mug. I do remember a TV celebrity who came over to watch with his young son. It was the actor who played the father in the ITV Oxo ads. Hardly a huge star, but still a nice man with both him and his young son enjoying the trick, and the mugs.

I pondered the gig on the way home, thankful once more for the Vernon book. Yet again it had come to the rescue with a wonderful little card trick from within its pages and again I had taken note of words of wisdom from Bobby Bernard and Pat Page, taking a trick created by somebody else and then transforming it by putting my own stamp on it. It was the same with the engagement ring trick - that was based on a sequence of moves originally created by Albert Goshman. How thankful and grateful I felt to have both

Vernon and Goshman at the heart of my creativity, and the likes of Bobby and Pat keeping me on the straight and narrow.

Babs hadn't been happy at home for quite a while, she needed a break. An opportunity arose for her to go off to North Wales with a few friends to have a go at rock climbing. I was more than happy for her to go, and she loved it. She phoned me when she got there and told me that the next day they'd be climbing on and around Holyhead Mountain. I'd have loved to have been with her. While she was there, I took Ben and Jay out for the day…

May 19th, 1991: *I took the boys to a farm open day near Brackley. We went to the allotment first thing to buy some seeds then off we went. We had some lunch as soon as we got there and then had a wander and saw assorted breeds of chickens, sheep, and cows, watched a sheep being sheared, saw some Punch and Judy (which wasn't very good), and then the highlight, a falconry display. We got home at around five o'clock and I treated the boys to a McDonald's, after that they helped me cut the grass and weed the garden. A really lovely day.*

It's nice to look back at happy days. I'd forgotten all about this one until I read it again some 30 years later.

The early summer continued pretty much as normal. Babs was still working at the gym, Clare was continuing with her course at Northampton, and Jeff had left school and was still working part time at McDonald's and enjoying the summer. I did a couple of gigs, including a charity do for Amnesty International at a local church. I'm happy to do the odd freebie job if it's for a worthy cause and from this one I did pick up a couple of others. We had a new boss at work who seemed ok and there was still enough coming in to keep me gainfully employed. There was one job which was memorable…

July 11th, 1991: *We did a job at Simpson village today, repairing a roof on a large old cottage, we all had our shirts off working in the sunshine. The best part though was having access to the property swimming pool. We certainly made full use of it. We were in having a dip during our morning tea break at 10 o'clock, lunch at 1 o'clock, and finally another quick dip at 4 o'clock before we packed up for the day.*

By the time August arrived, it was painfully obvious that Babs was unhappy. I was being rejected, she wasn't speaking, and in spite of a holiday in North Wales where things may have been resolved, they weren't. She left on August 22nd, initially to live with her brother, and eventually with the new man her life. They married later and have been together now for 30 years. We're friendly enough now, but things were difficult in those early years for all of us. It was agreed that to maintain stability for Ben and Jay (who were ten and eight), I would have custody so that their school and social life wouldn't be disrupted.

At times, during the rest of the year, there was a lot of anger and unpleasantness, but we got there in the end. Jeff left home to live with his Dad and grandparents at Wing, and Clare went to live with Babs where she had more space and light for her college artwork.

The rest of 1991 and beyond was full of every possible emotion, predominantly sadness. I'd lost somebody I loved, and it was all heart-breaking. Clare would come over and see us whenever she could, and we became really close. Any bad feelings we'd had when she went through her teenage angst period now totally dissipated.

The boys seemed ok and happy, and I gave them everything I had to maintain their wellbeing and stability. There were practical problems like getting them to and from school and somehow, thanks to friendly neighbours and family, so far, I was managing.

I had a long-standing arrangement with Anthony Owen to make a video. It was made by Derek Dexter at his home in Milton Keynes two weeks after Babs had left. Emotionally I was all over the place. However I got stuck in and performed each of the six routines straight to the camera followed by the explanations. Two of the routines were based on tricks from the Vernon book, including 'Ladies', which was the trick I did on Waterloo station; it began with the memorable lines…

"This is my Mum's favourite trick. I'm sure you've heard of Find the Lady, well this is Find the Ladies, although my Mum can never find a Ladies when she needs one!" Boom-boom. (It did seem funny at the time.) I did the best I could with all six routines, and we were pretty much done by lunch time. After that we adjourned to the garden where Anthony did a 25-minute interview with me about my philosophy and approach to performing. As far as I was concerned that was the best thing on the tape - a view shared by a couple of reviewers in the magic press. All in all I was quite pleased with it. Years later it was transferred to DVD format, but sadly the quality wasn't all that good, the interview with Anthony barely decipherable.

On the surface things were ok, but I wasn't coping at all well emotionally. The months up until the end of the year were particularly difficult. I wasn't sleeping or eating well, and weight just fell off me. I was exhausted. I didn't tell anybody at work what had happened, I just couldn't. I was a failure, that's how I felt. They must have known something wasn't right though due to my demeanour and appearance. Nobody asked me what the problem was apart from Dave the plumber (who was now back). I couldn't even tell him. The evenings were the worst when the boys were in bed, and I felt totally alone. There were a couple of friends who'd occasionally call, and family of course. Many of our friends didn't want to get involved or be seen to take sides, which was understandable I suppose. I phoned the Samaritans one night when I was at a particularly low ebb, not because I was suicidal, but because I knew there was somebody there I could talk to and who would listen. I dialled the number, and the phone was picked up. I didn't know what to say, I couldn't speak. After a while I heard the sound of a soft and friendly voice.

"Hi, my name's Bill, I know you're there. You can tell me anything you like in complete confidence. Take your time. I'll be here for as long as you need me to be here. If you choose to ring off that's fine and you can call another time. How can I help, are you able to tell me your name?"

I can't remember much of what was said apart from a lot of sobbing on my part. I did know however that I had to make the call and it was worth every second. I never did contact them again.

CHAPTER 19

Writing

I never was any good at expressing myself verbally. Annoyingly, I'd often think about what I should have said long after a conversation was over. I could write though, and it came fairly easily. I'd dabbled with poems when I was in my 20s but nothing too serious. One night, in the autumn of 1991, the boys were in bed, and I just couldn't settle. I had no interest in TV, music, magic, or anything else. I ended up pacing from the kitchen to the front room backwards and forwards with my head bursting with sorrow, anger, and confusion. I was losing it and cracking up. I couldn't let that happen. It occurred to me that all this stuff needed to come out somehow. I decided to write it all down, perhaps that would help. To make it more interesting why not write it in a poetical form, or better still a song? I found a pad and a pen and began to write. My first attempt was, *The Silence.* It was about the moment I was in - sleepless nights, hopelessness, pacing up and down and being alone in the silence. I picked up the guitar and worked out a tune and sang it into my old tape recorder. I played it back and it sounded ok, but was it any good? The next day Clare called in and I played it to her.

"What do you think?" I asked.

"I think that's the most miserable and depressing song I've ever heard," she replied.

Oh well, at least she was honest. I wasn't too despondent though; everybody has to start somewhere. I made no attempt to change it in any way; it was what it was, good or bad didn't really matter. I just knew it was great therapy. During the following months I wrote another 17. I took some of the better ones along to my friend, Charlie Hill, who had a studio and recorded them there. My nephew, Russ, also helped with backing tracks on a couple of songs. During that time, it gave my life a bit of purpose and all the stuff my head was full of, just poured out. Of the 18 songs, I reckon there are about 4 that are half decent, not so much in a musical sense (I can't sing for a toffee) but poetically and emotionally. I wrote angry songs and sad songs, one each for the boys, another for Clare and Jeff, and I had an idea for a song which I'd been pondering for a while. But meanwhile I had another idea involving the boys. I asked them if they'd like to go on an adventure to Great Yarmouth to the magic convention. I hadn't registered or booked anywhere to stay; we'd worry about that when we got there. They were up for it, especially if we might have to sleep in the car or on the beach! We left home at 8 o'clock on the Saturday morning and got there at 10.30. After parking in a side street, we went for a wander and found a cheap and cheerful B&B. I treated them to a McDonald's and then went to a music shop for Ben to have a browse; he loved them. His ambition from quite a young age was to work in Chappells music shop when he grew up. From there I took them to an adventure playground for an hour until it was time for the early performance of the spectacular magic gala show which was great. After a meal it was back to the B&B to watch 'Buster' on tv. The next morning I managed to speak to a few magician friends before we drove home. We'd had a great time.

September 28th, 1991: *If only Babs could have been with us.*

I was obviously still missing her; it was still early days.

During the week after our trip, I decided to follow up the idea I'd had just before we went. I was going to write a song that would portray our relationship from start to finish - beginning, middle and end. It isn't an uncommon scenario and has been done countless times, but where and how do you start? I thought the best way was to learn from the experts. One of the best songs ever written in my view is, 'The First Time Ever I Saw Your Face', by Ewan MacColl. I had a look at the words which are indeed beautiful, but it wasn't quite what I was after. I liked the idea of first impressions, but the song didn't tell the whole story. Mine would, I decided, from the first meeting in 1978 to the then present day of September 1991. I wrote down the first three words, (unashamedly ripped off from Mr. MacColl) and it all came together after that; it took about 2 hours. There is no bridge or middle eight, after all I was only an amateur. The melody came easily with a straightforward, basic chord sequence. Bearing in mind I only knew about six chords anyway, I was rather limited. All in all I was happy. It was the best I could do, and it does portray how I was feeling at the time.

Full Circle

The first time I saw you on that cold winter's night,
Pale, thin, and lovely to me, a wonderful sight.
We talked and laughed but in your eyes was sadness, and
I wondered,
I would make you happy again if it took 'till I was a hundred.

311

The second time I saw you the day was overcast,
Your love came shining through to me, happiness at last.
We laughed and loved and in your eyes no sadness and
I wondered,
We would be together 'till we were a hundred.

Those early years were full of love, my heart was overflowing.
Who'd have thought that ten years on such a cold wind would
be blowing,
My love for you has never stopped not even for an instant,
Not strong enough to keep you, and now you're oh so distant.

You're in my heart and on my mind every minute of the day,
I only hope you're happy in your chosen way.
For I have failed to keep you and lie awake and wonder
Could I make you happy again before I reach a hundred?

The last time I saw you the day was warm and bright,
Pale, thin, and lovely, still a wonderful sight.
We didn't talk, we didn't laugh, and in your eyes was sadness.
We've come full circle, don't you see?
It's pointless, wrong, and madness.

Up to now the boys had been ok. It seemed they had more resilience than I had. I did my best to control my emotions, but every now and then I'd snap at them if I was at a particularly low ebb. Towards the end of November I noticed that Jay was becoming withdrawn and quiet which wasn't like him at all. I tucked him into bed one night and asked him if he was ok, I could see he was upset. I gave him a hug and said…

"Tell your old Dad what the trouble is."

Then it all poured out as he explained to me through his tears.

"I'm in the school show, and I was going to be hornet, but now I'm not allowed to be hornet anymore. I've got to be a web dancer and I want to be a hornet."

I felt myself welling up and I wept, I wept for his innocence. I told him that he would surely be the best web dancer in the whole show and when I watched him perform, I would give him the biggest clap ever and so would everybody else!! He seemed ok after that. I stayed with him until he fell asleep. I went downstairs and wrote this;

Lullaby for Jay
Jay, close your eyes and lay.
In your bed at the end of the day,
Don't let bad dreams disturb you,
Sleep soundly my son, you deserve to.

Jay, rest your head and lay.
After a day of work and play,
Close your eyes and sleep,
Without worry, quietly and deep.

Jay, curl up snugly and lay.
Daddy's not far away,
To comfort you if you weep,
And hold you close 'till you sleep.
Jay, so peaceful in your bed.
Who knows what's inside your lovely head?
Don't worry we'll find a way,
For tomorrow's another day.

Ben and I went to watch Jay's show in December. His performance was upstaged somewhat when a little girl fell off the stage as they walked on. Apart from that the whole thing was lovely, and of course he was indeed the best web dancer in the show.

By the end of 1991 I was still emotionally all over the place. Late one night I sat with a cup of tea and couldn't help wondering when it was all going to end. It was a case of moving forward and feeling ok for a day or two and then having a relapse, often sparked by something banal like an old episode of Bergerac... I picked up my pad and a pen and the following was born.

Will the pain go away?

We've been through so much and suffered all that pain.
I could never go through such torment again.
Time is the healer, or so they say.
Nothing else seems to make the pain go away.

It all seems so pointless to break my heart.
Nobody's gained since we've been apart.
But you've got your freedom and your own way,
And left me to wonder, will the pain go away?

Life is a struggle but I'm starting to cope,
With you not being here and to live without hope.
You're not coming home, you're with him to stay.
Now I accept it, will the pain go away?

This year's nearly over, the worst of my life.
Will next year bring happiness and peace of mind?

As long as I think of you all through the day,
At night-time I pray, make the pain go away.

And what about you? Have you peace of mind?
Has it turned out ok? What you expected to find?
I doubt it, and know that in your own way,
That you too are wondering, will the pain go away?

This sudden burst of writing creativity would carry on for about another year. It dried up as suddenly as it appeared. I took that to be a good sign, everything that needed to be expelled suddenly was, I was over the worst and moving on. I've just looked back at the many pages of stuff I wrote during that period and there are some that capture a time and a moment and still stand up as being half decent in a personal way, most of them however are embarrassingly awful. There are two more worthy of publication here. These were both written for beautiful girls I really cared about.

I always wanted to write something for Clare. The moment came when it was her birthday, I thought it would make a nice present. I discovered that the songs written quickly, almost in a matter of minutes were often better than the ones I'd take weeks toiling over. This didn't take long at all.

Oh Clare

With your shy little smile and your lovely brown eyes,
The way that you toss back your hair.
So full of fun, as bright as the sun,
You light up our lives, Oh Clare.

You try and keep happy and smile when you can,
You're always so tired night and day.
But behind the smile that lights up your face,
The tears are not far away.

It hasn't been easy, you came through ok,
You've survived with a quality so rare,
With so much to offer and so much to give.
You make me so proud, Oh Clare.

I could have done better, I gave what I could,
You know that I always did care.
You're so understanding, and you forgive.
So easy to love, Oh Clare.

With your shy little smile and your lovely brown eyes,
The way that you toss back your hair.
So full of fun, as bright as the sun,
You light up our lives, Oh Clare.

I played it for Clare soon after her birthday. She didn't realise the song was about her until the first *Oh Clare* at the end of the first verse. She tossed back her hair, looked at me with the smile that really did light up her face, and cried. Oh Clare xxx.

The following final song was the only one I wrote that had nothing to do with my family. It did however have a lot to do with how I was feeling at the time.

It was the beginning of 1992. We had an interesting project at work involving a conversion job in a house in Milton Keynes. The tenants were Barry and Trish. The job entailed fitting a new roof over the rear garden, converting it into a fully equipped bathroom and bedroom for their severely disabled young daughter, Gemma. It was a big operation, often noisy and dusty. The roof went on ok which included a couple of skylights. The new area was floored and tiled, and new bathroom equipment with a state-of-the-art hoist was also installed. The final job was the decorating. Gemma's room was painted a lovely shade of pink with her bed situated directly underneath a skylight. During the roofing work, Gemma was elsewhere for obvious reasons. I didn't meet her until the work was almost done. She had beautiful thick red hair, and I took to her straight away. On the face of it she had little going for her, confined to a wheelchair, unable to speak or hear and fed through a tube. I was really touched with the love and care shown to her by both parents. I wrote the song for her in about 20 minutes. It was written from the point of view of us the builders. I took it along to Charlie who put a lovely backing track to it, and Don Mahon played finger-style guitar.

Gemma

We gave you daylight in your life of silence.
The sun shines through to your room of pink.
You touched our hearts oh little Gemma,
But more than that you made us think.

We may have problems, but they fade away,
When we see how cruel nature can be.
You touched our hearts oh little Gemma,
You opened up our eyes and made us see.

Your body is frail, but your heartbeat is strong,
Your smile says the words that you can't say.
You touched our hearts oh little Gemma,
We'll never forget you, you're with us to stay.

As you lay in your bed and look at the sky,
And gaze at the stars that shine above.
Rest your pretty head oh little Gemma.
You've nothing to fear you're surrounded with love.

Trish, Barry, and family loved it. They both cried on the first hearing. Sadly Gemma passed away in 1997. xxx

CHAPTER 20

Single Parenthood

There was more bad news in the middle of November 1991. With little work coming in, I was laid off for a couple of weeks. That was all I needed just before Christmas. Luckily, I had a number of seasonal gigs which would help. I had further good fortune from the local school. Paul, the head teacher, had learned what had happened and offered me work for the entire fortnight. There was loads to do, so I'd be doing him a favour. I turned up at the school with my tools on the first Monday and was kept busy for the whole two weeks. Both me and the school benefited, and I enjoyed it as well. I owed Paul a lot, he was supportive in every possible way.

It turned out to be a busy end of the year with Christmas gigs all over the place, from Milton Keynes to Ruislip.

It came as some relief when the year finally ended. 1991 had been traumatic to say the least. It was obvious moving forward that I would have to get myself into a better place emotionally, not just for the sake of the boys, but also for my own wellbeing. I had the love and support of my family who had been great throughout, always being there with advice and practical help and not being judgemental in any way. I knew there would be difficult times ahead as a single parent, but I was up for the challenge. Looking back now there were also some moving, rewarding, and proud moments too.

I began 1992 in a positive way. I really felt the need to spend as much time with the boys as I could. On January 2nd I suggested we have a day at the seaside. They were up for it (although somewhat bemused by going in the middle of winter). We set off for Bournemouth and with little traffic on the roads we had a trouble-free journey from start to finish. The boys were really good on car journeys, they could always keep themselves amused by playing the card game Top Trumps, or more often than not playing a game of their own called 'The Chase'. This involved point scoring, which was dependant on the number of cars I overtook, or which overtook us (I think). With rules that were constantly changing, I never did understand it. I would often hear one of them say,

"Oh Dad, you've just lost me two points!"

We got there at midday, had a nice pizza lunch, and then wandered around the town until it was time for the matinee performance of *Jack and the Beanstalk* starring Max Boyce. It was a good day; the boys slept all the way home.

Throughout the rest of January and February we'd have days out all over the place, this was fairly typical…

January 19th, 1992. *A really full day today. We started at Luton Airport where we watched a couple of planes land and take off, after our packed lunch we went to The Shuttleworth aeroplane collection near Biggleswade which was really good. We ended the day at Woburn Sands Table Tennis Club watching an inter-league match. The boys sat through it all as good as gold.*

The Shuttleworth Collection was where the cover photograph of Deke Leonard's album 'Iceberg' was taken… nothing wrong with a bit of trivia.

If I could afford it, we'd go out in the evenings as well, particularly to the local swimming pool, sometimes twice a week with friends of the boys. We visited the cinema quite regularly too, usually followed by a McDonald's. I took them to the table tennis club for coaching for the first time - Jay loved it, Ben didn't. The following week Ben loved it, Jay didn't! There was one venue in Milton Keynes they were both anxious to visit, 'Rollers', the recently opened roller skating rink in Bletchley. Determined to go, they hatched a cunning plan. They came into my bedroom early one morning with my breakfast on a tray. They stood in the doorway and said,

"You can have your breakfast in bed, but only if you take us to Rollers."

I didn't know whether to laugh or cry. I had to tell them that I just couldn't afford it, we'd go there another day. The tray was left on the floor and as they thudded down the stairs Jay shouted,

"No wonder Mum left you!!"

This was something else I had to deal with, although thankfully it didn't happen often. As time went on, they realised that comments like that were counterproductive anyway. When I got up, I picked up the tray, went into the kitchen and sat them down. I told them that I wasn't in a position to do whatever they wanted whenever they wanted as I just couldn't afford it. There were bills to pay, clothes to buy, and other things that just had to be paid for that were more important than days out. I did make it very clear but told them that if they were good for the rest of the day, I just about had enough money to take them for a swim at Bletchley Leisure Centre.

"Ok then," was the subdued response.

Later on at the pool, I picked up Jay in the water, gave him a hug and we made up.

For Ben's birthday treat I decided to take him and Jay out for the day along with their cousin William. As money was a bit tight it would have to be somewhere free or cheap. I plumped for Heathrow to have a look at the aeroplanes. We parked up and made our way to the viewing area. After an hour of watching planes take off and land we'd had enough (having decided that one plane is very much like another). I suggested we go somewhere else. We sat in the car for a while eating our packed lunch and I had a look at the map.

"How about Portsmouth?" I said.

The boys were happy to go anywhere other than back home so off we went, not only to the seaside but also to look at the old boats and the Naval Museum. Another good day, always nice to see the boys happy.

Ben was really getting into music by this time, always playing his keyboard and his new drum machine. He was often joined in his bedroom with his young friend Anthony, soon they were writing songs together. This was to be the beginning of Ben's passion for creating music. A channel and a way to express himself which he continues to enjoy to this day.

Where Ben was into music, Jay was getting into football. I noticed there was a coaching course taking place at Woughton Campus on Saturday mornings (the same place as the swimming pool). Jay was up for it, and we signed up. It was a bit stop and start to begin with but eventually he did stick at it and loved it. Those early days as a nine-year-old led to a regular team place in Youth Football which would last well into his teens and earned him a cupboard full of trophies.

By the spring things settled down and we began to get into a routine. I had to decide how to deal with school holidays as well. The boys would usually go to my sister Jean for half-term which wasn't always straight forward. Sometimes they didn't want to go, and it was a battle to get them there, yet when it was time to pick them up, they didn't want to come home! As the weather improved, we spent a lot of time outside including one memorable afternoon flying a kite at Campbell Park. There is something exhilarating about getting a structure made from canvas and bits of wood to soar into the air by running with a piece of string. After three hours we'd had enough, happy but worn out. That evening we went to the cinema to see 'Stop or my Mom will Shoot' which was quite funny. We enjoyed the cinema, the boys more than me usually and I did have to sit through some real turkeys. One of the worst was 'Bill and Ted's Bogus Journey'. For days afterwards the boys had picked up the strange language where everything was 'Excel-lent'!

I wanted the boys to have as good a childhood as I'd had. It made some sort of sense to me for them to have a go at the things I'd enjoyed when I was at their age. We'd been swimming a lot and had also started going on bike rides by this time. I wondered how they'd take to fishing.

June 27ᵗʰ, 1992: *I took the boys to the centre this morning and bought bait and a new reel for Ben's rod, all ready for our first fishing trip this evening. Jay managed to catch a couple of little perch, and I had one bite and that was it. They both got themselves in enormous tangles, and the last straw was when they knocked the tin of maggots into the water.*

A couple of days later we had an evening in Northampton. First, we visited Clare's college to have a look at an art exhibition

Ben and Jay with Paul Daniels

featuring some of her work. She really had a lot of talent as a creative and original artist. We were very impressed! From there we drove down the road to the Royal Theatre to see 'It's Magic' with Paul Daniels, his son Martin, and the lovely Debbie McGee. It was a great show. The magic club had hired a room upstairs where Paul was presented with an Honorary Vice President Diploma. All three stars signed our programme and were more than happy to chat to us and pose for photos. We were all thrilled.

I was still going along to the magic club whenever I could but had to resign from both the committee and as Junior secretary. My heart wasn't in it, I didn't have the time either. Ben and Jay had lost interest and I didn't want to drag them along or ask family to baby sit; they were doing enough. Hopefully though it wouldn't be too long before the boys would be old enough to be left on their own.

I did a lecture at the British Magical Society in Birmingham in the summer which went really well. Anthony came with me to help sell the videos and lecture notes afterwards which was kind of him. I sold three videos and five sets of notes which was pretty good I reckon. Later, in October, I popped down to Eastbourne to the IBM Convention and spent the day behind a stand with Anthony, doing some of the stuff on the video. We managed to sell a few more which was nice. I watched the early gala show and travelled home straight afterwards. I missed the boys.

The video had got good reviews from various magic magazines and was selling well. I've just discovered a press release that young Anthony had written and had sent to the local press. Apart from the usual promotional stuff about how wonderful I was (Bobby Bernard had given me some good advice years before, "Never believe your own publicity"), there was a paragraph that caught my eye which I thought was unintentionally hilarious. The following is exactly how it was written by Anthony.

"Local magician Ken Hawes is creating magical history this month as he releases many of his award-winning secret routines for his fellow magicians to learn, but he is teaching them through the new medium of video.

Ken explains, "You get instructional videos on keeping fit, passing your driving test and even on making love. So why not learn magic that way too? For years magicians have had to study books following the descriptions and the pictures exactly, but with video they can freeze frame to get the secret moves and positions exactly and see how it should look when performed correctly."

To this day I don't know if it was written that way to raise a smile, it worked though, as I did get a mention in the local press!

With the school summer holidays approaching I had to sort out child minding for the duration. Luckily it all fell into place. Clare came over to stay for the first week and the boys were over the moon. She was really good with them, and they loved her to bits. The three of them spent hours on the play area behind the house playing football and cricket to the point where Clare could hardly move. At the end of the week she went to a wedding and in the late afternoon I had a call to go and pick her up. Too much wine, she fell asleep on the sofa. Playing hard and partying hard, that was Clare in her late teens and early twenties, and why not? I'd booked two separate weeks off work, one at the end of August and the first one following Clare's stint. I felt the call of Wales again and was toying with the idea of a week away on the West Coast. Sod it, we'll go!

"Right then boys! Shall we have an adventure?"

"Yeah!" they chorused.

"Let's go to Wales, to the rock pools and the beach, and the harbour with the honey ice cream!"

"Yeah! Will we be staying in a caravan?"

"No idea, we'll worry about that when we get there."

"Does that mean we might have to sleep on the beach?" asked Ben.

"Or in the car?" added Jay.

"We'll find somewhere, we might even have to sleep in the same bed," I said.

"Ughh, gross!" they said together.

Looking back now, I did take a bit a chance travelling over two hundred miles with two small boys with no accommodation booked and at the height of the season too. Anyway I was committed. We set off early on the Sunday and had a good journey, arriving there late morning. I tried the holiday park where we'd been before - full up. I drove down the coast towards Newquay and tried a few more - all full. I was beginning to get a bit concerned and we were feeling hungry by now. We parked in the town and walked towards the beach. On the corner facing the small harbour was the Newquay Hotel with a 'Vacancies' sign displayed.

"Let's try here," I said.

We walked into the bar, and I spoke to a chap who turned out to be the owner. There was a family room available for £30 a night bed and breakfast. Perfect! I told the boys I could only afford a few days and we'd have to go home on Thursday and not Saturday. They didn't argue, they daren't. I paid for it there and then as I didn't want to take the risk of searching elsewhere and coming back to find it fully booked. We had a drink and some lunch in the lounge and then went for a walk on the beach, feeling content, relieved, and looking forward to the next few days. The room was comfortable, and we slept well that night.

We got up the next morning and went down to breakfast. I felt tired and a bit depressed. The boys were tucking into their cereals and with a mouth full of Weetabix Jay said,

"Sean hasn't been in a hotel like this has he Dad?"

"Don't talk with your mouth full. I don't know, you'll have to ask him when we get home."

"I bet he hasn't."

"I'm going to buy a honey ice cream because I've got some money," said Ben.

"That's not fair!" wailed Jay.

"Don't worry, I'll buy the ice creams," I said, "and we can go to the Bee Museum and look at the fish in the Aquarium."

"Cool!" they said in unison.

As I sat there it occurred to me that perhaps I shouldn't be mourning what I'd lost but be grateful for what I had. I looked at them chatting away, happy, and innocent and looking forward to the day ahead, and in that moment, I don't think I'd ever loved them more.

August 3rd, 1992: *A really nice day spent at Aberaeron. We did the Bee Museum and Aquarium as we usually do, and of course the Honey Ice Cream. We went to the beach at Cai Bach in search of crabs with some success and had a meal in the clubhouse there. We went for a swim in the Aberaeron town pool which was lovely. I bought the boys puzzle books and felt tipped pens and they've been terrific. We ended the day walking along the front, too tired for the sunset though.*

All the days were of a similar vein. One evening we went to the wrestling, featuring 'The Stoke Stomper' and 'Big Daddy'. What an entertaining night that was. On our last day it was more of the same. Ice cream, a swim, a boat trip, searching for crabs and playing ball on the beach. We were still building sandcastles on the beach at 9.30 that night. None of us felt like going home. Thursday came along much too quickly and after stoking up with a huge breakfast we said our goodbyes and set off for home at 10.30. We stopped off to visit friends in Stratford for a while and set off once again. The boys slept virtually all the way home and were still tired when we got there. Soon it was bath, bed, memories, and sweet dreams.

Clare decided to stay for a further week which certainly helped the boys to get over their after-holiday blues. Jeff came over to stay for a couple of days as well, and by the end of the week they were all aching and knackered after hours of football and cricket. The following week the boys spent with Babs, which gave me a chance to catch up on washing and housework. Then I had my final week off, and that was it! Well, not quite, we did have a trip to Alton Towers to end what turned out to be a great summer.

Ben and Jay were generally well behaved and were doing well at school. Each had their own set of friends, and they played well together, but as is often the case, boys will be boys. At the beginning of September Jay had decided that he wanted to join the karate club after all. I took him along one Friday evening and he seemed to enjoy it. The following week I had several visits from some of his playmates, complaining of him being a bit violent. I didn't take too much notice until I had a complaint from a mother. I put it down to the excitement of being in a new school but did wonder if there was a connection with his foray into karate. After a word or two from me along the lines of, "Naughty boys don't go to the cinema, or the swimming pool, or Alton Towers, or anywhere else," he was ok.

No problems after that, he didn't go to karate anymore.

"I'll stick to football."

The rest of the year went quickly. Life was full and often overwhelming. I was still all over the place emotionally but was coping. I had no social life of my own to speak of and was happy enough to share my time with the boys. Clare and I would occasionally have a game of table tennis, followed by a pint or two which was great. She could certainly sink the 'Pils!' In November, I did manage to get to see BB King at the Hammersmith Odeon, and what a great show that was! The audience was in the palm of his hand as soon as he walked on. I loved it. It was a great night.

November was a busy month for all of us. On the 1st we went to Alton Towers again, along with Clare and Jeff. It was a long day - we got there at about 9.30 in the morning and got home around midnight. During the day Clare and Jeff did their own thing, and so did the boys really, I was happy just to watch as I find those rides terrifying. The day ended with a huge and impressive firework display. Another good day.

At three o'clock one morning in late November I was woken up by a knock on the door. There were two policemen standing there. My knees buckled. Surely not bad news. They pointed to a car parked near my drive and asked if it was mine.

"No, I said, but where *is* mine!?"

It seemed the car on view was stolen then dumped and then mine stolen.

"We'll let you know when yours turns up," they said.

Two hours later, another knock on the door. My car had been found a few miles away. To cut a long story short, I had to get a couple of quotes for repair work (a hole in the door panel) which was eventually done and paid for by the insurance company. It was yet more stress to deal with on top of everything else. If only those 'joy' riders could see the aftermath of their actions. Bastards.

At the beginning of December, I was asked by a furniture store in Aylesbury to do the magic in store, every Saturday from 11.00 till 5.00, and Sunday 10.30 till 4.30. It was a huge commitment, but I wasn't in a financial position to say no. I told them I'd do it for a month, which I did. Then they offered me another month after Christmas which I accepted. Somehow, I'd found the time and money to buy Christmas presents and we all looked forward to the big day.

December 24th, 1992: *Mum came over today. I picked her up this afternoon after getting a few last-minute stocking fillers. We popped into the hospital on the way here so that she could pop in and see her neighbour and pick up dirty washing! The boys went to bed at around 9.30 all excited, and Mum went up at around 11.00 o'clock. We'd done the veg between us and put the presents under the tree. After watching a bit of tv I went to bed at about 12.30 - the boys woke up* *ten minutes later! I let them open one present each from their stockings and they went back to sleep.*

We had a lovely Christmas day and despite all the vegetables and turkey with all the trimmings, Ben decided he didn't want any of it. He had a solitary fried egg.

The end of my first year as a single parent came to an end. I'd got through it. I was able to hold my job down thanks to friends and family helping out. The boys were happy and had lots of friends and were doing well at school. My mental state however was nowhere near being back to normal, it would indeed be a case of 'Time being the healer'.

I was coming up to 43 and the man from 'The Foresters' (my financial advisor) suggested it was about time I thought about putting money away for a pension. I told them I'd think about it in a couple of years, once the cooker was paid for and I'd bought a new Hoover - I knew where my priorities lay but was also made aware of the importance of saving for the future.

January 1993 was busy and by the end of it I was worn out. I worked at the furniture shop every weekend throughout the month, so I was on the go seven days a week. As luck would have it, the car was being repaired for a couple of weeks, so I had to rely on my neighbour to provide transport. By the time I'd given him petrol money, half the fee was gone. I soon realised what the plan was in the store. If a family turned up, they would deposit their children with the magician who would keep them entertained while Mummy and Daddy looked at the furniture. They should have booked a children's entertainer; it was pointless doing stuff for adults, as I'd be preventing them doing what the store wanted them to do - buy furniture. The store management didn't get it and didn't realise there was a difference between adult and children's entertainment. As far as they were concerned a magician is a magician. Anyway, I adapted and got through it, and it did go well with the older children. By the end of the month I'd had enough, and so had the boys. They were missing out on weekend treats, and I missed out by not being with them. I quit.

As well as music, roller skating, and swimming, Ben had discovered a new interest - CB Radio. He had a rig set up in his bedroom and for a few months I spent a lot of time sorting out licences, aerials, and bits of equipment to stop the interference on the tv. I was a bit apprehensive with some of the people he was talking to, particularly when they suggested meeting up. Thankfully it was a short-lived hobby, the whole thing was dying anyway. He was 12 now and beginning to have his own set of friends, obviously wanting to do his own thing which often didn't include Jay. Although the boys got on really well together there were moments when I would hear the wail of...

Mum's 75th Birthday - what would I have done without her?

"It's not fair!" from ten-year-old Jay, or "Dad! Ben hurt me!".

By the end of the year Ben was going to Rollers every Friday evening (yes, we got there in the end) which meant I would stay in with Jay, after visiting the video shop to hire a film and buy bags of sweets - all to make life 'fair'. They would have to find out for themselves as they grew up that life is decidedly unfair, and you just have to live with it.

My birthday rolled around again. Mum had given the boys presents from the family to hide and to give them to me on the big day. As can be seen from the following, they were beginning to develop a quirky sense of humour. They wrapped some 'extras'…

March 9ᵗʰ, 1993: *The boys woke me up with a cup of tea this morning and an assortment of packages to open. There was a purse/wallet from Jean, slippers from Maggs, and a mop and bucket from Mum (always practical).*

The boys wrapped up - an old prayer book, my guitar capo, an apple, and two paper clips! I thought it was great, and they really had fun watching me open them. I love them to bits. We finished the day at the Pizza Hut (for them more than me).

The next birthday was Mum's seventy-fifth. She spent the afternoon with us and had a lovely time. Clare and Jeff were there too to wish her a happy birthday and she was over the moon to see them again. Mum was a Godsend in those early days of single parenthood. Often, she would drop everything, get on a bus, and come over whenever she felt she was needed.

The day following Mum's birthday I went into work until about 10.30 and then came home to change and set off for Stockton-on-Tees. I was lecturing at the Middlesbrough Circle of Magicians a journey of some 200 miles. I'd got the job after speaking to the club secretary at a recent convention. I'd known him for years. He would enter the IBM close-up competition regularly from the late sixties to the mid-seventies. He never did win it but certainly deserved a prize for tenacity. He was tall and thin, and I would often see him walking around the convention wearing an old raincoat and always carrying a small brown case. I didn't know him that well, but our paths would often cross at conventions. Judging from his appearance I assumed he lived in a small, terraced house and would be a shop keeper or perhaps a librarian and do children's parties at weekends. Anyway I'd soon find out, as he'd kindly agreed to give me a meal on my arrival and also overnight accommodation. The journey was good, and I found his house without too much trouble. It was quite large and in a really nice, secluded spot. So much for a small terraced! He invited me in, and we had a nice chat before sitting down to a lovely meal prepared by his wife. Far from having a menial job, he was something along the lines of a scientist or research chemist and highly educated to boot. I'll never judge anybody by their appearance again. The lecture went really well. I sold a few sets of notes and videos and also some old props I'd acquired from a recently retired magician. It was lucky I did and got some cash, as the treasurer forgot to bring his cheque book! (I was paid eventually.) Soon it was over and back to the house. I spent some more time chatting and unwinding over a cup of tea before retiring for the night. What a lovely man. I got up at five o'clock the following morning and after leaving a thank you note for my kind hosts, I set off home. I arrived at about eight o'clock, and after a hurried breakfast I went to work. I couldn't afford time off. I was managing ok, but I always had the fear of impending redundancy or ill health, and fear of being unable to provide for the boys. I had to work.

We had a run of school classroom conversion jobs which kept us busy for the first half of the year, including Water Eaton Juniors, my old school, and scene of many happy childhood memories. It all seemed so small now. The smell was the same though, floor polish and canteen food. While I was there, I learned about a school reunion that was happening later in the summer. I went along and met my former teacher Mr. Vince; since then we kept in touch, and I'd get a Christmas card each year with a message written inside with his still beautiful Italic handwriting.

We would try and do the work in schools during holiday time to minimise disruption, but it wasn't always possible. I had my own problems with school holidays in May. My sister Jean called to say that she wouldn't be able to have the boys for half term. They were going away for that week and taking Mum with them. That gave me a headache for a while, but it was resolved when she kindly invited the boys to go with them. A week at Bracklesham Bay! Life was like that, ups and downs continually.

At the beginning of July after a lot of thought I traded in my Metro for a brand-new Vauxhall Corsa. With the amount of travelling I was doing with both the magic and days out with the boys I needed a reliable car. I spent hours with a calculator and pay slips before going ahead with it. The one thing I didn't check out was the work situation. Two weeks later we were all summoned to the office and were told that due to lack of work our wages would be cut by £40 a week! - so much for keeping up with the car payments. Soon after that I had some welcome good news - I received quite a hefty cheque from an insurance policy I'd surrendered which put me back on track. As I said, ups and downs continually. I'd also discovered that I might qualify for the Family Credit benefit. The lady in our office helped me fill in the huge form and I sent it off at the end of August. Then came two months of correspondence asking about all sorts of stuff, most of which they should have known anyway. It was finally resolved at the end of October.

Meanwhile, Jay was sticking to his football and attending regular coaching sessions and was now wearing his first pair of boots (that was a proud day). In July he took part in his first tournament in Bletchley. It was huge and took all day. His team got through to the semi-finals and he won the first of many shields, cups, and trophies. He played well and had a great day. It was the first of many tournaments and matches for me as well. Standing on the touchline in all weathers on a Saturday or Sunday morning (often getting soaked) for several years. As a parent I didn't take it too seriously as long as Jay enjoyed it and was having fun with his pals that was good enough for me. He was disappointed when he lost but it was all character-building stuff and he soon got over it. I soon discovered that not all parents had the same attitude as me, some took it much more seriously. There was one match when a lad was about to take a throw in and was shouted at by an irate mother,

"My son takes the throw ins, not you!!"

On another occasion a referee was so shaken up by continual touchline abuse he phoned the police and refused to leave the pitch until they arrived and escorted him off; incredible really, for a match with ten-year-old lads. Occasionally there would be a lot of shouting and bad language from some parents, much of it directed at their own child. More than once I watched as a lad came to the end of his tether and walked off the pitch never to return. Unacceptable parental behaviour reflected on the club of course. They were told by the manager they were supposed to set an example to the youngsters and if they weren't prepared to do that they'd be banned from the touchline or the club, or both. And some were. Days out continued, often football related.

"Right then boys, who's up for another day out?"

"Meee," they said in unison, "Where are we going?"

"Somewhere we haven't been to before, how about Manchester?"

"Yeah!! To Old Trafford?"

"We'll see."

July 30th, 1993: *A really good day today. We got up early and set off for Manchester at six fifteen. We stopped off for a drink at Sandbach and got to the Granada Studios quite early. It was great there and we really enjoyed it. From there we went to Old Trafford and spent some time in the Mega Store. I told the boys we'd do the stadium tour another day; we did catch a glimpse of the pitch though. We had a good journey there and back despite delays on the M6. We're all knackered and in bed by 10.15.*

A good day out at Old Trafford

Just to see that beautiful well-kept green pitch was worth the trip. We saw Alex Ferguson that day as well.

What a difference there was between my two sources of income. In early September I'd spent the day working in a grubby old empty butcher's shop in Wolverton on a conversion job (ironically into a venue for Relate, formally Marriage Guidance). We had to make up sound-proof partitions which included a lot of insulation both inside the panels and underneath the floorboards. It was hot and dusty work. That same evening I had a gig with the magic performing at Luton Hoo, one of the most beautiful mansion houses in the country. What a difference! It was still daylight when I got to Luton, so I was able to see the impressive grounds. It is a remarkable place, more of a palace than a country house. The event was a corporate job given to me by friend and magician Roy Johnson from Leicester. He gave me several gigs over the years which was kind of him. It was a good night. A lovely venue with lovely people. The next day it was back to reality and the grubby butcher's shop. Things were looking up locally with the magic as well. A new agency had opened in Bletchley called VIP Promotions run by Vic Graves and his wife. We did a lot of work together over a two- or three-year period including a regular booking at a bar/restaurant in Milton Keynes called Muswell's which was only a five-minute drive away. I worked there every Saturday evening for four months September to December. It all came to an end due to 'senior management changes within the group'. Shame really as 'junior' management were all set for it to continue indefinitely. Oh well nothing lasts forever, and it was great while it lasted. All sorts of people frequented the place, most of them pleasant enough and some not so nice. There was a couple in one night and as they were drinking their coffee, I approached the table and said,

"Hi, my name's Ken, and I flit from table to table doing a few tricks."

I didn't get any further than that. He looked me up and down and said,

"Well you can just flit off then!"

"I'd like to see some magic," said the girlfriend with a smile.

"Well I wouldn't, and we're not!" growled the man.

"Ok," I said, "Perhaps another time," and walked away feeling really sorry for that lady.

I don't know what his problem was, perhaps he'd just had a bad day, I certainly wasn't going to argue with him. Most people who don't like magic are polite enough and just say no thanks and I move on. Sometimes however there are individuals in a group who behave really strangely. The following has happened on a couple of occasions. I'd approach the table as I normally do and make a start, and even if everybody else on the table is watching and enjoying it, there is one person (who is usually sitting right in the front) who will make a point of not watching. They turn their head away and ignore everything that's going on including the reaction and laughter coming from everybody else, they behave as if they're sulking. It is quite bizarre. I wonder what's said to him or her after I've left. "If you don't want to watch then go to the bar," would be my reaction and, "Don't spoil it for everybody else," would be another. My only explanation is that perhaps he or she is some sort of control freak and I come along and steal their thunder, or perhaps they're jealous or even envious that I can do something they can't. Who knows? It does take all sorts.

There are some things that can be labelled every parent's worst nightmare. One is when your child goes missing. I suspect many parents are familiar with that awful feeling when in a busy shop you suddenly discover that your child has disappeared. For the time they're missing, even for a minute or two, you feel an awful and overwhelming sense of panic, until suddenly they turn up smiling and wondering what all the fuss is about. It happened to me once on a sunny evening in September 1993. Ben was in the house, and I'd just got home from work. It hadn't been a good day; I was still working in the butcher's shop and was covered in dust and felt generally miserable. I made a cup of tea and opened the mail. Yet another letter from Family Credit, now they want to know how income tax was paid on my earnings with the magic. For God's sake I'd already told them that! I threw it on the table, my mind full of it as I prepared the dinner. When it was almost ready, I gave a shout to Ben. He came down and as he walked into the kitchen, I asked him where Jay was.

"He's out somewhere with Sean."

I glanced up at the clock, he should have been home an hour ago. Sean was Jay's best friend, and they were always together, a nice little lad.

"Did he say where they were going?"

"I think they might have gone down to Woolstone Pond," said Ben. This was an old pond about half a mile away. Deep enough to drown in I thought, as I gave Ben his dinner.

"I'll have a walk down there, you stay here."

I walked down the road towards Sean's house (which was on the way) thinking the worst and cursing myself for allowing this to happen, praying that he'd be safe. Sean's Mum was outside her front gate anxiously looking down the road towards the pond. As I was about to speak to her, she pointed and smiled. There were two small figures walking towards us. They were chatting and laughing. Sean was carrying an old net with a bamboo handle, and Jay, wearing his baggy floral shorts and a grubby yellow T-shirt, was carrying the seaside bucket we'd bought in Wales.

"Dad, you'll never guess what we saw!" he said as they got to the gate.

"Newts!" said Sean, as his Mum ruffled his hair and took him inside.

"See you tomorrow, Jay."

I took the bucket from Jay and took his hand as we walked up the road home.

"What's for dinner, I'm starving?"

"You've got Turkey Twizzlers, chips and baked beans - and it's the little children in Africa that are starving; you're just hungry."

"Ben doesn't like beans 'cos they make his mouth go all furry," we said together.

That night after his bath, I tucked him into his bed and explained to him the danger of deep-water ponds. Even though he was a strong swimmer he could still get tangled up in weeds, and did he know that it's possible to drown in only one inch of water!? I looked at him and he'd fallen asleep, his Manchester United book still open.

I went downstairs a lot calmer than I'd been a few hours earlier. I got stuck into a pile of ironing and thought about the emotional highs and lows of the day. Who'd be a parent?! In spite of it all, I wouldn't have it any other way. It was my love for them that was keeping me sane. Whatever happened we'd do it together. Life went on...

September 25th, 1993: *Ben didn't get up until ten o'clock this morning which was a bit of a surprise. I took Jay to his football training, and he did really well playing in the pouring rain (heading a wet ball!) He was caked in mud, but I put him in the bath when we got home, and we all had tomato soup and crumpets which he loved. I took Ben to the Centre in search of his computer magazine, no luck though. Muswell's continues to go well, and I'm booked for another month. I think it'll go on now until Christmas at least.*

With the proceeds of the Luton Hoo gig I bought the boys a bike each from a local cycle shop. It was owned by the former landlord of the pub I'd done all the carpentry work for a few years previously. A small world. With the boys now cycling came the added worry of accidents and safety. Luckily in Milton Keynes there is a cycle network throughout the city called The Redway which is brilliant. When Ben cycled to his new school, he barely touched a main road. My mind went back to when I was his age and cycling all over the place often on busy roads. The thought of my Mum and Dad worrying didn't enter my head. With my two I worried constantly. Health wise the boys were quite different. Ben had more time off school than Jay particularly in the early nineties. His problems can best be described as from the neck up. Swollen glands, sore throat, earache, and persistent headaches. He also had asthma which was treated with the aid of an inhaler. Many times we would hear the cry of,

"Has anybody seen my inhaler?"

If it couldn't be found Ben would get in a panic which would make his asthma worse. Invariably it would be found either under a cushion or more likely down the side of his mattress. His persistent headaches were a bit of a worry. One night there was a knock on my door and Ben was standing there leaning against one of his friends. They'd been to the fair and Ben had suddenly been taken ill. He looked concussed to me. He hadn't banged his head or anything like that, he just looked as if he'd been on something. I put him to bed, and he went straight to sleep and seemed better the next morning apart from having no memory of the previous night. During the day he was sick, obviously still not right, so I took him down to the surgery. From what he told the doctor and from what I was able to find out from his friends, the catalyst appeared to be the drinking of a can of orange Tango, and it had happened before. Perhaps it was a sudden rush of sugar that his metabolism couldn't cope with, who knows? His regular headaches continued throughout the following year which necessitated a referral to a paediatrician at the hospital. He was prescribed regular medication which didn't do a lot. They never did get to the bottom of it and as he grew up thankfully the headaches became less common and less severe. Jay's health problems tended to come from the stomach area, sickness bugs in particular. Often, I'd have to get up in the middle of the night and change his sheets when he didn't make it to the bathroom, and there were times when I'd have to do it all again when he missed the bowl on his bed. With Ben I would have trips to the doctors or hospital for antibiotics, headache pills, and throat lozenges. For Jay all I'd need was a bucket and a bowl and plenty of washing powder.

Work was rather hectic towards the end of the year with pressure to get jobs finished and on time. We had another school job on the go converting two classrooms into a library among other things and I was struggling to cope with it all. My head was still all over the place, I wasn't sleeping well either and there was the constant worry about the boys. At times it would all catch up with me and on one occasion I was summoned to the office (after I'd had a falling out with the foreman) for a talk with the boss. He was ok about it once he knew exactly what the score was and was very supportive. I made him aware that there might be times when I'd have to finish early or take Ben for one of his check-ups or any number of things that could crop up given my situation. I was quite relieved to have got it off my chest at last.

The year did end happily though with some great news. Clare was in love. She bought her boyfriend Tony over to meet us soon after Christmas. The boys took to him straight away, christened him 'Tony Maloney' and spent all afternoon jumping all over him. It was lovely to see Clare so happy. They got engaged on New Year's Eve 1993.

As Clare was beginning her new relationship, I had made the decision to formally end mine. At the beginning of 1994, I set legal wheels in motion regarding divorce proceedings. In August it would be three years since we'd been apart. Babs had now set up house with the new man in her life so I couldn't see the point in prolonging it any further. My first visit to a solicitor was in January. I wasn't in a particular hurry; it would take as long as it takes.

The year started well for all of us. A good and lucrative gig for me in January thanks to VIP, and I had some furniture making to do as well, a corner cabinet for Clare and Jeff's Dad. I still liked to keep my hand in with jobs like that. Jay was as keen as ever with his football, and Ben was doing really well with his music too. Jeff was doing ok and had a regular girlfriend, and Clare and Tony were living together in a small house in Buckingham. At this point regarding music I was pretty much an old fart and had no idea what the latest thing was. I discovered that Tony was in the middle of it all and a member of hip hop band, Criminal Minds, which had a strong national following. I was well impressed!

January 16th, 1994: *We went over to see Clare and Tony in Buckingham this morning and we didn't leave there until half past three. Ben took his keyboard and played a few bars of his own music and then Tony went to town and created a computerised tape incorporating Ben's tune. It's really good and Ben's over the moon, and if that wasn't enough Tony gave the boys a "Criminal Minds" coat each as well. It's been a really nice day.*

There was more good news at the end of the month. An excited Clare phoned to tell us she was pregnant! She also said they were planning on getting married in March, things were looking up at last. Work was improving as well with a temporary transfer to maintenance. This involved sorting out minor problems in recently built houses. There was little pressure timewise as all my boss wanted was to get the work done well and to make sure the tenants were happy. I spent as much time travelling in the van as I did working, driving as far afield as Harrow and Stevenage. It was nice for the few months it lasted. Although we appeared to have regular work, rumours were circulating that there wasn't much in the pipeline. All I could do was sit tight and wait and see what happened. It was a good year for the magic club as well with lectures from a variety of quality magicians. Ali Bongo did a great one and must surely be one of the best ideas men ever. He was the advisor on the early Paul Daniels tv shows, often making an appearance as Alistair the 'assistant'. Another great lecture came from Pat Page, who had moved on from Davenport's magic shop to also work as a TV advisor, particularly with Wayne Dobson. There were also lectures from Tony Griffiths, Roy Baker, Bob Swaddling, and a particularly nice one from Janet Clare who gave a talk about her life with the great Ken Brooke. These were all big names within the magic fraternity. Not bad for one year. Another good night was when the members had to give a presentation on who they thought was, 'The world's greatest magician'. I went for Dai Vernon. His influence and legacy will never be equalled in my view.

Jay was 'Man of the match' in his game on March 5th, we were all chuffed to bits! For my birthday treat I'd got tickets for the three of us to go to Wembley to see England play Denmark.

March 9th, 1994: *I finished work early and came home for a quick shower, and then it was off to the station to get the train to Wembley. We got there at about six o'clock and I bought the boys McDonald's which they munched as we walked to the stadium. We arrived just before seven o'clock and watched the players warming up before the kick off at eight o'clock. England won 1-0 in a good match. We got home at midnight tired out.*

It was exciting for the boys to see some of their heroes from Manchester United. It was a good crowd too, all hoping that the new Terry Venables era would pay dividends (ready no doubt to cheer him on if he did and slag him off he didn't). My first memory of that night was being impressed by how graceful the players were, particularly during the warmup. To say that Peter Beardsley moved like a ballet dancer might seem an odd thing to say, but that night he did - I was there!

The other, not so pleasant memory was the sheer crush in the crowds on leaving. I had Jay by the hand but almost lost Ben at one point. Anyway it was an enjoyable night out and certainly made a change from watching ten-year-old youngsters play.

Life followed its usual pattern of good times and not so good. One thing that happened in late February that had mixed blessings was the Woughton Campus fire. This was Ben's school and some of it was completely destroyed by arsonists. We were given the contract to board up and make safe the remaining partly burnt buildings (which gave us much needed work). Ben had to have a week off school, and I rescued a rather nice partly burnt teachers chair from a skip which I have to this day. In those days of the mid-nineties there was a lot of petty crime about which affected a lot of people in the area including us. A few weeks after the fire we'd decided to spend another day at Alton Towers. My nephew William stayed overnight to enable us to have an early start in the morning. We woke up to find the shed door wide open and the boys new bikes gone. I was able to pacify them by explaining that my insurance would cover the loss and we'd soon get new ones. I did a repair on the shed door and made it safe and off we went to Alton Towers. They soon forgot about the bikes once we got there. Luckily the insurance company were really efficient, and it was only a matter of weeks before the new bikes were delivered.

The highlight of March was Clare's wedding. She looked beautiful and radiant and with Tony looking smart as well they made a lovely couple. It took place in a registry office and Clare came in on the arm of Paul her very proud and smiling Dad. It was a short but moving ceremony and soon after it was back to the house in Buckingham for refreshments. As much as I tried, I just could not get the boys to even entertain the idea of wearing something smart for the big day. They were the only ones not booted and suited, both wearing identical hoodies. Oh well, nobody seemed to mind, and it certainly didn't detract from making it a lovely day.

I always tried to treat the boys equally, as seen by the following diary entry. If Jay had a day out, then I would try and do something with Ben. As they got older though they inevitably began to do their own thing and the regular wail of, "It's not fair" began to decline.

April 2nd, 1994: *Jay went to Watford Football Club today with the club and had a great time. They did some training in the morning and watched a match in the afternoon. Me and Ben spent the day in London. We drove down to Amersham and took the tube into the West End, we had a McDonald's, walked into Trafalgar Square via*

Carnaby Street and Broadcasting House, and ended up in Hamley's. A nice but cold day.

The rest of the year sped by. Jay played in a lot of tournaments and picked up yet more trophies at the club presentation evening and now joined by his pal Sean he was having a great time. They played their first match in the Milton Keynes and Border Counties League in September and lost 14-2, he still enjoyed it though and they could only get better! The boys had a week away with Babs, and then I took them to Newquay in Cornwall for a few days. This time I booked a small B&B in advance, bearing in mind that this Newquay would be busier than the one in Wales due to the popularity of the local surfing beach. We had a nice time there swimming in the waves and playing ball on the sand.

Things weren't looking good at work. The school jobs had come to an end and there was little coming in. I was given a job to do at the local Council Dump, painting the rather grubby toilets. If that wasn't a sign of desperation, I don't know what was. I was fairly busy doing other stuff though, I made and fixed shelves and bits and pieces for Clare and Tony. I also made a bunk bed for a friend of mine and a picnic table for Clare's Dad. Again it was a case of visitors looking at what I'd made and asking, "Could you make me one?"

It was getting close to Clare's delivery date, so it made sense for her and Tony to stay with us for a few days as the hospital was only just down the road. They arrived on the 12th of September, and so began what turned out to be a long waiting process. A week later, on the 18th with no sign of anything happening, Clare glanced out of the kitchen window and suggested we do some gardening. The rockery needed sorting out and the borders needed weeding too.

The fact that she was 9 months pregnant didn't bother her. She was fed up with waiting and hoped that a bit of light gardening might get things moving. Despite a day of weeding, bending, and hoeing nothing changed (apart from the fact that the garden looked great). A week later I took Clare and Tony down to the hospital for her check up on the morning of the 26th. They would start inducing her that night!

September 27th, 1994: *Opal Shakira was born at 5.00pm this evening, 8lb-9ozs. Mother and daughter are doing very well. Me and the boys and Nainy went over to see them tonight, I even had a little cuddle!*

CHAPTER 21

All change again

A week after Opal was born, the workforce was summoned to the office and were told that the Small Works department was closing down. Letters were handed out explaining all and it looked as if we'd be gone by the end of the year. Although it was more or less expected it still came as a shock.

I was handed my official redundancy notice on October 7th, 1994. My employment would be terminated on the day we broke up for Christmas. Not a good time to be out of work. Oh well, at least I had something to do for a couple of months. I was back on maintenance, working with a painter and travelling up and down the M1 to Harrow every day. Yet again I was faced with mixed feelings. Happy of course for Clare and her family on the one hand, but uncertainty hanging over me regarding employment on the other. Three weeks later, on October 25th, I was called into the office and offered a job within the company on the Truss Department. I'd be based on the premises doing the joinery work that was normally given to sub-contractors. Would I be interested? Definitely! I had a formal interview with the boss of the department and a company director, and it was agreed that I'd give it a trial up until the end of the year and give a definite answer then. I started on November 10th and accepted the job at Christmas. What a relief.

Where Jay was succeeding with his football, Ben was doing well with his music. He'd play his keyboard every day and although only 13 he was already on the way to becoming a good self-taught musician. I didn't realise how good he was until I spoke to his music teacher.

November 1st, 1994: *Quite a busy day at Harrow, and quite busy tonight as well. I took Ben over to his school for a parents evening where he played his keyboard for an hour. I picked him up later and spoke to his music teacher who is really impressed with his playing. I did feel rather emotional.*

I realised then how my Dad must have felt all those years ago when he insisted I performed to anybody and everybody who came to visit. Unsurprisingly, I found myself doing exactly the same thing.

"Ben, play 'The music of the Night' for Nainy."

"Just listen to this Mum, it's note perfect."

"Now play that tune you composed all on your own - brilliant!"

Music was a huge part of Ben's life from this point on.

The end of the year arrived and thanks to me being gainfully employed, Jay was able to have what he wanted for his birthday in December - football boots and a football. No surprise there. I was managing to keep the boys clothed despite their rapid growth. I did have problems with Ben regarding trainers though (the brand being more important than the quality). We had a lovely Christmas. Jeff came over to see us along with his now pregnant girlfriend, so all in all it looked as if 1995 was going to be a good year.

It began well with a visit to Southend on January 2nd. We got there around midday and had a walk along the front for an hour before going to the matinee performance of Dick Whittington, with Bobby Davro, Rod Hull, and Emu, and of course Des King as the Dame.

So much for 1995 being a good year and starting well.

January 12th, 1995: *What a nightmare today has been. Jay came home from school to discover that the house had been burgled. He went off to Sean's Mum in tears. She phoned the police who arrived shortly after. I'd gone to the supermarket straight from work and by the time I got home they'd been and gone. Poor Ben was really upset, his keyboard was gone, as was the ghetto blaster he'd won in a competition. Tony came over from Buckingham to sit with the boys which was nice of him. As soon as they'd calmed down, I went into work to pick up my tools so that I could repair and make the back door safe. I feel totally wrecked.*

That whole experience was just awful, and I really felt for the boys; Jay for the shock of finding his home trashed, and Ben who just looked so lost and bewildered with the heartbreak of losing his keyboard. They also took some of Jay's Christmas presents including a Game Boy and our stereo. When I went upstairs, I discovered my empty magic case tossed in a corner and the contents dumped on the bed. There was nothing of any real monetary value just a few coins and sponge balls etc. Annoyingly they'd taken a giant old English penny which I'd had for years, surely of no use to anybody else. During the following days we discovered other stuff missing presumed stolen which caused more heartbreak. In spite of the police and fingerprint people arriving quickly, the burglars were never caught. The police were familiar with the method however, of gaining entry through the back door and wrapping all of the stuff in a duvet cover and walking off with it, even in broad daylight. The following day Ben had to have a day off school; he was still in a state of shock. I finished work early that day and went to the police station to write out a statement and get a crime number for the insurance company. From what I was told, it seemed burglaries such as this were rife all over the city. During the weekend I spent hours sorting out insurance forms and doing my best to put a value on the stolen property. The Insurance Assessor came to visit a few days later and it wasn't too long before a cheque arrived. It wasn't as much as I'd hoped for but certainly enough to sort the boys out. I decided to buy a new keyboard for Ben, a new Game Boy for Jay, and give both of them a bit of cash to do whatever they wanted. A stereo and video player I'd buy some other time. I took the boys to the Centre on February 4th. It was great to see them happy, and so nice to hear the house full of music once again.

The police were right about burglaries being rife in the area. A couple of months later an intruder climbed through the bedroom window of my Mum's bungalow. It was the middle of the night, and she was in bed at the time. I can only guess how she must have felt to have woken up to find a stranger in her room. He didn't steal much as Mum didn't really have a lot. The police were called, and she was given books of mug shots to look at, all to no avail. She was almost 77 at the time and although she put on a brave face, I don't think she ever got over it.

In November our shed was broken into again and Ben's bike was stolen. It was more than annoying. I could have killed those morons. Property can be replaced, but I found the emotion and stress involved really difficult to deal with.

A week after our burglary I did another lecture at the magic club. I was a bit apprehensive as I hadn't had the time or the inclination to do a lot in the way of preparation. It went ok though and luckily there were a few new members who hadn't seen me before. I sold a few videos and lecture notes which was nice. It was also useful to iron out a few things before my next lecture which was for the Leamington and Warwick Magic Society in early April. Judging from what was written in my diary, it looks as if it had a mixed reception.

April 3rd, 1995: *I did the lecture tonight at Leamington Spa. It went quite well but most of the members were too old.*

Make of that what you will. These days perhaps that sentiment should be reversed - "Ken did a lecture tonight, it went quite well, but really he was too old!"

I'd go along to magic club meetings whenever I could and there was always something on offer. If a lecture wasn't booked, then we'd organise something for ourselves. There was an interesting one early in the year based on the BBC Radio 4 programme Desert Island Discs. Rather than choose records we had to decide what we'd take to the island relating to magic and instead of the Bible and Shakespeare (as with the radio programme) we had a choice of two magic books. I can't remember too much about it, but I'm pretty sure one of my books would have been the Vernon book and no doubt I would have related the story about Ken Brooke and the book being his Bible. Coincidentally, around that time I was asked by Anthony (Owen) to give it a review for a magazine he was editing at the time. Strange how that book has continually cropped up in my life over the years.

We managed to get along to the magic club annual dinner and presentation evening in the spring. The boys were happy to go, but again I had the problem of what to wear, not for me particularly but for them. I wore my usual suit and as Ben had just about grown to my size by now, he wore a pair of my black trousers and one of my black shirts. Jay wore his Manchester United team shirt which did get a lot of positive comments. According to my diary, *"They both looked very smart"*. More to the point though, they were happy and had a good time there. While I was doing some close-up, Ben was watching the band and Jay was talking football to anybody who would listen. A good night all round!

On February 14th, Valentine's Day, I had a booking at Muswell's. It was nice to be back there, even though it was only for the one night. The conditions were perfect as far as I was concerned. Just about every candlelit table was taken up with a couple, there was subdued lighting, and the music was provided by local singer and guitarist Martin Hartup who did a great job. I'd made him a custom-built guitar case some 12 years previously which was still going strong; it's always nice to work with people I know. Prior to the gig, and bearing in mind the date, I wanted to do something a bit different to suit the occasion. As well as my usual stuff I thought it would be nice to do a final trick on each table that would be memorable in some way. I had a think and decided to do the ring production (as performed at the garage gig a few years back). I approached the table and said,

"I did something really romantic at a garage once!"

That made them smile and also encouraged a bit of banter. I went on to tell them the story, exactly how it happened, of how and when I produced the engagement ring. As I spoke, I performed the trick and produced the ring again which got a great reaction, "Oh! what a lovely story," the lady would say; she'd look over to her partner and say something like, "All you did was get down on one knee!" Because the lady was happy then so was her partner, and because they were both happy then so was I - job done I reckon!

The following night I was out again. This time I had to travel down to The Lakeside Country Club in Surrey. It was an Agents' Showcase where a show was put on featuring various acts on their books. The audience was made up of venue reps and bookers. I was there representing the VIP Agency with Vic Graves. Ideally, I would have liked to have had the afternoon off work to rehearse and then a slow drive down there, arriving nice and early. Alas I couldn't afford time off and my life was just hectic. The aftermath of the burglary was still rumbling on, hence the visit to the police station. A typical day really.

February 15th, 1995: *I finished work at 4 o'clock and then went down to the police station for an interview with our local police officer. From there I rushed home to get ready to go down to Lakeside for the Showcase. Before that I had to mend Ben's puncture, then the zip went on my trousers as I was getting changed. I had to get petrol on the way which put me back a bit, and finally after a bit of a panic I ended up going in the wrong direction up the M3. By the time I got there (stressed and late) I didn't want to do anything. I did, though, and it went well.*

That night I was given free range to wander about doing stuff as and when I liked, handing out cards from the agency as I went. It was a strange night at times, as the 'Lookalike' thing was all the rage. Specialist agencies had suddenly sprung up from nowhere. It didn't matter if these people had no talent as long as they looked like somebody famous. What struck me as funny was when some of them were gathered around a table, which wouldn't have been possible under any other circumstances because some of them were dead. I saw Ian Botham chatting to Mahatma Ghandi (complete with loin cloth), Jack Nicholson was with Elvis Presley, and Dolly Parton was deep in conversation with Dame Edna Everage. I have to say a few of them were dead ringers, but many weren't. I did hear somebody ask one of them who he was supposed to be. (He probably went back to the day job.) I'm not sure how successful the evening was for Vic, but I did get a mention in The Stage newspaper; "On the list of acts represented by VIP, Ken Hawes Close up magician."

I had stopped going to the Magic Circle by now as I couldn't afford the subscription or the train fare. I did go to one special event though, having had an invitation for the final close-up competition organised by Harry Devano. The idea was for past winners to perform as a sort of tribute. I was happy to do that and had a lovely time. In 1995 I was invited again, this time to take part in a special evening dedicated to Ken Brooke. It was a great night sharing the stage with David Berglas, Geoffrey Durham, and my old friend Bobby Bernard among others. Yet again I performed my party piece of my impression of Ken Brooke and the Vernon book for the umpteenth time. I'd never done it in front of such distinguished company before though. I would always begin my lectures with the same story until it got to the point when many magic club members had no idea who Ken Brooke was. Often, I'd do it anyway. His name and reputation deserve to be remembered as one of the greats. I'd made a note in my diary on that night, March 6th, 1995, regarding the price of the rail fare. It was £12.90 return. A lot more expensive then than when I used to go to the Circle every Monday evening back in the 70s… just 25p!

Things were still ok with the family. Clare, Tony, and Opal were happy in their little house in Buckingham, and on February17th

Jeff phoned to tell us some wonderful news, his girlfriend had given birth to a beautiful little girl, Amy Louise. He was over the moon! Jay was still football mad, and Ben played his keyboard at every given opportunity.

March 7th, 1995: *The really cold weather continues, in fact it snowed some more today. Ben got soaked coming home from school at lunch time. He just puts his wet clothes in the tumble drier while he has his lunch and plays his keyboard and puts them on again just before he cycles back to school.*

The following day, on March 8th, the Divorce Absolute arrived in the post. That was it then, the day before my 45th birthday. I didn't consider it to be a happy event. The opposite really, it was a sad day in many ways, but I was free which is one way of looking at it I suppose. Free to do what? I certainly had no plans to get involved with anybody else then or ever. I just looked at it as another step in putting the past behind me and moving forwards. Life went on.

Work was going really well, and I loved it. I was making a lot of one-off stuff including a series of solid 6" x 6" handmade roof trusses for a new golf club in Bedfordshire. I was cutting joints by hand, which not only had to be right, but they also had to look good as they were exposed internally.

Luckily, I had the space to lay out big jobs like that. I was based in a large warehouse which, at the time of moving in, had no doors or heating. I did get both eventually, but it did take a couple of years. I think at the time nobody was too sure if my job would be permanent or not. The company certainly didn't go to town money-wise when the decision was made to heat the place. They

Busy working on the 6"x6" handmade roof trusses

provided me with a wood burner which was positioned outside the building with a pipe attached, which went through the wall entering somewhere near my work area. It worked ok providing I had the time to load it up with timber off cuts regularly. Around the same time new roller shutter doors were installed which made a huge difference. It was still quite cold in the winter though and like an oven in the summer. There was a large circular saw installed along with a cross-cut saw and bench, and eventually I also had a wall saw. Finally I was given a router and a planer and then had everything I needed to produce all that was required. A small crane was installed later to enable the lifting of heavy panels and stuff. I coped with it all, happy to have a job and doing something I loved. The hours were often long and hard with the bulk of the overtime early in the mornings. I started at 6.00 o'clock, had half an hour for lunch and finished at around 5.00 o'clock. I would also work regular Saturday mornings from 6.00 until noon. No wonder then I was permanently knackered. I did the housework over the weekend and Mum was more than happy to get stuck into huge piles of ironing during her weekly visit. I couldn't have coped without her. It was coming up to her 77th birthday and she was invited to spend some of it with us.

April 24th, 1995: *Mum spent her birthday with us today, all the afternoon and evening. Ben gave her 77 hugs, and Jay gave her a big 'luvvy' earlier on when she got here. She opened her presents and cards and had a nice time, I'm sure. The rest of the family came over tonight bearing yet more gifts, cards, and hugs.*

As you can tell from that, Mum was loved beyond words.

Although there had been a magic club in Milton Keynes on and off for a number of years (usually run and organised by the same small group of people), I had always declined their offer to join. It wasn't a personal thing as I mentioned earlier, I had even less time now. I did however consent to be a judge at their annual Originality Competition. It took place on a Wednesday evening in May, in a small room in a pub not too far away. I sat through a few performances of the type of magic you'd expect from a group of magicians, cards, silk handkerchiefs, rope tricks and the like, all well-presented and of a reasonable standard. The final act was announced, and a lady bounded onto the platform in full clown make- up. The first thing she did was to rip open a packet of condoms, blow one up and make a balloon animal (which I have to admit was rather colourful) - my mind is a bit hazy as to what she did next (thankfully perhaps), but I do remember the big finish which can only be described as a colour-changing dildo. She did a complete act with sex toys! It was bizarre beyond belief. The fact that she was dressed as a clown added to the spookiness of it. In some ways she deserved to win as the originality of her act was beyond doubt, but because it was so embarrassing to watch, she didn't come anywhere (pun intended). The prize went to an original presentation of a card trick, which from my point of view was about as unoriginal a decision as I could have made. Oh well, it was an interesting night out.

I hadn't booked a holiday away in the summer of 1995, as the boys were going away for a week on the coast with Babs, along with Clare and little Opal. It still meant I had a lot of organising to do regarding packing clothes and other stuff though. Ben was growing fast, and I could hardly keep up with him. I didn't fancy going clothes shopping with him anymore than he did. Up until then I'd bought clothes and Christmas presents by mail order (the good old Kay's catalogue), which enabled me to spread the cost. Ben was 14 and old enough by now (I thought) to choose his own clothes. Prior to his holiday he was desperate for more trousers, so I took a risk and gave him £20 to go up to the City Centre and buy a couple of pairs.

"Make sure you try them on," was all I said.

Off he went, and a couple of hours later came back with a carrier bag looking a bit sheepish.

"Did you manage to find some?" I asked.

"I did," he said. (Ben has always been a lad of few words.)

"Where did you get them from?" I asked, expecting C&A, BHS, or John Lewis. He gave the name of a shop I'd never heard of, which should have set alarm bells ringing.

"I hope you tried them on."

"I did."

"Let's have a look then."

He reached into the bag and pulled out a pair of trousers which looked ok to me.

"Just the one pair then?"

"Yep."

"How much were they?" I asked, expecting some change.

"£19.99, but they were reduced from £30," he added quickly.

Oh well, at least he'd wear them. I'd bought both boys trousers not too long before which they never did wear. I found that out when I found them screwed up in the bottom of their wardrobe.

"Why didn't you tell me you didn't like them when I bought them?" I asked.

"Because you were getting in a mood, and it was easier to say, Yes," said Jay.

The day of their holiday arrived. I drove the boys over to Lowestoft and got them settled into the chalet with Babs. After a cup of tea and a chat I drove straight back. A round trip of 280 miles. 'Knackering' is a word that springs to mind. I didn't fancy doing that again, so the following Friday afternoon I drove there and stayed the night in a B&B, and we travelled home early the next day. They'd had a great time. All very well, but I was stuck with a huge pile of washing and ironing, and of course it poured with rain, and I struggled to get it dry. The next day I had a Sunday lunchtime gig at The Warwick Hilton, more travelling, and more ironing when I got back. I fell into bed at 10.00 o'clock, then up at 5.00 am to start work at 6.00. This was the pattern of my life throughout the nineties. I didn't stop.

The rest of the summer consisted of hard but enjoyable work during the week and football with Jay at weekends - there were a lot of tournaments, many of them all-day events. It seems Jay and his pal Sean were up for anything.

June 28th, 1995: *Jay went Gaelic Football training with Sean tonight at the Irish Club - he's been picked for the team! He plays in a cup match on Saturday.*

The pair of them played a few times and really enjoyed it.

We also had yet more football-related days out during the summer. We went down to Wembley Stadium and did the tour, which was great fun, and good value too I thought as we were there for almost two hours. The tour included the dressing rooms and a basement room which housed something really special - the very same goalposts that were used in the 1966 World Cup Final. We were allowed to file past and touch them (more thrilling for me and the other Dads than the boys). Another highlight was walking up those iconic steps to the Royal Box and holding up a (pretend) FA Cup. A good day. We visited Manchester twice during that summer. In July we did the Old Trafford tour, which the boys loved. (Jay was a bit naughty though and came home with a blade of grass from the pitch.) We ended the day with a ride up the coast to Blackpool.

For our second visit we decided to try and get a few autographs at the first team training ground, The Cliff. One of the boys suggested making a video of the trip which seemed like a good idea, so we went to Radio Rentals in Bletchley and hired a video camcorder. We spent the evening getting the hang of it and charged-up the rather bulky batteries, all ready to go the following day. Ben reckoned he had it sussed, and I told him he could have control of it providing he looked after it and hung it round his neck at all times,

"Ok," he said, and took it up to his bedroom to film some of the Man U posters on the wall. Sometime later I heard a thud from upstairs and the familiar wail of Jay,

"Daaad, Ben's dropped the camera."

Luckily no damage done.

August 22nd, 1995: *We set off at quarter to six this morning and were in Manchester at eight o'clock. It took us a couple of hours to locate the Cliff Training Ground only to find the gates closed to the public. It was a real disappointment. We stayed on though and spent the rest of the morning filming the players coming and going and the boys really enjoyed themselves. We were allowed inside the gates at about 1.30 and they were able to meet some of the players, they were over the moon to meet Eric Cantona. From there we drove up the coast to Southport for an hour or two before coming home. A great day.*

In September, I found myself back at the beautiful Luton Hoo for a gig organised by VIP Promotions. It was a huge affair where the clients appeared to have a never-ending pot of cash and were prepared to throw everything at it. It was for Cranfield University Business School and was a large-scale ball and dinner to mark the end of studies for a group of mature students. I always smile to myself when I see those two words together - it sort of implies that they're not immature. Anyway, there were enough tables to warrant two close-uppers, so Anthony Owen came along as well (heaven knows I owed him a few favours). It would turn out to be a great occasion.

All credit to Vic (from VIP) who certainly pulled all the stops out that night. When the guests arrived, all looking smart with dinner jackets and ball gowns, they were piped into the Pillared

Hall by two Scottish pipers. There they were served with drinks
from silver trays and entertained by a string quartet. A formal area
was set up where a photographer took pictures before they were
piped into the ballroom for a four-course meal. During the meal
they were entertained by me and Anthony while a classical harpist
played quietly in the background. After the meal and presentations
there were a few speeches after which the clients could play at the
casino, set up in a room upstairs, or find out what the future held
by visiting a fortune teller. Later, back in the Pillared Hall, me and
Anthony were continuing to entertain while a caricaturist drew
informal cartoons. Soon there was a change of mood as a steel
band (complete with Limbo dancer) set up and began to play. If
the clients felt the need for something more adventurous, they
could go outside to the grounds and have a go on the bumper
cars, rodeo bull, or bouncy castle. Finally, at midnight, a live
band played in the ballroom for dancing until 3.00 am (while a
photographer wandered around taking photographs). I felt like a
small cog in a very large machine that night.

In early 1994, I spotted an advert in the local paper regarding
Woodhill Prison in Milton Keynes. They required a fresh intake
of prison warders. The money was good, as was the pension
scheme (and they retired early). It looked a secure job. As this was
during the time when things weren't going too well at Llewellyn,
I applied. I wasn't too sure if I had it in me to be a warder, but
I thought there might be something I could do in the carpentry
shop. The application form was huge, and I spent a lot of time
filling it in before I sent it off. It was some time before I had a
reply. In April of that year I was invited to go along there for an
aptitude test. I didn't really know what to expect and was quite
surprised to discover I wouldn't be alone, there were about 20

of us. We were led into a large room which was set out as per examination conditions. There were individual desks arranged evenly with a document face down on each one. We took our seats and were told that the test would take about 20 minutes and would be scrutinised immediately on completion. We were told to begin. I turned the document over and was confronted with an array of questions about general knowledge and basic arithmetic and the like. I didn't find it too difficult and soon got through it. Once the time limit had been reached, we were told to stop, and the papers were collected and marked by two men at a desk at the front. I noticed they were making two piles one considerably bigger than the other. I wondered which one was the pass pile. While that was going on, I chatted to the chap on the next table who told me that this was his second attempt. He went on to say that very few candidates make it to the final interview. Obviously not a stroll in the park then. It wasn't long before the invigilator stood up and announced,

"Would the following people please leave the room."

As he went through the list, I wondered if they were the passes or failures; I soon found out when the chap next to me was called, as he stood up, he muttered to himself, "Oh shit, oh well, third time lucky," and off he went no doubt to brush up on his general knowledge and basic arithmetic.

Those of us that were left were congratulated and told we would be notified at some point over the next 18 months regarding the next stage of the recruitment process. A lot can happen in that amount of time I thought, as I made my way out to the car park.

I didn't hear any more until over a year later in the middle of June 1995. I was invited to go along for a conducted tour, which was the next stage in the process. I found myself in a bit of a dilemma. I had by now fallen into a job I loved. Should I take a huge leap into the unknown for more money and job security? Or take the chance of staying where I was and risk the uncertainty of the building trade? I decided to go for it and anyway the tour would be interesting and give me a chance to look at the woodwork shop. If it didn't work out, surely Llewellyn would take me on again as they had several times before? I got to the prison on time (along with 13 others) and found the tour really interesting. The woodwork shop was small and quite crowded, but workable I thought. I was through to the final interview.

August 16th, 1995: *I went into work at six o'clock and came home around half past eight, had a shower, and went over to Woodhill Prison for the interview. The booklet, 'The Inside Story', arrived this morning so I was able to look through it while I was waiting. It was like being at the dentist and surprisingly I was quite nervous. I was called in and the interview was conducted by two ladies. It was all very chatty and nice, but I don't think I came over as being tough enough. We'll see.*

A few days later (which happened to be the last day of my summer holiday), I had the letter from the prison. I didn't get the job. I was disappointed, but soon cheered up when later in the day I had a phone call from John, my boss. I hadn't told anybody at work about the prison job, which was just as well perhaps. Anyway, he told me how much I was missed during my week off and there was all sorts of interesting work coming up, and could I carry on going in at six o'clock on Tuesday after the Bank Holiday? I told him how nice it was to feel wanted. I'd be happy to.

Meanwhile there was still a weekend to fill...

August 27th, 1995: *We set off for 'Cadbury World' at eight o'clock this morning and got there just in time for our booking-in time of ten past ten. It cost me £13 for our guided tour and it was really interesting with quite a few free samples! We left there around midday and called in at Clare's on the way home and stayed for a couple of hours. Opal is almost walking now and really giggles out loud. We left there around four o'clock. I suppose that's the end of the summer now, I did think about going to the seaside tomorrow, but the money situation is rather desperate at the moment.*

Desperate was the word. Despite working long hours and picking up the occasional magic job, at the end of September I had no savings and only £34 in the bank. The boys were growing up fast. Clothes and the ever-expensive trainers had to be bought (Jay was getting as fussy as Ben by now), football expenses, bills, food, days out, the car, all took their toll. Somehow, I managed to keep my head above water by being as frugal as I could. Jay's Christmas presents were ordered on the Kays Catalogue Hot Phone Line, and Ben's computer stuff from a company called Electric Boys which turned out to be a bit hairy, as rumour had it, they'd gone bust. The stuff arrived just in time. I had a few gigs over the Christmas period including two at the same venue, 'The Old Shanghai', a lovely Chinese restaurant in Olney. (I've been back there many times since.)

The end of the year was fast approaching, and November 10th would mark my first year of working for the Truss Department. It was still hard work but always interesting and the team of John, James, and Kevin, were great. The boys were doing well at school with no problems at all, and the magic club had a good second half of the year with lectures from Roy Johnson and Aldo Colombini.

On the rare occasions when I had a spare minute I still managed to work on John Ramsay or Albert Goshman inspired material, all put together using the philosophy of Dai Vernon. I was still enjoying the creative process.

Jay scored the winning goal in his final match of the season sending his team to the top of the division! Ben was improving all the time with his keyboard playing and continuing to compose some great stuff. Clare and Jeff were happy, both enjoying their beautiful little daughters. Their Dad, Paul, had married during the year and so had Babs. It had been an eventful year for all of us. All I could do was carry on as usual, work hard, take each day as it comes and do my best to provide for the boys.

CHAPTER 22

The teenage years

At the beginning of 1996 I had a welcome letter from Family Credit, but things were still difficult.

January 5th, 1996: *I heard from the Family Credit people today, I'm to get £10 a week which isn't bad at all. I had a sort out of the boys' old clothes and managed to sell some of them for a fiver in Bletchley.*

I managed to keep the food bills as low as I could by shopping at a new cut price supermarket a few miles away by the name of Netto. I'd get what I could there and the rest from Sainsbury's. The boys didn't mind, providing I didn't use the bright yellow carrier bags with the word, "Netto" emblazoned on them in large black letters. It seems there was some sort of stigma attached to the place and they didn't want their friends to know that we might be on the breadline! I didn't know whether to laugh or cry. At the time Ben was coming up to 15 and Jay had just turned 13. They got on well together most of the time, but they had their moments as you'd expect. Ben would always come along to support Jay's football matches and occasionally run the line as well. Because of their love for the game it made life easier when it came to present buying. I'd bought them a football game one Christmas which was similar to the classic old Subbuteo. It was a good game but, because it needed a flat surface on which to lay the green felt pitch, and the front room carpet was a touch lumpy, I made them a custom-built table to put in the front room. It had drawers fitted at both ends to house the players, goalposts, and other bits and pieces and it worked well. When not in use as their stadium it would double up as a coffee table and was made to match the existing furniture, so job done. I also made some stands to go along the sides and as an extra feature there were floodlights too. Whenever they had a 'Tournament', I wasn't allowed in, and quite a few times I was relegated to the bedroom to do the ironing. The only sound to come out of the room was Jay's commentary, with his team always being Manchester United of course.

They were growing too fast. Not my little boys anymore. They even told me they were too old to have a 'luvvie'. Gone were the days when I'd suddenly announce, "Who wants a luvvie?!" and I'd chase them all over the house and they'd be squealing in the vain attempt to escape the inevitable hugs that would ensue when I caught them. When they were really young and in their beds, I'd pretend to be a monster walking slowly and noisily up the stairs breathing loudly as I entered their bedroom, where I discover them curled up in a small ball trying to hide in their beds. I'd thump the bed all around them, and then they'd reveal themselves laughing, relieved to discover it was their old Dad and not a monster after all. I really missed the lack of hands-on affection. I needed it as much as they now didn't. Age is no barrier to love. They would always be my little boys.

There wasn't too much work about at the beginning of the year, but I did have a couple of gigs and a bit of private work (which helped to keep the wolf from the door). I made some boxes for a chap at work to house some of his record collection which earned me a tenner, and both magic jobs were at the same venue, a rather nice upmarket pub/restaurant in Bedfordshire, called 'The Knife & Cleaver'. The first one was on a Friday night at the end of January (as if Fridays weren't busy enough).

January 26th, 1996: *I managed to keep busy at work making a pair of fancy gallows brackets. After a hurried meal I managed to get Jay sorted out with his video and get Ben down to Rollers and get to The Knife & Cleaver for the gig. I was half an hour late though, but it went really well, and I got a booking for Valentine's Day. I picked Ben up from Jean's on the way home.*

The other gig on the 14th was a very busy night with 31 couples booked in. I much prefer it to be busy and the evening flew by and went very well. Luckily, I now had a bit of spare cash to spend on Ben's birthday on the 18th. The three of us went up to 'The Point' to see 'Jumanji' with Robin Williams; we loved it! A week later I had a night out myself. I'd bought a ticket at 'The Stables' to see The Australian Pink Floyd show. I always felt guilty about spending money on myself. What if one of the boys needed new trainers or something unexpected happened or even if I got made redundant? To be honest I needed a night out. I talked myself into it... it would do me good, I deserved it, once in a while wouldn't do any harm. Feelings of guilt or regret however soon faded. I took my seat to the sound of a heart beating from the stage as the lights dimmed. Soon the beautiful and haunting opening sequence of, 'Shine on you crazy diamond', filled the auditorium (and my heart) once again.

My diary also covered world events as well as my own life. Occasionally something would happen that would eclipse everything.

March 13ᵗʰ, 1996: *A man called Thomas Hamilton walked into a primary school in Dunblane Scotland and shot and killed 16 five- and six-year-old children, he then shot himself. The whole country has been numbed by it all, and all other news pales into total insignificance.*

March 17ᵗʰ, 1996: *There was a national minute of silence at 9.30 this morning. I stopped for a moment in front of the service on tv. Just then Ben started playing his keyboard, and Jay was having a tantrum on the computer, both of which cut through the silence. It seemed to make that minute all the more poignant. I felt incredibly sorry for the bereaved parents, and at the same time thankful, grateful, and very lucky for all that I had.*

In the spring of 1996 I attended my first meeting in my new role as a school governor. I was asked to do it by a chap I knew who had recently stepped down. (I did the magic at his wedding - just saying.) I was made to feel welcome at the meeting and I'm sure Paul, the headteacher, was pleased to see me. I felt out of my depth to begin with and didn't feel qualified to contribute a lot, and to be honest I found a lot of it boring. In time though I did sort out quotes for building work and I also offered to do odd carpentry jobs myself. I contributed what I was capable of. At the end of 1996 the school had an Ofsted Inspection which resulted in the school being put into special measures. At the time Paul's health wasn't too good and sadly one of the Special Needs pupils had suddenly died. It was an emotional time for everybody at the school; it was just one thing after another. The Ofsted Report was a total surprise to all of us; as far as we were concerned it was a well led and thriving school. A meeting with the inspector was arranged which didn't go well as she wasn't prepared to listen to anybody from the floor. The word I used in my diary was *"intransigent"*. I was really annoyed as I'd seen for myself how hard Paul and his staff had worked, and more to the point how good and dedicated they all were. I wrote a letter to the then head of Ofsted, Chris Woodhead, and told him exactly what I thought of the whole process. I ran it past the other governors before I sent it off, most of whom approved although one or two didn't (which I found surprising). I had a reply, and the word intransigent sprang to mind once again. I did what I could. As far as I was concerned, based on the fact that all four of our children loved it there and did well, the report was a travesty. It made me wonder why parents don't have any input or aren't consulted in some way when school inspections take place, rather than take all credence from what is no more than just a spot check. Oh well, what do I know? I went on to complete my five-year stint and it certainly gave me an insight into the often stressful and frustrating profession of teaching and education - and parenting. Speaking of which it was coming up to decision time for Ben. When I went to see his teachers in the middle of October, he had no idea what he wanted to do. Two weeks later he was given an option.

October 29th, 1996: *Ben saw the careers officer at school today and was given a written sheet of information which was discussed and also an action plan. It was quite impressive I thought. It had an instruction for Ben to phone Bedford College where there is a full-time course on sound engineering. When I spoke to Ben about it, he virtually dismissed the whole thing and insisted, "I'm not going to any college!"*

Argh, teenagers! Here we go again; that wasn't quite the end of it though. A week later he did in fact phone the college to get more details, the reason being one of his pals was thinking of doing the same course. I went along to another parents evening in November and spoke to several of his teachers. The general consensus was that he's quite bright and could do much better than he is - a memorable quote from one of them being, "He's so laid back, he's horizontal." I spoke to the careers officer who was very helpful, but he did make the point of how competitive the music business is and not that easy to get into. Ben really needs higher grades to stand any chance. It was a worry. He filled in the application form for Bedford College and sent it off. At least that was a start.

Jay was doing well at school with no problems at all. He was also having some success with his football. In March he played for his school team, scored two goals, and was voted man of the match. Later on in the season he played in a great cup final with the final score at 7-7. Rather than have a penalty shoot out to decide an overall winner, both teams agreed to have the cup for 6 months each. It was a great evening and both sides played really well. Yet more silverware for Jay.

June 14th, 1996: *It was Jay's football presentation evening tonight at Wilton Hall. I felt a bit sorry for him as he was the only lad without a shirt and tie. He was ok though once he'd picked up his trophy.*

As is typical with the building trade regarding workload you either have too much or not enough. Throughout the summer of 1996 I was working 7 days a week on a regular basis. I grabbed whatever was going as by the end of the year due to the unpredictability of it all there might well be nothing. The work continued to be interesting with a lot of one-off projects as well as the run of the mill stuff such as dormer sections, shaped barge boards, and a huge variety and all sizes of gallows brackets. Although I was permanently knackered it was nice to have money in my pocket, albeit not for long.

August 30ᵗʰ, 1996: *Me and Jay went to the Centre this morning to buy him some new clothes; T-shirts, tops, etc. For the first time I quite enjoyed the experience. Ben didn't want to come which is fair enough for a 15-year-old. Instead I drew out £70 from the Building Society and let him get on with it and buy his own. He did better than I thought, and I did get a fiver in change.*

We had another visit to Manchester during the summer and this time saw a match at Old Trafford. It was a reserves game but enjoyable none the less as there were a couple of first team players involved, including Andy Cole, which pleased the boys. It was reasonably priced too at about a fiver each for all three of us. We also had a little holiday that summer - a week away in a basic caravan on the east coast. We had a nice time visiting various beaches up and down the coast. I spent a lot of time with Jay, Ben was happy to stay in and around the caravan playing computer games and watching the Olympics on tv, all fair enough, I wasn't about to get into an argument with a teenager. We did all go to the cinema together a couple of times to see "Twister" and "Mission Impossible," and a typical end of pier show at the Brittania Theatre in Great Yarmouth starring magical entertainer Joe Pasquale. It was packed and a really good show.

Gigs picked up throughout the year, including regular Saturdays at a local pub/restaurant, 'The ship Ashore', and at the wedding of local radio personality Steve Riches. I did yet another evening at the magic club which this time was in the form of a Teach-In (more than likely the same old stuff!) Later in the year the club had a bit of a scoop when David Berglas came to lecture, mostly on sleeving as I remember - another good night.

In the summer of 1996 I had a call from a magician friend of mine Mark Leveridge. He asked me if I was available to perform on the opening gala show at the 5th British Close-Up Magic Symposium which was taking place in Bath the following year. Of course I was up for that, it was like a mini convention and a chance to catch up with pals I hadn't seen for a while. The deal was for me to do a 15-minute spot (which was a long time for me) and also write an article for inclusion in the symposium souvenir book. Luckily for this Mark had given me and the other performers a wide range of ideas. It could be an original close-up effect, or a discussion article related to close-up in general. The length and subject matter were entirely up to us. He went on to say that he was particularly keen on non-card items, which wasn't a problem as I did very little with cards anyway. After a bit of thought I decided to write an article called 'Influences'. It was dedicated to Bobby Bernard, Ken Brooke, Mick Chardo, Albert Goshman, Sam Hawes, John Ramsay, Tony Slydini and Dai Vernon. Much of it you'll find within the pages of this book. Happily it was written, delivered, and accepted on time. Regarding the act, I can't honestly remember much of what I did. I do know, however, there were a lot of 'in' gags and bits of business, and I do remember the opening. I was introduced by Chris Payne (who happens to be a doctor). He came to the front and said:

"Our next performer is Ken Hawes who is a past winner of both The Magic Circle and IBM close-up competitions. What I like about Ken is you never know what you're going to get."

"You can say that again!" – Yes, I heckled my own introduction.

"Ladies and gentlemen, please welcome Ken Hawes!"

There was a nice round of applause and I said,

"Thank you, Chris, for that lovely introduction - I think."

I looked at Chris and then looked at the audience and said,

"What a great name for a doctor – Pain!"

It went well and everybody was happy. It was a good day out in the lovely surroundings of Bath University.

I did another interesting job in September with Mick Hanzlik and John Shaw from the magic club. It took place on a boat on the Thames in London. It was a corporate event and also featured a live band and a really good girl singer. The conditions were rather cramped, and we did what we could and made the best of it. After an hour of wandering the decks doing the mix and mingle stuff, we had a break and went to see the singer in the enclosed bar area. This was in the days before the smoking ban, and I said to Mick what a shame it was for a singer to have to perform in such a smoky atmosphere. An hour after that we returned for more and it was still smoky and there was no sign of the singer.

"I've just seen her," said John as he came to join us, "She's up on the top deck having a fag."

December saw me at The Landmark Hotel in London for a repeat booking with the Japanese bank. Yet again it wasn't all plain sailing. This time they insisted I have a meal along with the other entertainers at the same time as everybody else. The problem with that was I couldn't work as I normally do. I would have preferred to have been available to circulate around the tables and perform between courses. I do like to earn my money or more to the point, I like to be seen to be earning my money which was a substantial fee. I skipped the last course and managed to do a few tables as the coffee was served. At that point an announcement was made.

"Mr. Yakamoto will now entertain us."

There was a smattering of applause and one or to groans as the familiar middle-aged gentleman walked on to the dance floor clutching a music stand and an acoustic guitar. He bowed and smiled, sat down, and began to sing a selection of Beatles songs while strumming his guitar and peering myopically at the music stand. There was a polite round of applause between each song and a half-hearted attempt from some of the guests at joining in. It was all very pleasant, but he went on, and on, and on. By this time there was a steady trickle of people leaving the dining room and making their way to the bar, and still he played. He did get the message in the end though as a substantial number of guests began to wave white napkins as a form of surrender. The upshot of all that was, because the timing was now all to cock, there was no time left for me to perform. I don't think I earned my fee that night due to no fault of my own. Anyway, they paid it.

Life was as hectic as ever. We went over to see Clare to celebrate Opal's second birthday in September, and for Jay's thirteenth in December I took him and a group of friends ten pin bowling. Both boys were often a source of amusement.

November 3rd, 1996: *Jay played football this morning and won quite convincingly at 6-2. The team played well and John the manager seemed happy enough. Me and Jay went to the Centre this afternoon to buy him some swimming shorts and "something for pudding"; I had in mind a couple of cakes, but it turned out to be a 2-litre pack of toffee ice cream. It was the firework do at Campbell Park tonight but me and Ben decided not to go (although he did lean out of the bathroom window with a pair of binoculars). Jay went up with Sean and family.*

Just before Christmas we visited Clare and Tony to do the usual present swap, and thanks to Tony we came home with an amplifier, mixer, and tape deck. This would be the first step for Ben into the world of recording and backing tracks. At the age of 15 he certainly had an early start and with his youthful enthusiasm came a dedication that knew no bounds.

We had a lovely Christmas shared with Mum. I was able to buy a new TV and a Play Station for the boys, thanks to the gig money. Needless to say, me and Mum watched TV and the boys didn't. 1996 came to its inevitable end and I wondered what 1997 would bring. Hopefully Jay would continue to do well at school and football, but somehow I knew it wouldn't be plain sailing for Ben. He didn't really know what he wanted to do apart from something to do with music. I continued to encourage him with my first shed job of the year, building units to house the new equipment. I decided to give our smallest bedroom over to Ben and call it 'The Music Room'. It took a while to sort out (to Ben's specifications) and when it was finished, we were all happy. The equipment had to be paid for and luckily, I had a couple of gigs which helped. Yet again magic was coming to the rescue. The first one at the end of January was a return visit to 'The Knife and Cleaver'. This time it was advertised as an evening of magic. Again it was a well-supported, good night. Because it was such a lovely and well-run venue, I'm pretty sure the regular clientele (which was considerable) would have supported anything there. The next one in early February was lovely. It was for my childhood friend, Alan Fraser. He'd moved to a delightful village in the Cotswolds called Charlbury. The evening was billed as a comedy night and took place in the Charlbury Corner House which was a beautiful old stone building in the centre, and at the heart of the community. I love this sort of job, local people getting together for a bit of fun and bringing their own refreshments and tea and coffee provided by the Women's Institute. It was such a great night with music as well as comedy (with me working the tables during the interval). It took me a couple of hours to drive the 50 miles there and I got about 30 quid. It was one of those nights when none of that mattered. As much as I enjoyed working in posh hotels and stately homes, nothing compared with the joy of being a part of the entertainment in a quintessentially English village hall.

A few days before the visit to Charlbury I had another night out. This time I felt no guilt. I'd have begged, borrowed, or stolen money to visit 'The Stables' on that particular night. It was to see my all-time guitar hero Peter Green. I'd been a huge fan since his time with John Mayall in the 60s and the very early days of Fleetwood Mac. He was one of the few musicians who had the ability to give me goosebumps and bring a tear to my eye, just by playing a few notes. His feel for playing and the emotion he was able to generate was legendary. On top of all of that was his remarkable voice and talent as a song writer. Sadly his mental health wasn't good and everybody in the audience that night was well aware of his history over the past 20 years or so. Although he was a shadow of his former self it was still a good night, and I wouldn't have missed it for the world.

At this time young Anthony Owen was doing really well. He had formed his own company called Dynamic FX with three of his pals and was still involved with the Magic Circle. He came up with a really good idea to involve members who lived outside the London area and also to raise much needed cash for the Magic Circle coffers. As well as continuing with the 'Country Members

Day', why not have 'Magic Circle Regional Days'? His idea was to have a day of magic in various parts of the country organised by The Circle which would include lectures and shows etc. The first one was in Wolverhampton, the second in Newcastle, and the third was to take place in Northampton. Anthony asked me if I'd like to take part in the close-up show. I was up for that - it was a Sunday afternoon and I had nothing else on. I rehearsed all morning and decided to try something a bit different. I've never been all that comfortable performing for magicians, much preferring to entertain the public with my tried and tested stuff that makes them laugh. Anyway, whatever I did that day died a terrible death. According to my diary, *"As soon as I got there, I knew it wouldn't work and it didn't."*

It isn't a pleasant feeling to die in front of an audience, especially when it's made up of your peers. It goes with the territory though, it happens, don't worry, learn from it, and onto the next. I had a chat with Anthony afterwards and he wasn't too bothered, and I did get a nice thank you letter from him (which I still have). It ends with:

"The day was a big success with over 170 magicians attending and over £400 being raised for The Magic Circle Appeal.

Thanks again. *Your support and participation were appreciated.*

Best wishes,

Anthony."

His italics - whatever help and guidance I was able to give Anthony when he was a young lad was reciprocated several times over during the ensuing years.

Later in the summer I took part in a one-day convention in Milton Keynes organised by another local magician, Gary Young. This was the first of quite a few that Gary organised over the years. For this I didn't have to perform as such but took part in a question-and-answer session in a close-up forum. There were several of us on the stage and we answered questions from the floor. I thought it was a great idea and certainly the first time I'd seen anything like it. It went really well, with sensible questions - how to approach a table, the length of time spent on each one, appearance (should you wear a dinner suit?). Each of us on the panel had various ideas and it was good fun as well as being well-received. A week after that I was off again. This time to the seaside to do a lecture for a club based in Frinton-on-Sea near Clacton. The club was called 'The Magic Triangle' and the secretary was Alan Norman, a former member of our club. It took place on a Sunday evening, so I had all day to prepare. (Not quite all day as the first Ashes Test match was on tv.) I picked Mum up, who was staying the night, even though the boys would have been ok on their own, she wanted to come anyway - any excuse to see them. I set off at about three-thirty and got to Alan's house in Clacton at about six o'clock just in time to watch the end of the cricket which England won! I knew Alan would be watching as he played both football and cricket for the county as a young man. After a bite to eat, Alan drove us the short distance up the coast to a community centre at Frinton, picking up a couple of others on the way. The lecture went really well, and I had a great time. Usually at lectures I do the stuff, answer questions, and sell the notes and videos at the end and then head off home. On this particular night it was going so well that it was agreed we'd carry on somewhere else after we'd been chucked out of the community centre. Luckily, one of the members owned a holiday club in Clacton and that's where we ended up until almost midnight, doing tricks and having a laugh. What a friendly bunch they were. The journey home wasn't without incident, however; I somehow mistook the M1 for the A1 and ended up in Stevenage, arriving home at 2.00 o'clock the following morning. It wasn't an unusual occurrence for me - my lack of a sense of direction is legendary. This was of course in the days before SatNavs. I navigated everywhere in those days with maps and written instructions sent by club secretaries. I have kept many of them for both lectures and gigs and they do make amusing reading. I call them my 'hysterical documents'.

I didn't get too may gigs in the summer, apart from weddings and family events, though I did have quite an unusual job in the July of 1997 at the Villiers Hotel in Buckingham. I arrived on time not really knowing what to expect. The contract was fairly non-committal - "After dinner entertainment from approximately 9.00 pm in the Tack Room." I was shown into a small room where there was one table with eight people sat around it. I soon discovered that they were to be my only audience for the evening. I didn't have a problem with that, in fact the conditions were pretty much perfect. I had a minute or two to prepare as the table was being cleared. As soon as that had been done, I approached the table and introduced myself and opened with the bottle of wine production which got me off to a good start. It was an enjoyable evening, and I did about an hour. In this situation where there was no pressure, I was able to relax and work at my own pace. It never ceases to amaze me how interested people are in how I got into magic in the first place. During that hour I virtually told them my life story. They asked me if I'd ever entertained anybody famous, so I related the Sting story. I told them that the set up with him was as it was here, with me performing at the end of the table a trick at a time. I went on to say that I could tell how well it was going by the look on his face, puzzled if he couldn't figure it out, and a pleased look if he thought he had - "Rather like you lot," I added. That made them smile. I pondered the gig on the way home feeling quite chuffed. I'd had a whale of a time, as had the audience. They had watched tricks with coins, cards, thimbles, sponge balls, banknotes, handkerchiefs, postcards, and cups and balls, and heard the story of my life. A veritable variety show. I didn't care if they figured out how the tricks were done, or if they'd been impressed that I'd entertained a celebrity. The relationship I had with them yet again was more important than anything. Loved it.

Another fun thing I did that year was going along to BBC Radio Northampton. The presenter was John Shaw who was also a magician and a member of the club. It wasn't an interview as such, it was more like two pals chewing the fat and having a laugh. It was really enjoyable. I tried to keep it fairly light, and we chatted about some of the strange and funny things that had happened during my years of performing. It was a much-needed relaxing afternoon. A few weeks later I did yet another evening at the magic club, this was to be a coin magic workshop with me teaching basic coin moves and sleights, including a handling of the Okito Coin Box. According to my diary, "It went ok although it was hot in the room." Yes, banality was still creeping in. While I was playing with my coins and chatting on the radio, Ben was in the middle of his GCSE Exams.

June 11th, 1997: *Ben seems to be coping ok with his exams, but I've yet to see him do any revision.*

The truth was he'd had enough of school and couldn't wait to leave. He told me that once he'd left, he'd get himself a part-time job until his college course began in September (assuming that would actually happen). He'd already made a few enquiries in some of the shops at the City Centre but with no luck. I thought the fact that he was actively looking was encouraging – but as it happened to no avail.

Both boys had a good summer after taking their exams. They had a nice week away with Babs on the east coast, and then Jay spent another week away with one of his friends at Centre Parcs near Nottingham. Meanwhile Ben had a letter from Bedford College offering him an interview for a BTEC course in Popular music. (He'd abandoned the idea of Sound Engineering.) The day of the interview arrived and off we went to Bedford on a Tuesday afternoon in August. We were shown into a music room and introduced to a young chap who was to conduct the interview. There was a piano and a couple of chairs and also a guitar on a stand. I thought it best to keep my distance and let them get on with it. I couldn't help thinking to myself what would have happened if I were in a similar position to Ben with me applying for a place in a school for magic with my Dad sitting where I was now. He'd have said to me, "Show him that coin trick you showed me last night boy." Then he'd turn to the interviewer and say, "You watch this, I've never seen anything like it!" Despite me wanting to say something similar about a beautiful and haunting tune Ben had come up with recently, I stayed silent. Ben was asked general questions about his taste in music and how he thought he'd got on with his exams (at which he shrugged). Typical. Next, he was asked to sit at the piano. The tutor picked up the guitar and said to Ben, "I want you to play a 12-bar blues in the key of E."

I thought, oh God, he can't do that. My head was in my hands. Then I heard Ben begin to play a perfect 12-bar blues with the tutor strumming along with a big smile on his face. I sat there gobsmacked.

"Now I'd like you to improvise a solo when I give you the nod."

When the nod came, Ben played a great improvised solo. I didn't know he could do stuff like that - all down to hours of practise. I could feel myself getting emotional. That's my boy! He was offered a place.

The summer continued with me trying to juggle long hours at work with all the other stuff I had to do at home, cooking, washing, ironing, shopping, and housework. Sometimes I'd get a bit annoyed when the boys hadn't seen the notes I'd left. It was the height of frustration to come home on what had been a sunny day to see the washing machine still full of washing, despite the note (which was in plain view) asking for it to be put on the line. Even when they read the note, they still didn't get it. There were times when the washing was on the line soaking wet because of rain. When I asked why it hadn't been bought in it was because it wasn't on the note!

"The note only says put the washing on the line."

It seemed to me the one thing not taught at school was common sense. Thankfully it didn't happen too often as the one thing that irritated the boys more than anything was, "Dad's in a mood." As time went on things did get better.

Ben spent much of his time in the Music Room with a few of his pals, and Jay was always out playing football somewhere. He was voted "Clubman of the Year" at the annual presentation evening with yet more silverware to put on the shelf. Throughout August Jay had been asking if he could have two of his friends over for a sleep-over. I'd been putting it off as I had to get up at five o'clock to go to work and I really needed my sleep. I had to relent in the end though as he'd spent the night at Billy's or Sean's on several occasions. This would be the first time all three of them would be together overnight. Surely it wouldn't be that bad, my diary says otherwise.

The following day was a long one.

August 20th, 1997. *What a night! I don't think I had any sleep at all. The boys certainly didn't. At one point I looked out of my window and all three of them were having a sack race with their sleeping bags up and down the drive! I just about got up in time to get to work for six o'clock, by which time they were asleep sprawled all over the bedroom floor.*

There was a lot of tearing about as well after work, to get Sainsbury's done, have a meal, and then get to Maggs' house for a lift to Aldbury with Ken and Mum for cousin Val's wedding. It was a really good do in a beautiful venue. Quite a few of my relatives asked me if I'd got another woman yet which I found rather tedious.

The family meant well but I found the word "yet" slightly irritating as if it would be a forgone conclusion that I would (and indeed should) get involved with another woman. When I told them I hadn't, they thought it was a great shame. There had been a brief infatuation for a month or two (from a distance) for a while, but it didn't come to anything. In all honesty my life was full, there was no room for anybody or anything else. The boys were growing fast and into their teens which was obviously an important time in their lives. They were more important than any relationship I may or may not have. They were more important than anything.

Things were on the move with Ben's forthcoming college course. I'd sent the cheque off for his travel to and from Bedford for his first term, (£96) and sorted his bus pass out. Next came results day.

August 21ˢᵗ, 1997: *Ben did quite well in his GCSE exams. He got one C, a few D's, and a couple of F's. I said I'd pay for the mixer from Tony as a present.*

The payment for the mixer was something Ben was going to sort out from the summer job he didn't have. Oh well, thanks to all the overtime I was doing, it wasn't really a problem and there was also some satisfaction and relief on settling a family debt. Another treat for all of us was another visit to Old Trafford and The Cliff training ground for yet more photographs and autographs. I do have to give credit to the players and staff of Manchester United, who stayed on the site happily signing and posing for as long as there were fans there - Alex Ferguson, David Beckham, Paul Scholes, Ryan Giggs, Eric Cantona, and many more. It was a great end to the summer holidays. We began that day at six o'clock in the morning and got home at five in the evening, and after dinner I did some wall papering! Heaven knows where I got the energy.

August ended on a sad note with the death of Princess Diana. It seems strange looking back now at how many of us were affected in such an emotional way. I spent all day in front of the tv on September 6ᵗʰ watching coverage of the funeral.

Clare phoned in the middle of it a bit tearful. It was the card on top of the coffin that did it for her (and millions of others too I suspect). The one from William and Harry, "for Mummy."

A week later, on the 13ᵗʰ I had a night out in London which did me the world of good. I went to the Shepherds Bush Empire, got drunk, and saw the Man Band. A combination of good ale and great music was just what I needed. A great night.

Life went on. Jay's first match of the season. Despite being level at 2-2 at half time, they went on to lose 12-2! Not a good start. Perhaps the next game would show some improvement - sadly that wasn't the case.

September 14th, 1997: *I spent the morning preparing the roast and setting up the timer on the cooker before we went over to St. Neots to watch Jay play in the 'Easy Cup'. They lost 8-1 but still played quite well - a definite improvement on last week. We had a nice buffet lunch afterwards which was nice, in fact it was a really pleasant afternoon.*

The food obviously better than the match it seems. At home, we had a regular Sunday roast, which I'd forgotten about. It was always chicken, roast potatoes, roast parsnips, and Yorkshire pudding, with added veg for me. We did eat well. I didn't have time to be too fussy with the boys, I gave them whatever they wanted because it was easier - I knew they'd eat whatever I put in front of them and there would be little waste. Some of it wasn't particularly healthy, but they were both fairly fit and certainly not overweight. Jay had his football, and Ben cycled a lot, so any excess fat was soon burnt off. Ben of course wouldn't be cycling to school anymore; he'd be going to college on the bus. His first day was September 16th and I spent all day being really nervous for him with all sorts of unanswered questions. Would he make friends? Could he cope with the work? And more realistically would he get there and back ok?

Day one went ok; day two didn't.

September 17ᵗʰ, 1997: *Poor Ben, I felt really sorry for him today. He should have been home by six o'clock at the latest but didn't arrive until 7.30. He got on the wrong bus and ended up in Cambridge. He'd had nothing to eat all day and he had one of his nasty migraines as well. On top of all that he's been given 7 assignments to complete in as many weeks, He's just totally worn out.*

I could understand him getting on the wrong bus (I've almost done it myself from Bedford). The service is the X5 which runs between Oxford and Cambridge and the bus stops for either direction are next to each other. Ben saw X5 on the bus and assumed it was going in the direction of Milton Keynes and then onto Oxford. It is confusing if the "wrong" bus arrives at the same time as the "right" one. He made sure the next day he got on the bus marked Oxford. By the end of the week he'd settled in and was happy to talk about his day and his college chums; he was even talking about a lift in every day with one of them from Bletchley. (Obviously unconcerned about the 96 quid I'd laid out for his bus fare.) As long as he was settled and happy it was ok by me. Over that weekend I bought him manuscript paper from Chappells music shop for one of his assignments and he got stuck in. So far so good.

We'd been invited to the wedding of my young nephew, Russ, on September 27ᵗʰ. This time I made sure the boys looked smart. I bought an outfit for Jay and gave Ben (yet more) money to buy something for himself. They both looked "well smart." Two days before the big day I was invited along to a local pub for the stag night. I wasn't sure how it would pan out as Russ wasn't really what you'd call a hardened drinker and his Dad, Ken, certainly wasn't. There were friends and family there all gathered around a couple of tables chatting away and having a laugh with a bit of banter as you'd expect at a do like that. After about an hour we had a visit from a lady from the Salvation Army. She wore the familiar uniform and was holding a collection tin and a bundle of Christian newspapers. This was quite a regular occurrence in the pubs in the Bletchley area back in the 70s, but not as common in the 90s. I didn't take too much notice, I'd had a few by then anyway but as I had a lot of respect for the 'Sally Army', I was more than happy to put a couple of quid into her tin. As I dropped the money in, I couldn't help noticing that underneath her bonnet she was quite attractive, and behind the copies of the 'War Cry' there was an ample chest. (I'm a bloke, I notice these things.) Suddenly she threw off her bonnet, tossed the tin and papers aside and made a beeline towards Russ, draping herself all over him and taking her clothes off! A strippergram - none of us was really up for it, particularly Russ, and it just didn't work.

September 25th, 1997: *I went to The Pickled Newt tonight to have a drink with Russ and a few of his pals before the big day on Saturday. The Salvation Army Strippergram fell rather flat, but it was a pleasant enough hour or so. Ken gave me a bowl of beetroot which will make a nice change.*

It was a lovely family wedding. The Service I remember particularly for the choice of hymns - one of them being "Fight the good fight". The reception was really nice which was held at Bletchley Park with lovely food, good speeches, and a disco in the evening. While that was going on I did the magic in a quiet area (showing my age). Russ and Karen have obviously fought the good fight and are still together after almost 25 years.

I was still doing the odd lecture here and there and on October 1st, I went to Luton to 'The Mystic Ring'. I can't help noticing the huge variety of names for magic clubs. I think it's great how the forefathers of some of these societies came up with something other than magic club. Although my own club, The Northamptonshire Magicians Club, doesn't have a memorable name, it did have an unusual emblem when the club was formed almost a hundred years ago - a green hand with lightening emerging from the fingertips. It has been changed now though, to keep up with the times and is now the Ace of clubs rising from an ornate card box with "est. 1926" underneath, and it looks great.

So much for "so far so good" with Ben at college. After only three weeks he came home and announced he was leaving. I couldn't get a lot of sense out of him, and he was adamant he'd had enough. He told me he wanted a job but didn't know or care what it was. (Ye gods, teenagers!) We went over to see Clare and Tony at the weekend and although they tried to talk to him and give him some encouragement to carry on at least until Christmas, it was to no avail. I decided to phone the college.

October 13th, 1997: *I phoned the college today and spoke to the welfare lady who is going to have a word with him and also his tutor. He was supposed to call me back tonight but didn't. He was also supposed to meet up with Ben this afternoon but didn't turn up! Maybe Ben is better off out of it. It's a bit of a worry.*

I never did get to the real reason why Ben left. He'd obviously inherited the Hawes family trait of stubbornness. Once he'd made his mind up to do (or not do) something that was it and there was no shifting him. I suppose it was no different to me leaving

Wolverton Works all those years ago when I'd had enough and knew it was time to move on. Although in Ben's case, after only three weeks, he'd hardly given it a fair crack of the whip. For Ben it was probably a combination of a lot of things. At the heart of it I suspect was his desire to work things out for himself. There's nothing wrong with being a self-taught musician or a self-taught anything particularly if you have a natural talent for it which he undoubtedly had. He was true to his word about job hunting and went along to the Youth Employment office for an interview and form filling and later in December a similar scenario at the Manpower Forum. Meanwhile he spent his days making music and recording and in the evenings the house would be full of his pals writing rap and performing to Ben's backing tracks. Although I was concerned he wasn't working in the traditional sense (yet), I was happy and relieved that he wasn't wasting his time. Had he spent all day moping and playing computer games that would have been different. Anyway he was only 16 with his whole life in front of him. Something would come up. Wouldn't it?

I had a change of scenery myself for a couple of weeks in November - Aylesbury Crown Court. I was on jury duty. I turned up on the first day not knowing what to expect and found the whole process fascinating. Everything was explained to us via a short video film before we were led into the courtroom. The first case involved a group of seven lads who were accused of violent disorder outside a night club. Nobody was actually hurt, although weapons were found on the site. Each lad had his own Brief and for four days we listened to police statements and then from all seven defendants. It was often dreary and repetitive and ultimately a waste of time as the judge threw the case out. While I was there, I realised I knew one of the ushers. She was the daughter of the lady who played the piano for our little concert party back in the sixties. It was nice to have a chat before the next case, which turned out to be more interesting than the previous one. It involved a group of yobs who'd beaten up the manager of a local store and then robbed it. Halfway through the case, the usher approached the bench to have a quiet word with the judge. He looked at the jury and said,

"I understand there is a Mr. Hawes serving as a juror today."

All twelve of us looked each other (along with everybody else in the courtroom) I stood up and said,

"Yes sir," feeling as if I was about to be sentenced.

"Please sit down Mr Hawes, there's nothing to worry about, but I do need to ask you if you are related to the victim of this crime who shares the same surname as yourself."

I looked quizzically at the man across the courtroom, who looked back at me in much the same way.

"No sir," I said with some relief.

"Proceed," said the judge to the Brief.

The case came to an end and we the jury retired to consider our verdict. It took about an hour and, as the video and photographic evidence was fairly conclusive, we found the defendants guilty. We trooped back into the courtroom and once the verdict had been announced the judge gave the defendants a real bollocking (there is no other word, a severe reprimand really doesn't cut it). His final words were,

"Take them down!" And with that he banged his gavel on the bench. And so ended a fascinating and (sometimes embarrassing) two weeks.

On one Sunday in November, Jay played football on the old Bletchley Town pitch in Fenny Stratford. While I was there,

I glanced over the allotment boundary fence and remembered how I would look over that same fence from my Dad's plot to watch the games. I was suddenly filled with nostalgia as I caught a whiff of a bonfire. Happy childhood memories came flooding back. On the way home we drove up the slope of the canal bridge, the same slope where me and Dad pushed sack loads of potatoes on an old bike all those years ago. We drove past my childhood home in Oakwood Drive, and I pointed it out to the boys.

"That's where I spent some of the happiest days of my life."

The following week Jay played his match on his home ground, and although they lost 3-1, they played well and did their best. You can't ask any more of the players than that and Jay was awarded Man of the Match. Babs was there to watch too. We were a very proud Mum and Dad.

It soon rolled round to Christmas, and I was very busy with the magic. I did a wedding in Northampton which was a lovely family affair with only 36 guests. That one gave me a lot of job satisfaction. As did the next one which was in a rather exclusive part of Northamptonshire. In those days, before the internet, mobile phones, and Satellite Navigation, much of the information was written on the agent's contract. This job came from 'Allsorts Entertainments' which was managed by Meg and Roy Gilbert. They were of the view that you can never have too much information written on a contract, which I agreed with. We were also like minded when it came to instructions of how to get to the venue. You can't beat landmarks (particularly pubs). This is what was written on the contract...

"Drive through the village from Northampton. Go past The George, past The Red Lion on the right, carry on round the bend and through an opening in a stone wall opposite The Coach and

Horses. The house is through there with a large marquee in the front. The client says that the area could get clogged up with cars so it might be advisable for you to park where you can get out easily when you've finished. The party is for their son Matthew, aged 21 on the day. He's a rugby player."

Most of the contracts from Allsorts were like that with loads of useful information.

A couple of days later I did a job in Oxford at the Randolph Hotel, another beautiful venue and one of Oxford's finest. This was via another agent who wasn't keen on any extra information on the contract apart from the basics which were the name of the client, the venue, time of performance and the fee. I was a bit concerned about parking so I phoned the hotel to find out if they had a car park and would it be available on the night. Luckily, they had, and it was to the right of the building, and I could drive straight in. That was a relief. The job was a Christmas party for a local company called Parchment Printers. What a lovely name. I assumed they were a specialist company that printed legal documents and the like. I imagined the owners to look like characters from a Dickens novel, elderly and white haired with a quill pen perched behind their ears - no doubt I'd find out more when I got there. I set off for Oxford in plenty of time and soon spotted The Randolph and the car park only to find it closed with a "car park full" sign displayed at the entrance (so much for being able to drive straight in). I drove round the block in search of a space, all to no avail, and ended up back where I started by the main entrance. I double parked and went inside the hotel to tell the client I was there and to find out where I could park. I was approached by a friendly looking middle-aged lady who said, "Are you alright love, you look a bit flustered."

I explained the dilemma I was in, and she said, "Come with me."

I followed her through to the front door and on to the street and she pointed down the road.

"Follow the road round to the left, get into the right-hand lane, and take the first right and there's a car park there. If that one's full keep going and there's another one on the left. Make sure you get into the right-hand lane otherwise you'll end up back here."

"I know," I said.

"You'll be ok," she said, "See you later."

I followed her instructions with no trouble at all and hurried back to the hotel where I was greeted with a huge smile by the same lady.

"You found it ok then?"

"I did. Thanks very much. Do you work for the printing company?" I asked.

"You could say that" she replied, "I'm Mrs. Parchment. Let me buy you a drink you look as if you need one!"

That was a bit of a surprise and what a lovely lady. I followed her into the bar where she bought me a welcome pint. After a while the bar area slowly emptied as the people took their seats in the restaurant. As I finished my drink at the bar, I was joined by a tall smart looking man in a dinner suit. I couldn't help noticing the obvious. Underneath his shirt a set of Christmas lights were colourfully flashing. I looked at the lights and then at him and said,

"I love the lights, but can't help wondering where they're plugged in."

"They work from methane!" he said, without a moment's hesitation.

We had a laugh and a bit of a chat, finished our drinks, and walked into the restaurant.

"Do you work for this company then?" I asked.

"You could say that" he answered, "I'm Mr. Parchment!"

They couldn't have been more different to the image I had of them, but what lovely people, needless to say it was an enjoyable evening.

I had yet another visit to the Landmark Hotel in London for the Japanese bank. This time all went well with no problems for me or from Mr. Yakamoto.

I was also lucky to perform at two beautiful local venues. The first was a Christmas corporate party in the rather stunning Sculpture Gallery at Woburn Abbey, and the second was at the beautiful Stowe School in Buckingham. This one from The Stardust Agency managed by Roger Tear who gave me loads of work in the 80s and 90s. I found this job particularly interesting as at the time I was reading David Niven's auto biography, 'The Moon's a Balloon'. He had a great time there as a schoolboy and wrote about those days with a lot of affection. The gig was for the background staff, gardeners, cooks, cleaners, and housekeepers and the like and it all took place in the original old kitchen. There's something about the atmosphere of old musty rooms in old buildings that I find really appealing. There were old saucepans and frying pans hanging on hooks in descending order of size, overhanging large ancient porcelain sinks, and on the other side were old dark ovens and hot plates. A couple of huge well-scrubbed wooden kitchen tables dominated the working area. On one of them a lovely buffet had been prepared with an assortment of fresh food on display with a pile of plates stacked at the end (proper plates, not paper). The other table was laid for people to sit at, with an assortment of chutney, pickles, and condiments, covering the centre. I couldn't help wondering how many meals had been prepared in that kitchen during the past 100 years or so. I took all of this in as I performed around that same table. The magic went well, and the people were lovely, and as I pondered the gig on the way home, I felt lucky and privileged, another lovely evening.

The final gig of the year was for The Villiers Hotel and Buckingham Town Hall on New Year's Eve. The contract was signed and delivered in October and all it said was, "Ken Hawes, Close-Up Magician. 7.30—11.30 with breaks." A normal gig then. On Christmas Eve I had a call from the hotel and was told that it was anything but normal. They had decided to give the evening a James Bond theme and would I be prepared to be a "Q" type of character? I said I was up for it and would do my best to adapt my material to suit.

"Leave it with me," I said, through gritted teeth (a bit more notice would have been handy). It was all very well to keep the hotel management sweet, but I only had a week to come up with something I could use. However, it's surprising how the old creative juices come to the fore when you have a deadline to meet. I came up with a card trick where the four queens (ladies) all disappear and change into images of 007, and then he too vanishes into the night. I also adapted an old trick whereby a piece of wood and a stick of chalk turn into an improvised calculator. That would have to do, I'd do my usual stuff later in the evening. The big night soon arrived. The venue (which was beautiful) was decorated with posters of our hero all around the room and each of the table decorations had a 007 theme. The staff there had obviously worked hard and did a brilliant job. There was a large screen on the stage showing clips of various Bond films and the guests were dressed in dinner jackets and ball gowns to be in keeping with a typical Bond film event. It all looked great. The highlight of the evening, which was at the beginning, was the appearance of the man himself (who I assumed would be from a lookalike agency.) The lights were dimmed and as The James Bond Theme blared out from the speakers, 007 strode out and struck a pose at the front of the stage. I have to say he did look the part, dressed in a white dinner jacket and looking like a combination of all the Bond actors - even the gun he was holding looked real and authentic. He left the stage to a huge round of applause which was my cue to begin to work the tables (and there were a lot). The idea was to start before the first course was served. Normally the serving is done from front to back and the staff tend to work in a line across the width of the room, all I had to do was stay in front of that. I approached my first table of the evening hoping the people would play along, I spoke in a confidential voice.

"Good evening, I'm sure you will have heard of my colleague Q. Sadly he's unable to be here tonight as he's busy elsewhere." (At this point I look to my left and right and tap my nose.) "I'm sure you understand. However, M has sent me along instead. My name is E. You can call me Mister E."

The man at the table looked at me and said, "Ok Mister E, obviously we're disappointed that Q is unable to be here tonight, but we are prepared to give you a chance. I do have to say, however, that this (he paused) had better be good." He then reached into his inside pocket and laid a revolver on the table. I did the tricks trying not to laugh and got a really good reaction.

"Can I assume then that you won't be using that revolver?"

"Not on this occasion," he said, "However, the night is young, and we do like to keep you on your toes, my spies are everywhere," he added.

"I'll certainly bear that in mind," I said, as he put the revolver back in his pocket. I love it when people get as involved as that.

I worked the room for an hour or two and finally ended up at the table where 'James Bond' was sitting; surely he'd play along. I did the spiel, then the trick, and he looked at me and said in a voice not dissimilar to Julian Clary,

"I don't see how that will help me on my next mission!"

The image gone in a second. I found out afterwards that he wasn't booked from an agency after all, he was friend of a member of staff there. Oh well, to be fair he did a great job and made his contribution to what was a really good evening. From that night, New Year's Eve was a regular booking for me for about ten years.

CHAPTER 23

Clare

1998 would turn out to be a terrible year for all of us. Both boys were growing fast, as I discovered at the beginning of January. I'd bought Ben a pair of slippers for Christmas and had to change them to a size 11! He was job hunting by now and was determined to get work of some sort. At the end of the month what appeared to be a golden opportunity came up. We'd spotted an advert in the local paper regarding work in Chappells music shop in the City Centre. Training would be given for a period of six months for which he'd receive £60 a week and there could be a permanent job at the end of it. He went along for an interview and filled in various forms and also had a short aptitude test. This was done via an intermediary company called Link. A couple of weeks later Ben had a call from them and was told he was unsuitable. I don't know who was more upset me or Ben. I felt so sorry for him, how could somebody with his talent be unsuitable?! I then did what my Dad would have done. I phoned the lady at Link, but she wasn't at all forthcoming, so I went up to the shop to have a word. I spoke to the chief salesman James who was really nice and suggested I give the manager a call in the morning. When I spoke to him the next day, he was pleasant enough and told me that the company had decided to pull out of the Modern Apprenticeship scheme and would be employing more experienced staff. It appeared that the *system* was unsuitable rather than Ben. He did say he would send him another form for part-time work which was kind of him. A couple of weeks later with no sign of the form I went back to the shop for another chat with James. He gave me the form and I gave him one of Ben's tapes, I told him to make sure he listened to the second track. I was intrigued to find out if that beautiful and haunting piece of music had the same emotional effect on him as it did me. The following day we had some devastating news.

February 22nd, 1998: *Clare collapsed at home this morning and was rushed to Milton Keynes General Hospital where various tests were carried out, all of which turned out to be inconclusive. We went to see her tonight where she's in Intensive Care and on a breathing machine. She had an exploratory operation, but no information was gleaned from that. More should be known when she regains consciousness. We were told that there is a danger of brain damage. It's just a waiting game at the moment.*

The following two weeks were just awful. We went to see her every day, but there was little we could do apart from talk to her and just hope really. Ben spent a lot of time there to keep Tony company and to give whatever support he could. The rest of the family visited at various times night and day, but just felt so helpless. I made sure the boys were kept in the picture and told them exactly what the doctors told me in a way they could understand. The nurses and doctors were kind, but as time went on it became obvious there was little hope. She never did wake up. Clare passed away on the evening of Monday March 2nd, 1998. She was 25.

The funeral took place on March 9th. Somehow, we got through it. Tony managed to find the strength to stand at the lectern (supported by Jeff) and gave his own moving tribute. Various pieces of music were played including the lovely tune of Ben's, which came to be known as "Clare's Theme". At the end of the service each family went their own way to support each other as best they could.

I can say in all honesty that all of us who loved Clare have never been the same since. We grieved in different ways, and some have coped better than others. The hardest part for all of us was trying to come to terms with the unfairness of it all. Why Clare? A beautiful human being in every sense of the word. She had so much going for her, a loving husband, a nice home, and of course a beautiful 3-year-old daughter, Opal. No wonder we all felt so numb and confused. Then there were the practical and often painful things to deal with. Tony asked me if I knew of a way to tell Opal that Mummy wasn't coming back. The only thing I could come up with was based on a passage in my recently read autobiography of David Niven. His wife too had died suddenly at the age of 25 leaving him with two small boys. My suggestion was that he take Opal outside when it was dark and point to the brightest star in the sky and say to her, "Look! There's Mummy!" Perhaps it would give her the impression that Clare would always be there watching over her, as indeed I'm convinced she is.

We all found it difficult to get back to normality. I decided to work the day after the funeral thinking it was better to keep myself occupied. It wasn't easy and it certainly took the rest of the year at least before I was anywhere near back to my old self. I would often get angry and snap at my workmates and managers, but they all knew what the score was. Ben buried himself in his music and kept himself to himself dealing with it in his own way. Jay was quiet but seemed to be coping ok and was soon playing regular football again. We all tried to get on with our lives as best we could. Tony and Opal would often come over to visit during the following months, Tony understandably often struggling and still trying to make sense of it all. The boys had a lovely bond with little Opal which certainly helped during those difficult times. Mum came over more often as well and would stay for a day or two throughout that spring and summer. Cards of sympathy and letters arrived in the post regularly for some time afterwards, all of them welcome and comforting. I think I can speak for most of us when I say it was three steps forward and one step back for quite a while. It was a difficult time, but thanks to the love and support of family and friends, eventually and slowly we began to move forward.

CHAPTER 24

Slowly moving forwards

Still with the mindset of keeping myself occupied, as difficult as it often was, I buried myself in work and magic. I did a lecture for 'The Guild of Magicians', in Nottingham which was a really good night. I even sold out of lecture notes. I also made a start on writing an article for the tenth anniversary book for The British Close-Up Magic Symposium. The article was called The Linking Ring and was the story of the night of me producing the engagement ring. Surprising how that evening has had all sorts of consequences. The magic club at Northampton was still going strong and I would go to meetings whenever I could. There was a particularly good lecture from Alan Shaxon there in April. I made him smile when I reminded him of the first time, I saw him perform - it was in the 'Tin shed' at the end of Clacton pier back in the Sixties.

I've performed in some strange venues myself over the years and for all sorts of events. From the usual weddings, birthdays, and anniversary celebrations to some of a more unusual nature. A job came in from Roy and Meg (Allsorts Entertainments) and once again in a rather exclusive part of the county. According to the contract the job was for, "A fundraising event for son Joseph's trip to Madagascar". As usual, Roy's information on access to the venue was immaculate… "Rectory Farmhouse, on the High Street, (opposite 3 Horseshoes pub. Door to house in courtyard.)"

I don't remember too much about that night and my diary has little to say, "*Not a bad evening, but I have had better.*" The one thing that does strike me looking back is why would a family book and pay me a hundred quid for a fundraising event? Oh well, let's hope young Joseph had a lovely time in Madagascar (assuming he actually got there).

I'm always happy to do the occasional freebie for friends and family, and charitable events too if I'm available; at that point in my life, anything to keep busy. I was asked to provide some entertainment at a drop-in centre in Bletchley early in 1998. The audience were mostly elderly, and it was a good laugh. I wasn't expecting anything for it and was pleasantly surprised when at the end of it I was presented with a WH Smith gift voucher for a tenner, what a lovely gesture. A couple of days later my sister Maggs asked me if I could do something for her ladies choir. When I asked her what it was for, she said, "Entertainment after the AGM." I was happy to do that too. I was well looked after with tea and some very nice homemade cake. It wasn't always just about the money.

At the end of March I travelled out of Milton Keynes to the lovely Cotswold village of Castle Combe and the rather stunning five-star Manor House Hotel. This was a job for a Tesco management team that I'd picked up from another gig a couple of years previously. If this one was going to be anything like the other, I could have trouble as they really did know how to party. The plan was to get there early and work the tables and finish before they got too rowdy. I was sent instructions on how to get to the venue, along with a printout of a map. (These were the pioneering days of technology.) I gave myself plenty of time to get there and was doing well until I came off the M4 where I got hopelessly lost.

With the absence of road signs it was turning into a nightmare, and panic was beginning to set in as I drove aimlessly around the country lanes as time marched alarmingly on. I hate being late for gigs, particularly this one as I needed to be early, never mind on time. Finally, and with considerable relief, I got to the venue, albeit an hour late. I made my way to reception and was greeted by the chap who was at the last gig. Before I could say anything, he asked me if I'd got lost. It seemed the instructions given were incorrect and everybody had come off the M4 at the wrong junction. (I did say they were pioneering days of technology.) The upshot was they were running over an hour late and there were still guests wandering around the local countryside trying to find the hotel. I was quite relieved until the manager joined us and slurred, "We're in the bar come and join ushh." I took up his kind offer of a pint (I needed it) and then decided to have a look at the dining room where I'd be working. As well as the usual cutlery on the tables I noticed plastic tubes about six inches long and boxes of small, round, and hard, paper balls. I had no idea what they were. I was about to find out. The door suddenly burst open and in came the guests wearing party hats and making a din with party blowers and whistles, all of them reeling after a couple of hours of solid drinking. They made a beeline for the tubes (which were peashooters) and began to shoot the small balls randomly all over the room but mostly at each other. It went on for some time until all the boxes had been emptied. That didn't stop them, they scurried around the room picking them up from the floor and began shooting them again, some of them on hands and knees crawling under the tables in search of yet more. It continued as they took their seats and the food was being served. Those small balls were everywhere including floating in the bowls of soup the waitresses were struggling to serve. I made a start with the magic as soon as they were seated, and of course I was a prime target. It was hard work, and they weren't particularly enamoured with the magic, more interested with target practice and yet again retrieving the small balls from underneath the tables and between my legs, even as I worked. All in all it was a riot, and they had a great time. I survived it somehow and I've still got the scars to prove it.

Nothing ever came of a job at Chappells for Ben. I'm not even sure he filled the form in. Tony's step-Mum, Anne, contacted him asking if she could use Clare's Theme for background music for the meditation classes she was running, of course he agreed - the first of many pieces of his music that have been used for all sorts of things in all sorts of places throughout the world. That would be years ahead though; meanwhile he needed a regular income coming in soon, as I'd just received the final Family Allowance payment for him. He applied for or had interviews with several places including Homebase, B&Q, WH Smiths, HMV, Comet, and even the piano factory, all to no avail. Then I had a brainwave. I asked my boss if there was anything going at Llewellyn, and luckily there was, in fact there were several fathers and sons working together at the time. He started at 8.00 o'clock on the 26th of May and by 8.30 he'd had enough. He barely made it through the day. Oh well, they did pay him 38 quid for his brief excursion into the building trade. Neither of the boys have ever shown any interest in following in their father's footsteps, whether it be woodwork, DIY, or even magic, not that I'm complaining, in fact they've done pretty well in ploughing their own furrow, or as we say these days, doing their own thing.

There was some good news in July. Ben applied for and got himself a job at 'Rollers', the roller-skating rink in Bletchley, working as a skate steward. He loved it and made a lot of friends there. Soon he was able to buy new recording equipment and pretty much every evening, when he wasn't at Rollers, his room would be full of his pals rapping and recording. It was a bit of a squash to get everybody in and it soon became apparent he would need more space. We'd have to do a swap. I'd move into the music room, and he could move into my (larger) bedroom. It would prove to be a massive undertaking.

It took until the end of the summer to get it all done. Both rooms were redecorated. I got rid of my double bed and, after seeing how expensive single beds were to buy, I made one each for me and Ben. Shelves were put up, new curtains bought and hung, and finally the custom-built units and studio desk were installed. All done to Ben's specifications, including mixers set into the worktops. Although I say it myself, it looked great. More to the point, it worked. I was more than happy to move into the smaller bedroom; all I needed was a bed, and a chest of drawers which was something else I made. Jay was happy too; he now had the other large bedroom all to himself and he could 'spread out' which he very soon did.

I had a welcome weekend away in May. It was a spiritual healing course organised by Tony's step-Mum, Anne Jones. It took place at her beautiful house in the New Forest. I approached it with an open mind and decided that at its worst it would be a relaxing couple of days away in a lovely part of the country. I found it fascinating, interesting, and most certainly relaxing. A lot was packed into the time available, including an explanation of chakras, cleaning the aura, meditation, crystal therapy and healing. It was emotional too at times, bearing in mind I was still grieving. I realised afterwards just how little we know about spirituality and how much there is to learn. I also realised that what is known these days as 'New Age' philosophy isn't the mumbo jumbo many people seem to think it is. It certainly opened my eyes, and I had a great time.

Speaking of having a relaxing time…

June 20th, 1998: *I went to the Australian Pink Floyd outdoor concert at The Stables tonight. It was a really lovely way to spend a pleasant summer evening. Wonderful music, a glass of ale, and a cigar.*

A week later I shared another gig with Anthony Owen in Stewkley, a village a few short miles from Milton Keynes. It was a charity black-tie ball which included a three-course silver-service dinner. We had the usual role of working the tables between courses. It went very well, and it was always nice to meet up and have a catchup with Anthony. The evening was a fundraising event in memory of a lady who had recently died of cancer and a lot of money was raised.

The next job I did wasn't a happy experience. It took place at a large hotel in London, The Park Court (which appears to be a block of flats now). According to the contract, I was the table magician for a wedding and the dress code was smart casual. The set-up time was 7.00 pm, and the start time and performance duration were to be directed by the booker on the night. It appeared to be a rather laid-back affair which was unusual for a London wedding; as always, I'd play it by ear when I got there. It was a really hot day and for some reason I decided to drive there. That was a huge mistake. I left the house at 4.30 pm and, due to delays on the motorway, and getting lost, and struggling to park, I arrived at the hotel reception at about 7.15 pm. Late, I agree, but not too late. In my experience weddings rarely run on time anyway, and if anyone was to complain I could always stay on later, for as long as they wanted, as implied in the contract. I asked the receptionist where the wedding was and she said,

"What wedding?"

For a terrible moment I thought I was in the wrong hotel. She had a look through her books and confirmed there was no wedding anywhere in the hotel (which was huge.) I showed her the contract to confirm I was at the right venue and asked her if she recognised the name of the booker.

"Yes, she said but it's not a wedding, I'll get him for you."

Soon after a chap came to see me dressed in jeans and a T shirt (so much for smart casual). He went on to explain what the function was all about. He was some sort of consultant who had been hired by a large firm of retail shops. His role was to give various shop managers from all over the country an opportunity to visit branches throughout London. They were split up into small groups of three or four and were given a task to do in each branch they visited. (The sort of thing that happens in The Apprentice tv programme.) They were all due to meet up back at the hotel around 7.00 o'clock to discuss what had been achieved during their visits. The culmination of the day was a disco and me working the tables, which should have been on the contract (and wasn't). By the time he'd finished explaining, it was about 7.45. Anyway, neither him nor me was particularly worried as groups of people were still making their way into the room. I followed them in with my pockets already loaded, all set to make a start. I gave a friendly wave to the DJ, who was making a huge racket. He glanced at me and instead of waving back he pointed at his watch. That didn't endear me to him. I don't know what it is about some DJs, many of whom appear to be locked into their own little world, with headphones attached and bobbing away to the music, forever flicking through boxes of records (as it was in those days) and not watching or caring about the volume or what's going on in the room. They don't seem to understand English either. "Do you mind turning the volume down a bit please," meant nothing to that bloke on that night, and nobody was up dancing anyway. I made a start on circulating around the tables and quickly discovered that hardly anybody was interested. Understandably, most were talking excitedly about the events of their day and the last thing they wanted was to watch a magic trick. Meanwhile the music was blaring out to the point where it was almost painful. I did what I could for about an hour and gave up. I explained all to the booker and he was ok about it, as far as he was concerned the day had been a great success. The fact that the magic hadn't really worked didn't bother him at all, in the great scheme of things it was pretty much trivial. The contract said that I would be paid cash on the night. That didn't happen either. A few days later I had a call from the agent who told me that there might be a problem getting the cash. It seems the DJ had complained that I hadn't worked hard enough! I explained all to the agent and he phoned back later in the week to tell me the money was on the way. The fact that it wasn't a wedding (and I had taken specialist material to suit such an event) and they didn't pay cash on the night, as stipulated on the contract, meant they didn't have a leg to stand on. He also said he wouldn't be booking the DJ again. I always feel disappointed when gigs don't go well, whether it's my fault or not. I look forward to performing and having a laugh with people and I do like to *earn* the money.

The summer soon passed and while the boys had a week away with Babs, I decided on a bit of a whim to go away myself.

September 14th, 1998: *First thing this morning I decided to go to Wales, then I changed my mind, then I packed and showered anyway and finally decided to go at twelve o'clock. I had a really good journey to Holyhead, and it took about 5 hours. I went for a walk along the front, and down Mackenzie Pier before driving to Trearddur Bay where I found a small hotel. It's really nice with my room looking out over the bay. I went out for a couple of pints, two cigars, and a lovely Broccoli Bake dinner before going to bed at half past eight!*

The following day was spent in Holyhead walking around the still familiar streets of the town centre, and then into Armenia Street and to Mum's childhood home, the scene of so many happy memories. Things were looking a bit different now though. The school at the top of the road was now a row of houses and the old laundry had been converted into a garage. A lot of it though was exactly the same as it was 35 years ago. The same alleyways still ran behind the houses and I walked through them again as I did when I was ten years old, all the way to the beach and the familiar promenade. The cast iron railings are still there as they were when Mum was a child. I walked all the way along towards the mountain and eventually to 'Rocky Coast', which was still as beautiful and unspoilt as ever. Memories came flooding back of the many walks we did as a family, carrying plastic macs "in case it rained," wearing plastic sandals and shorts while Dad wore his thick jacket and pullover with the ever-present cine camera over his shoulder. I wandered back into the town and then drove round the coast to the impressive South Stack lighthouse, and down the many steps (365), across the small suspension bridge, and this time I was able to go inside the lighthouse which was fascinating. Soon it was time to head home, back to the present and get the decorating finished and new carpets laid before I picked up the boys the following weekend.

September 18th, 1998: *I set off for Great Yarmouth at about 4.00 o'clock and stayed in the same small hotel as last year. I went for a walk along the front, had a couple of pints and cod and chips before heading back to my room to watch 'Rock Family Trees'. Brilliant!*

The next day I picked up the boys from Hopton where they'd spent the week having a great time with Babs in a huge caravan.

Jay had his first match of the season on the Sunday playing in a cup match. It wasn't what you'd call a good start. They lost 22-0! Outclassed and outplayed. There wasn't much they could have done. It was a shame, but the lads kept their heads up and weren't too disheartened. Yet again a case of things could only get better. At 14, coming up to 15, Jay was now working for his GCSE exams and Ben was doing ok and well settled into work at Rollers. He'd saved up and bought himself a new keyboard and his music and musicianship knew no bounds.

In early October, I heard of an event coming up at a local church hall. One of the church members knew of a retired former actress who lived fairly locally near Buckingham. The lady was approached to see if she would give a talk on her life and career. She was more than happy to do so. The actress was Hilary Mason, who I recognised as soon as I saw her; she had one of those familiar faces that you know but can't remember where. She'd been in countless tv programmes and films, but her biggest role was as the blind psychic in that iconic film, 'Don't Look Now', with Donald Sutherland and Julie Christie. I saw the film when it came out which I thought was a wonderful piece of work - disturbing, chilling, sad, sexy, and poignant, great cinema in my view. It did stir up some controversy on its release though, due partly to a rather explicit sex scene. Anyway, the tiny figure of 81-year-old Hilary took to the stage and spoke eloquently for over an hour about her long career as an actress. From childhood aspirations to drama school in London, and then her formative years in repertory, travelling up and down the country working in provincial theatres learning her craft. She talked of her many television appearances in the early days of drama when it was often broadcast live. It was just fascinating. She spoke about 'Don't Look Now' and the infamous sex scene and asked how many of us had seen the film. One or two people raised their hand (bearing in mind it was pretty much an audience of churchgoers). She then went on to tell us why that particular scene was necessary for the film. From her ten-minute explanation it was obvious that here was a lady who was not only a fine actress but also had a deep understanding of how cinema works. She ended her talk with a question-and-answer session; I can only remember one,

"Who was the finest leading actor you ever worked with?"

"Richard Burton," she answered, not even having to think about it. What a fascinating evening it was, and it only cost a couple of quid, which included a cup of tea and a slice of cake. Loved it.

I did a close-up job for VIP Promotions in November which I thought I may have problems with. It was for students at University College in London. I was convinced I'd get heckled, and they wouldn't be interested; taking the piss I can handle, in fact I encourage banter from the audience, but lack of interest can be a difficult one. As it happened, I needn't have worried, we had a great time. I do a trick where I borrow a ten-pound note. I asked the question at the first table,

"Could somebody lend me a tenner?"

Back came the immediate reply, almost in unison they replied, "Don't be stupid we're students!"

At the next table I fished out a tenner from my pocket and said, "You've probably never seen one of these, it's called a ten-pound note."

I'd found a theme for the evening. At one table I told the people that I started to get interested in magic when I was but a poor student myself and desperate for something to use, I even raided my old Mum's sewing basket and all I found was a thimble. Then I'd go into my thimble routine and when I produced the big one at the end, I told them the true story of how I spotted it in Bletchley market. It was a great night spent with a lovely crowd of young people. From that job I picked up their Christmas party which was held at the Cafe Royal. Another fun evening (with many of the students wearing ill-fitting hired dinner jackets) they all made the effort and were certainly up for having a good time. The place was packed, and it was a huge venue covering several floors. Conditions weren't ideal, it was noisy and had lots of long tables. I wanted to cover as many tables as possible but was limited as to what I could do. I thought about it and decided to do just the one trick over the whole evening. I stood at the end of each table and did the bottle of wine production. It didn't need patter, so I didn't have to shout, the audience just had to watch (and hopefully clap at the end of it!). I must have performed it 30 times that night. Job done I reckon. I was more than happy as were the students, the booker and the Agent. It was one of those jobs that gave me a lot of satisfaction. I was more than happy as I pondered the gig on the train on the way home.

There were a couple of gigs at Buckingham Town Hall during Christmas week, and another in Northampton on Christmas Day which I did for a friend of mine who'd fallen ill. It was a quiet New Years Eve; I stayed in with the boys watching tv.

It was with some relief that 1998 had come to an end. Our first Christmas without Clare. It had been a difficult and emotional year which we coped with as best we could by keeping busy and occupied as much as anything else. Ben was into his music, Jay had his schoolwork and football, I was busy both at work and at home, and gigs were still coming in.

1999 was a year of hard work, exhaustion, and frustration. A typical year then! The first magic club meeting of the year was an interesting one. It was organised by three members, Mick Hanzlik, John Percival, and John Shaw. The highlight of the evening was an appearance by local entertainer Professor Stanley Unwin. He was introduced and agreed to say a few words... "Good evenlobe. How trickywonderbold to be invited to this meeting of the magiclode clublocus of tricky tricky cardlopers." Or words to that effect. It was just hilarious. The longer he went on, the funnier it got. It was a mixture of real words which began to make some sort of sense, but then he'd go off at a crazy tangent using words which had no meaning, well they did, but only sort of. It was great fun. I had a chat with him during the evening and told him about a way of speaking that me and a couple of mates had been using for a few years, taught to us by a chap who used to be in the navy. The idea is to take the word "arag" and either put it in front of the word if it begins with a vowel, or after the first letter if it doesn't. So, "Jack sat on the mat," would be spoken thus – "Jaragack saragat aragon the maragat". With a bit of practice you soon become fluent, as indeed a few of us did. He listened with interest but told me the obvious really, that his method defies all logic and therefore gave him scope to take it wherever he wanted –

"Flights of nonsensical fantasy," was the way I put it to him, or "Flaragights aragof naragonsensical faragantasy!"

"Yarages," he laughed.

I did a couple of jobs in January that couldn't have been more different. The first one was for MK Mind, the mental health charity. It was a social evening with soft drinks and a buffet. I wandered from group to group or person to person performing my usual stuff. It went ok for the majority of people but for others who appeared to be on medication it was difficult. There were people there I recognised and had no idea they were having problems; no wonder then that mental illness is often referred to as being invisible. That evening was an eye opener in many ways; I was impressed too with the staff who were caring and obviously dedicated to what at times must be a very difficult job, a true vocation. A couple of weeks later I did another job for Tesco Management in Gloucester. This time I was prepared. I got there well before the start time and had a look at the tables in the restaurant. Sure enough the pea shooters were out again. I had time to pop out to the car to get my extra props. I made my entrance wearing a hard hat and a pair of goggles.

Things were busy at work, and I was quite surprised when in January the company offered me a job as foreman for a new department they were setting up. This involved working on pre-made and ready decorated steel units. I provisionally accepted but it didn't come to anything. In fact during my 25 years with the company I never did rise above the factory floor. I wasn't really bothered though, for me it was all about job satisfaction, as long as I enjoyed what I did and earned enough to pay the bills I was happy. Speaking of which, at the beginning of the year I had a run of gallows brackets to make, which kept me busy for weeks.

They came in all sorts of shapes and sizes, some of them quite unusual. Stair bulkheads and preformed dormer roof sections were also a part of my workload. The idea of making all this stuff in the factory was to save time on site. Each finished item was craned off the lorry and dropped into position straight into the house. It saved the on-site carpenters a lot of work as well as time.

Later that year, my usual work had dried up and we were now making spandrels. These are triangular shaped panels which are clad on both sides with two layers of plasterboard and insulated inside. The panels sit on top of the party walls and replace the more traditional block construction. They were heavy, dusty, and time-consuming, but gave the company much needed revenue and us, much needed work, and job security. Despite working long hours, I somehow found the time and energy to do a lot of work in the house. I made high level cupboards for my bedroom and made and fitted a bookcase between them. Once they were done, that completed both mine and Ben's room. Meanwhile Jay was having an understandable whinge about his room, and what was I going to do for him. I couldn't really say no, so between us we came up with the idea of a snooker parlour. I decorated the room with mahogany panelling and shaped moulding from the floor to halfway up the walls, topped with a fancy dado rail. When that was done, I painted the walls above it a nice shade of green. At this point we chose and had fitted a rather nice dark green carpet which went well with both the walls and the panelling; we were getting there. Next, I had to think about furniture. He needed a bed, a desk with drawers and cupboards, somewhere to put his clothes, and a half size snooker table! First, I made two chests of drawers and two cupboards topped with a green worktop (forming a desk). Above that I made and fixed high-level cupboards fitted with rails for his clothes. All the furniture was stained mahogany to match the panelling, and with fancy beading on the doors it looked really nice. The biggest problem was the bed. It would have to be movable to allow for the snooker table to fit in the centre of the room. I came up with the idea of fitting a long hinge on the base to allow it to be lifted parallel to the wall. The problem with that was the base of the bed would now be visible. I got over that by painting it the same colour as the panelling. It worked well and when it was raised there was room (just about) for a half-size snooker table in the middle of the floor. And when the bed was down, the table was stored underneath it. The final touch was a pair of green velvet curtains. It took months to complete but it was certainly worth the time, effort, and expense. The boys spent many hours playing snooker up there. Jeff would often come over and they'd have mini tournaments, playing their own variation of snooker which they called "Longshanks". I can't remember what the rules were - I'm not too sure it had any.

It was Ben's 18th birthday in February. Most of the family gave him money as a present as it was what he wanted. He wasn't a heavy drinker or a party animal at that time and he wanted to keep the day fairly low-key. Tony and Opal came over and I treated us all to a huge pizza dinner and he was quite happy with that. A few weeks later, after advice from Tony, he went out and bought a brand-new PC with his birthday money. With further advice and help from Tony, new software was installed to enable him to make and compose good quality backing tracks. He was in business. As was I, with magic jobs still coming in.

Although I'd performed in all sorts of restaurants over the years I'd never entertained in an Indian before. I was quite surprised when a booking came in for a local one for Valentine's Day.

Publicity was in the local paper in the form of a lovely, coloured poster, but with a glaring spelling mistake - "Treat your Valentine to a magical evening with Ken Howes". When I got there, I was told I could use a changing room which was upstairs. I went up the somewhat rickety stairs (it was an old building) and opened the door to the allocated room. It was full of laid out sleeping bags and beds. Obviously the staffroom I thought. It turned out to be a good night and I kept going from 7.30 until 11.00. The fee was good, and I got £15 in tips. That was quite unusual as I never work with picking up tips in mind. Two days later I entered the magic club close-up competition and won it again! Even though I'd won it several times before, I was still chuffed to bits.

March 2nd soon rolled round to mark the first anniversary of Clare's passing. A couple of days before, I'd driven over to Wing churchyard to lay some flowers on her grave. It's a lovely spot underneath a beautiful old oak tree with a stunning view looking out across the Aylesbury Vale. Each time I go I walk to the field at the bottom of the churchyard, climb over the stile and walk up the hill to gaze across miles of unspoilt countryside with the ever-present red kites floating above. From that point too there's a great view of the church. If it's open, I go in and have a sit down for a while. All Saints is a beautiful old Saxon church and every time I open the heavy oak door and cross the threshold I'm aware of an atmosphere of peace and tranquillity. It's the perfect place to sit quietly and remember Clare. A few weeks after that, I went over again with Jay which was an emotional experience. A few weeks later he played football at Wing, and as usual me and Ben went along to watch. I'd taken some flowers from our rockery with us and as Jay was playing, me and Ben went to the churchyard. This was his first visit and although he was understandably quiet at the time, it seemed to hit him the following day. I had to pick him up from work halfway through his shift. That is the nature of grief, it can hit you at any time in any place, as it does to this day.

The magic club continued to have a variety of lectures and themes and for the first meeting in March it was a, 'Try it out night'. A few of us went to the front to do exactly that, try something out to see if and how it would work before an audience. Comments and suggestions from other members made it into a good and constructive meeting. My old friend David Parriss had a go but struggled a bit as he was now battling the symptoms and frustration of Parkinson's Disease. He would turn up at the meetings with his wife as often as he was able and perform too. We all admired his courage and fortitude. A remarkable and lovely man.

I made another video in April. This time with Gary Young as producer and Bob Hamilton was the cameraman. I found it to be a happy experience, as this time I had two lovely people to work to rather than straight to the camera. I performed five tricks as I would to an audience, followed by the explanations. It came out a few weeks later to good reviews in the magic press and sold pretty well over the following 12 months.

I had a few run-of-the-mill gigs during the year, a couple of weddings and a corporate job with Mick and John, inside the brand-new Millennium Dome. It looked great from the outside but a bit of a building site inside. Another first for me was, 'entertainment after a christening'. It was a lovely family event in Oxfordshire. I've just had a thought; the baby will be 21 now. Wouldn't it be nice to perform at the 21st birthday party?

At the end of June 1999, I was having a look at my finances. I'd received a letter from the housing association informing me that the rent was going up again. It wasn't too much of a problem as it was affordable due to my long working hours. I did wonder though if it was worth pursuing the idea of being a house owner. The rent would always go up on a yearly basis whereas a mortgage repayment would stay pretty much constant, depending on fluctuations in the Interest Rate. If the rent and mortgage payments were similar, then it made sense to go for it. I was aware that I would be liable for repairs, which I thought I could handle, and luckily the housing association had replaced the complete central heating system the previous year, which meant I wouldn't have to worry about plumbing for a while. I made some enquiries and decided to go for it. I discovered there was something else in my favour. As I'd lived in rented accommodation all my life, I was entitled to a huge discount. I filled forms in, spoke to a solicitor, signed documents, had the house valued, and had a meeting with the Building Society. The whole process took four months. I took out a mortgage over 20 years and the difference between the rent and the mortgage payments was a fiver a week -I was a homeowner.

I went to the IBM Convention in Llandudno in September. This time however I had a job to do, well two actually. Being a judge for the close- up competition was the main one, and the other was taking part in a hospital show. Each year volunteers are asked to perform at hospitals and old people's homes, schools, and the like. It's a nice gesture from the organisers to make use of some of the hundreds of magicians that descend on convention towns each year. The close-up competition took place on the day after I arrived. It was a good standard with eight acts and one obvious winner (Trevor Stone) all the judges were unanimous, which is always a relief. From there I went to the hospital and spent an hour entertaining the patients. I can't remember too much about it and my diary was of little help - *"It went really well and I'm glad I did it."* I enjoyed that convention and as ever it was lovely to catch up with Bobby Bernard and a few other friends I hadn't seen for a while. While I was there, Mum came to stay to "look after the boys." It was more like cooking, cleaning, washing, and ironing. She just loved being with them. As a little thank you, I'd bought tickets for her, me, and our Jean for a show at the recently opened theatre at the City Centre. A competition had been organised for members of the public to come up with a name for it. I'm not entirely sure if the competition actually went ahead as it was finally announced that it would be known as The Milton Keynes Theatre, which is hardly an imaginative name for a competition win. Anyway, we had a great time watching a recording of the popular radio comedy 'I'm sorry I haven't a clue'.

The end of the year was approaching and with it a few Christmas gigs. A return visit to The Knife and Cleaver, and yet another for Tesco management. With repeat bookings I must have been getting something right, which is always reassuring.

The Tesco job was nothing like the previous two (thankfully). It was in the Sculpture Gallery at Woburn Abbey and a much quieter affair. There were only eight tables which was just about perfect.

Christmas day was lovely with just me Mum and the boys. New Years Eve was also a family affair at home with all the family. Eating drinking and silly games until the moment we toasted in the new century! 1999 had been an eventful year in many ways. Hard work, emotional at times, but a lot had been achieved. Ben, although still at Rollers, now had a studio at home and had met Rev. Peter Sharrocks. Ben had provided the backing tracks to a CD of Peter's self-penned songs. He'd also got together with a few of his pals to form Playaz Klub, an original rap band. He was on his way.

Jay was working hard at school and would soon have to decide his future direction. Tony and Opal were doing reasonably well and had now moved to Hampshire to be close to his Dad and step-Mum. (I suspect there were too many memories in Buckingham.) Jeff was ok too with his girlfriend and daughter, Amy. I was doing well at work in as much I had a job which appeared to be secure. The house was taking shape, and it was mine!

CHAPTER 25

Wings beginning to spread

Early into the new year Ben had had enough of Rollers and left. I was fed up with it as well to be honest because of the late pick-up times. (I was still the family taxi.) He concentrated on his music and made enquiries about work at a local recording studio which didn't come to anything. He did go back to college one day a week for a computer course which thankfully he did stick at. Meanwhile Jay had come to a decision regarding his future.

January 25th, 2000. *Me and Jay went to the college this evening to find out about a sport science course. It looks really good. Jay's full of enthusiasm as well which is reassuring. We only hope now he gets the grades he needs.*

He filled in the form and sent it off and sometime later I went with him for his interview. It all went well, and he did get the grades he needed for a two-year-course beginning in September. It cost me over £200, but I looked at it as an investment with no expense spared when it came to education. Both boys were now having a social life. Ben was happy to hang out with his mates and Jay had discovered girls (or perhaps they had discovered him). He did keep his cards close to his chest though and I rarely met any of them. He was also reluctant to tell me their names, even the ones who phoned him regularly. Whenever I asked for a name, his answer would always be the same, "Phyllis". If I happened to answer the phone to one of his girlfriends, I'd yell up the stairs, "Jay! Phyllis on the phone!" Then I'd listen to him trying to explain to the poor girl who the mysterious Phyllis was.

I had a couple of January gigs which didn't amount to much. The first one was a birthday party which again I had problems with because of a disco. It's annoying when clients think it's even within the realms of possibility to perform around the tables in a small hall with loud music blaring out. It was happening more and more so I came up with some new material that I could perform without saying anything. It worked up to a point, but I did miss the banter. Another option was to perform away from the room. Over the years I've performed in corridors, kitchens, cloakrooms, on a staircase, and even outside, for the smokers, just to escape the noise. The fact that I could find groups of people congregated in out of the way places, shows that loud music isn't to everyone's taste. The other job I did was in a family home in deepest Northamptonshire. It was for an hour of close-up magic on a Sunday afternoon for a lady's 60th birthday. It went ok, but it was all rather dull, there wasn't any booze, and it didn't really take off. As I pondered the gig on the way home it occurred to me that it would have gone much better had they had a disco. The irony of that thought made me smile.

Thankfully, most people do get it right. I did a corporate job in the summer of 2000 at the Saints rugby ground in Northampton. The contract from Allsorts Entertainments stated - "Artiste to provide Close-Up Magical Entertainment at the tables either side of the Bar-B-Q Approx. 8.00 pm, before disco. Act as known. Car parking available in usual Saints car park." Roy and Meg at the top of their game yet again. Here's another example. It was a corporate job at Billing Aquadrome - "Artiste to provide Close Up Magical Entertainment before guests sit down at 8.30 pm, and then at the tables during the meal as appropriate (except during the period of the competition) until the disco commences at approx. 9.30pm. Act as known. There will be 24 tables, ten guests to a table." There it was in black and white, all the information I required. It was a great night with the organisation spot on.

For my 50th birthday treat I took the boys to the theatre to see a Ben Elton play called 'Gasping'. I quite enjoyed it, but I don't think the boys were too impressed. They found it difficult to concentrate, as many people do with live theatre. Anyway, it was a night out. Although being 50 is supposed to be some sort of landmark, I had no plans to celebrate it any more than I did. The family called round on the day bearing gifts and cards, that was good enough for me.

Both boys embraced new technology. Ben had his PC, and later in the year I bought one for Jay as it was essential for his college work. These were also the early days of mobile phones. I was never interested myself and knew they'd never catch on.

March 23rd, 2000: *Jay has bought himself a mobile phone now, and so have Sean and Billy. They're treating them like toys! I expect the novelty will wear off in time.*

I remember when the boys pleaded with me to buy them walkie- talkies one Christmas when they were quite young. By the end of the holiday (once the batteries had run out) they were thrown into the bottom of the cupboard and forgotten. Mobile phones would surely suffer the same fate. I bought my first one some seven months later, on October 14th. (Ben bought his on the 19th.)

The house was slowly taking shape and the final room to be decorated was the kitchen. I'd already made and hung ten new wooden cupboard doors but there was still painting and tiling to do. I was making plans to make a start when Ben pointed out a problem with his bedroom window. It was rotten. I had a good look at the rest of the windows in the house and was alarmed to discover there were more showing signs of rot. I did some research and got a local family run company to give me a quote for replacement double-glazed windows and doors. I went along to my Building Society and obtained a loan without too much trouble and added it to the mortgage and they were fitted in July. Another job done. By the end of the year the kitchen was also finished. I don't have much idea about colour sense, what goes with what and all that stuff, but Ben does. He came with me to choose paint and tiles and I have to say, at first I was a little apprehensive, but he was spot on with choosing the bright and airy colours he did. It was the same for his bedroom/studio, perfect. The boys were too old now for holidays with me, so I got stuck into the decorating when I had my summer break from work. Jay had a pre- booked holiday away in Venice with the school for a week and Ben spent a lot of time sorting out the garden. He's got green fingers just like my Dad and Clare. He dug the borders and chose the plants, and I left it all to him. Meanwhile he'd applied for several jobs working in retail at the City Centre and eventually got one at The Discovery Store. He seemed to enjoy it and at last money was coming in. He told me that he would like to work with children in some way, perhaps getting involved with after- school clubs or even a teaching assistant. I pointed out it would require qualifications and courses and he might even have to go back to the dreaded classroom, but he was up for that. He'd realised by now that to say you're good at something isn't enough, you have to have a piece of paper that proves it.

During the summer Ben started a Fantasy Football league which was really popular locally. He did print-outs of league tables and even bought a trophy for the winner. He got into T-shirt printing and was also working hard and enjoying his music. He had a full and busy life. Meanwhile, Jay was anxious for some cash to fund his social life (he'd now discovered clubbing). He managed to get a job at BHS but needed something smart to wear for the shop floor.

"Go up there and buy your self something," I said.

"What with?" came back the inevitable reply.

July 14th, 2000: *Me and Jay went to the Centre this afternoon to get him kitted out for his job at BHS. I bought him shoes, trousers, a shirt, and a tie for less than £60 which I thought was quite reasonable.*

He did say he'd pay me back. Oh well, good old Bank of Dad came to the rescue again. Luckily, I had a couple of gigs. The first one was at Northampton for a company called Hawes Signs. I'd often seen their vans buzzing about, but as far as I knew, they were no relation to my family. The manager (unsurprisingly a Mr. Hawes) confirmed that fact to the agent. I got to the venue, and as soon as I found out who he was (and hoping he had a sense of humour) I went up to him and gave him a hug and said "Uncle!!" It was a good night! The other job I had was for a 40th birthday party. It was about as far removed from my 50th as you could get. It was at Buckingham Town Hall and a formal black-tie function. According to my diary it was quiet to start with but ended up being a good night. I always had a good time there, such a lovely venue, and by now I was on first name terms with the management and staff.

The summer soon passed. I was really busy both at work and at home. The boys were working and having good social lives. Jay was still taking part in football tournaments and adding to his collection of trophies. Ben was putting the finishing touches to the first Playaz Klub album, and still skating at Rollers with the occasional all-nighter with my nephew Stuart at a rink in Derby. He also played a bit of golf with his pals.

August 27th, 2000: *Jay went out clubbing again tonight with Lee, Billy, and Sean. Ben went out playing golf, so I had the evening to myself. It did feel a bit strange. The boys are almost men.*

I had a good night out myself in September.

September 21st, 2000: *I went to see the Man Band at the Roadmender Club in Northampton tonight. It was great to see the lads again. I gave them a couple of packet card tricks and a book. Deke signed my copy of the 'Rhinos, winos, & lunatics' book, and gave me a copy of his new one. A great night!*

A couple of days later I had a gig in Oxford. It was the "21st Birthday charity dinner dance for the National Association for Colitis and Crohn's Disease." Looking back now and noticing it was a dinner, and bearing in mind who it was for, I wonder what was on the menu?

I got back late that night and was able to watch Steve Redgrave win his 5th consecutive Gold Medal for rowing at the Sydney Olympic Games, a good way to unwind after a long night.

I spent an interesting afternoon in London in early October 2000. It was to make a video with Pat Page and Vic Pinto (an American magician/photographer living in London). This was to be number 3 of a series called Lounge Lizard Sizzle Sessions and was called 'A tribute to Ken Brooke'. I was asked to do it because Pat had seen my impression of the great man at the Magic Circle and thought it would work well alongside other contributors. He also asked me to perform some stuff incorporating some of Ken's moves and ideas. It all took place in a rather nice restaurant in Finchley Road. I arrived at about noon to find the rest of the participants already there. Pat (who was the anchor), Janet Clare, Terry Herbert, Harry & Mary Nicholls, and Lionel Russell. I'm pretty sure that was it (though there may have been a couple more). Vic was the cameraman. After a welcome from Pat and a chat about the format, each of us took our turn in relaying happy and funny memories of Ken from the 1960s up until he died in 1983; after that the tricks came out and some of us performed classic Ken Brooke material with yet more stories and anecdotes. As well as the impression and the story of buying the Vernon book, I did a coin box routine using a move taught to me by Ken in 1967 and still use to this day. It was a lovely afternoon of fun, magic, and memories. It went on until about 4.30 when we went our separate ways. Sadly the video never did see the light of day and was never released which is a great shame.

Christmas soon rolled around again, and I had a few seasonal gigs including a rather strange one for a model-makers club in Windsor. I was sent a computer printout of directions to the venue (a local football club). It looked fairly comprehensive, but with the absence of landmarks it was difficult to follow. I assumed it would be easy enough to find once I got to the general area. Needless to say, it wasn't. The weather was awful with heavy rain and strong winds which didn't help. I stopped to ask directions several times. Some were tourists who couldn't speak English, others had never heard of it, and there was a spate of, "sorry mate I'm a stranger here myself." At last though, with time marching on, a little old lady pointed me in the right direction and off I went feeling relieved. After about ten minutes I found myself outside a rather dilapidated clubhouse next to a floodlit muddy field. I parked the car, grabbed my case, pulled my coat over my head, and made a dash to the nearest door and walked in. What met my eyes wasn't the family audience I was expecting but a dozen burly men all naked. Needless to say, all eyes turned towards me as I stood there open mouthed - all I could think to say was, "Hello, I'm the magician." At this point I was met with laughter and a barrage of comments along the lines of, "Can you magic this bigger?" It turned out I was in the dressing room of a local rugby club. After a few minutes of humorous banter, I was directed to what I hoped would be the right venue, namely the football club. As I drove off, I glanced at the muddy field and spotted huge rugby posts in plain view, silhouetted in the floodlights, and falling rain - I blamed the little old lady. After studying the map for a few minutes I set off again, peering through my rapidly moving wipers until at last I found what I was looking for, goalposts. Luckily, I got there with time to spare and was able to drive down the narrow lane and park close to the front door of yet another rather dilapidated building. I made sure it was the main entrance (for obvious reasons) and walked into the foyer. Thankfully I was in the right place and as I glanced into the clubroom, I noticed a reasonable amount of people already there. I met the organiser and was shown into the makeshift dressing room which turned out to be the club boardroom complete with trophy cabinets and team photographs. In the middle of the room was a huge boardroom table with chairs all around it. In the centre of it sat an old enamel bucket, collecting drops of rain that were falling at an alarming rate from a hole in the ceiling. I put my case on the table as far away from the bucket as I could and got myself loaded up ready to make a start. I wandered into the bar and spotted a middle-aged chap supping a pint. I went up to him and cheerfully started to chat and showed him a trick; he watched with no reaction at all. At the end of it he turned back to his pint and said nothing; complete indifference. Oh well, I thought, it can only get better. By then an assortment of people were continuing to arrive. There were flat-capped elderly men with their wives, several families, and middle-aged men on their own. A mixed audience that to me had a 1950's feel about it. The clubroom soon filled up (model-making obviously popular in that part of the world). I made my way along the bar to a couple of elderly gentlemen who seemed to be having a good time. I showed them the same trick that 5 minutes earlier had failed miserably. This time the reaction was totally different, and they loved it. I was itching to find out what sort of model- making they did and was just about to speak to the nearest of the two gentlemen when I noticed that his left hand (which was holding a cigarette) didn't have any fingers, just stumps. I glanced at his other hand which had two fingers and a thumb. I thought it best not to say anything. I carried on happily working the tables for about an hour and then needed to have a change of material. I went back into the board room and noticed the bucket on the table was now half full of rainwater. I thought

I'd better tell someone, so I went back into the bar and found a committee man (he had a badge fixed to his lapel, "Committee"). He peered into the bucket and told me not to worry as it was only half empty. I wasn't going to argue with a 'Committee' man. I went back into the club room and did my final stint of about an hour which went really well; the people had turned out to be lovely. The evening finished with not a disco (thankfully) but a raffle. Even that was strange. The prizes were made up entirely of small boxes which I assumed contained a small model, but of what I had no idea. There were hundreds of them piled high on a table. I could see this was going to take hours, so I thought now might be a good idea to collect my money and run. I found the Committee man who told me that I'd have to wait for the treasurer to arrive. My heart sank, I'd had enough by then, it had been a long night. "Ah there he is now," he said and pointed towards the door. I looked over and couldn't believe what I saw. There was a tall youngish man standing there with a bright orange Mohican haircut. He wore a multi-coloured leather jacket, bright green trousers, and sported a pair of calf length blue Dr Marten boots. As he came towards us, I noticed he had a face full of metal, studs, and rings everywhere. All around and through his ears, on his eyebrows, on his nose, through his nose, and when he smiled and said hello there was a huge one on his tongue. We shook hands and he said, "Pleased to meet you, I'm the treasurer." He was a really nice bloke (there was no reason of course why he shouldn't have been). He went on to say how sorry he was to have missed the magic. He gave me the cheque and I told him I'd show him a trick before I went. I knew exactly what I'd do. I had a quick delve into my case and came out with a coin and told him that this trick was especially for him. I slapped the coin onto my forehead, and it stuck there. I told him that anybody could do it and I said, "You have a go." I prised the coin from my head and set it on the bar. The studs nearly popped out of his head when he saw that the coin had a huge nail fixed to the centre of it. I didn't think he was ever going to stop laughing. It was a great way to end the evening. I picked up my case, said my goodbyes and headed out into the rain and my car, which was hopelessly boxed in. I went back inside, and it was obvious I'd have to wait until the bitter end. The raffle was still going on, with a large amount of small cardboard boxes still waiting to be presented to the happy recipients. I bought myself a pint, had a chat to the treasurer and a couple of others and found myself back in the boardroom. I had a closer look at the photographs of a bygone era. Players with baggy shorts and Brylcreamed hair, smiling and looking proud. Then the trophies - winners and runners up, names and dates etched permanently on the now fading silverware. I sat at the end of the table and pondered the gig as the occasional drop of rainwater plopped into the bucket. After a while the noise from the clubroom reduced to a gentle buzz as it slowly emptied. It wasn't really about the tricks, and it never was. It was all about the people and the laughter. I felt truly blessed. It was quiet now as I made my way outside to my car. Case in one hand and the bucket of water in the other. I emptied it into the gutter and then took it back inside and placed it back on the table. It was the least I could do.

Into 2001 and an encouraging start. Now that the boys were doing their own thing, I decided it was time for me to have a bit of a social life and perhaps get back into sport. I'd heard there was a new custom built table tennis centre in the Kingston area of Milton Keynes.

January 5th, 2001: *I called in at the Kingston Table Tennis Centre to find out where it was and to find out opening times. I went back there tonight at 7.30 for a knock and had a great time. I hope I can make it every week now.*

I went along there every Friday night. I even joined a team and played in the league once again. Although it was in one of the lower divisions, it was still good fun, and I did that for a few years. One evening I came home from my usual Friday night knock and mentioned to the boys that I'd been playing with a man who was in a wheelchair. This chap was really good and up to Olympic Games standard. When they asked me if I'd beaten him and said I'd said, "No", they thought it was hilarious. "Beaten by a bloke in a wheelchair!" They've never let me forget it.

Jay was working hard at college and was doing well. He'd made his mind up to go on to university at the end of his course, so it was important that his grades were good. He was also still working hard at BHS and putting in a lot of hours. He did apply for another job at a computer game shop (imaginatively called 'Game') where the pay was better and one of the perks was a 25% discount on all games; the hours were more flexible too. I also suspect street cred' played a small part as well. Working in Menswear at BHS with middle-aged women didn't really cut it. He went along for an interview which seemed to go ok, but obviously didn't.

January 18th, 2001: *Jay didn't get the job at the Game shop. The interviewer thought he was too quiet. Sounds a bit of a twat to me.*

Oh well, he carried on working at BHS, a case of better the devil you know. Meanwhile, Ben was thinking about employment of an entirely different nature.

January 15th, 2001: *Ben's friend Toby has been at our house for most of the day and he's thinking about going to 'Camp America'. He's got all the information and Ben seems interested as well. I don't blame them.*

The next day Ben had got himself a passport form, had filled it in and sent it off. He was going and that was that! For him it was a win win situation. An adventure of course, but also an opportunity to work with children, which was something he knew he'd be good at, and gain some experience. There was a lot of form filling to do, and it went on for months with some of them going missing presumably lost in the post which meant they had to be resent; it was all rather frustrating. He had to get several references and have a check-up with our GP who also had a huge form to contend with. By the time April arrived it was all pretty much done and dusted. All that was left now was his induction course which took place in Birmingham. He got through that and was formally accepted. At that point he had no idea where in America he was going, although it seemed that many of the camps were in the New England area. Ben wasn't too bothered though; just happy he was going. He completed the second year of his computer course before he went and left 'The Discovery Store' in April. They gave him a good send off with a lovely card signed by all the staff with a present of thirty dollars (which would turn out to be useful). His departure day arrived all too quickly and we set off for Heathrow on Saturday June 2nd at 7.00 o'clock in the morning. The arrangement was to meet up with a company rep' outside a coffee shop. Of course we waited by the wrong one for a while, but eventually found the right one and Ben joined the group which consisted of a selection of young people from all over Europe. There were also some anxious parents and a couple of friendly reps. We were told that all the youngsters would be housed in a holding area (which was a college in Richmond) until a place and a flight became available. I watched him go, rucksack over his shoulders, a quick glance back and a wave, and he was gone. I did feel a tad emotional on the way home but rather proud as well. The whole thing was Ben's idea, it wasn't discussed, and my opinion not sought. He'd made his mind up and that was that. He was about to set off on only his second flight (the other one to Jersey) and his first visit to a foreign country. It was a brave thing for a 20-year-old to do. My attitude can best be summed up in a diary entry in March of that year several weeks before he went.

March 7th, 2001: *Jay went football training tonight and really enjoyed it. He has to do a minimum of ten hours for his college course. He told me again today that he's looking forward to going to university. Ben sent off his final application to Camp America, so it looks as if both boys are flexing their wing muscles. Good luck to both of them.*

As with Ben and his trip, Jay's decision to go to university was entirely his. So different from my experience with my Dad who would have been distraught had I'd suggested something similar. Times and attitudes were different in those days and thank God youngsters of the 21st century have more scope and freedom to do much more with their lives than we did. I was proud and pleased that both boys had the vision and wherewithal to follow their dreams.

Of course I worried about Ben as he left but luckily I had a busy weekend with the magic. As soon as I got back from the airport it was a quick shower then off to do a wedding which took up most of the afternoon. The next day I was helping at a one-day convention in Wolverton, organised by Gary Young. It was a really good day, and I spent a lot of it teaching youngsters coin moves. I always find that rewarding especially when they suddenly get it. The only downside to the day was losing my mobile phone. Bearing in mind where Ben was, it couldn't have been a worse time, luckily somebody had found it and put it in a drawer - unluckily the key to the drawer had gone missing. When the key was finally found (about a week later) the phone wasn't in it. The chap who had found it had now left the venue and had apparently taken it home. I finally got it back some three weeks after I'd lost it. Luckily Ben phoned the landline on June 6th from a noisy pub in London to tell me that he was flying out to California the following day. He was excited of course but a bit concerned about how he was going to get home when his stint had finished. It seemed the trip to Sacramento was one way. What a time to tell me! I put a brave face on it and said we'd worry about that nearer the time. A week later he sent an email to Babs (I was totally technology ignorant then) saying that he'd got there ok and was on the California and Nevada border where it was really hot and he's there with a bunch of Australian lads. He phoned a couple of days later (reversed the charges of course, but I didn't care). He was doing ok and enjoying himself but sounded a tad homesick - he said he hadn't had any mail yet. I gave his address to friends and family and quite a few of us sent regular airmail letters. He phoned every couple of weeks or so throughout the summer and feeling quite chuffed at one point as he'd mended the camp computer. In August we had to face the problem of getting him home, the easiest way was to send him enough money to cover his flight plus additional expenses. Luckily my long working hours literally paid off and the bank of Dad was able to send him 300 dollars. After travelling around California for a while with his Australian pals he finally got to New York. His flight home was on September 5th. Six days before the attack on the World Trade Centre.

Jay had decided to spend some of his hard-earned cash on a holiday in the sunshine in July with a few of his pals. He spent all day packing and re-packing and finally got it all finished in time for me to drop him at the station that evening. There were a couple of Mums there seeing their lads off fussing and worrying and almost in tears as they waved them off. I had to smile to myself as I thought about Ben's recent adventure.

A couple of days later I decided on a bit of a whim to head off for a few days in Wales. I left the house at about 5.45 am on a lovely sunny morning heading for the west coast. I stopped off at Hay-on-Wye to have a long browse around the many book shops there. Something I'd always wanted to do. In the past with the family in tow I'd had to drive right passed the place. I had a cup of tea there and then continued on to Aberaeron and found myself a nice B&B overlooking the harbour. As much as I wanted to get away from it all for a few days I never quite could.

July 25th, 2001: *I went for a walk round the town, had a honey ice cream, and wandered round the aquarium which isn't as big as it used to be. I spent the afternoon in Newquay and Cai Bach beach where it was really beautiful and quite hot and also deserted. I had a shower* *at 6.00 o'clock and went to the Cai Bach clubhouse for a pint or two and a huge lasagne. Finally I watched the sunset over Cardigan Bay which was wonderful. I was in bed at 9.30. Meg phoned just as I was nodding off about a gig in August.*

The following day I travelled up the coast to Aberystwyth where I stayed for an hour and ambled around the shops and museum. The weather was beautiful, and I carried on round the coast to Borth, Barmouth, Porthmadog, and Criccieth where I found a cheap B&B (£15) for the night. The next day I drove around the coast still heading north to Caernarvon, right across Angelsey to Holyhead. There I visited the usual haunts and had a cup of tea in the beach cafe before heading to Llandudno. It had been a long day. There was a road full of B&B houses and I chose one at random. I rang the bell, and it was answered by a familiar looking chap.

"Hello Ken," he said, "Still doing the magic?"

It was the same place I stayed at two years previously at the convention. It was lovely to have a chat and a catch up. I got up early the next day and after a huge breakfast set off home at 9.00 o'clock arriving at about 1.30 pm. It was a Saturday, so I had all of Sunday for washing and ironing and preparing myself to go back to work the day after that. It had been a great week and I wasn't particularly looking forward to going back to the grind. Although I was only 51, I couldn't wait to retire. Only another 14 years to go! Luckily my first day back at work went ok with no problems and that evening I was able to relax.

July 30th, 2001: *I had sausages for dinner which went down a treat. I spent the evening on the crossword and had yet another plonk on the* *guitar trying and struggling to learn Stairway to heaven. After that I watched an interesting tv documentary about flashers.*

I picked up Jay from the station after his two weeks away in the sunshine and although he'd had a nice break, he got sunburnt and came home with a cold. Generally speaking, he thought the island was a bit of a dump. No idea which island he was referring to - no doubt they're all pretty much the same. It doesn't appear that he had much luck with the girls either, but he wouldn't have told me anyway; if I had asked, it would probably have been another Phyllis.

I had a couple of summer gigs one of which was for Tesco. I arrived at the Watford Hilton with some trepidation, half expecting the pea shooters to make an appearance. I was almost disappointed when they didn't. According to my diary it went ok although the new trick I planned on trying out (a pack vanish) didn't work. It was one of those instances where I came up with the idea at home and rehearsed it all day (and it worked beautifully) yet when I had a couple of attempts before I started, it just wouldn't. I daren't risk it. Can there be anything more embarrassing than having to pick up a full pack of cards off the floor in front of a room full of people? Anyway, I did go on to perfect it over the following years and it worked - most of the time. A couple of weeks later, I had another job which according to the contract was for 200-300 people in a marquee. When I got there, I discovered about 75 people in a rather grubby rugby clubhouse. Anyway, it went ok, helped by the fact that I was quite experienced by now at entertaining in football and rugby clubhouses. A few weeks later I was at the other end of the social scale, performing at a function at Warwick Castle along with a few friends from the magic club, organised by Kevin Burke. This was on September 1st. A memorable day if you're a football fan. England were playing Germany in a World Cup qualifying match. There was one particular table that were listening in on a little radio. As luck would have it, I found myself there just about every time an England goal went in. There were five all together and of course a huge roar went up on each occasion. Everybody would look over and I'm sure the other performers must have thought, *Ken's going well.* According to my diary it was a really good night, although it ended on a bit of a frustrating note when I got lost in the car park.

I had another week off in September to go to the IBM Convention in Scarborough. It was nice to meet up with my pals, Mike Alan, Kevin Fox and the Manchester lads and others. It was the only time I got to see them. Kevin was a lovely man, who gave me a lot of advice about everything. To meet up and chat with them all was always the highlight of conventions for me. If the organised magic was good, it was just a bonus. The undoubted star of Scarborough was Dominique Duvivier. He did an act of card magic with his daughter Alexandra. Seated at the same table they would pass the cards to each other, shuffle and cut, and miracles would happen. Some of it was done to music which added to the overall effect. The presentation was just wonderful. During his lecture Dominique would speak in French while Alexandra acted as interpreter. Not really being a card man myself I was more than happy to listen and just look at the beautiful Alexandra.

By mid-September we were all back to some sort of normality. I was still working long hours starting at six and still managing to find some energy to play league table tennis once a week. I soon found myself playing in a match at the AHW Club where it all began for me back in the 60s. The place hadn't changed a bit. The same three tables were there, the paintwork hadn't been touched, and my photo was still on display in the same spot on the same wall (with probably the same drawing pin). It was taken when I was 16 in 1966. It was great to be back in the old place for the first time in almost 50 years. I think I would have been disappointed if it had changed to be honest.

Jay was busy doing some research online into various Universities, and Ben (finally over his jet lag which seemed to last for weeks) was back at college. Both boys were still huge football fans and had been pestering me for weeks to buy into Sky Sports so they could watch Premiership matches.

September 21st, 2001: *Me and Ben went to the Centre tonight and signed up for Sky Sports. It cost me £60 to start with and it'll be £28 per month which the boys have promised to pay for.*

I've just fallen off my chair laughing at that last sentence. Oh well, I was able to afford it providing I kept putting in the hours and got some gigs. Luckily with the Sports Channel package there were about 60 other channels, several of which were of interest to me, which of course meant, from the boys' point of view, it was reasonable for me to pay the subscription, which I did until they left home some years later.

A couple of days later we sat down to watch a Manchester United match against a team from Greece. It was on ITV which was a bit annoying. We were joined on the sofa by an Australian friend of Ben's he'd met in America. This was to be the first of many visitors from all over the world. Ben would invite them ("Dad won't mind.") and they stayed for various lengths of time. Often, I'd have to pick them up from railway stations and even airports at all times of the night and day. It was hard work having to feed and accommodate them but always worth it. There seemed to be something inherently adventurous about Australian youngsters who came to visit. One of them scanned the local paper one night, asked to borrow the phone, and bought himself a car. He needed to insure it and sort out a new logbook, which I'm assuming he did as a couple of days later he drove a battered old Ford from our house to "the West Country" to continue his travelling. Meanwhile Ben was still pursuing his music with his pals and in October he ventured into the public arena.

October 14th, 2001: *Ben and Dale did their first gig tonight at Bar Central. It was an Open Mic night and in spite of Ben's almost reluctance to go, he seemed to enjoy it. Jay went with him to give support and I picked them up at 12.30.*

I don't think Ben was too keen on performing, he was more of a creative force behind the scenes and was happier composing and creating music in the comfort of his studio. By now the excitement of his trip to America was behind him, but I was still feeling the aftermath.

October 19th, 2001: *The phone bill arrived today and Ben's reverse charge calls from America came to £105! As a result of that my monthly payment has to go up to £45. I went to table tennis and had a good knock.*

You can't beat a good game of table tennis to get frustrations out of your system. There is something very satisfying about hitting that small white ball as hard as you can for an hour or two.

I didn't seem too bothered at the time, as work appeared to be plentiful, and I also had a bit of private carpentry work (I made two beds). Yet again though, as befits the building trade, a couple of weeks later the workforce was summoned to a meeting. We were told that owing to lack of work there would be imminent redundancies and we were all handed the standard letter explaining all. It obviously wasn't the first time, and I was banking on being transferred to the maintenance department if I happened to be on the list. Luckily though I was given work to do around the factory site for a few weeks, doing fence repairs and building small sheds to house machinery etc. Luckily, by the beginning of November, work had picked up again and we were told there would be no more redundancies. It was a huge relief as three days later I went to a meeting at Jay's college to find out about university expenses. It looked as though I might avoid a considerable amount of the fees as my earnings were just about below the threshold; I was also told that I might get help with his living expenses (one of the few perks of being a single parent). However, I knew that the years ahead would be difficult financially for both me and Jay. I do have to give him credit for the amount of hours he was putting in at BHS as well as his college work, and he was having driving lessons. The year ended on a positive note. Ben was asked to go back to America as the camp photographer the following year, and Jay had come up with a shortlist of six universities, and I had a great New Year's Eve with a gig at Buckingham Town Hall. It was all to look forward to.

CHAPTER 26

Further Education

2002 didn't have a good start when I discovered there was no money in my bank account. My Christmas wages hadn't gone in. Fortunately, I was able to transfer some money from my ISA to cover for a while. The money in that account, though, was put by for Jay's uni expenses and to bail-out Ben if he got stuck in America again. I couldn't really afford to use it for too long on day-to-day expenses. Meanwhile, I was being hit with bank charges because payments were due which obviously couldn't be paid. It seemed the wrong numbers were quoted from my company which meant my bank couldn't release the cash. It took four weeks to sort out and for me to get my money back. Soon after that we had trouble with the boiler. Why is it, I wondered, that heating problems always seem to arise in the middle of winter? I also discovered the downside of being a homeowner - I had to pay for a plumber. Gone were the days when the council would come out and fix it for free. It was eventually sorted by a chap in Yellow Pages.

As Jay was getting himself prepared for uni, Ben was searching for work; he even asked at the local school if he could do something on a voluntary basis. He definitely knew what he wanted to do, and he eventually did reach his goal. Some 20 years later, he is still involved with youngsters and enjoys every minute of it. It was in early 2002 when he discovered yet another talent - film making. He and his pals would go out into the community with a video camera and make short films which turned out to be really good. There was one called Urban Cartwheeling where Ben filmed his pal Dave doing cartwheels around the local landmarks of Milton Keynes, including down the aisle of a large recently- opened supermarket. They were well edited, and Ben also wrote and performed the music. They were original, funny, and brilliant! (Well, I would say that wouldn't I, but they were.) I've made a guest appearance in a couple of them - one was called, 'How to annoy Dad', and the other one was a film of him and his pals doing 'keepy-uppy' with a football around the landmarks of Milton Keynes. This one was particularly good and had a good response when it was on YouTube. It was eventually pulled though because of copyright reasons having been made with the music of Jamiroquai. I'd have given that one an Oscar.

Jay was applying for university places, and getting offers. He obviously had to make the right decision as his future depended on it. His shortlist of six was Canterbury, Leeds, Winchester, Warrington, Worcester, and Walsall (sounds like a firm of solicitors!). We had a long talk one night and had a good look through each glossy prospectus and other information and concluded that we really needed to go and have a look at a couple of the more promising ones. In the end though we took no chances and visited them all. Luckily each of the open days didn't clash and I think we both enjoyed the overall process. The first one we visited was Canterbury and my diary entry for that day is fairly typical of the other five.

February 14th, 2002. *I went into work from 6.00 o'clock until 10.00 this morning and then it was off to Canterbury with Jay to Christ Church College open day. We had a good journey down with lovely* *weather, arriving at the park and ride in Canterbury at about 12.30. We walked into a circular underpass in search of the correct exit and ended up where we started! We found the college in the end though and had a snack in the refectory before queuing for an hour to see the sport science lecturer. From there we had a conducted tour which was followed by a short presentation. All in all it was quite impressive. The accommodation works out at about £65 per week and there is a BHS in Canterbury. Not a bad journey home. I'm exhausted.*

The financial implications were clear, and the importance of having access to a potential part-time job for Jay needed to be considered. Obviously I'd help out whenever I could, providing I was still in work with plenty of overtime. Although impressed with Canterbury, we didn't have anything to compare it with. However, a couple of weeks later we set off early on a winter's morning to travel up to Leeds. The day was a familiar format to that of Canterbury, beginning with two very professional presentations followed by a conducted tour of the accommodation block by a young student (in the middle of a blizzard). Jay had an interview in the afternoon, and he wasn't impressed by the interviewer who by all accounts knew little about the course and had no interest in what Jay had to say. Despite that he was offered a place. Too soon to decide yet, so onto the next - Winchester. As luck would have it, this visit was on a Saturday, on my birthday. Again the same format of a welcome, presentations, and a look at the accommodation. This was one of the better ones, but we were by now beginning to realise the end decision wasn't going to be easy. My diary entry for the next day made me smile.

March 10ᵗʰ, 2002: *Jay bought me a CD single for my birthday, it was called, "Nothing" and was by a band called "A". Ben just bought me nothing!*

Oh well, he probably had more important things on his mind.

Three days later, me and Jay travelled up the motorway to Warrington and this time, to save money, we took a packed lunch. We sat in the car park munching away and looked at the buildings, which were very school- like and a bit tatty. The day was again well organised and interesting, and to match the slightly run-down appearance of the accommodation, it was only £35 per week. My attitude was beggars can't be choosers – however, it was never going to be my decision. Three more to go.

Onto the next - Worcester. We were impressed with this place right from the start. The chap who gave the sports presentation was really passionate and it was certainly the best one yet. Worcester had something many of the others hadn't and we could feel it as we walked around the campus; it just seemed more friendly and positive somehow. The downside though was they weren't too strong on the Media Studies side of things. (As an option Jay was considering sports journalism.) On the way home Jay had decided on a shortlist of two, Winchester and Worcester. I was hoping he'd go for Worcester, but we still had to see what Walsall had to offer. This was an afternoon event, so I was able to get a few hours in at work before we travelled the short distance up the M1 to Birmingham. Again a very slick opening presentation in the main hall after which we made our way to one of the gymnasiums to see what was on offer for the sport courses. This rather short presentation was conducted by two young chaps wearing rugby shirts and jogging bottoms. They came swaggering in and told us how wonderful the place was, but they weren't particularly well prepared, and we weren't impressed; at one point one of them made a derogatory remark about Worcester which we found annoying. As luck would have it there was no media studies course available there which meant it was off the list anyway. It was all down to Jay now.

April 22nd, 2002: *Jay finally filled in his UCAS form and has chosen Worcester as his first choice and Winchester as his second. Relief all round. I went out and posted it this evening. Ben and mates went out golfing tonight at Wavendon. When they got back, they went out onto the play area and filmed themselves hitting fruit and veg. All good clean fun.*

Jay would be leaving college in June and was looking around for a job other than BHS to raise some extra cash for uni in September. He did go on a lifesaving course at the beginning of the year and worked as a lifeguard at a local swimming pool for a while but, being on the wrong side of town and not an easy place to get to, it didn't last. BHS was getting him down and it wasn't something he really wanted to do anyway. Soon though he heard from UCAS confirming his choice of Worcester and things were on the move. All through the summer various forms and letters arrived in the post connected with uni. They had to be read deciphered and sent back. It was never-ending. It went on right up to early September and I thought he was never going to get there. The good news was he did leave BHS and got a job at the cinema which kept him going for a couple of months.

2002 was just a crazy year from start to finish. The house was always full. Ben's musician friends would be there recording in his studio most evenings, and on one memorable occasion when he was making a CD for a local Minister, a small choir was crammed in there. He was under a bit of pressure to get it finished, and the Playaz Klub CD, and a video he'd made for one of Jay's college projects - all before he went to America. He just about managed it. When Jay wasn't working or getting his final college assignments finished, he would have a room full of his pals playing computer games or snooker. I was in the middle of it all, cooking and washing up and trying to win a losing battle against endless piles of ironing. Somehow, I found the energy to play table tennis once a week, go to the magic club (I won the 'Magic of the Mind' competition) and even the occasional gig. A full life.

With the often heavy work and long hours and unpredictability of the building trade, I was always on the lookout for something else. I spotted an advert in the local paper for a cabinet maker and decided to go for it. I went for an interview.

April 4th, 2002: *I went for the interview at Rubens and did quite well I thought. The place is run by two quite young chaps, and they seem friendly enough. The stuff they do is at the top end of the market and looks rather complicated. They asked me point blank if I could hack it. I said I could, given the time to get into the swing. I was shown around and was quite impressed. I reckon I could settle there ok. They're interviewing 13 men this week and next, and they'll let me know in a fortnight.*

A shame I didn't get the job, but they did send me a nice letter and would keep my details on file. That was the last I heard from them.

Ben was getting prepared to jet off to America again and had got everything sorted out after the usual endless form filling. I was a bit concerned about him being on his own in New York for a couple of days, but he was fearless. He was more concerned about how he was going to watch the England games in the World Cup than anything else. As it happened, he was able to watch one of them in a bar in Los Angeles sitting next to one of the Goss brothers from the band Bros. We never have let him forget about that! We did manage to watch one match together before he went...

June 2nd, 2002: *We travelled down to Tony's this morning leaving at 8.10. We had a good journey down apart from a slight hiccup at the end. (I drove in the wrong direction on the M27.) Even when we got to Totton, none of us had Tony's number to contact him, or the whereabouts of his house. (We blamed each other of course.) Anyway we got there just after 10.30 and in time to watch the match. We played well in the first half, scoring first, but the second half was pretty awful with Sweden equalising. We spent a lovely sunny day relaxing with Tony, his Mum, and of course Opal who's gorgeous. She's doing well at school and has started ballet lessons. The poignancy of that affected us all I think. We had a good journey home. A really lovely and memorable day.*

Four days later I dropped Ben off outside the departure lounge at Heathrow. He got his rucksack out of the boot, put it on his back and strode through the door, and I drove straight home, neither of us keen on goodbyes. Three days later he phoned to say he was at the camp and had travelled over with two Russian youngsters. Always a relief to know he'd got there safe and sound.

That same weekend I had a busy time with the magic, two gigs and a one-day convention. Coincidentally, the gig on 8th June was at another rugby club. Perhaps they're cheap to hire, or perhaps the chap who was celebrating his 50th birthday was a former player. Who knows? Anyway, according to my diary all went well if a little noisy. The gig the next day was totally different. It was another birthday party (a 60th) and was in a marquee at a large house in a small village in Northamptonshire. I'd done several of a similar nature like this before for Roy & Meg. According to the contract there would be around 200 people there which is a lot of people for one performer to cover. I was booked from 12.30 until 3 o'clock. I got there early and made a start doing some mix and mingle stuff as the people were standing around the bar area. It was an hour before they sat down. Their timing was all over the place. I didn't have a break but made a start on working the tables, desperately trying to remember who'd seen a trick and who hadn't. I did what I could and finished at just gone 3 o'clock. I said my goodbyes and was about to get into my car when one of the guests came over to me remonstrating that I hadn't been to his table. I offered to unpack and do some stuff for him, but he said I was obviously finished for the day and stomped off. It left me with a sour taste but as far as I was concerned, I'd followed the instructions on the contract to the letter. When I got back, I phoned Meg and explained all, and she said she'd make a call the next day and let me know of any developments. Two days later Meg sent me the cheque for the gig with a small note from the lady who had booked me and whose name was on the contract... "Thank you so much! Thoroughly enjoyed the party, the magician was excellent!" What a relief. I hate it if the customer isn't satisfied. Thankfully it doesn't happen very often. My final comment is one that is often used by entertainers like me when referring to an audience. There's always one!

When I got back from the gig, I went over to another one of Gary Young's one-day conventions. It was pretty much over by the time I got there but I did have a chance for a chat with my old friend Bobby Bernard (enthusiastic as ever). I was also able to watch an excellent gala show. A good end to what had been a rather exhausting weekend.

Jay finally finished college on 28th June. His hard work had paid off, earning him grades of two merits and six distinctions. I was really proud of him. He spent the afternoon drinking with his mates and then went out clubbing with them that evening. The college part of his education was complete and well worth celebrating. He was now looking forward to the next phase of his education - three years at Worcester University. He spent the rest of the summer working at the cinema and getting everything ready for the big day in mid-September.

I had a week off work at the end of July and decided to go up to Wales for a couple of days to unwind, relax, and charge up my batteries. In some ways the urge to go there is almost like a calling. I drove up to Anglesey arriving in the early evening and found a cheap B&B. It was only £17 and was pretty basic with a bed, wardrobe, and a rickety old chair, and that was it. I had a quick shower in the equally basic (but clean) bathroom and walked into the village to find a pub and a much-needed pint and something to eat. After polishing off a large pie and chips I made my way back along the seashore and ended the evening watching the final day of the Commonwealth Games on a small TV in the small lounge. By the end of that I was nodding off and went to bed. I was woken up around 7 o'clock with the unmistakable screech of seagulls and the scratching of its feet from the roof top directly above me - sounds that always fill me with happy childhood memories. The milkman arrived, noisily parking below my open window, and chatting to the owner with his wonderful Welsh lilt. By now I was wide awake and feeling a bit peckish. Soon the smell of bacon came wafting up the stairs and in less than 10 minutes I was sat at the breakfast table.

August 1st, 2002: *I had a terrific breakfast this morning - fruit juice, cereal, two mugs of tea, and then a cooked plateful which consisted of fried bread, fried egg, grilled tomatoes, bacon, sausages, mushrooms, and black pudding. After all of that, toast, and marmalade. Yum yum!*

Although the accommodation was pretty basic, it was certainly more than made up for by the quality and quantity of that breakfast which kept me going for the rest of the day. It was a short break but none the less enjoyable.

I went back to work the following Monday where all sorts of rumours were circulating. It went on for a couple of weeks and some were confirmed when the workforce was summoned to the conference room. We were told that the company was to be taken over by another company called Rok. It appeared that nothing would change, and we were to carry on as normal. Easy to say. A couple of months later we were driven by coach to a hotel near London to listen to a presentation led by the CEO of Rok, a rather charismatic figure by the name of Garvis Snook. He confirmed that as far as the employees were concerned it was indeed a case of carry on as normal as the company was being taken over as a going concern. My attitude was to sit tight and see what happened. My overriding memory of that evening was the journey home. Many of the lads had taken advantage of the free bar and were as pissed as newts!

One of the perks of Jay working at the cinema was being able to get free tickets.

August 24th, 2002: *After dinner Jay suggested we go to the pictures. We went to see 'Reign of fire' which was about dragons invading the British Isles. It was good escapism and we both enjoyed it. I was really quite touched that Jay would want to go with an old git like me. I have to say I felt quite conspicuous as I'd nothing to wear, it felt strange to be out and about with so many young people.*

I didn't really have a social life, but I wasn't bothered. I was either too busy, or too tired. The thought of buying new clothes never occurred to me, not that I could afford them anyway. My life was totally wrapped up around the needs of the boys, more so now with both of them on the cusp of adulthood and about to launch themselves into the world of work and career. My life, I decided (then) would become my own when they'd left home, or I'd retired. Whichever came first. Meanwhile, back in 2002 life went on.

Soon it was the end of Ben's stint in America, and it was time to go down to Heathrow to pick him up. I made sure I was in plenty of time and set off at seven o'clock (after working for an hour). The traffic was awful and by the time I got to the Arrival lounge he should have been ready and waiting. He was nowhere to be seen. I went to the Virgin desk where, after scanning their computer, I was told he'd been booked on a flight arriving the next day! I didn't know whether to laugh or cry. It was annoying I had a wasted journey, but I was so relieved he was ok. He phoned that evening and told me the details of his flight the next day which could well be delayed. The best plan was for him to give me a call when he arrived at Heathrow, and that's what happened. I picked him up mid-morning. He looked fit and well but as thin as ever and strangely taller. He was quiet in the car driving back which was understandable as I remembered his problems with jet lag from the previous year. As soon as he was able over the following weeks he set to and busied himself editing over 3 hours of footage he'd taken during the summer. The end result was just stunning with a beautiful film of life in a California children's camp. Once that was done and sent off, he soon settled back into his routine of composing and filming, and also job hunting. It was at this time too that he discovered another hobby. Fish. He'd bought himself a small tank (with colour coordinated gravel to match the décor) plus electric filters and a small light. He called it his Benny Fishery. Around this time he was called Benny by all his friends, but to family he'll always be known as our Ben. I fixed a shelf to the wall and soon several small fish were happily swimming away. As the years passed the tanks got bigger, as did the fish. His interest never waned. He's got quite a large fish tank in his own lounge now, and it is very relaxing.

Always on the lookout to make a few quid I spotted something in the local paper in early September put in by the police. They were after volunteers to line up in an identity parade. I (just about) met the general criteria of the type of man they wanted and applied. What could be an easier way to make fifteen quid than walking into a room and standing still for a couple of minutes? The boys thought it was hilarious.

"What if somebody recognises you?" asked Jay.

"What for?" I replied.

"Well, you know."

"No I don't!"

"What if you're picked out?" asked Ben.

"I won't be because I haven't done anything!!"

"That's what you say! And we can't afford to bail you out!"

And so it went on until it was time to go. I got to the police station and joined a group of blokes who I do have to say looked a bit younger than me. As we filed through to another room (I was the last) I felt a hand on my shoulder.

"Excuse me sir but we won't be needing you tonight after all."

I looked at the sergeant who went on to say,

"You still get the fifteen quid, and can you come back at the same time next week?"

"Certainly Officer." I replied; easier money than I thought.

The following week I duly turned up and joined the queue and filed into a well-lit room clutching a piece of card with a number on it. We were told to face the front and to maintain a normal expression and look forward into what I assumed was a long two-way mirror. A voice came through the speaker.

"Would number 331/AVU turn to your right and leave the room please?"

The chap next to me gave me a nudge and whispered,

"That's you mate."

And indeed it was. I went through the door to be met by the same sergeant who said,

"Sorry sir but you're too old, but here's fifteen quid."

That was the last time I ever set foot in a police station. The thirty quid was very useful.

Jay's big day finally arrived and on Sunday September 15th, 2002; we set off on the 85-mile trip to Worcester with the car loaded up full of everything he'd need. Well, sadly not quite everything as we'd find out later. He got himself registered and signed on for the library and Students Union with no trouble at all. I drove the car round to his allocated flat and after a chat with his new flatmates we began to unload the car. When it was done, we realised there was no duvet for the bed. We re-read the accommodation letter and discovered that he was indeed supposed to supply his own. I wasn't surprised that something would be missed despite having a car full of stuff. The next day he phoned to tell me he'd need an extra plate, and could I bring one of his old bank statements so he could open an account. Later that day he phoned again; he couldn't find the confirmation letter from UCAS stating that he was actually allowed to be there. I knew that was in a file with him somewhere because I'd seen it. Ye gods! The following day I travelled up to Worcester straight from work. The duvet was in a bin liner along with a plate and a bank statement. I'd worry about the missing letter when I got there. I arrived at about 7.30 and the first thing Jay did was tip up the bin liner and break the plate! Regarding the missing letter, he said he'd been through the files and just couldn't find it.

"It's in the black file" I insisted.

He passed it over, I opened it, and there it was on the top! I got home at ten o'clock that night knackered after a 170-mile round trip but relieved he was sorted out at last.

At the end of September I had a week off work and reckoned I deserved a break for a while from the pressure of family life, so off I went down to Eastbourne for the IBM convention. Again it was great to see my old friends and share stories and do tricks for a few days.

Meanwhile, back in Worcester... Soon after I got back from Eastbourne Jay phoned again. He'd lost his bank card. He applied for another one and could I send him £100 to keep him going until it arrived. Thanks to my ISA I was able to do that. A week later he phoned again to say he was now down to his last three quid and could I send him more. I sent him another £20. A few days later he phoned to say his new bank card had arrived but no PIN number. For security reasons it was being sent separately to my address. Once that had arrived, I was able to give him the number over the phone, another problem solved. The burning question now was could I afford to keep him there for three years? He'd cost me a fortune and he'd been there for less than 3 weeks! Luckily it was all teething trouble and he soon settled into uni life and was loving it. Usually he was quite good with his money and always managed to find work when he came home for holidays. He only asked me for money if there was no other option. Ben was exactly the same. They knew what the score was. If you want money you have to go out and earn it.

December soon rolled around, and on the 17th, I went to the Stables to see David Penn's magic show. (David was one of my first magic club juniors.) He did a great job and at one point he had the spotlight trained on me. As I stood, he thanked me for the help I'd given him all those years ago and led the applause. What a lovely thing to do.

A few days later I did a corporate Christmas gig for a local company which took place in their head office. There were several rooms nicely decorated that were set up for a variety of things. There was a bar and a disco in the large dining room and a rather nice buffet in the room adjacent to that. Just down the corridor was another room with a roulette table. My brief was simple, wander about performing as and where I liked. Because of the usual problem with a disco (and sound travelled) I ended up staying put and sharing a room with the roulette table. The people there were ok about it, and it turned out we'd shared gigs before. It was an unusual situation in as much as the people would come to me rather than me wander about from group to group or person to person. It was a matter of adapting to the conditions and it worked quite well. As I finished for the evening and the crowd dispersed, one middle-aged man stopped to have a chat.

"That was marvellous," he said, "I have no idea where those coins came from, you even had your sleeves rolled up!"

"To be honest, it's a bit of a myth that magicians use their sleeves," I said.

"I can't do anything like that," he said, "Look at my hands."

He held them out, they were normal if a bit podgy. I went on to tell him about John Ramsay who had similar hands and he was one of the best that's ever been.

"I still wouldn't be able to do it, I can't do anything with my hands, in fact I'm no good at anything. I've been a failure for most of my life."

His face dropped, he thanked me for the magic and wandered off into the night. It left me with a bit of an empty feeling. Magic isn't supposed to be like that. It's a form of entertainment that fills people with wonder and makes them laugh - doesn't it? For that chap the opposite had happened, watching me perform had made him miserable, which in turn had made me miserable. Apart from that, it was a good night.

2002 had been eventful in all sorts of ways. I wondered what the future would bring regarding work and the takeover. Would Jay do well at uni? What would happen with Ben? I think we were all up for the challenge as 2003 dawned.

CHAPTER 27

2003 & 2004 Some good, some not so good

I had some idea how Jay was coping with domestic arrangements at uni when he came home for Christmas.

January 8th, 2003: *Jay did himself a fry up at lunch time which Ben filmed for posterity. What a mess! He also crammed the washing machine with a pile of his dirty clothes and put washing powder in all the compartments including the one for conditioner. It took me ten minutes to dig out solidified powder.*

I thought it best if me or Mum did the ironing, for health and safety reasons. Although now well into her eighties she would still get on a bus and come over once a week. She'd cook the dinner and tidy up the house and get stuck into the never-ending pile of ironing. A godsend. It was her 85th birthday in April and we celebrated it with the family taking her out for a nice meal. While the rest of us had salmon or lasagne or something equally exotic, Mum was more than happy tucking into cod and chips.

Winter isn't a pleasant time in the building trade due to most of it involving the great outdoors. The timber was stacked outside and if it had been raining, followed by a frost, the planks would be iced together and would have to be prised apart with a crowbar. Snow covered timber was something else that had to be dealt with. Even with gloves my hands were often in a dreadful state. *I shouldn't be doing this because I'm an artiste*, didn't carry any weight with management. By now we were heavily involved with another company based locally called Pace. As well as making roof trusses and spandrels we were now making Pace panels for timber framed houses, rather like the old days. We were busy once again and with that came the inevitable long hours. Bearing in mind I'd worked for the company for about 20 years, I was conscious of the fact that if I were to leave, I'd lose a good sum of redundancy money and the threat of that was always hanging over us. Even so, yet again I decided to apply for another job I saw advertised in the local press. This was teaching woodwork at the local college. I thought it would be rewarding and interesting to pass on my skills to a group of youngsters (and be in the warm; I bet their timber wasn't covered in ice). I called in at the college one night on the way home and picked up a form (which took over an hour to fill in) and I handed it in the next day. A few weeks later I was summoned for an interview. I thought the set up at the college would be similar to that of the old Wolverton Works training school, with youngsters working on benches. It turned out it was nothing like that. The job consisted of helping apprentices get through their City & Guilds Carpentry craft examination. This entailed regular visits to building sites to set up tests, along with marking and monitoring. There was a certain amount of workshop work, but it was all connected with the building trade - a bit of cabinet making would have been nice. I took some photographs of some of the work I'd done over the years with me to the interview and, although I soon realised I didn't want the job, I showed them anyway. The interviewer looked at the photo of one of the fancy gallows brackets I'd made and said,

"That's interesting, is it made of hard wood?"

"No," I said, "It's pressure treated softwood and painted with a high grade of preservative, and then it'll be stained or primed and painted on site."

"Tut tut, it should be hardwood." he said, a touch condescendingly I thought.

I didn't want to get into an argument with him, although he was probably right, but I'd followed the architect's instructions on the drawing to the letter. Just as well perhaps I didn't get the job.

Spring was around the corner. Ben was busy recording and mixing the PZK album called City of Circles and also recording some young local rap outfits. Yet again he was asked to go back to camp in California. By now he was used to the form filling and the annual medical which took place at our local surgery… he was in there for about ten minutes and charged 72 quid!

I went over to Worcester to pick Jay up for his summer break at the end of May and couldn't believe the amount of stuff we had to cram into the car. Of course I asked the obvious question,

"Do you need all of this stuff, and what's in those two huge black bin liners?"

"Washing," he replied.

Oh well, ask a silly question.

Somehow, we crammed it all in and got home after a slow journey (due to the weight) in two hours.

The next day stepson Jeff came over for one of his periodic visits.

May 26th, 2003: *Jeff came over this morning and stayed for a couple of hours. All three of them played footy out the back. Ben now has a*

bad back, Jay has hurt his ankle, and Jeff could hardly breathe when they came in.

Not as fit as they thought!

Summer soon arrived and with it a busy weekend with the magic. On the evening of Friday June 6th I travelled over to the Old Warden Airfield in Shuttleworth near Biggleswade. This was a huge charity event called 'The Primrose Grand Gala Ball' and was for The Bedford Hospitals Primrose Appeal; there were almost 700 guests, and it was a fund-raising event for a purpose-built cancer unit. A worthy cause indeed. I got there at 7.30 pm and met up with the seven other 'close-uppers' I'd be working with, to plan a strategy. Because of the amount of people there, and the size of the venue (most of it outside), it was fairly easy for us to spread out and just do our own thing. We did the 'mix and mingle' stuff to begin with for about an hour and once the people were seated, we worked the tables in the marquees. It was a great evening, and the weather was perfect, as was the atmosphere. We kept going until almost sunset and were then given a lovely buffet meal inside an equally lovely building. Afterwards, and as we walked out, I could detect a buzz of excitement in the air. There was to be a fly-past of an iconic Spitfire aeroplane to commemorate the anniversary of D-Day. We stood on the steps of the building and looked out across the airfield and towards the setting sun. A military band was playing just below us and just as it began to play the familiar Royal Air Force march, a small speck appeared in the distance. We watched as it grew into a Spitfire heading towards us. There were one or two elderly ex-servicemen sitting close by, proudly wearing their service medals. As soon as they realised the plane was approaching, they struggled to their feet, stood to attention, and saluted as it roared directly over our heads. In the silence that followed, I'm sure there were mixed emotions from the elderly people who were watching, no doubt thinking of the many young pilots lost, but at the same time feeling grateful and proud of the iconic few. It was a moving experience. A week later we all received a letter from the organisers thanking us for our input. The evening raised the amazing sum of £10,000.

The next day I was in more familiar territory - Buckingham Town Hall and Villiers Restaurant. I've always loved working there, a great venue and great staff. This was for a wedding reception and according to my diary *"It was one of the best gigs I've ever done."* It appears I was on a bit of a roll.

I dropped Ben off at Heathrow on Friday 13th June. Luckily, I'm not superstitious, but I was concerned about Friday afternoon traffic, which as it happened didn't materialise. By now, I wasn't worried about his stay in the States; he always seemed to have a good time and was obviously good at what he did and was well liked. All didn't go so well though on this trip. He somehow cut his hand which required stitches, and even more painful was the medical bill of 300 dollars. He was told he may have to pay for it and then claim it back through the insurance. A few days later it went up to 800 dollars, but luckily the insurance company paid up, which was just as well, as I barely had enough in my ISA to cover it.

Jay, meanwhile, home for the summer was job hunting and getting a bit desperate - even applying for a job at a city centre bingo club. I asked him how he'd feel about venturing into the building trade and working at Llewellyn for a few weeks. Obviously more desperate than ever, he said yes. I made some enquiries and he agreed to start on July 1st. I wasn't too sure how he'd cope with all the heavy work involved in the truss department (and the boredom), I just hoped he'd last longer than Ben did. It was also a completely new environment that he'd never experienced. He'd have to work with a bunch of blokes and all that goes with it - banter and piss-taking on a daily basis. Luckily it was the summer, and he wouldn't have the cold to contend with, which was something I suppose. It was difficult to begin with and it was hard work, but once his blisters had healed and he had his first pay packet he managed to stick it out until he went back to uni in mid-September.

Jay's stint with on-site accommodation at Worcester was now over. For the rest of his time there he'd be living in a private house, sharing with other students. (Think of the TV programme 'The Young Ones', and you wouldn't be far wrong.) I'd agreed to drive him there after work on a Friday afternoon. He'd spent all morning sorting his stuff out packing it in suitcases and the inevitable black bin liners, and again there was loads of it. I packed the car as far as I dared (after pumping the tyres up), but there was still a lot left. I couldn't believe it. It would take two journeys; I'd have to take the rest of it the next day. We set off and got to the house at about 7.00 pm. It was a large Victorian mid-terrace, and we were met by the landlord who spoke to us along with a couple of other students who had just arrived. He laid down a few ground rules and seemed ok, but it was obvious he wouldn't put up with any crap. My mind went back to our kitchen full of smoke after Jay's attempt at a fry-up, and the blocked washing machine, and also the permanent untidiness of his bedroom.

"He'll be ok; he's really neat and tidy at home," I lied.

It was all down to him now though.

I had a good journey home and the next morning travelled back again and delivered the rest of his stuff. He made me a cup of tea before I left, thanked me for my help, and I drove home in the sunshine. When I got back, I spent all the afternoon tidying his bedroom and ending up with yet another black bin liner full of rubbish. Afterwards I sat with a cup of tea in the quietness of the front room. Both boys were away, now grown up and doing their own thing. I was proud but I did miss them.

In late September I set off to Southport for the IBM convention. Yet again to meet up with my pals for a chat, a beer, and late-night sessions, swapping moves and stories into the early hours. The close-up competition was well supported that year with 12 entrants, including young Sean Heydon from the magic club; although not a prize winner, he did a good job I thought. Some 20 years later he works as a busy professional working on the comedy club circuit, good luck to him.

Ben arrived home from America while I was in Southport and had a great time again. I arrived home on the Sunday.

September 28th, 2003: *I travelled home straight after breakfast. It was raining first thing but brightened up after an hour. It was a good journey and I arrived home some three hours later. Ben seems fine and has already written a new CV in preparation for yet more job hunting. He had a great time and has been invited to go back again next year. I spent the rest of the day washing and ironing Ben's stuff, as well as my own.*

Some things never change!

Another thing Ben did was to get the house wired up for broadband, which he offered to pay for. I had no idea what that meant or what it would do. I might have had more enthusiasm if it was something that helped with the ironing. I have to give him credit though for just getting on with it and making sure we made full use of modern technology. As many of his friends lived abroad, it certainly made it easier to keep in touch with them all. Soon after, an Australian friend of Ben's came to visit who stayed for quite a while.

I was still reasonably busy with the magic and was invited for a return visit to The Mystic Ring, this time to be a judge for their close-up competition. There were only four competitors, but the standard was good. It was a really pleasant evening, and it made a nice change. I was still going along to my club at Northampton whenever I could and in October, we had a return visit from Ali Bongo which was another great night. He began his lecture at 8 o'clock, performed for an hour before a short break, and then carried on until 11 o'clock. The sheer amount of material (all of it brilliant) was just staggering. Needless to say, he received another standing ovation at the end of it.

In the middle of November I had a gig at a rather up-market pub in a village near Slough, a distance of some 55 miles. The contract wasn't all that forthcoming - "Close-up magician. Function. Evening dress." I was booked to do two hours from 8.30 to 10.30. I found the place ok and the couple who ran the place seemed pleasant enough. I was told to wander around the two small bar areas, and a conservatory where people were sitting at tables, and perform as and when I liked. I was also told that a couple of singers would be performing at the same time. That didn't bode well, and I knew I'd have problems as soon as they started. They were too loud. I did the best I could for the few people that were there, but I was being deafened. When they had a break, I went over to introduce myself and explained the situation. To give them credit, they did offer to turn it down a touch. I made the most of the relative silence while they were having their break and got stuck in. The next problem I had was complete indifference from the people there. The response to the event obviously wasn't good as there were a lot of empty tables. Hardly anybody had any interest in watching the magic, and those that did weren't particularly pleasant, and a few were worse for drink. I struggled along for about an hour, but it just didn't take off. The atmosphere was just dead. Obviously, the landlady could see what was happening (or wasn't) and her response was to go over to the singers, get them on again and turn the sound up, in a forlorn effort to get some of the audience up and dancing, at which point I gave up - the phrase 'flogging a dead horse' springing to mind. I got my fee ok but was disappointed that it didn't take off, as were the managers. We were philosophical about it though, and as we'd all been in the entertainment business for years, were more than aware that there are occasions when things just don't always go to plan - another example of you can't entertain all of the people all of the time.

The following night was a better one - a public school Dinner & Dance which took place in a marquee in the grounds. I was booked to do a mix and mingle in the bar area and then work the tables during the meal. I decided to bite the bullet and try out some new material, which had a mixed reception but nonetheless I felt it was worth pursuing. It takes more than one gig before I know if it's workable or not. Routines tend to evolve over a long period of time and the only way for that to happen is to stick at it and perform in front of people as often as you can. Luckily the good old thimble routine came to the rescue and according to my diary did go particularly well.

The final gig of the year was a bit of a strange one but nonetheless enjoyable. It was at the table tennis club where an exhibition match was taking place with some of England's top players. There was a presentation afterwards with a buffet and drinks and I was booked to do the usual stuff. I did it for nothing so there was no pressure, and it was also nice to perform for table tennis friends, many of whom didn't know I was a magician. A fitting end then to what was an interesting year for all sorts of reasons.

2004 would turn out to be a depressing year. It was a hard slog from start to finish with all three of us struggling with our own particular issues. As soon as one problem was rectified another would emerge. I was still working long hours and saving money in case I had to bale out Jay. His student loan was fast diminishing at this point, he was often struggling and on more than one occasion I paid for his accommodation which was about £200 a month. Ben had similar problems throughout the year but was able to manage better once he returned to working at the Discovery Store. Mum gave the boys the occasional 'present' as well, always ready, and willing to help out in whatever way she could. It was rare for the boys to actually ask for money (there was a pride issue here) but if they did, I knew things were not going well.

Luckily Jay was doing ok with his uni work; he phoned me in late January and told me he had achieved good grades in his first semester. He was also job hunting in Worcester, which portrayed the other side of the story.

Back at home Ben had another short trip to America; this time to Baton Rouge to meet up with friends and to distribute the new PZK album. I was able to drop him off at Gatwick as it was an early morning flight, and I didn't lose too much time off work.

He had to make his own way back on his return though. I think he understood the situation now.

All sorts of things have been written in my diaries over the years. It's mostly family stuff and of course work. The following entry covers a host of things that pretty much covered my life at the time.

February 2nd, 2004: *I've got trouble with my jaw and teeth now. The jaw crunches and the tooth near it aches. I'll give it a week or two. A new lad started at work today and apparently there's another one coming too. I still don't know if I'll be on the crosscut or the wall saw, there's no way I can do both. Time will tell I suppose.*

I had a nice dinner tonight, mashed potato, carrots and swede, peas, corned beef, an omelette, a tomato, diced raw mushrooms, and a pilchard. We played in the Challenge Cup tonight against a team that's top of Division 1 and we lost by 4 points! One of the players said he might have a gig for me if I'm interested.

My eating habits are legendary amongst the family. I just like as many different flavours on my plate as possible, and Jay wasn't averse to experimenting, providing it was cheap. He phoned me one evening to ask if you can put cheese in a pancake. I think I convinced him that the more traditional pancake of butter, sugar, and lemon juice is tastier than anything savoury. As I put the phone down it occurred to me that perhaps he was asking the question because it was all he had. It was soon apparent he was struggling when he phoned a few days later and told me he now qualified for a hardship allowance from the university. That made me think. I decided to send him money every week if I could, directly into his bank account. He did apply to the university and was eventually granted £600, which was a godsend. I told him to accept it gracefully as he was entitled to it.

Luckily, gigs were coming in bringing in much needed income. One was an anniversary party job at a venue in Milton Keynes in February. Yet again it was difficult because of the conditions and the noise. As well as a disco there was a live band, and as one finished the other would start. I got through it ok though and it went as well as it could. The worrying thing was that it was getting to the point when most of my gigs were of a similar nature, and I was doing them purely for the money. Things weren't the same anymore.

Ben was still busy with his music and his band now had the addition of a drummer, guitar player and a bassist, and was far removed from the original line up which consisted of a series of rappers with him on keyboards. Rehearsals were fairly regular both at home and in a studio in Buckingham, for which I was often utilised as the band taxi which I was happy with. It was around this time at the beginning of the year when Ben had all sorts of equipment failures. His mixer, computer, video camera, and recorder all had glitches which had to be resolved. Jay had problems with his computer as well. It wasn't a good year for technology in the Hawes household. By the beginning of March the band was ready for a gig at the Xscape building in Milton Keynes. Jay came home for the weekend to give his brother some support along with three of his mates from uni. They arrived mid-afternoon and I decided to feed everybody with a buffet. I'd been to Sainsbury's the day before and bought ham, chicken nibbles, sausage rolls, and small sausages and cocktail sticks amongst other things. It was quick and easy, and I put everything out on separate plates on the kitchen table where they could help themselves. It was only then that Jay whispered to me that one of his mates was a vegetarian. It was sorted by a quick visit up to the local shop to buy a couple of quiches and veggie burgers and everybody was happy. After a quick visit to Maplins for Ben to pick up some last-minute cables, I dropped him off at the gig, to be joined later by Jay and pals who walked there, as did I later on. It went really well, and the place was packed. Needless to say, I felt conspicuous due to my age, but I enjoyed it as much as everybody else.

Work wasn't going well; things were changing, and the carpentry work had dried up. I was now working as a sawyer. It was quite interesting to begin with, with the arrival of an additional saw which cut angles in quite an ingenious way. It must have been at least 30 years old, but it was as solid as a rock and made of high-quality steel (unlike modern machinery). Far from being automatic, it worked with a revolving table with the angles marked around the circumference. It was operated by pressing two buttons at the same time at the front; this was a safety device which made it impossible for the operator's hands to be anywhere near the blade as it came up through the middle of the table. It was accurate to half a degree, which was useful as angles of 22.5 degrees were quite common. The main large saw in the factory that cut the bulk of the heavy trusses couldn't have been more different. It was completely automatic with the sizes and angles and cutting lists entered into it from a computer in the office. I know what I preferred. I was happy enough, providing I had stuff to cut that required angles, the more complicated the better. The problems arose with the advent of Posi Joists. These were floor joists that were made up of two lengths of timber and V shaped metal plates which made the joists into frames. It was a brilliant idea which revolutionized this area of building construction. The company invested heavily in new machinery and purpose-built benches. Soon Posi Joists were being churned out by the thousand. It was my job to cut most of them and because they were square ended it was mind-numbing. All I was doing day after day was loading timber onto the saw, pressing two buttons, and putting the cut timber onto barrows. It was obviously boring but more to the point, it wasn't carpentry. Time once again to look for something else. By this time the company, Rok, were a separate entity and doing their own thing, but still had offices on our site. I heard through my mate John (who worked for them) that they were setting up a small works department, so I made some enquiries. I applied and had an interview on March 17th. I was told what the pay would be and what the job involved, and I was offered the position and accepted. He couldn't give me a start date as he was still in the process of setting everything up. He'd be in touch. A month later I saw John again who told me they'd be taking on people over the next two weeks. A month after that on May 28th, I had a call from the interviewer who reassured me that I hadn't been forgotten and things were on the move. Three months later, on August 19th, there was an advert in the paper from Rok asking for carpenters and builders. Still I didn't hear anything. On August 27th, I rang Rok, explained the situation, asked to speak to the interviewer and was told he wasn't available. After almost 6 months I gave up and didn't hear any more. It was frustrating but at least I still had a job. I tried to make it more interesting by writing stuff in my head as I worked. I wrote enough material for a stand-up comedy routine and even considered trying it out at a comedy club. I taught myself the phonetic alphabet, Alpha, Bravo, Charlie, Delta, etc. Then I had a small radio with the headphones hidden inside my ear protectors tuned to Radio 4 all day. It all made the job more bearable.

I went into work as normal one morning to discover we'd been burgled. My cupboard was wrecked, and tools scattered. They had used my screwdriver to remove a small chop saw and they'd also stolen some welding gear. Luckily, I had taken most of my own tools home as I just wasn't using them. The one thing I did leave was my Estwing (the Rolls Royce of hammers) which was stolen. To give the company credit, everything was replaced by the end of the day, including my hammer. As this wasn't the first time something like this had happened, over the following weeks and months security was improved and we ended up with alarms, CCTV, and the presence of much needed night-time security guards.

Ben wasn't too happy at the Discovery Store either; there was a lack of customers, and he was as bored as I was. In late March he was summoned with other senior members of staff, to a meeting in High Wycombe to discuss the future of the stores moving forward. They were told of a name change which was to be, "Must Have It" (which certainly didn't have the same ring as the Discovery Store) - a few weeks later Ben decided, "he didn't want it" and left.

He kept himself busy song writing and filming, and also working on another CD with the Rev. Peter Sharrocks. I was asked to participate in the film making on the odd occasion, probably as a last resort.

April 7th, 2004: *Mum came over as usual today and was quite bemused with the filming we did with fake guns and pretend deaths. She's going to the chiropodists tomorrow on the Lakes Estate.*

Easter arrived and with it another trip to Worcester to pick up Jay and his friend Frag (the vegetarian) who was staying for the week.

April 15th, 2004: *I reckon I've coped pretty well with the cooking this week. Frag has eaten everything I've put in front of him which is good. Speaking of cooking, Jay did his infamous upside-down cake for Ben to film tonight. He said he may not be able to use it as it turned out pretty well and he didn't make any mistakes.*

While Jay was here, we (me actually) filled in yet more forms regarding his delicate financial situation, including one to the taxman. Who knows, we may have caught him on a good day, and he might even consider giving Jay a much-needed rebate.

A good lecture at the magic club in April from Pat Page. All his material is relatively easy to do; it's always effective, original, and entertaining. As I watched him perform, my mind went back to the sixties when I met him for the first time, almost 40 years ago. He was still exactly the same, extremely knowledgeable, and as helpful as ever. To this day I use one of his ideas I picked up on that night. A lot of his stuff was put out in the form of notes and small booklets and to quote Arthur Askey, "Every one a little gem."

Throughout 2003 and 2004, I'd been working on a Goshman type act which lasted about 20 minutes. It was self-contained, complete with a custom-made table. I used some Goshman material intermingled with some of my own. Music was involved as well, and I'd spent a lot of time and effort in putting it together. It never did take off and I only performed it for the public a couple of times to a mixed reception. The problem was there was nowhere to perform it. It had to be somewhere quiet for a start which was becoming increasingly difficult, and without performances it would never evolve into something half decent. I gave it up in the end.

Early in the year Deke Leonard had sent me an unusual pack of cards that he'd picked up somewhere and thought I might be able to use. It was towards the end of the Iraq war and the pack consisted of photographs of members of Saddam Hussein's regime who were still at large and were on the Wanted List. Unusual indeed. It was the Originality competition at the magic club, so I came up with a routine that might just work - I thought I'd have a head start with the cards alone to be honest. The thing about competitions like this, when it's a one off (and will only be performed once), is the fact that I had no idea how it would be received.

May 25th, 2004: *It was the originality competition at the magic club tonight and I won it with my trick with the Iraq cards. It went quite well, and I got laughs when I didn't expect them, and nothing when I did. Just goes to show you never know until you get out there.*

I have no memory of the routine I performed that night, but thanks to Deke I had another little trophy to put on my sideboard.

In the summer of that year I began another project which I hoped would make me some much-needed cash. Now was the time, I decided, to go into furniture production in my shed at home, making davenport desks using the drawings I'd bought back in the mid-eighties. They would be based on a similar design to those I made when I was in the cabinet making industry. I loved making them as there was so much involved. Four drawers on the side, a desk with a leather inlaid lid and small drawers on the inside. The idea was to make a prototype, make careful notes and add my own drawings where necessary, and keep copies of cutting lists and receipts. The profit I made on the first one would then subsidise the second. That was the plan. I already had a table saw, a router, and other bits and pieces and made a start on No.1. Every spare minute I had was spent in the shed working away and slowly it began to take shape. By mid- September it was done, apart from the leather inlay on the lid and polishing. Luckily, I still had a few contacts in the trade and was able to get the leathering done fairly soon. The original plan was to polish it myself. I'd bought French polish, wire wool, linseed oil, methylated spirit, cotton wool, and muslin… and a book on how to French Polish. I had dabbled with it over the years, but it is a highly skilled job and in the end I decided to get it done professionally by an expert. I took it over to him and we had a bit of a chat, and he asked me if I had a buyer for it. I told him I hadn't and would advertise it in the local paper.

"You might struggle," he said.

The reason being that the reproduction style of furniture was pretty much over. The one (and obvious) thing I hadn't thought of was, would they sell, and is there still a market for them? Sadly the answer was a resounding no. I put an advert in the paper that got no response. I asked people who expressed an interest when I started, and even they, although sympathetic, said no. In the end I only made the one and I sold it to my sister Jean where it still sits in pride of place in their lounge.

Almost 20 years later I'm still waiting for reproduction antique furniture to become popular again. I still have the drawings and cutting lists; well, you never know.

I picked up Jay from Worcester for his summer break and gave him a hand to clean up the house before we left. It wasn't too bad actually (surprisingly). After about a week of searching he got himself a job in a shoe shop in the city centre. All that can be said of that experience is that it was a job. Somehow, he was able to deal with rude customers and ineffective managers too. There are some people who seem to resent higher education. Jay was about to start his final year and once he got his degree the world would be his oyster. It seemed whenever Jay made a mistake in the shop he'd have to put up with snide comments like, "And I thought you were supposed to be clever." The obvious response would be, "I have a future, which is more than you have. Because of your lack of education you're limited to working in this shithole of a shoe shop or somewhere similar for the rest of your life." But as usual he just bit his lip and said nothing, he needed the money. Now that he did have money in his pocket he was getting out and about with his mates and having a well-deserved social life. One particular night, after spending an hour or so getting ready, three of them were still in the house - I thought they were never going to head off to the nearest club. Finally, just as I was thinking of going to bed, I heard the door slam. I went into the kitchen to find two empty bottles of vodka on the table and three glasses - that's what many youngsters did in those days before they went clubbing, to save queueing for vastly overpriced drinks.

Appearance was important, as you'd expect for a 20-year-old. He came home one day having been for a haircut. I couldn't see any difference. That night as he was getting ready for another night on the town, I could hear a lot of banging about and swearing emerging from the bathroom. I went upstairs to explore. He threw open the door, pointed to his hair and said,

"How can I go out with it looking like this?!!"

"Looking like what"? I replied, I was really struggling not to laugh.

"It's a disaster!"

"Nobody will notice in the darkness of a club for God's sake," I said.

"You just don't understand!"

And with that he brushed past me and went out to join his mates, who had been waiting outside for some considerable time.

What made me laugh was the fact that I did understand, as I was exactly the same when I was his age, probably worse. It took me hours to craft my hair with a hair dryer and a brush, and if it was raining, I just wouldn't go out. Jay was definitely a chip off the old block.

As jay arrived home, Ben was off to camp in America again. As luck would have it, the trip down to Heathrow clashed with another one of Gary Young's one-day conventions. I managed to catch the first lecture and half of the next one from Tommy Wonder, before we set off. Tommy was just great, one of the few performers who has studied and made use of misdirection with amazing results. I'd put him up there with some of the greats. Luckily, I got back in time to catch all the evening show which again featured Tommy who was just outstanding. It was another great day and a shame I had to miss some of it.

I had another good evening out in Leicester in June when I travelled up to the Musician pub to see Deke Leonard's one-man show. It was a great night with him telling stories and singing the odd song, much of it based on his series of autobiographies, which are hilarious. If you are familiar with the books, it will give you some idea of how entertaining the evening was.

June 27ᵗʰ, 2004: *I spent all afternoon working on the davenport and lost track of time. Too late for dinner as I had to leave at six o'clock to get to Leicester to see Deke's new one-man show. It was a really good night and at last I met the lovely Mary. It was nice too to meet up again with the equally lovely Pete Williams who was the roadie for the night. When I got back, I had a bite to eat and did some ironing while watching the last of Glastonbury. It's about 1.30am. It's been a full and enjoyable day.*

While Ben was away, Jay borrowed his bike to go to work. It saved him walking, and bus fares, and indeed me as a taxi. In July it was stolen from a city centre bike rack despite it being secured with a hefty "D" lock. We reported it to the police and got a crime number and then went through the process of claiming on the insurance. After previous bike thefts, I made sure the word 'Bicycles' was on the policy. The problem I had was I couldn't find the receipt for it and didn't know the make either. In the end I went to the bike shop where it was bought and luckily, they had all the details on file. Then there were forms to fill in for the insurance, it just went on and on. Ben finally got his new bike at the end of September. I don't think the mindless morons who steal have any idea of the inconvenience and stress they cause. Another episode we could have done without during the year.

A week after Jay had gone back to Worcester, it was time to pick up Ben from Heathrow. Luckily, I had a week off, so I was able to have a leisurely drive down there to meet him. I had to wait an hour at the now familiar arrival railings and stood amongst a small crowd of people, some holding pieces of cardboard with names on. The thought did occur to me that perhaps I could do that just for a laugh. A trickle of passengers walked towards us pushing the inevitable trolleys loaded with suitcases. Soon the trickle turned into a sizeable crowd, and I tried to spot him. I had noticed a tall figure wearing shades and a baseball cap with a blue rucksack and a small flight bag, but that was a cool well-travelled dude, no sign of Ben. I was just starting to panic when there was a tap on my shoulder, it was the cool well-travelled dude.

"Hello Dad," he said with a grin.

I took his flight bag as he hitched the blue rucksack further onto his back. He strode towards the car park with me following and struggling to keep up feeling proud and relieved, he was home.

At the end of that week, it had rolled round to convention time again. It was back in Eastbourne, which is one of my favourite venues, and popular too with the many magicians who registered that year. The events were well supported; in fact there were 15 acts in the close-up competition, which was encouraging. It was won by Mel Harvey who years later became President of my magic club. There were lectures from Eugene Berger, Max Maven, and Paul Gordon, in fact there was something for everybody. Yet again though, it was meeting up with my old pals that was the highlight. I had an interesting chat with Geoff Ray and his son Paul who had a furniture business at the time, and they were kind enough to send me some samples of beading I could use for my davenport project (should it work). I always enjoyed conventions if only for a change of scenery and a chat and a laugh with my mates. Some of my pals at this time were looking older (same as me no doubt) and a few had quite serious health issues. I did say to one or two of them in a bar one night, when it was late and I was three parts pissed and a touch melancholy,

"When you lot kick the bucket and go to the great convention in the sky, I'm not coming to them anymore."

Eventually that's what happened.

Work wasn't going well again, as I discovered on the following Monday. There wasn't much work about but there was plenty in the pipeline. We'd heard it all before. A few weeks earlier we'd all been given new contracts of employment. I refused to sign mine as I'd been demoted from carpenter to general operative. I could see the dilemma faced by the company, as at the time I wasn't doing much carpentry. I insisted on it being changed back though, as if and when a carpenter was required, no doubt I'd be expected to do it, even as a general operative. I ended my little rant with, "I *am* a qualified carpenter." They couldn't argue with that. Sometime later, common sense prevailed, and it was changed back to carpenter. A few weeks after that, they might have regretted that decision as I asked to be made redundant. I had a good case, I thought, as according to my contract I was a carpenter and there was no carpentry work at the time. I think they thought I was joking, perhaps I was. Anyway work did arrive, and I carried on regardless.

By the end of October Ben was job hunting again and at a bit of a loose end. Jeff came over quite a lot and was in the process of doing tests in his quest to be a driving instructor. Jay meanwhile was in his final year at uni and doing a dissertation on refereeing decisions in the Euro 2004 football tournament. He'd had to record many of the matches on video tape (there were piles of them, paid for by his Mum). He made notes of all the decisions and the effect they had on results, morale, and all sorts of other things. He even pondered on the future - could or would robotic and video refereeing ever be used? It was an interesting read. The only team that didn't have any controversial decisions against them in the tournament was Greece, the eventual winners.

In early October, I spotted a book in a charity shop written by Desmond Douglas, who was the English table tennis champion on 11 occasions. He peaked at equal World number 7 and European number 3. A star of English table tennis. I bought the book for about a quid. Desmond had retired from playing competitively some years previously but still worked as a coach. A few weeks later he was running a course at the Table Tennis Centre in Milton Keynes which I went along to. It was all basic stuff for an hour or so but great to be there; he helped me with a problem I'd had for years. I would continually over-hit whereby the ball would overshoot the end of the table. He told me that the angle of my bat was too open and to slightly close it. It was great advice, and he was very helpful. I had a chat with him afterwards and showed him the book, which made him smile as it was written when he was quite young. I asked him to sign it and I eventually donated it as a raffle prize at a league fund-raising event. I gave him one of my cards, which again made him smile. A couple of years later he was a guest at another function where I was doing the magic and I was able to show him some stuff. He loved the old 'paddle' trick called 'I'll start again', which I bought from Ken Brooke back in the sixties. It consists of a small piece of wood, shaped like a cricket bat on which are marked chalk lines which move up and down, and disappear and then reappear - it's a lovely little trick. I had the perfect opening line, "I bet you've never seen a bat like this!"

I was still playing in the league but had got to the point when by the end of the working day I was exhausted. With long hours coupled with housework and worrying about the boys, I was struggling to concentrate. I wasn't winning the matches I should have, and felt I was letting my team mates down. I gave up playing competitively at the end of the season but continued to go to the club for a knock once a week to keep my hand in and for some exercise - something I still do to this day.

I was still getting gigs fairly regularly, some of them just run of the mill and more or less forgettable, and one or two memorable. While I was at the convention at Eastbourne somebody came up to me and said,

"Hello Ken, how are you doing, haven't seen you for years."

I looked at him and had no idea who he was. He wasn't going to tell me either. He looked at me smiling for a couple of minutes and then suddenly the penny dropped.

"Noel from Preston!"

Noel did a very good 'manipulative' act. He appeared in countless convention shows and I believe he'd also been a prize winner. Our paths had last crossed probably back in the 70s. He told me he was now busy working as a children's entertainer and had moved to Greenwich in London and had changed his name to Dave Andrews. We had a lengthy chat and I told him what I'd been up to with furniture making and table tennis and other stuff, and he went on to tell me that he was heavily involved with The Boys' Brigade. From that conversation I was invited to attend the 19th Annual Fund-Raising Dinner of the 2nd West Kent (Blackheath) Company of the Boys' Brigade.

"You'll love it," said Dave, and after a brief description of the format I was more than happy to accept. Dave offered overnight accommodation, staying with him and his wife Sally, along with a free meal and petrol money. For that I agreed to do the magic around the tables at coffee time. Sounded like a good deal to me. I travelled down to Greenwich on a Saturday afternoon in early November and spent some time chatting with Dave and Sally before going over to the Boys Brigade Hall in Blackheath in the early evening for the dinner. It was a lovely old building and had the atmosphere of a village hall. The tables were already set, and people were beginning to arrive, excited and smiling, all dressed smartly in evening dress (even the youngsters). There was a kitchen attached to the hall with a serving hatch from which the unmistakable aroma of cooking was already emerging. When everybody had arrived, we took our seats at the well-arranged tables. Once settled, Grace was said and the six-course meal began, all of it cooked, prepared, and served by volunteers. The quality of it all was stunning, just as Dave said it would be. At the end of the meal, as people were relaxing, there came the unmistakable sound of a spoon tapping on a glass and we all rose for the Loyal Toast. During the following 20 minutes or so, the tap on the glass would be heard several times and a voice would ring out,

"The Company Captain would like to take wine with former Boys' Brigade members."

There was a shuffling of chairs as a surprising number of gentlemen stood up to raise a glass, obviously delighted and proud to be there. Later, after the now familiar chink of spoon on glass…

"The Company Captain would like to take wine with Members of The Magic Circle."

From memory, three of us stood up for that toast.

Soon it was time for responses and speeches including one from special guest of the evening, Terry Herbert from the Magic Circle, and past President of the IBM. After that it was my turn to perform around the tables (along with another close-upper, Barry Miller). It was such a lovely evening, and everybody was up for having a laugh and entered into the spirit of it all. The atmosphere created by the enthusiasm of the many people there made it a truly memorable evening. I loved it.

A few weeks later in mid-December, I had a booking to do close-up at a club in Bedfordshire. It came to me via an agent I knew but also involved another I'd never heard of. The job was originally given to a lady magician who for some reason was now unable to do it. The name of the club was unusual and as the contract didn't give any information, I decided to get in touch with the other agent to find out what I was letting myself in for. I also thought it a good idea to have a chat with him and tell him a bit more about myself (you never know it could mean more work). I gave him a call and he came across as quite an unpleasant individual. He was rather abrupt and told me that as far as he knew it was a bingo club and, "You'll find out when you get there." and that was that. I had another look at the rather sparse contract and judging by the stipulated performance times, 5.30 to 7.00 and then 8.00 to 8.30, I'd be working between games, and I would indeed find out when I got there. It also said that payment would be made by cheque within 7 days - I found that a bit annoying too as I would have preferred cash or cheque on the night. Anyway I wasn't particularly worried, after 30 years of experience I should be able to cope with most situations and treated it as just another gig. I spent an hour or two rehearsing during the afternoon and dressed to suit the venue as I normally do, which in this case I assumed to be a sort of Working Men's Club. I wore a smart black casual suit and a black shirt which would make me recognisable as, 'The man in black', should that be required. This was before the smoking ban, so I didn't really want to wear a smart suit and end up smelling like an ash tray. There wouldn't have been time to have got it cleaned in time for the next gig anyway (a wedding) so in that sense I didn't have much choice. I arrived in plenty of time and introduced myself to the manager, who was another unpleasant individual. He wasn't happy because the agent hadn't had the foresight to inform him of the change of performer (no surprise there). He was expecting the lady magician and was really disappointed and annoyed when a middle-aged bloke like me turned up - a thank you for me stepping into the breach at the last moment would have been nice rather than taking it out on me. Not a great start to the evening. He confirmed that I'd be performing between the games and to make sure I was nowhere near the punters once they got underway. Off I went to get loaded up and I made a start straight away. After a couple of tables I was into my stride and it was going well. I did notice the manager looking over and got the feeling I was being scrutinised. Luckily, the customers were great, and I'd tell them to give me a loud cheer and lots of applause. I don't think he was that popular with them either as they were happy to oblige, in fact going way over the top. I finished my first stint with no problems and felt all was going well. After my break I made a start on the final half an hour and went up to an elderly lady who was sitting on her own facing the stage, I explained who I was and why I was there, but she wasn't interested. She asked me if I was aware that the building used to be a cinema and pointed out some of the Art Nouveau plasterwork still visible between the rather tacky Christmas decorations. She went on to tell me that she visited it a lot when she was courting with her husband some 40 years previously. It became apparent she had a lot of affection for the place as she spoke about some of the films they'd seen together over a long period of time. She smiled at the happy memories. She told me that her husband had died a year ago and had only just decided to get out and about.

"My daughter's idea," she said, shaking her head.

"And a good one too," I said, "If you hadn't been here we wouldn't have had our nice little chat."

"That's very true, thanks for talking to me."

What a lovely lady. After the final game of Bingo I picked up my case and after chatting to a few people I went on to tell the manager I'd completed the job. He was waiting and not happy. We stood by the open door of his office, in full view of the customers as they walked out. He'd noticed me talking to the lady and went on about me being paid to perform magic and not for chatting to the customers. Just then the same lady came past, shook my hand, and said, "Thank you very much, I've had such a lovely evening."

The fact that she thanked me and not the manager spoke volumes I thought.

"Thank *you*," I said, "It's been a pleasure."

As the lady went out of the door the manager turned to me, slightly flustered, and said,

"And for what it's worth, I don't like your appearance!!"

I really couldn't figure out what this man's problem was, and I was getting annoyed. As I hadn't been paid yet and didn't want to fall out with the agent, I had to be careful what I said, so rather than tell him that his establishment was hardly the bloody Ritz, I looked him up and down and told him that I thought what he was wearing was entirely appropriate. He was wearing a clown costume complete with silly hat. I picked up my bag and left the building.

I got my cheque ok for that gig and got a nice (standard) thank you letter back from the agent. That was a relief. Cash on the night is always a better option and I could never figure out why that couldn't be done more often. As I drove home that night, I pondered the gig. The lead up to it and the beginning wasn't too good, but the middle and the very end of it were great! And how strange I should get praise and thanks from a lady who hadn't even seen a trick. It's a funny old world sometimes. It could be argued that during the ten minutes or so we spent chatting, we were having fun anyway and a trick was surplus to requirements. She just wanted somebody to talk to. Regarding the manager, I reckon he'd seen the lady magician somewhere before and really fancied her and that's why he was so disappointed she hadn't turned up. Mind you, if she had been there, his clown outfit wouldn't have done him any favours.

Soon after, I had car trouble - in fact it started on the way home from the Bingo job. I was hit with a bill for £500! Not the sort of thing I needed just before Christmas. Luckily it was paid for by seasonal gigs. Thank God for the magic. Jay was having health problems with his knee, 'swollen like a football' and Ben was poorly at the time too. It was a worrying time. Luckily though he was feeling better by mid-December and had begun doing some really good artwork (something else he was good at) which was probably good therapy along with his music. The really good news was that he'd applied for and got himself a job at a local school, supervising at an After School Club. This could well be the beginning of a career. Time would indeed confirm that would be the case. I didn't have a New Year's Eve gig (I spent the evening ironing), but I did do a wedding at Knebworth House on the 29th, another beautiful venue.

The end of another year – onto the next…

CHAPTER 28

Feeling Poorly, and Proud

2005 began with some interesting and exciting family news. My brother-in-law Steve, who is married to my sister Jean, was offered a Deaconship post in Birkenhead. He'd completed his rather lengthy training, and this would be his first post. It took about half the year to sort everything out regarding property and moving and all the hassle that entails. They finally moved in August to begin what would turn out to be an enriching time in their lives.

Jay was now on his final year at uni and had a regular girlfriend. She had a car (which saved me a few journeys to Worcester), but I did have to take him back there at the end of January and then face the aftermath in his bedroom.

January 29th, 2005: *We set off for Worcester at about quarter to two. It was a good journey there and back and I arrived home at five thirty. After a bite to eat, I attacked his bedroom. It was in a dreadful state and took me two hours to sort out. I filled up a bin liner with his junk, and a large carrier bag full of recyclable stuff, including three empty vodka bottles! It's been a long day.*

Both boys were now in their early twenties and Jeff was now thirty. All of them making their own way in the world and beginning their adult lives, but as far as I was concerned it was the end of an era. I really did miss their childhood days and would often spend an evening poring over old photograph albums, reliving those happy days at the seaside and a host of other memories. I could see now why people would often tell me to make the most of their childhood days as time goes so quickly. "They're not children for long!" - Never was a truer word spoken.

In February I began to feel ill, but life as always had to go on somehow. This was the beginning of it.

February 11ᵗʰ, 2005: *I've felt really awful all day today. I had a Lemsip at lunchtime at work which saved me from going home. This bug is awful, it leaves you totally exhausted. I struggled around the Centre after work and when I got home all I could do was sit on the sofa and doze. I managed to change Ben's bed linen but wasn't able to clean the bathroom or Hoover. I put Ben's dinner in, and after he'd had that I went to bed for a while until it was time to pick up Jay from the station. As soon as we got home, I went straight back to bed. I honestly don't know how I'm going to do the gig tomorrow night. I think I'll try and survive the night with no tablets and really dose myself up throughout the day tomorrow.*

Luckily (or so I thought at the time) this was a Friday which would give me the weekend to get over it. The Saturday gig which was in Enfield was cancelled which was a relief. I struggled through Sunday and woke up on Monday morning feeling reasonable.

February 14ᵗʰ, 2005: *I really thought I'd beaten it when I got up this morning. I woke up at four o'clock in a lake of sweat. I changed all the bed linen, had a shower, felt great, and went to work. By lunchtime though the red-hot rivet was back in my skull, my lungs were on fire, and my nose was pouring. By four o'clock I'd had enough and came* *home and phoned NHS Direct, who were kind but not practical. Maggs phoned and gave me the number of 'MK Doc' which is where I eventually went. By this time I was suffering with a painful chest as well, but despite listening to my lungs, looking down my throat, and peering into my ears, nothing. Back to the paracetamol and ibuprofen.*

The rest of the week was really grim; I was still going to work and wasn't getting any better. On the Friday I phoned my GP and was able to get an early appointment. She immediately gave me a week off work with a diagnosis of acute bronchitis. I was given a prescription for antibiotics and asked to go back and see her on the following Wednesday. I took the tablets as prescribed and completed the course over the following five days. By the time Wednesday finally rolled round it was obvious they hadn't worked. I was feeling dreadful and with a strange pain in my lower chest. I sat down in front of the doctor and spoke about my kidney removal operation, of when I was told after a chest X-Ray that if the cancer were to spread, it would probably go to my lungs first. I then mentioned the pain I felt in my chest.

"Ok," she said, "Let's have a listen."

She used her stethoscope as I breathed in and out, in and out. She then went back to her desk and picked up the phone.

"X-Ray department please. Thank you. I have a patient here, Mr. Kenneth Hawes, who requires a chest X-Ray with some urgency. No, that's not good enough. Now please. Thank you very much."

She put the phone down and told me to go straight down to the hospital X-Ray department where they would be waiting to take one of my chest. She was obviously concerned and at that point so was I, bearing in mind my head was all over the place after taking a mixture of ibuprofen, paracetamol, and antibiotics for days on end. I hadn't slept well with the sweats pretty much every night and my appetite wasn't good either. As I walked out of the surgery, I was convinced I had lung cancer. I got to the hospital and parked my car where I shouldn't have as I assumed I'd be in and out in a few minutes. I made my way to the X-Ray department, explained who I was and took a seat. I waited for a worrying ten minutes or so and was called in. The X-Ray was taken and I was told to take a seat until it was developed and a doctor had had a look at it. I waited for what seemed a lifetime, worrying and thinking the worst. Finally a nurse came out holding a large brown envelope containing the dreaded photo.

She said, "Mr. Hawes, I'm afraid we'll have to send you to the CDU department where you'll be told what happens next."

The colour must have drained from my already pale face as she insisted I go there in a wheelchair. As I'm being wheeled along clutching the envelope it occurred to me what CDU must have stood for. It had to be the Cancer Diagnostic Unit. By the time I got there some ten minutes later my head was all over the place. I was led to an ante room where there was a bed along with a desk and chair. Above the desk was a noticeboard on the wall. I was told to lay down on the bed and a nurse would be along soon. As I waited, I glanced at the noticeboard expecting to see information on cancer help lines, or chemotherapy and the like, but there was nothing like that apart from contact details of various hospital departments. It wasn't too long before a business-like nurse came in. She asked me if I was ok, took the envelope and removed the X-Ray plate and began to read the enclosed notes. She looked at me with some concern and said, "I'm afraid Mr. Hawes I have some bad news for you. You have pneumonia."

"Thank fuck for that!!" I almost shouted, "Excuse my language nurse but given the choice I'd rather have pneumonia than lung cancer!"

The nurse was experienced and had heard it all before and one swear word didn't faze her at all. I told her the story which made her smile, but she made it very plain that pneumonia is also a serious illness and for that reason I'd be staying in overnight for observation. I wasn't going to argue with her. She asked me if I had any questions.

"Yes, I do actually. What does CDU stand for?"

"Clinical Decisions Unit," she answered, trying not to laugh.

I woke up the following morning in my sweaty hospital bed not really knowing what to expect.

February 24th, 2005: *Another 'wet' night but at least I didn't have to change the bed linen. I reckon that'll be the pattern now until all of this is over. I had some breakfast and a shower and did a few crosswords until Dr. Smith came to visit. He allowed me home later on and I have to see him next Tuesday at his clinic. Around midday I was wheeled down to the waiting area where I was given some lunch which was really nice. Once the tablets had arrived from the pharmacy some two hours later, I drove home. Rev. Peter Sharrocks was here when I got back recording some more songs with Ben. I could tell by the look on his face I must have looked poorly. I phoned Jay tonight who was quite surprised when I told him the events of the last few days. Ben seems ok. We had faggots for dinner.*

Once the tablets had kicked in, I slowly recovered. I did have an allergic reaction to one of them which gave me a shingles type rash. That was sorted with a couple of over-the-counter antihistamine tablets. I finally got the ok to return to work on Wednesday March 9th, my 55th birthday. I still went for regular check-ups over the following weeks at Dr. Smith's clinic and was finally given the all-clear at the end of May. I was warned that it would take some time to get over and it did, and as my GP said soon after, "You really were quite ill you know."

When I look back now (not having read the diaries since they were written some 15 years ago) it's apparent that I should have gone to the doctors much sooner than I did, and I certainly shouldn't have gone into work when I was obviously so ill. In those days there was no sick pay to speak of, so I didn't have a lot of choice. My mindset then was all would be well by the next day, or the end of the week, and most of the time it would be, I just *had* to work no matter what. Both Mum and Dad were exactly the same. I don't remember Dad ever having time off until his final illness.

Mum would also work for as long as she was able. She was still coming over on the bus every Wednesday afternoon to help out in any way she could. By the time I came home from work, she'd be there wearing the blue housecoat and purple slippers with the little white bobbles that she left in the cupboard. Vegetables would be on the hob peeled and ready, and there was always ironing to do. She was 87. In her world of total family dedication, she was convinced that her presence in our house every Wednesday was essential and relied upon. Some years later there came a time when she was unable to walk to the bus stop from her bungalow. That didn't faze her - she'd come over in a cab and I'd drive her home in the evening. When she became too infirm for even that, and realised she couldn't visit any more, she sat on her chair and cried, not for herself but for us. Concerned that I'd have too much to do without her input every Wednesday, in spite me telling her otherwise. Soon there would be a change of roles where we would have to care for her. My sister Maggs and her husband Ken who lived close by did a wonderful job for many years caring for her and making sure she had all she needed.

Mum was cut from the same cloth as Dad and as dedicated to her family as he was. I suppose it was inevitable that I'd turn out in a similar way, you worked until you literally dropped. It wasn't because we felt heroic or even expected any thanks; as a parent and grandparent it's just what you do.

I had to have extra cash somewhere in case the boys needed help, or I'd have unexpected expenses. I'd go to the Building Society every Friday afternoon after work and transfer some money into a cash ISA. It wasn't a regular sum, just what I could afford. Much of the earnings from the magic went in there as did private chippy work. It had been invaluable over the years for all sorts of reasons as it was when I was ill. At work there was no company sick pay scheme (unless you were staff), so all I had coming in while I was ill was Government Statutory Sick Pay which at the time was £66 per week. To had insult to injury the first 3 days "didn't count." For my first week off I had to make do with about £35. It was lucky I had the ISA to bail me out for a change. I was quite annoyed that there was no company scheme for the bulk of the workforce and was rather peeved that 20 years of service counted for nothing. I wrote to the CEO and put him in the picture and to give him credit he did come and see me when I got back to work and was quite sympathetic telling me the company was looking into it. That was the last I heard and luckily, I was never ill again for it to matter anyway.

Jay came home from uni for a 3-week stay and he spent much of it working on his final projects in his now tidy bedroom. Well, it was. Something very strange happened in that room that could have been catastrophic.

March 19th, 2005: *Jay's been busy on his college work all day in his bedroom. He had a bit of a scare this afternoon when his curtains started to burn, caused by the sun reflecting off his shaving mirror which was on the windowsill – quite bizarre really. Ben had the PZK boys round here all afternoon and they had a good session. We watched some rugby, with Wales winning the Grand Slam.*

Luckily Jay smelt the burning curtains and quickly removed the offending mirror; it only resulted in a small hole, which we could live with. I didn't buy new ones until I redecorated some ten years later.

I did my first gig after my illness in April. I was slightly apprehensive as I was still feeling tired, especially after a day's work. My suit fitted better though, having not replaced the stone in weight I'd lost during the previous couple of months.

April 15th, 2005: *I went to the Building Society after work and put £20 into my ISA and got the fruit and veg from the market. After I'd put it all away, I did the hoovering and then got ready for tonight's gig near Hertford. The journey to the golf club was awful down the motorway. I left at quarter to five and got there at just after 6.30 which was my time of arrival according to the contract. They didn't sit down for dinner until 8 o'clock so I sat in the car for a while. It was a good night, I did the bat, sponge balls, and thimbles. I had a vote of thanks at the end and almost had a standing ovation! I got a bit lost on the way home on the country lanes, but it was certainly a better journey.*

I suppose I could have done some mix and mingle stuff at the bar before the meal, but I just wasn't up to it. The contract said, "Close-Up Magic Services", so I was under no obligation. Anyway, once I got going, it went really well, and adrenalin got me through two hours of table hopping. Ken Brooke was right when he told me you only need three tricks. It all worked out well on that night as the number of tables was perfect for the way I prefer to work - perform one trick at a time at each table so everybody had seen three tricks. It's a good way to make sure every table is covered, especially if there are a lot of them.

A couple of weeks later I did another lecture, this one for a magic club in Bicester called The Thames Valley Magicians Guild. With the applause still ringing in my ears after my last gig, I went through all my tried and tested routines, explaining how and why they work, using misdirection, timing, and bits of business, and suggesting they apply the reasoning behind it all to their own tricks and routines. It seemed to go well but according to my diary the venue wasn't all that good, it appeared to be some sort of leisure centre. *"The room was rather dowdy, and I had to put up with the noise of a football match going on in the next room."* - I've worked in worse places.

Manchester United played Arsenal in the FA Cup Final of 2005, and at the time one of Ben's American friends was visiting and eagerly looking forward to watching her very first game of Cup Final soccer. Jeff came over to watch the game on TV so there were just the four of us in the front room. The match kicked off, and although the teams were fairly matched on paper, Man U definitely had the edge, and needless to say Ben and Jeff got quite excited as their heroes missed chance after chance. Meanwhile the American girl sat there bemused by it all.

"When is something going to happen?" She asked as half time arrived with no score.

"I'll make the tea," I said.

The second half started with more of the same with Man U being the better side but just could not get the ball into the net. By now Ben and Jeff were shouting at the TV and that poor girl really didn't get it. She couldn't understand why Ben and Jeff were calling the United players all the names under the sun as they kept missing the net.

"I thought you supported them," she said in all innocence.

The second half followed the same pattern as the first and after 90 minutes it was still goalless. Extra time would have to be played. The players lined up, the whistle was blown and 30 minutes later and with more yelling at the TV and yet more missed chances the result remained unchanged, stalemate. This meant it would all be down to the first penalty shoot-out in Cup Final history. Needless to say, feelings were running high as at last the Red Devils slotted the ball between the posts. Then -Paul Scholes ran up to take his turn which was saved by the goalkeeper! Oh no! Both boys had their heads in their hands and could barely watch as Patrick Vieira, the Arsenal striker, placed the ball on the spot, ran up, shot, and scored, and that was that, game over. Had Manchester United been the victors, Ben and Jeff would have watched the presentation and danced around the room "whooping and hollering" and been over the moon. As it happened, the TV was immediately turned off, plunging the room into an almost spooky silence. Jeff stormed out of the house and got in his car and went home, and Ben went into the kitchen to hide his disappointment as he noisily filled the kettle.

"Did you enjoy that"? I asked our American guest.

She didn't say anything, merely spread her hands speechless.

"That's soccer," I said, "And for what it's worth I don't get it either."

Ben had decided not to go back to camp that year. He was busy in his studio most evenings and had enough work during the day. He had the job at the school in term time and worked for an out-of-school childminding company when it wasn't. He was obviously well thought of, receiving loads of cards and presents from both children and staff, each time term time ended. Jay meanwhile was coming to the end of his time at university. Five days before I was due to pick him up for the final time, I had a phone call asking if I could lend him £110 for his final rent instalment, somewhat wearily I said yes. His three years at Worcester, (which had sped by) had cost both of us a lot of money and stress, but worth every penny. Jay had loved his student days and when I picked him up on the Saturday, he was quite sad to leave. We had a look around the house which in my view looked filthy. I remember saying to him something along the lines of, "Leaving it as you found it," and "It's a bit of a shit hole, hadn't you better…"

"Naah," he said, "The landlord's had his money, and anyway he gets a cleaning company in."

I bet they earn their money, I thought.

Before he closed the front door for the last time, he had one final long lingering look around the room that had been his home for the past two years, probably thinking about the good times he'd had there, of beer drinking, pizzas, and debauchery, but more than anything else the friendships he made there that would last a lifetime.

By the summer things were getting back to normal with full days once again. I had a booking for a wedding from the Allsorts agency with yet again more helpful info from Roy and Meg to make sure everything went well on the day. The contract had arrived in March with this little note pinned to it.

"Hi Ken, please could you phone the couple approx. 2 weeks before the job (that would be around June 4th) as she would like to give you the final numbers etc. Hope you're feeling A1 now.

All the best, Roy & Meg.

PS. The lady has a baby so is available much of the time on her landline number."

If only all agents were as lovely and helpful as Roy & Meg. I phoned the lady on her landline and sure enough she was there. It was nice to chat to her and explain exactly what I did and put her mind at rest. I told her I was self-contained and would blend in and adapt to the circumstances as I found them and was looking forward to meeting her and her new husband on the day.

The day of the gig was indeed full and long.

June 18th, 2005: *The hottest day of the year today. I managed to get up in time to get to work for six o'clock and worked four hours until ten. From work I went to the centre and got my fruit and veg from the market. It was really crowded, a shame I couldn't have gone yesterday as I normally do on a Friday. After I'd put it all away and got the housework done, I had a cold shower and set off for Kettering and the wedding gig. Despite the really hot weather it went remarkably well. The atmosphere and the people there were terrific. I would have stayed longer but there was a drunk who was starting to be a pain. I did a couple of hours and was home at 7 o'clock. After a nice fish pie I watched a documentary about Live Aid. That was 20 years ago!*

Thankfully it wasn't that often I had problems with people under the influence. There isn't a lot you can do apart from avoid them as best you can. In a pub or bar it could go with the territory, but it rarely happened. At a wedding or family event it happened occasionally and most of the time it was easy to humour them and just walk away; the problem on that day was the chap kept following me around - luckily, he was a happy drunk and known to most of the other guests and they were more than happy to tell him to shut up or lead him away back to the bar. It was a bit annoying, but it happened as I was finishing anyway.

Ben, meanwhile, was spending a lot of time in his room chatting to his overseas friends over the internet. I'd often wonder if he was ever going to come out.

June 26th, 2005: *Ben's been in his room all day and finally emerged for dinner (and Glastonbury) at six o'clock. Ironically the first performer on was Brian Wilson singing "In my room."*

A couple of weeks later I had another wedding to do, this was through an agent I'd never used before (which would turn out to be nothing like Roy & Meg's agency.) The contract arrived in April and the gig was on July 2nd. It was good money, but it was a shame it clashed with the Live 8 concert, and I'd miss Pink Floyd. Oh well, a booking is a booking. The front of the contract stated the usual venue, time of performance, fee, and contact details etc, and also the legal blurb that must be on all contracts from all agents. On the back of this one however was a huge list of rules and regulations (with sections and sub-sections) about using legal and tested equipment, insurance, performance & presentation, and liability. The list went on and on and if that wasn't enough, a week before the gig I had a confirmation letter reminding me that I was representing the agency and to make sure I abided by the rules - they wished me well almost as an afterthought. Health & Safety was everywhere at this time, or to put it another way, "Let's do everything in our power to prevent us getting sued." Anyway it all seemed to go well, it was yet another full and long day.

July 2nd, 2005: *I worked six until eleven this morning, and after some lunch I watched the start of Live 8 but had to rehearse for most of the afternoon as I was determined to try out some new stuff with the table at tonight's gig (which I did). I set off for Cheshunt at six o'clock and was there in an hour. I chatted to the couple running the casino for a while before making a start. Quite a good night I thought. Luckily, I didn't have to work the tables in the main room, which was just as well as a disco was in full swing. I caught the end of Pink Floyd's set on the way home and hopefully Ben has recorded it and I can watch it tomorrow.*

The new stuff with the table was an idea I had with the mix and mingle set up. The idea was to move around the bar, or large room, where people were standing, using a small tripod table to entertain small groups of people. It gave me something to work off rather than use the hands of the audience where choice of material can be limited. It worked well that night as the conditions were pretty much perfect, just as well really as the contract did state "Close Up & Mix & Mingle Magic." I certainly wouldn't have wanted to have been in breach of contract!

A few days later I had another job which couldn't have been more different. It was in a garage in Dunstable for another car launch. It wasn't particularly well attended and the whole event never did really take off. It was on July 7th the day of the London bombings, as I wrote in my diary…

July 7th, 2005: *London had its September the 11th today. Bombs were planted in several underground stations or trains and even one on the top deck of a London bus. Carnage reigned for a few hours and the complete transport system came to a stop for most of the day. So far there are 37 confirmed dead. It's hit the country hard, particularly after the Olympic announcement yesterday. None of it makes any sense and I suspect most people like me are going through a whole gamut of emotions. I finished work at four o'clock and set off for Dunstable at five. I got there at six and started at quarter to seven. I finished at half past eight.*

As you can see from that diary entry, many people were in a state of shock including those of us who attended the car launch. I spoke to the manager who had the dilemma of deciding whether or not to go ahead with it having had a few cancellations. The garage was nicely decorated, and the salesmen were in place, and everything was set to go. He was of the opinion that it had to be business as usual. Good for him. It went well in spite of a small attendance. There was one lady there who told me she was a teacher and was wondering what and how she was going to tell her class of 7- & 8-year-olds. Luckily there was some support in place with a staff meeting early the following morning where help and advice would be given to staff members who were struggling emotionally. The school, which was in the Luton area had a high proportion of Asian children with many of them from Muslim families.

"Who'd be a teacher?" she said with some irony.

Who indeed I thought. I wished her well.

The following day Jay had confirmation that he'd been awarded his BSc degree. A proud moment for all of us. He too was toying with the idea of teaching as a career.

Ben meanwhile was also doing various courses. With a Youth Leader qualification under his belt he got a job at Bletchley Leisure Centre for a day or two a week and was also continuing with the child-minding company. Both jobs would last throughout the school summer holidays and would give him much needed cash to fund a proposed trip to Australia. There would be no year out or travelling for Jay though - he couldn't afford it and had to get a job and some cash to continue with his driving lessons and buy a car. Luckily, he was able to work with his brother Jeff at a local warehouse. As it happened both Ben and Jay started work on the same day. I got the impression neither of them were particularly happy.

July 25th, 2005: *Both boys got to work ok this morning. Jay just about got in on time and got an early lift home with his mate's Mum. He spent most of the day watching safety videos. Ben had a long day without a break with about 40 kids. I picked him up at about six fifteen, knackered!*

I was still very much the family chauffeur. I was able to drop Jay off if he had an early shift and I could usually pick them both up after work. It made my already long days even longer. Somehow, we got through the summer without too many problems. I had a weekend away in Birkenhead helping Jean and Steve move into their new home which gave me a bit of a break. Soon it was September and Ben was back into the school job, and Jay applied for and got voluntary work at the local school between his shifts at the warehouse. Ben was also busy in his studio working on more backing tracks for a local girl singer. There was certainly nothing wrong with their work ethic. I was proud of them both.

Ironically, I did a magic job on the 4th anniversary of the Trade Centre attack on September 11th. This one however went really well; it was at the Crossroads Hotel in Weedon and was a "Grandparent's Day". It was the usual format of working the tables and it was very much a family event with many of the tables seating three generations. I worked solidly for over two hours and had a great time. The venue was very nice with a friendly atmosphere and staff, and I went on to work there twice more before the end of the year.

I went to the IBM convention in Southport at the end of the month which according to my diary was a bit of a lack lustre affair. There were some highlights though with some great performances from Simon Lovell. He did a straight-jacket escape which was hilarious - as he released his final arm, his hand clutched a full pint of beer! That bought the house down. The other thing that I warmed to was the Fringe show and banquet organised by Faye Presto. That to me was a breath of fresh air. A welcome change from the same old same old.

In early October I had a call from Gary Young asking if I could help him and Bob Hamilton in making a video. This would be unusual as although I'd be in it from start to finish, I wouldn't be performing. My role on that Sunday afternoon was to be a spectator, sat at the table, while Paul Gordon performed and explained several card routines. I wondered how I'd cope with trying to look amused and interested during several hours of card magic. I needn't have worried though as Paul, as ever the consummate professional, went through his tried and tested material. At the end of it he asked me if I had any questions. I did have one. I asked him if he did anything else apart from card tricks. From memory I think he answered, "I don't have to.", which was a fair comment! It was a fascinating afternoon and I really enjoyed it.

At home I had a domestic problem when the washing machine ceased to work. It had been playing up for some time with it making a noise like a bag of spanners. I got an engineer out to look at it and he found over a pound's worth of loose change rattling around inside it. So much for the boys (and me I suspect) checking their pockets before throwing what seemed like several pairs of jeans per day into the drum. Anyway, that was a minor event compared to Jay's graduation which took place in Worcester Cathedral on November 3rd. It was a memorable and proud day. We travelled over with Jay and his girlfriend and my Mum. Jay was really pleased that Mum was able to go, and she was delighted too to be able to be there at the age of 87. We met Babs at the university at nine o'clock and made our way to a large room, where we sat down and had a chat while Jay went off to get his gown and mortar board. Twenty minutes later he was back, looking smart with a carnation buttonhole attached to his gown. His tie was a bit wonky, and bits of his hair stuck out from underneath his mortarboard. Babs straightened out his tie and kissed his cheek as I was trying desperately not to get emotional. We stood back and looked at him.

"You'll do," we said.

We took some photos until it was time for him to make his way to the cathedral with the rest of the students. Soon after, we were told to join the queue of equally proud parents outside. It rained a bit as we waited for the bus to take us the short distance to the cathedral. Umbrellas were opened and spirits weren't dampened as we chatted excitedly together. The cathedral was spectacular and the atmosphere inside was buzzing as we took our pre-booked seats. They weren't the best in the house by any means, but CCTV and a screen close by meant we could see everything. It was a long morning, and it was some time before Jay's name was announced and he walked up to the front to pick up his scroll. Babs took a small video camera out of her bag. I pointed out a notice that said no video was to be taken inside the building.

"What notice?" She asked, as she gazed myopically around her. It seemed she wasn't the only parent who suddenly had bad eyesight as I glanced around me. After the ceremony it was back on the bus for a lovely champagne reception and buffet and yet more photos, including the (then) traditional throwing the mortarboards in the air, now sadly banned from some establishments for health and safety reasons. By mid-afternoon it was all over. Jay returned his gown and mortarboard, no doubt to be used again and again. He chatted with his friends whom he'd shared so much with, reminiscing about both good times and bad and vowing to keep in touch. We said our goodbyes to Babs as she went off to catch her train home. Soon after we headed home ourselves arriving at around five o'clock. What a day it had been; in fact what a three years it had been - expensive and often traumatic, but worth every penny. I knew Jay was a hard worker. He was on his way, even if he was in debt to the tune of some £12,000.

Things were happening at work with the appointment of a new manager. I liked him and we got on well, unlike some of the lads who were kicking up about the bonus scheme. He called a shop meeting.

November 9th, 2005: *We had a meeting with the manager after lunch and he wasn't happy about the fact that although he allowed the truss line to be in early this week, once they realised it was going to be a crap bonus, they didn't bother. Most of what he said didn't affect me, so I just counted how many times he said, "The bottom line is...". It was 16. I sat with Mum tonight doing a crossword, and after dropping her home I watched the film, "The Bourne Identity." It wasn't all that good. Ben went to see his friend in London.*

My working hours were still long but the work interesting with more angled stuff to cut. It was hard work and often heavy. I was cycling the mile and a half to and from work every day which took about 20 minutes. It was a good way to keep fit and save on petrol too. I noted in my diary that the price of petrol in early December 2005 had gone down to 84p a litre - what a difference to today's prices. My diaries have been fascinating to look back on how much prices have risen over a period of many years, and wages too, speaking of which Jay was busy job hunting again trying to get work in retail at the City Centre over the Christmas period. He went for an interview at a chocolate shop but ended up at "Lush" the company that makes handmade soap and cosmetics. It was ok but he'd come home reeking of the stuff. I told him once he smelt like a tart's handbag, which didn't go down too well.

2005 came to an end with a really nice New Year's Eve gig at a rather nice up-market pub in Oxfordshire. We had a lot to look forward to in 2006 - Ben and his trip to Australia, and Jay with a lot of decisions to make and really excited about his future. Me? Who knows? More of the same I expect.

CHAPTER 29

Poorly again but surviving

I took Ben to Heathrow on 5th January, and we soon found his travelling companion Jennie who had driven down with her Dad. The youngsters (Ben was 25, and still young) were off to Australia and New Zealand for three months - what an adventure! We had a chat for a while and after a final goodbye off they went happy and excited. They had friends who lived there so on this particular trip I wasn't too concerned about the potential need to bail Ben out and send him money. Four days later he got in touch.

January 9th, 2006: *We had an email from Ben today. He seems ok and is going to travel north on his own while Jennie is going off somewhere else with her pals. Hopefully he'll be staying with friends which should save on hostel accommodation. He did warn me however that I might have to bail him out - he's only been there for two days! I can foresee another expensive January like last year. The car's going in for a service tomorrow, then there's the MOT as well.*

Unfortunately, the car failed the MOT, and I had a bill for £275. Luckily the magic earnings I'd earned over Christmas helped but it was still a worry; it was always a worry. I was permanently in a nervous state and terrified I'd run out. I'd have to put more hours in at work which was ok as long as the overtime was available; luckily at the time, it was, and included regular Saturday mornings. The downside of that was having little time for myself and somehow, I had to find time to rehearse yet another lecture for the magic club. I'd shown the same material so many times I was desperate to do something different. The only thing I hadn't done was the Goshman act which didn't fill me with confidence as I knew it wouldn't work, based on past experience. I decided to go for it anyway and came up with an unusual presentation. I called the lecture "The Flying Lesson" and divided it into two halves. The first half was about *how* to perform and the importance of connecting with an audience and learning how to relax and fly. I used as a text (not quite a sermon but almost) that wonderful little book 'Jonathan Livingston Seagull,' by Richard Bach. The lecture was perhaps a little hairy-fairy and new age-ish, and most certainly different, but nonetheless it went ok, and I was quite pleased. After the interval, I set up the table and invited two lay volunteers to sit with me. To say that it died a terrible death is an understatement. Having said that though, as far as the audience were concerned it was watchable and there were one or two good bits in it, but I wasn't at all happy having spent an hour in the first half explaining how to fly, and in the second half remaining firmly grounded! It reinforced my view that it just didn't work and that was the last time I did it. Oh well, it passed an evening, and a lot of people did ask me for more information regarding Richard Bach's book. That being the case they'll be able to read for themselves some memorable and useful advice about practise and having the freedom to be yourself where nothing can stand in your way.

With the lecture not going well, and potential money problems looming with another email from Ben talking about running out of money (and being sunburnt), I found myself in a rather poor mental state.

February 15th, 2006: *What a sad life I have. No social life whatsoever, nowhere to go, and no friends to go with anyway. It's just work. The magic isn't happening, and I've abandoned the act as unworkable.*

Re-reading that particular diary entry makes me look a bit pathetic. I think a lot of it had to do with overwork. I was always knackered and always worried. Not a good place to be especially when I was depended on so much. Luckily, I always managed to claw myself out of those dark places to survive another day.

I was still struggling some two weeks later...

March 7th, 2006: *I went to the club tonight and it was a 'Try it out' night. Again because of lack of material I decided to do something different. I remembered a fascinating passage from one of Deke's books about when the band met Tommy Cooper, so I read that out. It went ok but the newer lads just wanted to see tricks. Some of them are doing some nice stuff and I'm getting the feeling I'm being left behind. Things aren't happening. I suppose I do need to get out more.*

My response to that now is, I definitely did need to get out more.

If ever I needed cheering up, I'd pick up one of Deke Leonard's books. In this case 'Rhinos, Winos and Lunatics'. The passage in question was when he and the band did indeed meet Tommy Cooper when they found themselves in the same hotel in Manchester. I decided to read the passage out because it portrays exactly the effect that one of the world's greatest clowns had on the public. Deke writes of how he walked into a room full of people who were in hysterics, their eyes glued to a small table in the corner, and there was Tommy just sitting there. "He wasn't doing anything, but I burst out laughing, and so did everybody else in that room." It is a beautifully written piece. The point I was trying to make was that Tommy cooper didn't *have* to do anything - *he* was funny, and that's how and why personality is so important. Us mere mortals can learn so much from successful entertainers like Tommy Cooper. But no, they'd rather watch card tricks.

I did eventually take my own advice and started to get out more. I discovered walking and the countryside. I'd go out for hours absorbing it all with my spirits gradually lifting. I would get home tired perhaps, but certainly in a much better place mentally and it didn't cost me anything. Although I wasn't in a position to spend too much on myself, I was more than aware that my time would surely come when the boys had left home and I'd retired, something I was already looking forward to.

On March 9th, 2006, I was 56 and it was a Thursday. I went to work as usual and when my workmates found out it was my birthday, to a man all of them said, "What are you doing here then?" They would have had the day off. Times and attitudes were changing and not always for the better. I wonder what my Dad would have made of it all? I was reminded of him a few days later when I had a call from my nephew, Stuart. He wanted to transfer Dad's old cine films onto a DVD format and would I be up for it. I certainly would. It seemed a good way to get myself into a happier state of mind as well as making the films available for the rest of the family. Stuart came over a couple of days later and I set up the old projector which luckily still worked. There were 17 reels altogether, many of them with the same stuff on - holidays in Holyhead with the local scenery, the factory outings to Great Yarmouth or Clacton, and Leon recreation ground and the canal in Bletchley. (Dad didn't get out much either.) I set up the screen and put the first reel on. Even the sound of the projector and that distinctive smell of old films bought back so many memories. Stuart set up his camera and the old sometimes grainy films and memories burst onto the screen. It was a happy few hours reliving my childhood. Happy days.

April soon arrived along with Ben and Jennie from their adventures in Australia, both looking fit and bronzed. He'd taken loads of footage and was soon busy editing it into a finished film. It took him a month and we had the grand premier here at home with friends and family. It was really good and what a wonderful keepsake and memento of what was undoubtedly a memorable trip.

Thankfully my mental health improved along with the weather. The boys must have picked up on it as they were now helping out a bit more around the house. Jay was back working at Lush and he would clean the bathroom on the odd occasion when even he couldn't stand the remnants of their products plastered around the sink and bath. Ben was happy now to run the vacuum cleaner over the carpets once a week and even clean the kitchen floor. He had regular visitors during the year from all over the world which may have had something to do with it, anyway it was still appreciated. Jay had re-started his driving lessons, thanks to Babs who had paid for a batch of them as a Christmas present. Bearing in mind he hadn't driven for a couple of years, he soon got back in the swing and passed his theory test at the end of April. He put in for his practical test and the big day soon arrived – however, things didn't go smoothly (typically).

July 7th, 2006: *We had a bit of a panic here tonight, Jay lost his driving licence (again) which he needs for his driving test tomorrow. We found it after about 2 hours of searching, underneath his snooker* *table which was under his bed. Huge relief all round. I reckon he's going to be really nervous tomorrow morning and he hasn't got a lot of confidence.*

His instructor didn't have a lot of confidence either, based on a trial test ten days previously which he had convincingly failed. He told Jay he hadn't a hope in hell of passing. I tried to cheer him up by telling him he was in a similar situation to me when I took my test (and passed) and my instructor had said exactly the same thing. "But it wasn't my first test," I added (and immediately wished I hadn't.)

"Thanks Dad," said a gloomy Jay.

July 8th, 2006: *Jay passed his driving test!! To be honest I didn't think he had a chance, based on what he and his instructor have been saying recently. He left here at quarter to eight for an hour's practise and then had his test. He reckons he had no real problems, so that's it, job done!*

Jay left the world of retail and soap and got a temporary job at the local school, working on a one-to-one basis with an 8-year-old lad. It soon became apparent that his future was in teaching, but to pursue it any further he would need to retake his GCSE Maths and obtain a better grade. He was up for that, but it would cost £300 to do the course; I agreed to fund that, should it be required (which it was).

Ben, meanwhile, had been to Oxford for an interview for a job at a summer children's camp in the Lake District which he got. He had to go to Derby for a training course first and I was able to drop him off there on my way for a much needed few days away on The Wirral with Jean and Steve. I spent the first day alone.

July 12th, 2006: *A full day today. I got up early and walked into Birkenhead. I spent an hour or two wandering around the shops and bought the Marvin Gaye CD, 'What's going on', for a couple of quid. I caught a tube train to Liverpool and spent the rest of the day there. I wandered around the shops first of all and was asked if I'd mind doing a survey in a small office. I sat down at a desk with a computer for 20 minutes for which I got a cup of tea and a pen! I had a drink in the pub opposite where the original Cavern Club used to be and then strolled down to the Albert Docks. The museum was closed but I had a nice chat with the doorman and also a busker who was playing a banjo brilliantly. I had a look round The Tate but wasn't impressed and after that went on an open topped bus tour which was terrific. After that I caught the ferry across the Mersey and walked back to Jean's at around six o'clock. A great day!*

The next day I was woken at 8 o'clock with a tap on my bedroom door and Jean asking if I'd like to go for an early morning swim at the local pool (this was something she and Steve did quite regularly); I was up for it and off we went. It was a decent sized pool in a local leisure centre. We joined a small group of mostly elderly people swimming up and down in roped off lanes for about an hour. It certainly gave me an appetite for breakfast. After that I drove to Port Sunlight not really knowing what to expect. It's a peaceful Merseyside village which was founded by the Victorian entrepreneur William Hesketh Lever to house the workers of his soap factory; his company eventually became the global giant Unilever. The Cadbury brothers of chocolate fame did a similar thing with the village of Bournville in Birmingham. Firstly I went to Lady Lever's art gallery which was wonderful and from there to the Heritage Centre where I learned all I needed to know about the history of that remarkable place. I wandered around the village for some time ending up in the rather stunning church. I found the atmosphere in there and indeed the whole place really special and peaceful.

That evening we drove to West Kirby and joined a walking group of four ladies from the local church and walked across the sand to the island of Hilbre. It's a journey that for obvious reasons can only be made when the tide's out. From the shore it didn't look too far away, but it took us two hours. We were met there by the Island's only inhabitant a young chap who looked after the nature reserve. He showed us the remains of an old chapel and spoke about the history of the place and the work he was doing there. It was a lovely spot, but we couldn't stay too long as we had to trek back to the shore before the tide turned. Before setting off home we sat for a while looking back across to the island and a glorious sunset. It was a fitting end to what had been a great day.

More of the same the following day, with a trip to New Brighton and a long walk in the sunshine along the banks of the Mersey to the Seacombe Ferry Wharf in Wallasey. By the end of the day we were more than ready for a visit to a local pub. I'd had a great time and the next day I somewhat reluctantly travelled home.

Back to the inevitable grind. Work, and a few summer gigs. Usually I wear shorts from May to September and I find putting on a suit for a function a bit of an ordeal. Anyway needs must and as ever I needed the money. A new club had opened in The Point in Central Milton Keynes called 'Talk of the Town'. The management there had extravagant plans and ideas for it, which was encouraging but sadly it didn't last long. I did my usual walk around stuff which went really well and there was talk of regular work, but it never did come to anything, and it closed down soon after; shame really as I could have walked there in 15 minutes. I did a couple of open-air jobs in August, both wedding anniversary family events and both in Kettering on consecutive days. The proceeds paid for Jay's GCSE maths course, which was handy. He was now actively car hunting on eBay and scouring the internet for cheap insurance. Luckily his girlfriend's Dad was in the motor trade and was looking out for a possible bargain as well. All in all he was better equipped for his first car than I was - all I had to help me was the bloke in the pub.

Ben came home from camp on September 2nd and the next day a girl he'd met there came to visit. He'd had a good time up there in the Lake District. On that same day, I was struck down with the bug that gave me pneumonia some 18 months earlier. The symptoms were exactly the same, so I knew what it was. I got in touch with the doctor early the following day and luckily had an appointment to see him that same evening. Antibiotics were prescribed as there was a lung infection already there. I had the same night sweats and was taking paracetamol and ibuprofen, as well as the prescribed medication, just like the previous time. I felt awful yet I still staggered into work for a couple of days until I was sent home. It went on for a couple of weeks and I had to have stronger antibiotics to finally get rid of it. The only light spot during that time, which seems funny now, came from a diary entry...

September 10th, 2006: *I haven't really felt much better today, no doubt it'll take a bit of time for the new tablets to work. I had a reasonable night with no sweats. I still feel really tired and spent all day on the sofa in the front room. Every time I nodded off somebody would phone and ask how I am.*

I was getting a bit concerned about two things, the forthcoming IBM convention in Eastbourne (which was paid for), would I be able to go? And of course what would be the extent of money lost due to absence from work. Both were answered on the same day.

September 15ᵗʰ, 2006: *I went to see the Doctor Fagan at 9 o'clock this morning and got the all-clear. If it flares up again in Eastbourne (which is unlikely) he gave me a letter to give to a local doctor; I thought that was really thoughtful of him. I phoned the lady in the wages office who told me that next week I'll get nothing, and the week after that I'd get about £70. That upset me for the rest of the day for obvious reasons.*

She was right, I got £70 statutory sick pay and a tax rebate of £8. Being ill had cost me almost £300. Nothing however was going to stop me having a good time at the convention. Ben was home and settled, Jay had money put aside for his new car expenses, so I was able to dip into my ISA for some spending money and was all set to go. I'd also made the important and obviously sensible decision to stop smoking. I never did smoke cigarettes, I started with cheroots, and ended with small cigars. I wasn't a heavy smoker by any means, I'd have one with a pint or when I was wound up for some reason and that was it. Bearing in mind the smoking ban was looming anyway it seemed the right time to stop. The test would come of course when I was at the convention at the bar with a pint with my pals with adrenalin flowing and doing tricks.

September 19ᵗʰ, 2006: *I went to the Centre first thing and drew some money from my ISA and then went to Sainsbury's to stock up. The boys should be ok. I packed my case (which didn't take long as*

I haven't got many clothes). I had a shave and some lunch and set off for Eastbourne. I had a good journey and was able to park outside the hotel, and after checking in went for a walk to get paracetamol (just in case). After a lovely dinner I wandered over to register and had a quick look around the dealers and spent an enjoyable evening with Kevin (Fox). We ended up in the bar of the Landsdowne hotel. I haven't bought any cigars and so far have coped ok.

I'd had my last cigar. I missed them for a while, but it would have been crazy to have started again. Surprisingly I found giving up much easier than I thought and soon became an anti-smoker. As the ban approached it was fast becoming an anti-social habit anyway. I realised that even when smokers go outside, they still reek of tobacco when they come back. That could have been me at an event performing close-up magic; what could be worse than trying to entertain a group of possible non-smokers and smelling of cigar smoke? Luckily, I did the right thing and at the right time and my health improved as a result.

The first lecture I saw at Eastbourne was by American magician John Carney who was superb. He'd studied with Dai Vernon and was a huge fan of the magic of John Ramsay. We were kindred spirits, on the same wavelength, the same page, and everything else. It gave my confidence a bit of a boost as I often thought I was a voice in the wilderness. By now though there were other magicians who had new and fresh ideas who appealed to the young performers and sadly the names of my heroes were at times confined to history. It was still lovely to see and watch John Carney flying the flag of Vernon and Ramsay with so much enthusiasm. Later that day there was a trade show session. This was something that had started in America and was beginning to be popular over here. It takes place in trade shows or exhibitions. Magicians are employed by companies to be at their trade stand and advertise the product using magic. It's very hard work and long hours but also very lucrative. I dabbled a bit with that type of work over the years, but I found it a hard slog. That evening was the stage act competition with 14 acts, all of them watchable (which was a bonus as it isn't always the case). My old pal Noel/Magic Dave entered and performed very well I thought.

The next day I watched an interesting lecture by Shep Hyken, an American motivational speaker and advisor. I had to commend the convention organisers for even considering something like this for a room full of magicians. He pitched it really well and held the audience for about an hour. I've always been up for anything that's different from the usual format of doing tricks and selling DVDs. This was much more up my street and more about *how* to perform. I thought it was great and made a refreshing change.

The close-up competition came up next with 13 acts, and according to my diary was a good afternoon's entertainment.

The weather was really lovely that year, so I donned shorts and T-shirt and walked up to the Downs and Beachy Head. Walking was continuing to give me a lot of pleasure and good mental therapy, as was reading. No trip to Eastbourne is complete without visiting the world-renowned Camilla's book shop. I've spent hours browsing in there over the years and again came away with a pile of books. The next day the weather broke so I stayed inside the complex all day, and luckily there was a lot going on. John Calvert did his show and lecture, and it was hardly noticeable that he was in his 95th year. Still a great performer. Next up was a lecture by American magician/juggler, Charlie Frye. Brilliant!

Later in the afternoon there was another good lecture by American comedy magician Jeff Hobson. With his rather camp style of personality and performance he was hilarious making a simple trick like the egg bag into something big and wonderful. He too talked at length on the *performance* of the tricks and of the importance of style and personality, and whether he was aware of it or not, it was another motivational lecture - loved it! There was another great lecture the following day from yet another American comedy magician Mac King. He had his own show in Las Vegas and, as far as I know, still has. His style of performance is about as far removed from the huge spectacular illusion shows that are synonymous with the place as you can get. He does a family friendly comedy magic show, and it was a really enjoyable and informative lecture. It was turning into a great convention, and it wasn't over yet. The International close-up was great, as was the final gala show, and it all ended with a few beers at a fringe event. What a great time I'd had. I'd learned a lot, met up again with my magical friends, had a few beers, learned to live without smoking, and there had been no sign of a recurrence of the dreaded bug.

Luckily Christmas bookings were coming in, and not just for the magic.

November 8th, 2006: *I had a call tonight from the agency in Boreham Wood about a job in Northampton. It was something about opening the door of a limo for elderly people in a retirement village while wearing some sort of costume. It sounded odd to me, so I politely declined.*

Even though the money would have been handy, you have to draw the line somewhere; I never was keen on dressing up.

Soon after returning from Eastbourne I got in touch with the local football team the MK Dons to offer my services as a close-up magician to entertain their corporate fans before or after the match. We'd been to watch a few games at the Hockey Stadium, where they played at the time and where I got the idea. To be honest, I wasn't really a football fan but going with the boys was a good afternoon out and the opportunity to indulge in a bit of father/sons bonding (not that they saw it that way); they were at the age when taking the piss out of their old Dad was something to relish. When we first went, they insisted that I joined them in some home fans chanting; I can't say I was happy about it, particularly when some of them were what I considered to be in poor taste. Whatever happened to, "Two, four, six, eight, who do we appreciate?" We watched them play Shrewsbury once, and even though the town isn't in Wales and an abundance of sheep was doubtful, the fans would still roar at the opposition, "Sheep shaggers! sheep shaggers!"; the reply back was invariably a gesture involving a finger. The other one that was used a lot was, "Who are yuh? Who are yuh?"

I asked the boys what it meant as I didn't have a clue - "Who's who?" I asked; they just laughed. The only chant that I did join in with some gusto, particularly after a poor decision, was, "The referee's a wanker!" Anyway, a rep from MK Dons got back to me and it was agreed that I'd do a trial run with the magic for free. I wasn't particularly happy with that, even when they said I'd be able to watch the game from the corporate area; that was of little consolation as I'd rather have the dosh. It turned out I'd be out of pocket anyway, as it occurred to me that I'd have to buy a new coat. I could hardly turn up and sit with wealthy businesspeople wearing an old Llewellyn donkey jacket. On the morning of the gig I went to BHS and bought a coat for 24 quid reduced from 40, which did the job. I arrived at the specified time and the corporate area was packed, I worked solidly for an hour until it was time for the match to start and we all took our seats. I was really pleased; the magic had gone well. The Dons won 2-0 which I thought would bode well when I spoke to the rep at the end. It seemed obvious to me, however, that even though the idea and the entertainment had worked, they were reluctant to part with any cash. I got the impression they wanted me to do it for a free ticket to watch the games. Sod that! They said they'd get in touch, but they never did.

In early December I did another job for Allsorts Entertainments. Yet again Roy and Meg excelled themselves with loads of information written on the contract. It was for a 60th birthday party and thanks to Roy's notes I knew there would be: 2 nine-year-old children, 6 teenagers, and the remainder (some fifty people) aged between 50 and 60.

The address of the venue, which was a village bowls club, was written on the contract thus:

"The Bowls Club is off Station Road, passed the Bakers on the left. Go down the alley on the right and the club is halfway down and up some steps. To avoid the steps, turn down Park Street opposite The Boot pub, go down to a T junction at the bottom and turn left. You're now at the other end of the alley thus avoiding the steps."

One thing's for sure, you'd never get that amount of useful information on a satnav. When I actually got to the venue (which I found easily) there were only 4 people there and one of those was the barmaid. As people arrived, they began to organise themselves into a semi-circle, as though I was going to do a stand-up show.

Once they realised what I did though they soon got themselves into groups and it turned out to be a really good night.

A couple of weeks later I did a job that couldn't have been more different. This one took place in the Great Room of the Grosvenor House hotel in London. It was vast with 108 tables. There was a large team of us working that night each allocated some 15 tables. Each one was numbered, and we were given a map with our tables highlighted; it was still difficult to navigate around the room though as there were so many people and staff all doing the same thing. I got there at about quarter to six and when the rest of the performers arrived, we had a briefing from the organiser. As long as we visited each table we were left pretty much to our own devices. It wasn't easy; it was noisy for a start and with a quiet voice like mine I was never going to command the attention of the whole table of about a dozen people. I resorted to my usual tried and tested formula of doing one trick at a table and then moving onto the next. I'd scan the people, look for a friendly face, and show him or her the trick along with the people either side of them, so at least I was covering a quarter of the table per visit. If it went particularly well and it got a good reaction, I'd do it again on the other side of the table. It was one of those evenings where most of the people weren't bothered if they saw a performer or not as there was just too much of a hubbub going on. After I'd visited each of my tables I made a note of the ones that went particularly well and went back for a second visit. That was it, job done. It was a long and busy night, and I got home well after midnight. Although jobs like that paid really well, it was a hard graft and there was little opportunity to actually engage with the people, do the trick, and onto the next. Give me a village hall anytime.

The next job was another busy one, this was for McLaren, the Formula One racing people. The venue was better suited for doing close-up, with a large bar area and a couple of lounges as well. I was joined that night by Mick Hanzlik and John Shaw from the magic club. We all had a good time that night. There was such a mixture of people there from executives to mechanics and there were a lot of them. It made me realise just how big a workforce is required to enable a few cars to drive round a racetrack.

A couple of days later I found myself back at the Hockey Stadium for a gig. Nothing to do with the football club, this was a job for Homebase which at the time was a part of the Sainsbury's group. When I spoke to the rep, he asked me if I could be suited and booted and wear a dinner suit. I was ok with that and was looking forward to entertaining their top executives. (I'd come up with a trick using their loyalty card and was anxious to try out.) I got to the venue and had to fight my way through a noisy bar full of young people talking, drinking, and dancing, most of them the worse for drink. I walked all the way round searching in vain for a door or stairs that would lead me to where I needed to be. In the end I asked (shouted to) a young chap and asked him where the Homebase event was.

"Here," he shouted back, "Are you the magician?"

I was horrified. I told him I was indeed the magician and why was I wearing a dinner suit when I pointed out that everybody else in the room was wearing jeans and T-shirts.

"Well, I did ask them, but you know what young people are like."

I think I stayed for an hour. There was a huge raffle that went on for half of that time and at the end of that I'd had enough. The music was turned up, everyone was on the floor dancing and the alcohol was flowing. Close-up magic was out of the question (particularly when performed by an overdressed middle-aged bloke in a dinner suit). I found the young organiser, who was ok about it, and he gave me an envelope with my fee in full. I walked to the car park with ears ringing and glad to be out of the place but feeling a bit disappointed. It would have worked better perhaps if I'd have got there earlier before the punters hit the bar. Oh well, another one to chalk up to experience.

Another year gone, another year survived, and I was feeling pretty good by the end of it. Things weren't going so well for the planet though. I was quite surprised when I read this diary entry from the middle of the year.

June 1st, 2006: *I've just watched a David Attenborough programme about global warming which every person on the planet should be forced to watch. It was really quite frightening. While it was on, Ben was on his computer, and Jay was playing a game on his while watching Big Brother. Sometimes I despair.*

Unfair perhaps to bemoan the fact that the boys hadn't watched the programme. No doubt there were millions of others too who would rather get on with their lives in a similar way with most of them unaware of a possible looming tragedy. Politicians were aware though, or they certainly should have been. It's been 15 years since that programme was aired and at last world leaders are talking about it and making promises. Let's hope it isn't too little too late.

CHAPTER 30

Disappointed but wiser

Mum was visiting every Wednesday despite being in her 89th year and still bringing crisps and biscuits in abundance. By the end of the year though she'd had to give up bus travel and came instead in a taxi and I'd drive her home at about nine o'clock. Her general health wasn't too bad, but her hearing and sight had been failing for some time. She had hearing aids but at the beginning of the year was having some trouble. The following is a fairly typical Wednesday evening…

January 3rd, 2007: *Mum had trouble with her hearing aids this evening and it drove me mad. They were emitting a high-pitched whistle that was even louder than the washing machine. I got her to turn them down a bit which did the trick. We spent the evening in front of the TV. First The Archers (via the radio), then a true crime programme, and for the last hour the Biography Channel with Led Zeppelin, it was made on the cheap with archive footage, but it passed an hour.*

I would give Mum first choice of what to watch, but typically she wanted me to choose. As ever, it was always family and others first. We did manage to convince her to spend a considerable amount of money on herself however later in the year. She took delivery of new state-of-the-art hearing aids which added a tremendous amount to her wellbeing and quality of life (and ours).

There was yet another takeover at work at the end of 2006. I was now an employee of a company based in Ireland called Kingspan. Again we were told that nothing much would change apart from an increase in workload. That would indeed be the case throughout 2007; yet again I worked long hours six days a week. By now I had a good financial advisor and as well as keeping my ISA topped up for unexpected family needs, (just as well I did), I was putting away as much as I could into a pension pot. Jay, meanwhile, had begun his own journey into economics by venturing into the world of motoring. He bought his first car. It was second-hand and cost him £120. He had the cash to pay for half of it and I had to pop up to the cashpoint to get the other half (which he did pay back, eventually); I haven't mentioned in my diary the make of the car, as based on my own experience it was bound to be expensive and trouble whatsoever it was. He spent a lot of time on the internet getting it insured and by mid-January it was sorted and ready to go, but I wasn't sure that Jay was.

January 18th, 2007: *Jay got his car insurance sorted out but still hasn't driven it. He did put an air freshener inside though and checked the hazard warning lights! I was hoping he'd pay me back some of the money I lent him so I could go to Sainsbury's, but he didn't so I had to go to the cashpoint again.*

I was reminded of my first car and how nervous I was to begin with. Now the boot was on the other foot, and I was just as concerned as he apparently was. I was going through the nightmare that parents suffer when their offspring begin the often rocky road of driving for the first time.

January 23rd, 2007: *Jay drove up to the garage tonight to get petrol and did ok. I was really nervous after he'd gone; I realise now how Mum and Dad must have felt when I had my first car some 30 years ago. It'll be even more nerve racking when he goes on his first journey.*

The garage was less than a mile away and his girlfriend (who owned her own car) was with him, so I don't really know what I was worried about. A couple of days later he drove up to the city centre, and a few weeks after that went on his first really long solo journey, a visit to his girlfriend in Buckingham (a distance of some ten miles). After that I didn't worry so much and for a while he experienced trouble-free motoring, until the end of February when the car (unsurprisingly) failed the MOT. The car got him through most of the year and he finally sold it for scrap at the end of October for £60. He bought his next car from his mate for £40.

Ben was doing ok; he never did show any interest in driving and was happy to cycle or bus/cab (or get a lift from me) to get himself around. He was still working at a local school and filling his spare time with his music. One day when I was working in the front garden, he had a visit from his old boss who ran a children's after school club. He'd called round to pick up a key that Ben still had. He stopped for a chat afterwards and told me that Benny (as he was increasingly known) was one of the best workers he'd known. He had this natural rapport with children which was quite rare. He went on to tell me that he'd employ him again in an instant and that I should be really proud. I was, and again a tad emotional. Ben was quiet and didn't say much about his work. It was reassuring to know that he was guaranteed employment in a field that he was so good at and enjoyed. He'd also been busy with his artwork and displayed some of it at a couple of exhibitions with other local artists during the year.

Jay spent much of 2007 deciding his future. Would it be teaching or something else? He applied unsuccessfully to join the police force. I think I was as disappointed as he was when he got the news. He still had the part time job at the local school and left there at the end of the summer term. Judging by the amount of cards and presents he came home with on that day he was well liked by both staff and pupils. He went for an interview as a fitness instructor and despite 44 applicants, he got the job. He did that throughout the summer and worked long hours and wasn't particularly happy there. In October he was offered a job back at the school on a higher grade, which he accepted. By the end of the year he'd made his mind up to go from being a teaching assistant to actively pursuing a career as a teacher. He spent a lot of time on the internet researching the best way to do his training.

In April of 2007 I decided to enter the IBM close-up competition at the Southport convention in September. The application form arrived in the post, I filled it in and sent it off. I was committed. The plan was to at the very least enjoy myself performing in front of my peers at the four tables required and at best any prize money would be useful to contribute to convention expenses. Again I wanted to do something different. I had the material and a vague idea of the original tricks I wanted to do. It would be all about the presentation. I came up with the idea of doing an auto biographical theme. Of how my Dad gave me a lot of encouragement and would often go through the drawers in his shed in search of anything I could use for props in the early days before we discovered dealers. It took a while but by mid-August I had the act sorted out and timed. I did a trick with a screwdriver to open, then there was a coinbox routine with old pennies, followed by a trick with a large nut and bolt and three hazel nuts, and I finished with a card routine with the production of half a dozen washers. It was certainly original, but would it work? I had no way of knowing. Therein was the problem. My half a dozen tried and tested routines that I'd performed for the public for 40 years had all evolved over a long period of time. I *knew* they worked. The competition act was very much a one-off with hardly any exposure to an audience. I did try it out in June when the magic club visited the Pentacle Club in Cambridge. I received polite applause and that was about it. The conditions there were the same as I'd find in Southport with a table in front of rows of people where the surface of it could be difficult to see. I came up with an idea to make it more visual; I made a small, wedged-shape mini-platform that would sit on the middle of the table which enabled the audience to see the cards and coins more clearly. To be honest I was experienced in competitions, so I knew what to expect. I wasn't exactly brimming with confidence as can be seen from the following.

August 13, 2007: *I cut the base to my close-up "stage" today and also a small piece of ply to stop the nuts from rolling. I glued and pinned it altogether and it seems ok. It just needs filling, sanding, and painting, then I'll have to cut up an old close-up mat to glue onto the protruding piece at the back. It should be done by the weekend. I'm starting to get nervy now as it's only a month today before the actual competition. I still get two different feelings about the act. Sometimes I think it's crap and I won't come anywhere, and other times I think*

I'll win the thing easily. I'm trying to get myself into the state of mind where I want to just go out there and really enjoy it.

Meanwhile, I was still going along to the magic club, sometimes when I wasn't all that keen on the subject matter.

August 21ˢᵗ, 2007: *I went along to the club tonight which was a meeting on card moves and sleights. It was taken over entirely by one of the members who as a performer does absolutely nothing for me. In fact the highlight of the meeting was when one of the chaps farted rather loudly.*

By the beginning of the following month, I still wasn't happy...

September 2ⁿᵈ, 2007: *I spent the afternoon rehearsing the act, and as I see it the only dodgy part is loading the coin underneath the coin box lid. When I first came up with the idea a few years ago, the fact that you couldn't hear it drop was its strongest point. Now it just looks obvious. I'm convinced now that the material just isn't strong enough to win it.*

And again a week later...

September 10ᵗʰ, 2007: *I rehearsed the act again tonight and I solved the noise problem when loading the coin under the lid - a small piece of Blu-tac. I had a few run throughs tonight and it's now as good as it's going to get. So that's it, it's certainly been a time-consuming project. 172 times I've rehearsed it, let's hope it pays off.*

Until I re-read the diary, I had no idea that I'd actually counted the number of times I went through it; a strange thing to do.

The following day I travelled up to Birkenhead to stay the night with Jean and Steve before continuing my journey to Southport the next day. I went through the act for them, and it seemed to go reasonably well inasmuch as I remembered it and didn't drop anything.

It didn't take long to travel to Southport, and I soon found my hotel and the venue and registered before watching the opening show. After that I went for a wander before Bill Malone's lecture which was good if a little short. Next up was a lecture on sleeving from Rocco, and that was it until the stage competition in the evening. There were 8 acts, and the standard wasn't too bad that year. I had a couple of pints with some pals after that before an earlyish night and to prepare myself for the competition the next day. In the morning I watched a lecture from top American comedy magician David Williamson which was really good and almost had a standing ovation.

The Close-Up Competition took place in the afternoon, and I got to the venue early to check out each of the four rooms. They were all pretty much the same and I couldn't foresee any problems. There were ten of us competing so that meant there was a gap between each of the four performances, so it wouldn't be a case of finish one and straight onto the next. The organisation was very good with a steward in each room who made sure we had as much time as we needed to prepare. I was lucky in that I didn't need any assistance from the audience. It was all self-contained with everything I needed either in my pockets or behind my small platform; all I had to do was walk on and place it in the middle of the table and off I'd go. The first table can be the worst or the best. If it goes well then you have the confidence and enthusiasm and can look forward to the other three. If it doesn't go well, you can have a problem. I walked into the room and was introduced; I was on. I had an opening line which I was convinced would endear me to the audience and get a good laugh. But I got nothing. I don't think there's anything worse than the profound silence that comes instead of expected applause or laughter. I got through it though. I performed the tricks well and nothing went wrong from that point of view. It just didn't work. The audience (and it would turn out the judges too) weren't enamoured with what they saw. I came off and went back to the meeting room along with the other lads and almost decided to give up there and then. For whatever reason, it just wasn't working. I certainly wasn't going to blame anybody, but I knew the same thing was likely to happen on the remaining tables. But there was still a slim chance it was just a bad room, which does happen occasionally when some are better than others. Sadly not in my case. The next two tables were just as bad, and I performed to total silence. I was a bit annoyed and disappointed because I wasn't enjoying it. The final table however was a bit different. I threw caution to the wind and changed my approach. I was introduced and said,

"Now listen to me you lot, I've just performed to three audiences to total silence and I'm on the verge of dying the death of a thousand dogs for the fourth time in an afternoon. Only you can prevent that from happening, so let me see a few smiling faces and at least pretend you're having a good time. It would also be a good idea to have a round of applause now before I start as there's little chance of getting any at the end. Thank you."

With that I got a huge cheer and a round of applause with lots of smiling faces. I went through the act with one or two extra gags and ad libs, and we all had a good time, apart from the judge who didn't quite know what to make of it all; by then I was past caring.

In spite of everything, I came equal third which isn't bad out of ten competitors. It could have been a lot worse. I was cheered up the next day as I was walked around the dealers. Gary Young called me over and told me there was somebody who wanted to meet me. I was introduced to the renowned French magician, Gaeton Bloom, who was there both as a dealer and a lecturer and had been a judge for the competition. He told me how much he'd enjoyed my performance and certainly would have put me in the top two, "But the other judges…" he said, and shrugged. He went on to say that my trick with the screwdriver caught him badly and was the best trick of the afternoon. What a lovely man. We had a chat for a while and then he mentioned that he'd heard I do a good impression of his old and dear friend Ken Brooke. I did that for him which he appreciated, and he then gave me a copy of his lecture notes with a lovely message written inside. "Dear Ken, I had a really good time watching you perform, not to forget the nice talk about our other dear 'Ken'. Most sincerely Gaeton Bloom."

That meant more to me than winning the competition.

The final evening after the final show was spent in the bar of the headquarters hotel getting rather drunk with my pal from Scotland Gordon Bruce. We were sitting at a table along with David Williamson and author and creator of great card magic, Walt Lees. Walt was waxing lyrical about how great David's lecture had been.

"In over 40 years of attending conventions and having seen hundreds of lectures, yours was without doubt the finest and most entertaining I have ever seen, the material and advice given was just exceptional!"

In the silence that followed, and before David could reply I said,

"Well I thought it was crap."

David Williamson laughed. That moment too meant more to me than winning the competition. Generally speaking, it was a good convention; the competition I've written off as experience - if you're not prepared to lose then don't enter is the obvious sentiment. I certainly had no regrets. I did suffer with a bruised ego for a while but felt happy in the knowledge that it wasn't the end of the world, nobody died, and it was only for a bunch of magicians anyway... and I didn't come last.

Back to work and Health & Safety came to the fore. I was given a job to build some large sheds to house packs of plywood and insulation in the yard. As usual I was left to my own devices, or so I thought. I'd built a couple of trestles and a platform to stand on. I was about to climb onto it when I had a visit from one of the managers. He insisted that I fit braces to the trestles and then connect them together with yet more bracing. Almost as an afterthought he asked to borrow my tape measure and checked the height of it, he then said I'd have to make and fit a handrail! It took me a couple of hours to make something just to stand on. That's how it was from then on. The argument that me and my contemporaries would often give, that we'd been doing it this way for thirty years, didn't mean anything anymore and we just had to go with it. It was more difficult for tradesmen on site to adapt to the new regime, especially when they were told what to do from youngsters freshly qualified just out of college, some of them girls. I could see the reasoning behind it though, you just had to look at the statistics of the previous 20 years regarding lack of safety and the sheer number of accidents (including the ladder one I'd witnessed.) A new industry had sprung up regarding Health & Safety. I've lost count of how many courses I had to attend during the 7 or 8 years I had left in the trade before I retired, with some done twice, the second one being a refresher course. There was everything from manual handling to erecting a tower scaffold and for most of them a certificate was issued at the end of it to prove that we were capable and had enough knowledge to perform the relevant tasks safely. A cynic might argue that the employers are merely covering their backs and I suspect there is some truth in that; however statistics have proved that the advent of Health & Safety has considerably reduced the number of accidents throughout the construction industry, even though it does occasionally 'go mad'.

The smoking ban was now in place on our premises which was difficult to deal with as most of the workforce were smokers. Prior to the ban, the blokes were given fag breaks and allowed to smoke in a hut in the car park. When that was dismantled and got rid of, they went outside the factory gates and off the premises for a quick smoke. That came to a halt when they were told they'd have to clock out and therefore lose money. For us non-smokers, it was quite comical. But they had little choice and for quite a few though it did give them the impetus to stop smoking which was good news. The next thing to happen, pending a visit from the company Health & Safety officer, was that white lines were painted on the floor as guidelines for where timber was to be stacked, and where the workforce and forklifts could and couldn't go. I also spent the best part of a day fixing signs and notices to the walls advising all sorts of things. It did seem strange at the time, but now it's very much the norm wherever you go. Jay too was not immune to it while he was working in the gym; he had to go on first aid and lifesaving courses. And Ben, working with children, has also had to do various courses over the years, as you'd expect. Health & Safety was definitely here to stay.

I was still going to the table tennis club for a knock once a week and in a moment of madness had entered the Bucks Open Championships. It took place at the club in November and was very nearly over for me before I'd played a ball. I discovered I had to be registered to a club to compete. I just turned up there every Sunday for a knock, paid a fiver and that was it, I was a non-member. I explained to the organiser there would only be a problem if I were to win something and that was about as likely as me flying to the moon. Luckily, common sense prevailed, and I was allowed to enter the men's singles and the over 55s intermixed, veteran singles. I was looking forward to it as it would be a good day out, even though it was a long one. It was due to begin at 8.30 and eventually finish around 7 o'clock. There was a group system with all the categories which meant everybody played each other once with the winner going on to the next round. I had quite a few games which I enjoyed but didn't win many so didn't progress. I was also happy to score matches to keep things running. It was nice as well to have a chat and meet up with other players I hadn't seen for years. For the most part everything went smoothly although the matches did tend to overrun and by 6 o'clock there was hardly anybody left. One of the last groups to be played was the over 55s and I did think I was in with a slim chance of winning something. It was duly announced, and I went over to Table 3 with a spring in my step eager to end the day on a bit of a high. I stood around for a few minutes and very little was happening. Then an official came up to me and told me there was nobody left for me to play - they'd all gone home. (2007 obviously wasn't my year for competitions.) There was a bit of a huddle going on with the organisers and one of them came up to me and explained that they'd decided to present me with a trophy anyway as it wasn't my fault nobody had turned up. I accepted gracefully and said that I did deserve something due to the number of games I'd scored. Let's not beat about the bush here, I was chuffed. I went home eager to share my victory with the boys. I showed them the rather nice Perspex trophy which was engraved, '55 plus intermixed singles consolation winner 2007/08'. I think I may have forgotten to mention that I hadn't actually played a ball in that category.

"What does consolation mean?" asked Jay.

"Never mind that," I said, "Just look at the word winner."

I placed it carefully in the cabinet, closed the glass door, turned around and both boys were grinning.

"Is it a consolation prize because you got beaten by that bloke in the wheelchair again?" said Ben.

2007 was a good year for my young friend Anthony Owen. I went along to his wedding in April which was just wonderful. (Ironically it was at The Landmark Hotel in London where I did those memorable Japanese bank gigs with Mr. Yakamoto.) Anthony's career as a TV producer was going from strength to strength with his production company involved in, 'Peep Show', with David Mitchell, Robert Webb, and Olivia Colman. There were various magic shows and series in the pipeline as well, and with a lecture tour booked in America, things were looking good for him. He lectured at the magic club in November which was a great night. Three of us had travelled over to Northampton from Milton Keynes for that and the next day I told my Mum all about it. She'd met Anthony quite a few times over the years and often asked about him. The conversation moved on to the weather (which wasn't good) and the journey to Northampton. I told her that three of us had travelled in one car and who the other two were. She'd heard of one but not the other. She then asked me if the one she didn't know was married. I found myself in a bit of a dilemma here and wasn't too sure how she'd react to the news that he was gay. It was a subject we'd never talked about. At the time, civil partnerships had been legal for a couple of years and generally speaking people were becoming more tolerant and understanding and accepting of different lifestyle choices. There were however still rumblings of discontent amongst some Christian groups and churches, and bearing in mind Mum was a practising Christian, I was rather intrigued as to how she'd respond. I told her he was gay and that he had a partner and was very happy. There was a moment's pause and she said, "That's nice," and didn't really react. She thought for a moment and then told me that she'd met a couple of girls like that when she was in the army during the war.

"They were nice girls," she said, "One of them looked like a man and the other one had a speech impediment."

The matter-of-fact way she said it made me roar with laughter. There was never going to be a problem with Mum. Her attitude of accepting people for who they are and not what they are and with love and compassion was a huge part of who she was. She'd accepted gay people since 1944.

2007 drew to a close and ended with some unmemorable Christmas gigs and the visit of a couple of American girls to stay who were great fun. On a less happy note the shower had broken and had to be replaced in a hurry, the washing machine seized up, and there was a problem with the ballcock in the loft tank which caused a leak in the kitchen due to a too short overflow pipe. Oh well, another year gone, and I wondered what 2008 would bring.

CHAPTER 31

The end of an era

Although my health was pretty good at the time (apart from being permanently knackered), I did have a problem with a small hernia that had been rumbling for a couple of years. It was uncomfortable more than painful and took the form of a small lump situated just below my belt line on the right-hand side. I dealt with it the obvious way. Whenever the lump appeared I placed my hand over it and pushed it back. Obviously not what you might call proper surgery, but it worked. I did go and see the doctor who confirmed it was indeed a small hernia and he gave me a choice, live with it, or he could refer me to a specialist. My mind was made up for me.

January 6th, 2008: *I went to table tennis tonight, but my hernia played up a bit which was a bit annoying. I spoke to Michael who had the operation and it cost him six weeks off work! I'll see if I can hang on until I retire in 7 years 2 months' time.*

And hang on I did. In fact it somehow cured itself and the lump stopped appearing altogether and that was that. You can also see from the diary entry I was already counting down the time to my retirement. I'd just about had enough of the drudgery of work and the incessant long hours. I was also hoping that my job was safe, and it would see me out the 7 years and 2 months I had left. At the age of almost 58 I really didn't have the energy to start doing something else.

The year started well for Jay. He'd spotted an advert in the local paper for teacher training on the job (paid) at a school in Buckingham. He went along for an interview and got the job. He obviously settled in ok as some 14 years later he's still there but now as Assistant Head. He'd also been house hunting for a few months with his girlfriend and they moved into a small flat in the Spring. Due to its size and the difficulty finding suitable furniture, I made a desk and a unit which were nice little projects for me. He'd moved out in a bit of a rush and left an enormous amount of stuff in his room which I had to sort out. It took me 3 hours just to clear up and bag the stuff on the floor. In the process I picked up and bagged a fair amount of loose change, the total of which came to £40 including a £20 note! It was months before the drawers were emptied but, in all honesty, there wasn't a lot of room in his flat to put it all anyway; some of it's still here.

Magic jobs were coming in including a memorable one at The Old Shanghai Chinese restaurant in Olney. It was for the Chinese New Year and the owner's family took part in the celebrations all dressed in national costume. The small children looked really cute as they handed out the raffle prizes after performing the dragon dance along the complete length of the restaurant. It was just lovely and as you'd expect the customers loved it too. I was lucky enough to get that gig for several years and it was always a good night there with friendly customers and staff.

I was still going along to the magic club whenever I could. We had a lecture from a young chap in February by the name of James Brown who I thought was quite exceptional. Everything about him was fresh and original and his misdirection was spot on - one of the few who actually use it and apply it to such great effect. Definitely on the same wavelength as John Ramsay and Dai Vernon. It was a good night and also encouraging to see a young performer use the techniques of my magic heroes.

Since the 1960s when I first got into magic, I've always been on the lookout for anything I could use in the act as a novelty prop or gag. Over the years I have amassed quite a collection of all sorts of things, some I use regularly and some I haven't used at all – yet - but one day I might so I don't throw anything away; if there were more than one available then I'd buy two. It's a strange logic but it has paid dividends on a number of occasions. As I wandered around Bletchley market one day in the mid-sixties, I spotted an absolute gem. It was a large metal thimble with the words, "Just a thimble full" engraved around the base. It was a novelty whisky measure. What made it so good was the fact it was proportional in size to the normal size metal thimble I was using that I nicked from my Mum's sewing basket (she had loads of them and wouldn't have missed one). It was just perfect. Over the next 40 years the thimble trick evolved into what has become my favourite routine which I've performed thousands of times. In March of 2008 tragedy struck. I lost it (the thimble and my cool). It was at the magic club dinner, and I didn't notice it was missing until I got home. I searched the car and my pockets and my case several times, all to no avail. The following day I phoned Roy, the club secretary, who took the trouble to visit the hotel and even searched the room, but there was no sign of it anywhere - it was gone. It may seem melodramatic to call the loss of a large thimble a tragedy but to me it was. I was heartbroken and quite surprised how the loss of it made me feel, it was like a bereavement. I realised and understood then how Ben must have felt when his keyboard was stolen, and I now have enormous sympathy for anybody who has lost anything that has sentimental value, whatever it may be. At the time it didn't occur to me to search for a replacement as I felt the chances of finding an identical one would be pretty much impossible. The internet would have been useful had I'd access to it, but at this point in my life I didn't know what Google was or indeed what it did. I did have to find something though as gigs were coming in and I wanted to carry on performing it. I looked amongst my old props and found a giant red wooden one that my Dad had made from the bottom of an old table lamp which I'd used as a part of my stage act as a teenager. Luckily, I'd kept it and the matching smaller version and managed to work it into the routine. It was never quite the same though but at least it was something. Meanwhile I was still hustling for gigs. The local papers were a constant source of information, and we took delivery of at least three of them each week, two editions of the MK Citizen which came out on Sunday and Tuesday and the MK Mirror on Wednesdays. They were useful for a host of things - publicity for the magic, a prize crossword (which I won several times), table tennis and local football league tables, and of course adverts for all sorts of things and events. Over the years though the quality declined, and they ended up having more adverts than news and eventually ended up as online newspapers. As I was flicking through one of the better ones one day in 2008, I spotted an advert for a large charity event taking place at the newly opened MK Dons football stadium. It was a formal dinner, auction, and cabaret, taking place in one of the large function rooms overlooking the pitch. Always on the hunt for new venues and anxious to have a look at the place I sent off for a ticket (which was £65). With my application I enclosed a letter offering the event a free evening of close-up magic. I couldn't see how they could refuse bearing in mind it was costing me 65 quid to be there. But refuse they did. Perhaps they thought I was trying to capitalise in some way on the charitable cause which I have to admit could have looked that way. They thanked me for the offer and told me they'd already booked a magician and went on to say that they'd managed to sell over 400 tickets. It was a bigger event than I thought and surely with that number of tickets sold they would have been glad of another magician, especially one working for free. Oh well, there wasn't much I could do about it; I'd go anyway as I was curious to know who the magician could be. If it was somebody I knew, then he or she might be glad of some help. I took my stuff with me in the car and put a couple of things in my pocket just in case and made my way inside. I had a pint at the bar and looked around at the groups of people that were beginning to gather and felt a tad frustrated thinking how well the mix and mingle stuff would have gone. I was very tempted to do something but thought better of it; I didn't want to run the risk of upsetting the organisers or the paid entertainer. I wandered around for a while wondering if there was anybody there I knew, while at the same time keeping a lookout for the magician but all to no avail. I found my table and was soon joined by three couples and another chap on his own. The meal was pleasant enough and I chatted to the people either side of me until the speeches began towards the end of the final course. The general mood of the evening changed at this point as the organising couple emotionally explained the point of us all being there. It was to raise funds for a little-known disorder their young daughter was suffering from called Niemann-Pick Disease. From what they said, funds were urgently needed for research into what was a debilitating illness that had no cure.

The meal finished and as yet there had been no sign of the magician. Next up was the auction and as that was going on I went for a walk round the room in search of him or her, again to no avail. It looked as if the auction had a long way to run so I had another pint at the bar and when that was gone, I decided not to stay for the X-Factor winner cabaret and went home slightly disappointed, but at least it had been a night out.

I pondered the non-gig on the way home and although a touch disappointed, I felt lucky because I still had a regular wage coming in and wasn't dependent on magic to make my living. I've known of wedding magicians who've attended exhibitions, along with photographers and hire cars and the like, for whole weekends to no response, and others who've written to agents all over the country for little reward, often enclosing expensive publicity material. The entertainment business can be frustrating at times, particularly when gigs aren't forthcoming. But those of us who love to perform and entertain, still plod on knowing that somewhere at some point is an audience ready and waiting. When I got home, I picked up my bag of assorted props and put it in my cupboard packed and ready for the next one, whenever or wherever it may be. I was philosophical about the evening, it hadn't been a complete disaster as at least I'd had a good meal even if it did cost me 65 quid - after all, it did contribute to a very worthy cause which in the great scheme of things was probably more important than anything.

Still with the mindset of needing to get out more I decided to have a day out in London.

July 22nd, 2008: *I walked over to Campbell Park and got the 7.30 bus to London. I got off at Golders Green as I was feeling a bit queasy. I walked from there through Hampstead and Chalk Farm and got to*

Camden Lock at about 11.00 am. I spent an hour browsing around various stalls and had some lunch before walking through Primrose Hill then along the Regent's Canal and St. John's Wood. I got to Abbey Road at about 1.00 o'clock. The outside of the studio is covered with graffiti, and of course the tourists were posing on the zebra crossing. From there I travelled to Greenwich by tube and the new railway and spent the rest of the day at the Maritime Museum and Observatory. It was wonderful! One of the best days out I've ever had, spoilt only by blisters on my feet.

Despite the blisters, the next day I set off for Wales. Yet again to Aberaeron and Cardigan Bay. I found a B&B and had a couple of pints and fish & chips before an earlyish night. Up early the next day to explore some more and walk the six-and-a-half-mile coastal walk to Newquay (again). I got a bus back to Aberaeron, a quick bite to eat and I travelled home arriving at around 9.00 pm. Shame I couldn't have stayed longer but I had a couple of gigs booked - I needed a day to get over it.

Luckily the first one was in the afternoon, so I was able to have a leisurely drive over to the venue in Leicester. I have no record of this job apart from what's written in my diary. It was a hot day and took place in the garden of a private house and I did 3 hours. It was more than likely a birthday or wedding anniversary. By the time I got back from that one it was almost time to set off for the next. This was a two-day two-person job between me and Roy. He had done the previous night and he gave me a call to warn me of the conditions. It was in a bar in Daventry where the brief was to mix and mingle and work the tables. I got there at the specified time of 8.00 pm and after an hour the place was heaving with young people intent on getting hammered and having a good time. The music was deafening, and it was becoming a bit of a struggle. Luckily there was a small outside area (for the smokers) which is where I spent most of my time. I somehow kept going until about 10.30 by which time my voice had gone due to shouting and smoke, and I was exhausted. I had a quick chat with the owner outside before I left and he told me that he'd seen a couple of young close-uppers working in the bars and clubs in London and had decided to try it, "out here in the sticks."

I pondered the gig on the way home and soon concluded that the writing could well be on the wall for a close-upper of my age. Youngsters were coming through and creating their own audiences and in new and different venues. Certainly I could do it based on years of experience, and I was always prepared to adapt, but one thing I couldn't do was hold back the years. Gigs such as that should have been done by performers of the same age as the audience, late teens, and early twenties and not by somebody approaching sixty. It was a bit of an eye opener, but I wasn't despondent, I'd had a good run and there would always be jobs where conditions, venues and audiences would be better suited for somebody like me. What I didn't think of at the time though was how much technology would come into play to actually get the gigs. Over the following few years agencies would all but disappear and clients would book performers directly from the internet. We would soon be in the era of websites and online booking.

After my good day out in London I decided to do it all again some ten days later. At the time, the new Milton Keynes Coachway depot was being rebuilt and there was a temporary one a short distance away across Campbell Park, just up the road from me. Again it was an early start and this time I travelled all the way to Victoria Coach Station, a journey of some two hours. I had no real plan of action, so I wandered down the road to Belgravia (to see how the other half live) and from there I walked to Sloane Square and down The Kings Road. Bearing in mind it was a Saturday morning, I was really disappointed. It was all but deserted. Not at all the buzzing thoroughfare I remembered from my youth. When I got to the bottom, I scanned my well-thumbed A to Z and on a whim decided to go to Portobello Road. The weather was nice, I had my walking boots on, the blisters had healed so why not? It was a pleasant walk in the sunshine ambling through Earls Court and the rather lovely Holland Park. I got to Portobello Road around midday and had a spot of lunch in a local cafe. As I sipped my mug of tea, I wondered if I could find a replacement giant thimble. Judging by what I saw on some of the stalls, there was certainly a chance. I decided to walk down one side and then back up the other, not really knowing or caring the length of the road or indeed how long it would take. On one of the first stalls I visited I spotted a large American dollar which was encouraging, and after buying that I looked closely at everything as I moved from stall to stall. It took about an hour to do one side, enquiring about a large silver thimble at those which were selling trinkets and the like, but with no luck. As well as traditional market stalls, there were, I noticed, shops as well, particularly on the other side. I began to make my way back up the road scanning each stall and visiting every shop. Some of them had quite big entrances and, tucked away in small alcoves and corners, there were single traders whose pitches were barely big enough to take a small table and a chair. I'd almost got back to the top of the road when I spotted one who had a selection of silver thimbles on display inside a glass case, along with other bits and pieces. She was a lovely elderly Jewish lady who greeted me with a smile.

"I know this is a bit of a long shot," I said, "But I'm looking for a large silver thimble which were manufactured many years ago as novelty whisky measures and were engraved with the words, 'just a thimble full' around the rim. Have you ever seen one?"

She reached under her table and came up with a small wooden box which she placed on top of the glass case. She opened the lid, reached inside and with a grin said,

"Like this you mean."

There was my thimble, displayed on the palm of her hand! I was over the moon; I couldn't believe it. I told her the story, but she'd never understand just how special that moment was. I asked her the price which was £10 and was happy to part with it, in fact I'd have given double that; to me it was priceless. I travelled back to Milton Keynes a very happy bunny.

I wasn't happy for long though. In the weeks and months that followed, the whole world was suffering because of the economic crash. Things weren't going well regarding my employment either. I'd lost count of the amount of times work had dropped off, followed by redundancies, only to pick up again with more work and hours I could barely cope with. This time things felt different. There had been a steady stream of redundancies throughout the year including office staff. By September work had all but dried up. In mid-October we were told that a part of the factory had been leased to another company which manufactured timber framed houses. Then followed weeks of rumour and counter rumour, meetings, and confusion, culminating with the news that Llewellyn was closing down. Redundancy notices would be issued in due course before Christmas. Meanwhile the new company called Framework had already moved in. It all came to an end in early December.

December 5th, 2008: *We'll be notified next week about a meeting with the personnel manager. It seems there may well be options for work elsewhere within the company at the factory they have near Bedford. If we don't take that then it will be redundancy for all of us, unless of course we can get a start with the company that has moved in. I sorted out my cupboard and tools in the factory and put them in the car and went back to say my goodbyes. There was a tinge of sadness as we shook hands - after all, 26 years is a long time. I gave my number to the Framework foreman who said he'd be in touch pending the meeting next week, that's my only option at the moment.*

By the time I went to the meeting I'd decided to accept redundancy whatever I was offered. I'd had enough of long hours and heavy work and despite approaching the age of 59 I was prepared to look for something else. Meanwhile I had a few Christmas gigs, one of them not a pleasant experience, not helped I suspect by the worry of my work situation…

December 6th, 2008: *I got to the golf club for eight o'clock and it was hard work from start to finish because of the bloody disco. I got by and got paid but the whole thing was just a chore. I tried out the new 4 Queen card trick a couple of times with some success, and also had a bit of a session just outside the function room but generally speaking not a happy night.*

It was another case of being thrown into a noisy room where I was expected to entertain a lot of equally noisy people many of whom weren't interested anyway. The gig on New Year's Eve more than made up for it though as it was the first of many at the Villiers

Hotel and Buckingham Town Hall, shared with singer guitarist Tommy Kavanagh, it was a great night and much needed.

Midnight heralded the end of 2008 and the arrival of 2009. I had no idea what the future held, it was a bit of a worry and the first time I had been without a job since I left school in 1965.

CHAPTER 32

A New Beginning

2009 didn't begin very well. I'd had a bad back for a few days which was really painful. The New Year's Eve gig didn't help as I was continually bending over to work the tables. Strangely I didn't notice it while I was there, probably because it was one of my favourite venues. It's such a beautiful place with a good reputation, *and* it was a dinner-jacket event which certainly added to the prestige of the evening. I soon got into the swing, and it was going well until the balloons were discovered inside the crackers. Not ordinary balloons but the ones that are inflated, released, and allowed to fly around the room with an annoying noise. There was nothing I could do about it apart from duck whenever one came my way. At least they were easier to avoid than the Tesco peashooters! The customers were lovely with most of them sitting in family groups of six or seven and there were several couples too of varying ages. It was a bit of a mixed bag really which is how I like it. There was one group of six who had travelled some distance and were staying at the hotel for a few days. They loved the magic and towards the end of the evening one of the ladies came up to me during my break and pressed something into my hand and said,

"Here's a little something from all of us."

I went through the motions of saying that she shouldn't have and thanked her very much, but she insisted. I decided it would have been impolite to refuse. A few minutes later I found a quiet corner, curious to find out how big the tip was. With six of them it had to be at least a twenty-pound note. I opened my hand to reveal a fiver, it worked out to be less than a pound each. I have to admit to being a little disappointed but at least it was something, and out of about 50 people, they were the only ones who offered. As I pondered the gig on the way home, I just laughed to myself and realised that at least it would buy me a pint.

During the first week of the year I'd heard the sad news that my old friend David Parriss had passed away. I'd known him since I was 13 and never forgot the help and advice he gave me right at the beginning of my magic career. We'd always stayed in touch and his enthusiasm never waned both with the magic and his other passion of steam engines and fairground organs. He'd coped with his debilitating disease for a number of years with courage and dignity. January 4th was a sad day for both his family and his many friends.

The first week of the year also marked the end of my long association with the staff of Llewellyn. Some of whom had been on the same often rocky road as I had for almost 30 years. The meeting with the company personnel manager took place on January 6th where I was told the terms of my redundancy and how much I'd get. As expected, the payment followed the letter of the law. At least I'd have something to live on for a few months while I searched for something else. Another thing in my favour was the fact that I didn't have to worry about bailing out the boys (as much). Jay was settled in his flat with a steady job, and Ben had also got a regular job training as a Teaching Assistant. He was still living at home and although saving hard for a deposit for his own place he was able to contribute to household expenses.

I decided to have a bit of a rest for a few weeks and get my back sorted out before looking for employment. I tried all sorts of self-help books and exercises, some of which actually worked. I think the best treatment was regular walking. Gone were the days of lying flat and not moving for days. By the middle of the month it was back to some sort of normality. Also by then word had got around that I had joined the ranks of the unemployed and I'd get phone calls from people I knew in the trade who were keeping an eye open for me. I got one from an old friend of the family who said he'd put a word in at a local firm of coffin makers. I was open to anything. I couldn't do a lot though until I'd been to the Job Centre and registered as unemployed once my finances had been sorted out. Meanwhile I got stuck into decorating Mum's bungalow. I was determined to keep occupied whatever happened. I went to the Job Centre a week or two later and had an interview with a nice young lady who told me I'd be eligible for the Job Seekers Allowance Benefit of some £60 per week. I had a look around while I was there and soon discovered that there were small computers around the room and most of the jobs were advertised online. I was lost. I was pretty much computer illiterate. A few days later I went to a job fair at the football stadium, which was full of stands of prospective employers, including Hanslope Park. This was a government establishment just outside Milton Keynes where there could well be maintenance work available. I spoke to the lady on the stand who explained all and suggested that I email them a copy of my CV. It soon became apparent that this was now the normal way of doing things. I felt like a ship out of water, not only was I unable to send emails I didn't have a CV either. For the past 26 years I hadn't needed one. I realised at this point that things could be difficult, and I soon came to the inevitable conclusion that I would have to drag myself into this new era of technology. This was reinforced when I discovered that even help with the benefit system was accessed via a government website. Everything appertaining to being unemployed was online and if I didn't embrace this new way of doing things I'd just get left behind. The following diary entry captures the moment of looking back to an enjoyable past and at the same time taking a tentative step into an unknown future.

January 20th, 2009: *I wandered up to the Centre this morning and in Middleton Hall there was a 'Living Archive' exhibition. I bought their book on Football in MK and later on I drove over to their office in Wolverton, having decided to give them my old Training School exercise books. I had a nice chat with the people there and then went to have a look at the Training School. It's a bed shop now but is virtually unchanged, even with the same décor. I hadn't been in there since 1966. So many memories. After lunch me and Ben went to PC World and Comet where I bought a laptop. The next stage is learning how to use it.*

Soon after that I bought a printer and was ready to take a leap into the unknown.

The people at the Living Archive project told me about a free computer course for the unemployed which was held in their premises every Friday morning - I obviously wasn't alone then, which was encouraging. I signed up for it and went along to the first one at the end of that week. It was pretty basic but certainly helpful. Certificates were issued as you made your way through each module over a period of time. I also bought 'A Beginners Guide to Laptops' book which again was useful. I was making the effort. Later that day I plucked up the courage to visit the Job Centre and have a go on a Job Seekers' computer. I went for one in a distant corner but just couldn't figure it out. I spoke to a lady behind the counter to get some assistance. She wasn't particularly helpful. She slammed her pen on the desk...

"For God's sake!" she said, "They're not rocket science."

I followed her over to the nearest unused one and she explained to me how to use it in the manner of a teacher talking to a 4-year-old.

"Got it now?" she asked.

I just felt humiliated. I was a craftsman and proud of it and didn't deserve to be spoken to like that. I didn't want to make a scene, so I just left. The following weeks and months could very well turn out to be more difficult and trying than I thought.

January 23rd, 2009: *I Just hated being in that Job Centre. I walked back home along the canal via Pennylands and Campbell Park. It was during that walk that I reached my lowest point so far. When I got home, I had another go with the laptop and read my new book, not too successfully but I'm getting there. Anni phoned tonight and said she'd type up my CV for me. I read it out and she made some suggestions which were really helpful.*

My friend Anni was a godsend; she sorted out my CV and explained how to file and send it using my laptop. Ben was helpful too in creating an email address. His advice was to spend as much time on the laptop as I could and just try stuff; I was ok with that once I realised that you couldn't break it by pressing a wrong button. I was also trying to get myself into a more positive state of mind. I'd certainly been through worse stuff in my life and thankfully once again I managed to dig my way out of it.

I signed on as unemployed for the first time in early February and as I approached the desk, I noticed it was the same lady who had given me grief during my previous visit. I'll never know for sure if she recognised me, but I think she did; she looked a bit sheepish for a moment before being overly helpful; anyway, I signed on. I was given several leaflets to peruse and also a diary to fill in every day to prove that I was actively searching for work. Over the following months I would put everything in that little book including checking out websites and looking through local newspapers, anything to fill it up - after 45 years of writing stuff in my own diary I didn't find it too difficult. The first company to receive my brand-new CV was the company that had moved into our old premises. I thought it would be a good idea to drop it off personally as I was anxious to see what the set up was. It was fairly predictable with similar methods to Llewellyn. Although I didn't particularly want to go back into the building trade (never mind the same building), it seemed to me that the "better the devil you know" scenario would be helpful while I searched for something else. That being the case, I delivered another CV to Rok who of course had owned Llewellyn in the past and where there might be a familiar face or two who could put a word in for me. But it didn't go too well…

February 9th, 2009: *I spent most of the morning checking out Job Centre websites, and then I clicked on Rok. After I'd dropped Ben off at work I called in at their office in Fox Milne to hand in my CV. I didn't gain many friends there as I walked through the door which* *said, "Use other door" and couldn't find the "other door." Oh well, it's done now.*

I did spot a familiar face as I entered the open plan office (that I obviously shouldn't have) to no response. In fact bearing in mind I could have been anybody (including a potential customer) they weren't very welcoming at all. As it happened, I got no reply from them or Framework.

By mid-February the days had formed into a regular pattern - half the morning checking out Job Centre websites and scanning the local papers, then practising typing until I got fed up (I'd bought a book on how to touch type), then burying myself in a book, or doing a bit of writing, or even working on the magic. After lunch I'd always go for a walk accompanied by my little radio tuned to Radio 4. I managed to keep myself occupied, soon realising how important that was.

It became apparent there was very little work about with an obvious slump in the building trade and nothing at all regarding furniture making. I persevered looking at familiar websites as I didn't know what else I wanted to do (apart from retire). I had another setback one morning when I spotted a job vacancy for making and erecting fencing. I clicked on it, and it stipulated that ownership of a CSCS card (Construction Skills Certification Scheme) was essential. I had no idea what that was. I did some research and discovered it was a recognised scheme where you can safely put all your qualifications onto a photo identity card with all relevant skills listed on the back. As time went on, I noticed more and more companies were asking for it, so it made sense for me to get one. At the time the cost was £17.50 for a Health & Safety test (which you had to pass), £25 for the actual card, and £8.50

for a book with questions and answers for revision purposes (not essential). I bought the book anyway as I really didn't want to do it more than once and it did turn out to be useful prior to the test. The venue for the test was in a small room on an industrial estate not too far away and I was able to walk there. The test was a tick-box, multiple-choice scenario and was easy enough using a small computer. I passed it with no problems and a couple of weeks later the card arrived in the post. It had cost me £50, was valid for 5 years, and I never used it. The book I took to a charity shop.

As Spring arrived, I was fairly busy doing odd jobs for a variety of people. One of the more interesting was helping my brother-in-law Ken with his work as a church organ builder and renovator. We would travel to mostly rural churches where Ken would maintain and repair those remarkable old instruments. It is a highly skilled job, involving electrics, joinery, and a knowledge of air flow and valves, and a huge variety of small components. Often it was difficult to get parts which meant they had to be made and improvised, all fascinating stuff. As we worked, he'd tell me stories of his work in churches and chapels all over the country over many years and the characters he'd met. I suspect Ken is one of the last of a dying breed.

I was still going along to the computer course in Wolverton every Friday and by now had my first certificate. As I left there one day I wondered if there might be work available in the Works (not really a sign of desperation, but close). I knew parts of it were still open but had no idea what was going on there. I had a word with the security chap who told me that carriage repairs were still being carried out and it was now owned by a company based in Germany; a far cry from when I was there and good old British Railways. He went on to tell me that all recruitment was done via an agency and was kind enough to give me the details. When I got home and clicked onto it, I discovered it was mainly for experienced engineers at the top end of the market, involving work all over Europe. I registered my CV with them anyway - you never know. Not unexpectedly I didn't get a response, but the idea of agency work was food for thought. Another place I tried was the Open University. It's a large site where I did a fair amount of work when I was on the Small Works department with Llewellyn. I was familiar with the buildings and was quite impressed with the feel of the place and wondered if there was anything available in their maintenance department. The OU is situated in the Ouzel Valley Park, so I walked past it pretty much every day. I called in there one morning and dropped off my CV at their personnel office. I was quite happy to do it that way, at least they can put a face to the applicant, which may (or may not) be advantageous. Of the many applications and CVs I sent out either in person or electronically, the OU was one of the few to take the trouble to reply even it was just the basic, "No vacancies at the moment but we'll keep your CV on file."

One morning I spotted a job that looked a possibility at a Special Needs school a few miles away but still in Milton Keynes. The advert was a bit vague, and I wasn't too sure whether they wanted a Teaching Assistant or a caretaker. I gave them a call and was given the opportunity to visit the following day along with somebody else who I assumed was another applicant.

March 3rd, 2009: *I got to the school just about on time. For some reason my watch had stopped at 8.30. There were four of us being shown around and from what the head teacher said, competition will be fierce. I was really impressed with the place; it has such a lovely* *atmosphere. She had a word with us all afterwards and I reckon I could do it and I'm in with a chance. The money isn't all that good but it's certainly better than nothing. I spent the rest of the day filling in the form and drafting the personal statement. I'm just grateful that I have a talent for writing and didn't find it difficult to do.*

The school had a small workshop which was perfect to teach basic woodwork skills to children who were capable, as well as being useful for doing any maintenance work that might crop up. I mentioned all of this during my chat with the head teacher and also told her I could teach simple magic tricks. I did my best to convey to her my enthusiasm for the job and how much I loved the place. The application form was lengthy, as they all are in the education sector, and I managed it quite well. The personal statement was a breeze too; I called it, "Not just another job" and wrote about how special the school was and what a privilege it would be to join an obviously caring and dedicated staff. I had to get the balance right though and didn't want it to be over the top. I sent it over to my old friend, Paul Freedland, to check out and make comments. I took his suggestions on board and sent it off with my CV attached and eagerly awaited a reply. Two weeks later and having heard nothing, I gave them a call and was told I hadn't even made the shortlist. I was disappointed and annoyed. What is it these people actually want!? My confidence really did take a knock, but the time wasn't wasted as it was all good experience in form filling and interviews, and heaven knows how many more of those I'd have to go through.

Now that I had more time on my hands and determined not to waste any of it, I had a spell of inspiration with the writing. I'd met a lady at a party around Christmas time who had quite an effect on me. Anybody over the age of fifteen knows how it feels when you meet someone you're mutually attracted to. You look into each other's eyes, can't stop smiling, and then your stomach does one of those flippy things, and not to put too fine a point on it you're in heaven. That's how it was for me while I was talking to her (for quite a while as it happened). Towards the end of the evening, I got waylaid talking or showing a trick to somebody else during which time she'd gone. Throughout the following week I tried to pluck up the courage to get in touch with her, but I just didn't have the nerve. I did however contact a mutual friend to find out if she was attached to somebody else - at least that would be a start. Surprisingly and sadly it turned out she was, so that was the end of that. I'd obviously picked up the wrong signals and nothing came of it. What a shame. Oh well, I suppose I should have been grateful as it was the first time I'd been besotted in 15 years, even if it was only for a week. I decided to write about it as I was quite surprised how I felt, bearing in mind I was 59 and not 15. The entire sad and ultimately embarrassing saga was written in a piece called, 'That Face'. It wasn't what you might call a poem, it was more of an outpouring.

A week or two later I heard of an open mic event taking place at the Madcap Theatre in Wolverton. It was called, 'Tongue in Chic' and was open to local aspiring poets and writers. I decided to go along and try it out in front of an audience (after all, I did need to get out more). I have to admit to dithering a bit to begin with, as this would be a first and I had no idea what the reception would be. The other unknown was the quality of the other performers; one thing was for sure, they'd certainly be better and more experienced than me. Seeds of doubt were beginning to set in. Is my stuff any good? I had another look at it and realised that nothing rhymed. But does it have to? - As long as it has a certain rhythm and conveys some feeling and emotion, I don't think it does; after all, everybody in the room should be able to relate to it having more than been through a similar experience themselves (although probably not at 59). Anyway, as Gilbert O'Sullivan wrote in his song, 'Nothing Rhymed' - "nothing old, nothing new, nothing ventured…", I decided to go for it. The next question that arose was how would I do it? I assumed I'd be announced and then walk up to the microphone and read it out from my well-thumbed piece of paper as, no doubt, would everybody else. Yet again though, in an effort to be different, I decided I wouldn't do it that way - I'd memorise it. I would perform it as a bona fide writer/performer and, with my experience as an entertainer, do my best to connect with the audience rather than be a mere middle-aged bloke reading out a poem. It took a while to learn, and I rehearsed it as I walked around the local countryside, forfeiting the afternoon play on Radio 4 for my aspiration of indeed being a stand-up writer/performer. The big night arrived, and I have to admit to being a touch nervous as I joined the queue to give my name as a contributor. The people I stood with were friendly enough and I was pleasantly surprised at the age range, from teenagers to pensioners which was encouraging. Tables and chairs were scattered around the room with the solitary microphone positioned in the performing area at the front. There was a small bar against the back wall and although desperate for a pint I thought it best not to have one before my turn but savour one afterwards. I took a seat next to a young couple who it turned out were teachers. The organiser was Mark Niel who got the evening off to a good start with a reading of some of his own topical stuff. He was just brilliant. Soon the ball was rolling, and I had the chance to see quite a few performers before it was my turn. It was a mixed bag of stuff from all sorts of people, some better than others but all of a reasonable standard. There were political poems, funny poems, and a few angry ones too. The lovely thing was that we had the freedom to talk about whatever we wanted with no constrictions on language or content. Soon my moment arrived. I pretended to be confident as I strode up to the microphone. I looked out at the audience and told them that what I was about to tell them was a true story and would more than likely appeal to the ladies in the audience. The gentlemen however will undoubtedly want to throw up, and now might be a good time to visit the bar. Nothing like starting with a laugh. (Laugh is perhaps a bit strong, a few random grins would be more like it.) Anyway, I took the plunge and gave it my best shot. For a first-time performance it went as well as it could. The applause and reaction I got was I felt one of encouragement rather than for the quality of the writing, a case of, "Not bad for a first attempt but don't give up the day job," (assuming I had one) was the vibe I felt at the end. As I walked off, Mark said,

"Thanks Ken, that was very good, you'll find the Relate office on the left just down the road. Our next performer is…"

He was the perfect host always finding something funny or nice to say about all of us. Ironically, I knew exactly where the Relate office was, having worked there a couple of years previously (the butchers' shop job). The two young teachers were quite complimentary as I rejoined them with a much-needed pint and feeling relieved it was all over. I had no regrets about doing it and quite enjoyed the buzz of performing in front of likeminded people, who perhaps like me had the need to express themselves with the written or spoken word. For me writing is a need. If I'm moved or angered by something it has to be written down, only then can I get over it and move on. For others that night, there may have been other reasons - to share, to inspire, or as a form of therapy. The one thing that I'm sure we all felt was the satisfaction and joy that is always derived from the creative process.

It occurs to me now that the lady who I fell in love with for a week, who inspired the piece of writing which led to a spoken word performance, and a page in this book, has no idea about any of it and is none the wiser. It also occurs to me that perhaps at some time in the future, one of my grandchildren when a teenager may well go through something similar (in fact that's almost a certainty) and may well bemoan the fact that I just wouldn't understand what they're going through. Should that happen then I would do a repeat performance of, 'That Face', just for them and tell them I do know exactly how they feel and how much it hurts, even at the age of 59.

Meanwhile I was still finding it difficult to shake off my low state of mind. Luckily my family were being supportive.

March 25th, 2009: *A bit of a sleepless night last night. I'm feeling all of the things connected to the unemployed - depression, lack of confidence, low self-esteem. It's all kicking in now. Maggs phoned tonight to say that she'd spotted a job in the MK News at the police station, and Jean sent me an email about a carpentry job in Bedford. I think I might go for the police one as it's local, and maintenance is a bit more up my street.*

The online form for the police job was a nightmare - nine pages with eleven pages of help notes. I also had a lot of technical problems with boxes becoming unticked among other things, and with the frustration of it all, I could've thrown my laptop out of the window. As it happened, it was a waste of time anyway as I didn't get the job. It was then that I decided to sign on with an agency. I went over to Stony Stratford where they were based and the next day, they sent me for an interview for a storeman type of job at a factory a few miles away. The manager showed me around and tried to explain his rather complicated way of doing things, but nothing came of that one either. Next, I applied for a caretaker job at another school in Bletchley where again I was asked to visit. There were three other chaps there, so it looked like being a similar scenario to the last school job I applied for. I was invited for an interview at 3.30 and felt quite confident as I made myself known to the lady on reception. After a few minutes I was shown into a room to face a panel which included the head teacher (who was lovely) and several members of the governing body, who really didn't have much idea how to conduct themselves at an interview. Rather than try to get know me as a person (as the head teacher did) they just asked questions that were written on pieces of notepaper held in front of them, reciting them parrot fashion. I wasn't impressed. As the number of applicants had risen to five, all of whom had to be interviewed, it was turning into a long afternoon. After the interviews we were shown around the school which took about half an hour. Following that we were led into a classroom to each sit at a desk and, with pen and pad, asked to give an overview of the grounds and buildings (inside and out) and suggest what improvements we would prioritise and do over the next 12 months. I did spot some health and safety problems and wrote those down which I felt had to have priority. I left the school at 6.15 feeling reasonably confident, but based on previous experience with school jobs, I felt a bit wary. Later that evening as promised by the head teacher I had a phone call to tell me I was unsuccessful. Again I asked myself the question, "What is it that these people actually want!?" Obviously not a craftsman.

After that I thought I might have more luck if I searched outside of Milton Keynes. I went for Bedford as it's only 18 miles away and only half-an-hour in the car. I Phoned an agency there and as luck would have it a job had just come in for a maintenance carpentry job at Cranfield University. I sent off my CV and an interview was arranged, which I felt went very well, and I got the job! At last, and what a relief. I was told that once my probationary period was over, I'd be transferred from working for the agency to be being employed directly by the university, something that never did happen. I started there on June 29th, 2009. I had been told by a friend of mine a month or two earlier that a job might come up there, but I didn't hold out much hope. Anyway, I was in.

CHAPTER 33

Counting the days

Meanwhile Jay had passed his final exam to become a qualified teacher in Buckingham and was still living locally with his girlfriend. Ben was also settled in his job at Two Mile Ash school in Milton Keynes and was still being creative with his music. Things were beginning to slot into place at last. I was getting magic jobs fairly consistently with a lot of weddings and private parties, including a memorable one at the rather nice Pendley Manor Hotel in Hertfordshire. It was a family event for a gentleman's 70th birthday. The contract stipulated evening dress which I was happy to comply with although I didn't relish the thought of performing in a warm room in mid-summer. This was in the days before air conditioning came into its own in recently built venues, but even today in some older establishments air conditioning means nothing more than opening the windows. Anyway it wasn't too bad at Pendley Manor, the room was large and airy with patio doors that could be opened. I was met by the organiser who told me to perform as and when I chose. "You're the expert, you know what you're doing." I love it when they say that. It just gives me the freedom to do what I feel is right appertaining to the venue, the conditions, and the general feel of the event. I made a start in the time available before food was served and then between courses. Things were going well. As I finished on one table a lady spoke to me, and although it was a long shot, she asked me if I knew a magician by the name of James Adams.

"Surely not Jim from Anglian Water?" I asked.

"That's the one!" she laughed.

Jim was from Northampton and a former secretary and president of the magic club who I hadn't seen for years. It turned out they were related and coincidentally were due visit him the following day. What a small world. People ask me quite often if I know of a magician they know and most of the time I don't, even if he or she is a member of the Magic Circle. Many times I've had to explain to the public that there are over a thousand members from all over the world and there's no way I could know all of them. There are one or two rare occasions when I do know them or know of them. While I was in hospital having my operation the chap in the next bed (who was a bit of a whinger) told me he was in the army doing his national service with Ali Bongo. It made me smile as I just couldn't imagine Ali in a uniform square-bashing whether it was true or not. The next time I saw Ali, I asked him if he knew him.

"I do remember him," he said, "A bit of a wet blanket."

"That's him," I said, "And he hasn't changed."

The Pendley Manor gig was a lovely job. Such a beautiful venue as well as a friendly audience. At the end, the man whose birthday it was came up to me and thanked me for the entertainment. We had a chat and I commented on a plaster he had on his chin.

"Cut yourself shaving?" I asked.

"If only," he replied, "It was a melanoma."

He went on to tell me that the prognosis wasn't good. He was philosophical about it though and would continue to have treatment for as long as it was required. He had the support and love of his family which was obvious to me as I worked the tables. He shook my hand and thanked me again and said,

"I hope your life will continue to be as rewarding and joyful as mine has been. Good luck."

"Thank you, and all the best to you too," I replied, wondering how his future would pan out.

As I pondered the gig on the way home, I had mixed feelings. Happy that it had been such a good night but tinged with a bit of sadness. I wondered how many more family events he would live to see.

Once I knew I was going to be gainfully employed again, I started having a social life. In mid-June I went to see a local band play in the back room of a pub in Stony Stratford. I love Stony for the number of pubs as much as anything else, most of them old and full of atmosphere and characters, all of them serving good ale. A pub crawl there is highly recommended. The band I went to see that night was, 'The great pig in the sky', a Pink Floyd tribute band made up of local musicians. I arrived quite early and had a pint at the bar and was soon joined by the saxophone player I'd known for years, Joe O'Halloran. We had a pint or two and chatted for a while. Then the band arrived on stage and soon the wonderful opening sequence of 'Shine on you crazy diamond' began to fill the room. Meanwhile me and Joe are still chatting and drinking,

"Joe, you're on!" I said.

"Not yet, this bit goes on for ages," he replied slurping his pint.

A few minutes later he glanced at the stage, left his pint with half of it left and said to me,

"Keep your eye on my pint, I'll be back in a minute."

With that he made his way through the crowd and onto the stage, picked up his sax and delivered an emotional, blistering solo that left us all open mouthed. Then he came back to the bar, downed his pint, and said,

"Where were we, your round isn't it?"

Somebody once said to Jack Benny, the famous and successful American comedian, how pleased he must have felt be to be recognised as one of the all-time greats. His reply was unexpected. He felt he was a failure. He began his career playing the violin and always wanted to be a classical musician. In his eyes he'd failed. Perhaps it was slightly tongue in cheek, but I know how he felt.

I always wanted to be a musician. I don't feel I've failed with the magic, I'm just a touch frustrated. How I wish I could master an instrument as Joe has, and indeed the rest of the band. I can bang out a few chords on the guitar and I'm persevering with my harmonica but it's a struggle. I've always hung out with musicians hoping that some of their talent and ability might rub off but unsurprisingly it never has. In all honesty though it's a talent you either have or you haven't. My Dad had it and I haven't, but our Ben has. I think it must be in your genes. You can work at it and achieve a modicum of success, especially if you started early and stuck at it, but to a born musician it all comes naturally, not always easy I suspect but it is a gift.

Oh well, I suppose I am good at something. There may well be somebody out there who'd love to be able to do card and coin tricks and for whatever reason isn't capable, who knows? Perhaps then we should be grateful for the talents we *do* have and be happy to share them with each other and as many people as we can. The more you give the more you receive, I think any entertainer worth his salt will tell you that. The final verse of a poem I wrote called Magic hits the nail on the head.

With me, it's magic. With you? Who knows?
Whatever it is, the same thing goes,
Give yourself and like me learn,

And feel what comes back in return!

My first few days at Cranfield University were interesting. I was introduced to the rest of the maintenance team and given a tour of the carpentry workshop. The machinery was of good quality, mainly because it was so old. A huge and heavy planer/thicknesser dominated the place with an equally old and heavy mortice machine positioned alongside a wall. Next to that was a fairly new cross-cut saw and spindle moulder. There was an old bench for each carpenter, accompanied by an old cupboard. I say old, which was true but well-made and solid. It was like stepping back into a bygone era, reminiscent I thought of 1960s Wolverton Works. I put my tools into my allocated cupboard and was given a map of the campus and a phone. Later I was issued with an ID swipe card which would give me access into most of the buildings. There were several vans for our use that had to be checked first thing every morning and ticked off on a check list. Lights, indicators, brake fluid, oil, water, and the horn. Bizarrely there were a couple of old electric milk floats we could use; they were slow but useful to transport sheets of ply or doors. For the first couple of days I worked alongside Tim one of the carpenters doing various small jobs and doing my best to remember the layout of the place as we trundled along with me driving one of the floats. In many ways the campus is like a small village with accommodation houses and flats for students and a variety of buildings both old and new used for a variety of things of all shapes and sizes. There was a launderette on site, a library, a couple of social clubs, and not forgetting the small airport. Each building was run by a facilities manager who we had to report to before we started work and afterwards to get the work ticket signed. The hours were reasonable (compared to what I'd been used to) 8.00 am to 5.30 pm Monday to Thursday, and 9.00 am to 5.00 pm on a Friday.

There was a morning tea break which for some reason we had to take in the canteen, which I found annoying especially if I was in the middle of something and at the wrong end of the campus. It seemed crazy to have to travel there and back just to sit at a table for 15 minutes. What's wrong with sitting in the van? It was ok if you gave the manager a call (depending on what sort of mood he was in) and told him you were too busy and couldn't make it, but it was certainly frowned upon if you made a habit of not being there. Later in the year, management did suggest in one of the regular department meetings that it should be scrapped but the workforce reps wouldn't have it.

When I walked into the canteen for the first time I was told where to sit. Every chair at every table "belonged" to somebody (again like Wolverton Works). As I got to know the people there, I discovered many of them had been there for a lifetime; 30 and 40 years was certainly not uncommon and I suspect they'd sat on those same chairs since day one, some of them playing dominoes on the same table using the same set since God knows when. They were all great characters and as time went on, I discovered they were really good craftsmen too. We had an hour for lunch which for me was too long, half an hour and finishing earlier would have been better but this, along with the tea break rule, was obviously set in stone. The reason given was that our hours had to be compatible with the rest of the place in case an emergency arose, which I suppose made sense. We had to fill in a timesheet each day and pretty much every minute had to be allocated somewhere. Sometimes it was difficult to do, particularly if you'd had a quiet day. The management seemed to think each of us were given a bundle of tickets in the morning and merrily went from job to job covering all of our daily hours and minutes. That wasn't always the case. Sometimes it was a battle to find hours from somewhere and something to book them to. Occasionally there were odd days when I'd find myself back in the workshop with nothing to do. I'd clean the machinery and sweep up and sharpen my tools and book an hour or two on 'cleaning the workshop' which was acceptable for a time, but eventually we were told we couldn't even do that. The question of where to book hours if there was nowhere to book them to never was answered. After a few weeks though and helped by my workmates I was getting used to it and worked out my hours at the end of each day. The work was charged to the building or department where the work was allocated. They all had a budget to adhere to and were within their rights to complain about the amount of money spent on maintenance work. Each ticket had to be signed on completion anyway and I can't recall getting too many complaints.

The buildings were a mixture of old and new and each had their own particular foibles. The newer buildings were a bit of a nightmare due to poor design. They may well have won awards for outstanding architecture and looked good, but they were really difficult to maintain. Whenever I'd get a job in one of those, I knew it wouldn't be straight forward and it rarely was. Anyway, after my trial period I was told the job was definitely mine, and soon I had my own van and into my final years of being gainfully employed.

Things were continuing to go well for the boys too, Jay at his school, and Ben at his. I was still getting work with the magic all over the place. An interesting one at Oxford for a group of people called, 'The United Kingdom Grand Priory Sovereign Order of St.

John of Jerusalem, Knights of Malta'. According to the contract I was booked for three hours to perform close up magic during drinks, reception, and dinner. I had no idea what to expect and treated it like a normal gig. I was a touch disappointed as that was exactly what it turned out to be. There were no costumes or rituals and nothing at all to suggest they were anything more than a group of like-minded people having a good night out together. It was a good night though with lovely people from all over the world.

Several of us from the magic club travelled up to Telford for a corporate job. It was organised by Mick Hanzlik and from memory I believe it was something to do with a Master Locksmith organisation of which Mick was a member. We did the mix and mingle stuff first and then worked around the tables in a vast restaurant totally devoid of atmosphere. I was glad when it was all over. It was a long day as well, setting off at 3.30 in the afternoon, and due to roadworks and diversions, not getting home until late in the evening. Oh well, a case of taking the rough with the smooth. At its worse it was night out with my pals.

A funny incident took place during a church service I attended in the summer.

July 26th, 2009: *It was a husband-and-wife team who led the service this morning. They performed a sketch about shining a light. At the end of it the husband turned to his wife and said, "I will certainly shine my light, will you?" She turned towards the congregation and said in a loud voice, "I will! - I **will** shite my line."*

I was experimenting with technology in quite a big way at this time. I used my laptop to buy something online for the first time. It was the David Roth book on coin magic which I bought from Davenports. Apart from almost ordering it twice I coped quite well I thought. I felt really proud that I'd crossed the barrier of giving my bank details to a complete stranger. I was relieved though when I had the confirmation email telling me it was on its way. The other thing I did in October was to sign up for Facebook which was something I thought I'd never do. I took to it straight away and soon got in touch with old friends I hadn't heard of for years. It also gave me a voice. I could write and post stuff that was of interest not only to me but also to my ever-increasing number of friends. The whole point was to share it and to make new friends along the way which is what happened and continues to this day.

By the time Christmas arrived things at Cranfield weren't going too well. I was having problems with my line manager. I'd seen him at his worst by the way he spoke to other more vulnerable members of the department and was quite shocked to be honest. I was warned by several people to be wary of him. I was getting nervous and my confidence in my own ability was beginning to waver. Although the thought of leaving did cross my mind, I concluded that compared to unemployment it was better I stayed to see it out until the bitter end, March 9th, 2015 - it couldn't come soon enough.

The winter of 2010 was very cold and icy with quite a lot of snow, often making it difficult to travel the eight miles or so along country roads to work. Luckily, I had several routes to choose from and I always got there somehow. For much of that first year I was in a steep learning curve. As well as carpentry maintenance (involving a lot of doors) the job also involved sorting out UPVC double-glazed windows and a selection of different types of metal and glass doors, some of which were sliding, and others had spring loaded hinges set into the ground. All new to me regarding repair and maintenance. I was dropped in at the deep end one day and sent to have a look at a particularly heavy metal and glass entrance door. I placed cones and barrier tape around it first, and 'No Entry' signs and arrows pointing to another door that could be used. Not that they made a lot of difference to some people who would either crawl under the tape or climb over it to get through a door that was obviously broken and potentially dangerous. The students at Cranfield came from all over the world and were some of the brightest on the planet, but I soon learned that intelligence doesn't always equate with common sense. The door opened outwards, so I was effectively working outside which was a bit of a pain in the middle of a severe cold snap. I soon spotted the problem; the door had a locking push bar enclosed in an aluminium box which was stuck in the closed position. I took the screws out of the casing and as I pulled it off to explore, small springs, washers, nuts, and screws sprung into the air and landed in a pile of snow. I retrieved what I could and then had to figure out how and where to put them all back - not easy with freezing fingers and having no idea what went where. Panic began to set in. I daren't phone for assistance as my line manager had recently told me that I needed to use my initiative more and not to keep pulling my workmates from their own work. I could see his point, but it didn't help me and my rapidly rising stress level. Anyway, after a couple of hours of trial and error (and left with a spring and two screws I couldn't find a place for) I got the door working and the ticket signed.

I struggled with windows in my early days too, particularly the 'Tilt and Turn' ones which were a pain for all of us. One of the problems with the windows was the huge variety. They may well have all been plastic and double-glazed, but because they'd been installed over a long period of time from many different manufacturers, it was difficult to get spare parts. There was a small selection available, such as hinges and handles, which helped, but it was a question really of knowing how to deal with the problems that occurred with each type. In time you'd know which windows were on which building and go prepared. I visited a building one day for the first time with a ticket for a window that wasn't working properly. (I'd only been there a short time) I tried everything with that window and didn't have a clue and was ultimately defeated. I went back to my line manager and told him it was obviously a job for the manufacturer. I assumed that's what you did and that there was a firm of specialist window people who came in to service broken mechanisms. (Not the case.) He raised his eyebrows, breathed out and told me he'd give the ticket to one of the more experienced carpenters. The following day he spoke to me at my bench and said, "That window you couldn't do yesterday? It was done in ten minutes." And he walked off.

Nothing was really solved as I still didn't know how to mend the bloody things. Nobody had shown me, and nobody ever did.

Much of the work involved wooden doors many of which had to be replaced to conform to fire regulations. There were others that had come to the end of their life and were starting to rot or twist. I replaced one such door on a Friday afternoon, finishing it just in time. The new door went on ok with no problems and I'd thrown the old one into the skip on my way back to the workshop. As I was sorting out my stuff ready to go home, I had a call from my line manager who was in a bit of a flap. He told me that the alarm system wasn't working in the building where I'd just been. It appeared this was due to a component that was let into the top of the old door and hadn't been transferred to the new one. Me and another carpenter rushed to the skip, retrieved the part (which I hadn't noticed when I took it off) and then hurried back to the new door, I drilled the hole and dropped it in. Relief all round when it worked. It was another example of the amount of stuff I had to learn and remember. A learning curve indeed. I owe a lot to my workmates at the time, Tony, Tim, and Darren. Always helpful and full of good advice.

There were regular meetings and reviews with management with graphs and pie charts and departmental reports etc. We were always kept in the picture of what was going on within the department and what the future may hold. Regarding us agency chaps being taken on by the university? Consultants were being bought in to review the situation. This was in January 2010 when I'd been there for 6 months. It still might happen. At the time though it was doubtful I'd still be there for much longer anyway. I was toying with the idea of applying for a housing maintenance job in Milton Keynes, but sadly that didn't come to anything. I even thought about training to be a Teaching Assistant, but Jay didn't think that was a good idea and he should know. I'd just have to stay put but keep my eyes open.

Somewhat ironically in early March a communication seminar was held for everybody in the department including management. We were put into groups and had to discuss how we could improve communicating with each other. After half an hour of that, each group was called upon to share whatever it was they'd come up with to improve things. I was never convinced that these things worked, as those that should have taken notice and acted upon some of the better suggestions, of course never did. There were a lot of meetings and courses during my time there, one or two of them hairy-fairy nonsense, but most of them related to health &

safety. Often, they were tedious, but I couldn't fault the university on making sure safety at work was a priority.

March 9th was my birthday, and I was 60. I celebrated it with Jay and his girlfriend in a rather nice Mexican restaurant in Central Milton Keynes, followed by a few pints in a local Wetherspoons pub. It wasn't so much my birthday I was celebrating it was more a case of 'Only another four- and- half- years to go until retirement'. A few days after I heard the sad news that Micky Jones of the Man Band had passed away. He was a great guitar player and provided the sound track to my life of my early twenties. A sad loss.

Work wasn't always doom and gloom, I was lucky to work with a really nice bunch of lads which included other trades as well as carpenters. There were electricians, plumbers, bricklayers, painters, and a locksmith. We would often have to work together doing all sorts of things. One day a job came up for two men to put up vanity netting all around the tennis courts. They were put up in the spring and taken down in the autumn and attached to the existing fencing with cable ties. It was a long job lasting about half-a-day. I worked alongside Martin who was one of the painters. We got on really well and chatted about a variety of things as we worked, including our childhoods and sport. I told him about Jay and his football and visiting Old Trafford, then he said to me,

"My Dad would often take me up the Arsenal."

I stopped what I was doing and said, "Could you repeat that?"

Then we just fell about laughing, it was one of those moments when neither of us could stop, we were almost on the floor waving our legs in the air, it was uncontrollable. Luckily, we weren't on stepladders at the time. I can honestly say that was a very welcome fun afternoon. Speaking of having fun, I went down to Swansea for the weekend.

April 17th, 2010: *I set off for Swansea at 10.00 o'clock this morning and got here at 1.30. I checked into The Red Lion and went to explore down- town Morriston for a while and had a rather nice 4 sausage bap and a cup of tea. After that I went back for a pint or two and a shower and watched a bit of TV before having a really nice salmon dinner with a pint. I set off for The Club at about 7.00 o'clock and got there just as Deke and Mary arrived. Terry Williams turned up soon after and from then on it was wonderful - a great chat, loads of beer, and great music. Rostok were great and Deke's band superb. I met some of the ex-wives and attempted the thimble trick, but I was a bit too pissed. I sat with a couple from The Red Lion and had a nice chat. All in all a bloody good night!*

As I approached the club on the way there, Deke and Mary were getting out of their car. He looked up and said,

"Bloody hell, Ken Hawes, what are you doing here?"

"I've travelled some 200 miles just to see you, Deke, because you're one of my all-time heroes." (Which was true.)

"You daft bugger," he said.

Terry pulled up across the road soon after and I wondered if he'd recognise me. It must have been at least 35 years since our paths had last crossed. He looked at me for a while and the penny suddenly dropped, "Kevin the magician!" That was good enough for me, we went into the club and chatted in the bar for a while until the first band came on. The ex-wives I refer to are obviously not mine, they used to be married to Terry, Deke, and Martin of the Man Band. It was great to see them all again, they all sat together around one big table, Linda, Fran, and George, and an assortment of relatives. According to George I looked exactly the same, but older.

In June, I experienced my first Cranfield graduation which was the highlight of the year for the university. It was a massive undertaking with all hands to the pump. Due to the large amount of work involved it necessitated working overtime for two consecutive weekends, where the extra money was welcome, but it was exhausting work. Separate ceremonies took place on Thursday and Friday in the sports hall, morning, and afternoon. On those days we'd start at about 6.30 am and get home some 12 hours later. There was so much to do to prepare the hall, laying carpet, erecting the platform for the small orchestra, hanging the huge backdrop curtains, and then positioning hundreds of chairs and placing a programme on top of each one for each ceremony and then collecting the unwanted ones at the end. Altogether, there were about 1500 students along with guests celebrating one of the most important moments of their lives, we had to get it right. As soon as the last person had left at the end of the final ceremony, we began to strike everything and return the hall back to normal, and it had to be done over the weekend ready for business as usual on Monday morning. I was involved in several graduations during my time there and they always ran quite smoothly. About a week later, when it was all over, we were treated to a lavish buffet to thank us for our hard work. Well-deserved I reckon.

I've always enjoyed live theatre and I'd go along to the one in Milton Keynes quite regularly. I saw a stunning version there of 'An Inspector Calls', when at the end, the set (which consisted of the house on two levels) sort of lurched and dropped, as did the shoulders of the characters as they came to terms with what they'd done. It was totally unexpected and raised a gasp from the audience. Another local venue is 'The Stables' which was created by John Dankworth and his wife Cleo Laine in 1970, literally in their backyard. It was rebuilt in 2000 and is a great venue. It has a wonderful atmosphere that's loved by performers and audiences alike. Obviously, it specialises in live music of the highest quality (The Man Band have played there) and over the years many world class performers have graced its stage. Comedy and drama have also featured and on July 11th, 2010, and on a bit of a whim, I bought a ticket to see a two-handed play called 'My Name with Yours'. It featured Maureen Lipman playing Joyce Grenfell, a role she was familiar with, having played her in the successful one-woman-show 'Joyce'. The play that night was written by Jane Bower and was about the influence that an American actress called Ruth Draper had on Joyce's career. Both Joyce and Ruth specialised in monologues which they successfully performed all over the world. Most of the material written and performed by Joyce Grenfell was familiar to me and I loved it all. As I took my seat and read the programme I wondered if Ruth Draper (played by Jane) would be as good.

The answer to that was a resounding yes. Jane Bower was just brilliant. From the moment she walked to the front of the stage and began to speak as a character created by Ruth Draper, the audience was hooked. One of her monologues was about immigrants arriving by boat into New York Harbour in the early 1900s. With just her voice and with no sound effects, somehow the screech of seagulls could be heard, the calls of the stevedores as they worked, intermingled with different languages from disembarking passengers. The clang of bells, small children crying, the smell of the sea, and I could even sense how strange this new country was. All of it portrayed by just the spoken word. It was as if I was there, and judging by the audience reaction, I wasn't the only one. It was a remarkable and moving performance. At the end of the play as both actresses took their final bow there was an immediate and spontaneous standing ovation that went on for some time. It was certainly one of the best performances I'd ever seen.

Some years later I came across the printed programme when I was having a bit of a clear out. Somehow, I found out Jane Bower's email address and told her how much I'd enjoyed her performance, and would it be done again? Not in the foreseeable future was her reply, but never say never. I did go back to The Stables a few years after that (along with my friend Kate) to see her new play based on her father's diaries of his life during the war. 'Daddy's Diaries' was again an emotional experience. We met her afterwards which was lovely, and a small seed was sown. Perhaps one day I could write something myself based on my own diaries.

In mid-July I had a welcome week off and set off as usual to Aberaeron. After visiting the usual sites there, I did a mini tour up the coast staying at various B&Bs along the way. The standard of these varied depending on the price. I wasn't too bothered though as long as the bed was comfortable, the food good and it had a bar, what more could a chap need? I was also aware that you get what you pay for. I stayed at Barmouth one night in a small hotel that stated 'ensuite' in every room, pretty good I thought for thirty quid a night. I was shown to my room and dumped my bag on the bed and realised there was no 'ensuite'. It had been a long day and I wasn't all that bothered. I emptied my bag and opened one half of the double wardrobe and there was the ensuite, actually inside the wardrobe. It turned out to be a really nice place with great food, good beer and perfectly positioned to walk the short distance to the seashore and watch the sunset over Cardigan Bay.

Next, I had a day of Welsh castles; Harlech first and then Caernarfon via Porthmadog which was a nice little town with a lake, steam trains and a couple of good book shops. I spotted a poster on a wall there advertising a gig by a Welsh Pink Floyd tribute band, shame I couldn't go. Needless to say, I eventually ended up in Holyhead and as I wrote in my diary, *"It still gives me a thrill entering the town as it did fifty odd years ago."* I found another B&B there which was pretty basic and unknown to me the bedside alarm clock was set to ring at three o'clock in the morning, probably to wake up somebody to catch the ferry to Ireland, but as it wasn't for me, I could have done without it. After breakfast I visited the usual familiar places and then drove home via Trearddur Bay. It had been a nice few days away. I really wasn't looking forward to going back to work.

At the end of July, Tony, one of my workmates retired. He'd been there, man and boy, since he was 15 and had served the university well. He was a brilliant joiner and he'd helped me out a lot during my first year. I felt quite envious and a touch nervous too as to what the future might hold for me. I knew I didn't have the experience he had so I hoped the chap who was to replace him would be as good. As luck would have it that would be the case. Meanwhile, there had been a development with my line manager.

August 9th, 2010: *It all came to a head this morning when he started having a go at me as soon as I got in. I had a go back at him which ended up with yet another one of his chats in the canteen. I did get him rattled though by threatening him with a phone call to the HR department, and I called him a bully. The upshot of it all is that he surprisingly shook my hand. Let's hope that's the end of it. Roll on retirement.*

I had looked at the formal complaints procedure, but soon realised that going through everything which was involved in that would've given me yet more stress (the irony of which wasn't lost on me). I decided the best course of action was to keep my head down and do my work as best I could and try and keep out of his way.

The new man, Colin, started a week later and was an excellent and experienced joiner and we got on really well. We worked together on all the two-handed jobs and were a good team. Things were starting to improve at last.

Outside of work I was beginning to have more of a social life. I'd discovered The Cross Keys pub which is within easy walking distance from home, and I'd go along there every Friday evening, as I do to this day. I've made a lot of friends there over the years and have had some great nights! I'd also teamed up with three of my cousins and joined their pub quiz team. We'd meet up regularly and join other teams at the quiz night at Shenley Leisure Centre. We had to decide on a name and came up with 'Four Candles' (not to be confused with fork handles!) We were a good team and had some success, often winning prizes (some of which were better than others).

I travelled down to South Wales again in September for another Man Band event and had a great time. I met a couple of people I hadn't seen for 35 years, Pip the roadie, and Richard Treece the guitar player with 'Help Yourself' who peered at me for a minute or two, then smiled and said,

"It's Ken the conjuror!"

As ever it was great to see Terry, Deke, Pete, and Pugwash again and enjoy some great music.

I was still getting magic work and was particularly busy around Christmas and once again New Year's Eve was enjoyed with a gig at Buckingham Town Hall and Villiers Restaurant with singer/

guitarist Tommy Kavanagh. Luckily, I finished my stint there at about 11.00 o'clock and was able to pop down to The Cross Keys to see the new year in for an hour or two. I couldn't help wondering as I staggered home what 2011 would bring. There was certainly an element of doubt regarding my future at Cranfield after almost two years I still hadn't really settled.

January 2011 didn't begin too well at home with a knackered boiler and no heating or hot water for a couple of weeks. No wonder Ben was now actively looking for his own place. Estate agents were leaving messages quite regularly. My workmate Colin had a major operation, and he was off work for quite a while, so I was on my own for a few weeks. At the end of the month I had a fall at work and damaged my shoulder which was a pain in every sense of the word and wasn't helped by my next big job which was replacing doors in one of the accommodation blocks. They were heavy and had to be carried up several flights of stairs. In the end I went along to the doctors and eventually had a scan at the hospital which revealed a torn tendon. Luckily it healed up reasonably quickly after a cortisone injection and regular exercises which I was able to do at home. The door job may have been heavy and often uncomfortable but at least it was inside and regular work. Me and another workmate, Tim, soon got into a pretty good system of working and things generally went well; luckily, we were left alone to get on with it. It was often hot work in the narrow corridors, but my abiding memory of that particular job was the various aromas of cooking from students from all over the world, preparing food from their own country of origin. For many of them English cuisine was considered rather bland.

Most of the time the flats were empty as students were attending lectures around the campus, but occasionally there would be one or two working from home so to speak. One day there was a young couple poring over a strange looking contraption which was on their kitchen table. Curiosity got the better of me and I asked them what it was.

"This," she announced quite dramatically, "Is a 3D Printer."

It must have been one of the very early ones and what an amazing piece of kit it was. Shame I didn't have the time to ask them what they were actually doing with it.

I was by now gaining some confidence and was prepared to take a risk or two as can be seen from the following.

February 11th, 2011: *I got two doors finished quite comfortably by before lunchtime today. I worked through the morning tea break for common sense reasons. It looks now as if it might be reviewed at the end of the month anyway. The new chap on the management team did say to me that as I work for the agency, I can do what I want. That was reassuring news.*

Just when things were dropping nicely into place, in early March I had another setback. I was on my way to a wedding reception near Oxford when I had a car accident. It happened on a dual carriageway on a windy and rainy evening at about 8.00 o'clock. I was driving along steadily and could see my exit ahead. I indicated left and drove onto what I thought was the slip road. A couple of minutes later I was confronted with a sharp left-hand bend which I missed completely and ended up driving straight ahead onto a service road with a wooden barrier at the end of it. It was a surreal moment knowing I'd never stop in time and would just plough into it. During those few seconds, my life didn't flash before me, and it didn't appear to happen in slow motion either. All I remember about those few moments was saying to myself, "Oh shit," as I did indeed plough into it. After the impact I was a bit shaken up and noticed a tiny cut on my left hand. It was obvious the car was a write off but more importantly I wasn't injured. A car had stopped just ahead of me and two people came running up to make sure I was ok and were kind enough to stay with me until I'd phoned the emergency services on 999. The police took all the details and weren't too concerned as long as I wasn't hurt, adding that they wouldn't be sending anybody out. I was at a bit of a loss then. Shaken up and stuck in the middle of nowhere not knowing what to do. I looked up the road trying to make sense of it all and could see the long sweep of the exit road I thought I was on ahead of me. For some reason I'd turned left too early. I opened the boot and took out my bag of tricks and decided to find the nearest village or sign of life. Just then a police car pulled up (so much for not sending anybody out). The two policemen told me they were in the area anyway and asked me if I was ok and what had happened. I sat in the back, and they asked me if I'd been drinking; I wasn't breathalysed, but they sat close enough to enable them to smell my breath. They wanted to know where I was going and was the car mine etc. Then surprisingly I was cautioned pending an investigation. They gave me the number of a breakdown vehicle or perhaps they phoned them I can't remember. Anyway it turned up while I was still in the police car and confirmed it was a write off. I was given a lift into Bicester and luckily was able to catch a bus home from there. What a pain!

Next, I had the hassle and worry of sorting out the insurance, getting to work and looking for and buying another car, plus the fact I might be in trouble with the law. Luckily that didn't come to anything. I had a letter from them saying, "After careful consideration of the available evidence and surrounding circumstances, it has been decided that no further action will be taken against you." I did wonder what on earth had made me turn left too early, I don't recall seeing a sharp bend sign or even a sign for the village that the road actually led to. I did notice however a nice shiny brand new one in place as I drove past there a couple of months later.

I do have to give credit to my insurers (not words you hear every day). They were very efficient and paid up within a few weeks. Things didn't go as smoothly when buying another car though ('twas ever thus). In all honesty I panicked, anxious to get anything to get me to work. I really should have spent more time looking for something more reliable and newer than the one I eventually bought. It was an old Citroen that had done 89,000 miles and cost me £2000. He must have seen me coming. By the end of the year I'd spent another £780 on repairs. Oh well, it did serve its purpose in getting me to and from Cranfield for as long as I was there.

Luckily, I was getting some magic work and did a really nice job at a hotel on the Thames in Oxford. This was on Easter Sunday at lunchtime and into the afternoon. There were a lot of families, some with young children which can make life difficult. It's surprising how many people assume that magic is a form of entertainment purely for children. A few of the parents expected a kids' entertainer and I suspected the management there assumed that's what a magician is. I coped ok though by doing the same material but changing the patter and style of working to suit. If they were from about ten years upwards then I was happy to teach them simple card or coin tricks; the parents loved that, and you never know it may have sparked a lifelong interest. All in all it was a really pleasant three hours in delightful surroundings. (Thankfully the car got me there and back with no trouble.)

By the end of May, I made the decision to retire a bit earlier than I'd originally planned. I'd be 65 on March 9th, 2015, and I decided to go at Christmas 2014. It was only 3 months earlier, but it was exciting to know I had an actual date. I worked it out to 1,311 days. From that point onwards I literally counted the days, I'd cross one off every night for three-and-a- half years. Occasionally when I was sitting in the canteen, I'd say to my workmates something along the lines of,

"When I retire in 1,112 days' time, I will be mostly having an afternoon nap." Or I'd be driving along in my van and a painter would call out and say, "Ken, how many more days?"

"Four hundred and seventeen and a half," I'd shout back.

Of course I'd be criticised for wishing my time away, but I didn't see it that way at all, I couldn't wait.

Meanwhile work continued, much of it the usual run of the mill stuff. Pinboards and whiteboards, shelving, easing windows, and of course the inevitable doors. Some of those were quite interesting and had to be made to suit and others had apertures cut into them which included making and fitting the beading. There was also a variety of different locks and handles to fit and maintain, some of which could be really fiddly. Graduation came around again and with it the usual vast amount of overtime. The money I earned from that I used to pay off another slice of my mortgage, the plan was to get it down to a point when I could pay it off completely, early into my retirement.

Soon after graduation I had a couple of weeks off which I'd decided to spend catching up with odd jobs at home for the first week and then perhaps have a trip to Wales for the second. The first week soon went and the following Monday I threw a few things into a bag and set off for Wales. I got as far as the outskirts of Worcester when I had a puncture, luckily not in a dangerous position so it was possible to change the wheel. I opened the small compartment in the boot and found the jack but no spanner to undo the nuts. I had no alternative then but to phone the RAC; meanwhile, I took the spare wheel out only to discover it too had a puncture. I'd committed the cardinal motorist's sin of not checking the car before I set off (as the mechanic reminded me when he arrived half-an- hour later). He did a temporary repair on the tyre which was safe enough to get me home. I couldn't face the risk of anything else going wrong had I carried on to Wales. This was typical of that car, there was always something. I hated the bloody thing.

Those two weeks flew by and it least they ended on a restful note.

July 2nd, 2011: *I walked into Fenny along the canal to check up on Mum this morning. It was really nice in the sunshine. I'd bought some sunblock during the week to prevent my face from looking like an over-ripe tomato. I walked back along the river and spotted a kingfisher! I got home around lunchtime and after a bite to eat I went for yet another walk to Milton Keynes village. I sat under a tree to watch some village cricket while listening to a play on my little radio. If this is what retirement's like bring it on! After a sausage and mash dinner this evening I spent some time on the Big Issue sudoku and then walked down to the pub. Graham and Sue were there, so my last drink of my hols was really nice.*

By this time Mum was 93 and I was visiting every Wednesday and taking her to church on Sundays. Maggs and Ken lived close by and would also visit regularly. Her general health was pretty good, but her eyesight was failing. Following a visit to the eye hospital in July it was discovered she was totally blind in one eye and the other one wasn't too good either. Mentally she was quite sharp but there were occasional bouts of confusion but nothing that gave us too much cause for concern, she was still coping reasonably well at this point, living in her small bungalow but we could see that things would inevitably get difficult as time went on.

The rest of the summer wasn't good at work, problems continued with my line manager and in the end a meeting was arranged with the general manager and my safeguarding officer. I told them my concerns and all that had happened to both me and former workmates since I'd been there. Another meeting was arranged with the HR department where I gave a written list covering several pages of things that had happened and had been said over the last couple of years, all gleaned from my diaries. I didn't know at this point if I was being overly sensitive, and he was just doing his job or whether he'd crossed a line and shouldn't have behaved the way he did. What I did know was that I'd got to the end of my tether, enough was enough. Anyway it was with some relief that it was now out of my hands and left to the HR department to decide one way or the other.

At the end of August I did the magic at a wedding for the daughter of a friend of mine in the back room of a pub in Stony Stratford. As I've alluded to before, I love the place and was looking forward to it. I got there on time and joined the queue of friends and relatives outside the function room. I wore a smart light casual suit which I usually wear in the summer. It was comfortable and practical with nice big pockets and as it happened, I didn't look too different from the other guests. I had a quick glance round and didn't recognise anybody but was happy to chat and begin the process of getting to know them when suddenly one of them said,

"I understand we've got a magician today."

"I've heard that too," I said, "And apparently he's really good."

"I wonder who it is?" said his girlfriend.

"Actually it's me." I said, which made them smile.

At this point a rather sedate and well-dressed elderly lady turned round, looked me up and down, and in a voice not dissimilar to Dame Edith Evans said,

"You're not very smart you?"

Then I looked her up and down and said,

"Perhaps not, but you look fabulous!"

"Oh, what a nice young man you are," she said, and then added, "You'd better be good!"

"Let's go and find out," I said as we made our way inside.

Happily she was a real character and loved the magic. What a great night that was.

In September I did a surprise birthday party for my old friend and neighbour, Ken Rainey, in Olney (another lovely little town) and later on in the year did a similar one for his wife, Lydia. This one took place in what I think was a cricket club in one of the surrounding villages. It was in the middle of a field I do remember that much. The guests arrived in plenty of time, and we waited as Lydia was driven there (blindfolded) and guided inside. As she uncovered her eyes, we all sang Happy Birthday with tremendous gusto which was a lovely surprise for her. There was a small disco set up in the corner and the party began to get going.

After a couple of records there was a sharp knock on the door and standing in the doorway was the DJ's wife, not looking very happy. A huge stand-up row ensued with some of the guests desperately trying to keep them apart. They were hustled outside where they continued to argue for ten minutes until she eventually drove off in an obvious huff. The DJ walked back inside as if nothing had happened, picked up his earphones and said,

"Who's for a bit of Abba?"

Ben was busy with his music, both writing and producing and also working on backing tracks for all sorts of people including poet/rapper, Soul Urban Poet. Once the CD was finished The Stables got wind of it and a gig was the result. It would be the first ever for a rapper at this prestigious venue. I went along to give moral support along with friends and fans, and it was a great night. A really good local girl singer opened the show and then poet Mark Niel from Tongue in Chic did a spot. As he was considerably older than both the performers and the audience I wondered how he would go. No worries on that score, according to my diary he destroyed them (showbiz parlance for, he went very well indeed.) Soul Urban Poet finished the show with Ben playing piano and bongos as part of the band. It went really well and was enjoyed by everybody and deemed a great success.

Ben had been playing bongos for some time and some six months after he bought them, I somewhat cockily said to him one night,

"Come on then Ben, give us a tune on the bongos."

He picked them up and began to play; surprisingly, I was really moved by what I heard and felt quite emotional. Who'd have thought? The lesson I learned on that night was that a percussionist is as much a musician as any other instrumentalist.

Thankfully, 2011 drew to a close, but with it I had to have a PDR (Performance and Development Review) with my line manager. It was an hour and a half of total bollocks. I let him do the talking (which wasn't difficult) and agreed with everything he said and let him write whatever he wanted. I was past caring. The way I saw it, I'd carry on the same as I always have, doing the best job I could while trying to get on with everybody and keeping my head down for the 1,107 days I had left, if I could last that long.

Thankfully it was another great finish to the year. Me and Tommy back at Buckingham Town Hall and Villiers restaurant, and to see the New Year in at the good old Cross Keys!

2012 began with a shortage of work which was always difficult when it came to filling in time sheets.

January 5th, 2012: *I had two tickets this morning both of which were done by half past nine. The rest of the day was spent in the workshop tidying my cupboard, then the van, then my screw box, and then the mastic tubes. Somehow, I have to find five and a half hours to put on my bloody time sheet. It's really doing my head in.*

There was a time when we could book half an hour for checking the vans first thing in the morning but that was stopped. The only other outlet for using up time was on admin. We could book about half an hour per day which was supposed to cover the time for filling in the daily time sheet and getting tickets signed etc. I used to take my paperwork home to pore over and just spread the load across whatever jobs I had. If I was really desperate, I'd book time on a job that was pending that I hadn't even started. Even that didn't always work, as the line manager would then give us a bollocking for spending too much time on a job. Time taken and time booked often bore no relation to each other when work was tight. The obvious solution, bearing in mind that management actually issued the tickets and must have known we had nothing to do, was to find something long term that we could book to whenever work was slack, or even send us home. Thankfully this situation rarely happened and for much of the year it was a steady plod.

The magic club at Northampton was still an important part of my life and I'd go along to meetings and lectures whenever I could. In early February I went to watch one of my favourite entertainers, Steve Evans from Wolverhampton. The first time I'd watched him perform was at an IBM fringe event several years previously, where in my view he stole the show. With his Midlands accent to the fore and lots of gags and bits of business he was hilarious. His self-deprecating humour was always a hit with any audience, whether the public or a group of magicians. His day job was a surveyor with his Local Authority, and he'd often introduce himself as, "The man from the council". His lecture didn't disappoint - great ideas and material, all of it really entertaining. Steve was diagnosed with a nasty form of incurable cancer which he fought bravely and with dignity. He was happy to share his thoughts and feelings on TV, and radio and with a regular blog on social media which soon had a huge following. Steve brought help and advice to people and families who were going through a similar situation as himself and by the time he passed away at the age of 52 he was loved and respected by thousands of people throughout the world. Although I didn't know him well, there is no doubt that Steve was a one off and a remarkable human being.

At the beginning of the year Ben went to have a look at a house a few miles away and decided to go for it. I took him over to the estate agent to pick up the keys and then onto the house. It was perfect for him with a room ideally situated to suit his studio. I don't quite know how, but somehow we got locked inside and had to call Jay to come over and let us out. A similar thing happened a few weeks later when Ben got stuck inside his bedroom, unable to get the door open. He managed to shout out to a neighbour from the window who contacted me with a call to my mobile…

"Hello is that Ken"?

"Yes, it is."

"You don't know me, but I live next-door to Ben, and he's locked himself into his bedroom. Could you come over and rescue him?"

"How can he get locked inside a room when the door doesn't have a lock?" I asked.

"No idea," came the reply.

"Ok, tell him I'm on my way."

When I got there, I soon saw what the problem was; the catch had broken while the door was closed and there was no way he could have got out with no tools to hand. Luckily, the frame had a moveable door stop and once that was off, I was able to force the door open and later fit a new catch.

Throughout early Spring, Ben, along with his Mum, worked really hard cleaning and decorating. I had a week off work and was able to spend it making a start on building the new desk for his new studio. He gave me a small sketch with some measurements and from that I was able to make a working drawing to scale and off I went. It was made in sections to make it easy to transport and manhandle up two flights of stairs. It took a few weeks, but it all went together really well. We slotted the mixer into the pre-cut opening and fixed the inspection panel on the side, and once his keyboard was positioned on the sliding shelf and the speakers placed in the right places, it was ready to go. It looked and sounded great (if I do say so myself). It took a few journeys to move the rest of Ben's stuff from my house to his, but it was finally all done by the end of April. After dropping him off at his new home for the final time, I drove back to an empty and quiet house. I went upstairs to look at his former bedroom and studio, the marks on the carpet still visible where his old desk used to be. There were transfers stuck to the doors from his visits to America, and in the middle of the room was the bed I'd made all those years ago, looking oddly lonely in the middle of the otherwise empty room. I walked across the landing to Jay's room; stuff still there in boxes and marks on the walls still visible from miscued snooker shots. Memories came flooding back to when he was young and would cry out,

"Dad! Ben hurt me!" "Dad! Tell him off!"

Then my memories took me further back to when Jeff shared the room with them with his Technic Lego and the music of Paul Young blaring out from his ghetto blaster. I closed the door and then stood in the doorway of what was Clare's room (now mine) and remembered the pictures she had on her wall. I could almost hear the sounds of Wet Wet Wet, Adam and the Ants, and Frankie goes to Hollywood, and me shouting to her to turn it down a bit. As I stood there lost in thought, it occurred to me just what a silly old fool I often was during some of Clare and Jeff's teenage years. I always meant well though and thankfully they did come to realise that. It was an emotional experience, as it always is when I think of Clare. I went downstairs where it was eerily quiet. It was the end of an era, and I was on my own. I felt a mixture of emotions confused as to what the future would hold. Every minute of every day for twenty years had been dedicated to the boys, keeping them fed and clothed and safe. Now they weren't there anymore, I was definitely suffering from 'empty nest syndrome'. I made a cup of tea and sat at the kitchen table feeling a bit empty but thankful at the same time. Ben, Jay, and Jeff had all turned out to be kind, funny, and independent young men, more than capable of making their own way in the world - Ben with his music and work at the school, Jay with his teaching, and Jeff was now following in the footsteps of his Granddad and Dad by working at Ascott House near Leighton Buzzard. I felt proud of them all.

Work continued in much the same way doing a variety of jobs, some big but most of them small, and others just plain daft. One day I had to fix a Fire Exit sign above a door in an office; nothing too unusual about that apart from the fact it was the only door in the room. I didn't question it; all part of my policy of keeping my head down. I had an awkward job to do one day in one of the newer buildings. On the ticket was written, "toilet door sticking". Usually this would involve packing the hinges or adjusting the indicator bolt and occasionally planing the door edge; generally speaking a small job as the doors were usually small and light. This door however was in one of the buildings where nothing was ever straight forward, and I knew there would be problems. The door turned out to be nine feet high and three feet wide! Crazy really, no wonder it had dropped. It turned out to be a two-man job the following day, along with Colin, both of us often muttering under our breath, "Bloody architects."

The regular health and safety courses continued throughout the year, including one on working at height and later a course on working in confined spaces. The height one was divided into two; the first part in the morning was on harnesses, and the second in the afternoon was on working safely with ladders. Most of the chaps on the course had a lifetime of experience working with ladders and we all knew instinctively the correct angle to place it against a building. However, technology was even involved with that. I think we were all surprised when the instructor checked the angle with an app on his phone, "You need to bring the base of the ladder out about 50 mill."

After several years of similar courses, we were way past answering back with, "Do you know how long I've been working with ladders? Since before you were born mate!!" We were dignified and did what we were told and put the resulting pass certificate on top of the increasingly rising pile of the others. There was one instance though that I did have a job getting my head around. It was towards the end of my time there (probably during my final 100 days) when we were told that we had to stop using all workshop machinery with immediate effect. It had come to the attention of management that most of us hadn't completed the latest course on safety with woodworking machinery. There was only one person who had, and he was a young lad of about 20 who had just finished his apprenticeship. It seemed crazy that three qualified carpenter/joiner/machinists, with combined practical experience of 120 years, weren't allowed to use the equipment, while a lad with only 12 months could. Experience (or lack of it) obviously counted for nothing. We eventually completed the course where we learned nothing new; it was the same stuff that had been taught to aspiring wood machinists for generations, most of it based on commonsense. For us it meant another course completed and another certificate to add to the pile and for management, another box ticked.

Most of the courses took place in a room with slides and a talk followed by questions and a short test. The confined space one however also had a practical element. We were lowered into a dark and narrow manhole and when we reached the bottom, we had to put on a rather complicated face mask; a nightmare if you suffered from claustrophobia (luckily, I didn't). Again though, it was something I'd never have to do during my time there. There were regular courses on the risks of asbestos and the training was comprehensive and often long. I was involved with some low-risk removal and had to wear all the available protection, as you'd expect. This was an area where no chances were taken and was taken seriously by all of us.

It was often interesting to see how the students at Cranfield lived. Most of them were from overseas and some were cleaner and tidier than others. The quality of accommodation varied too depending on how much the student was prepared or able to pay. While I was there some of the older buildings were being revamped and updated and generally speaking the standard for a university, pretty good I thought, having seen what Jay had experienced. As well as single room flats there were also houses provided for mature students who had their families with them. There were all sorts of cultures and rituals which we had to be aware of. For Muslim households it meant covering boots on entering and notifying the man of the house so he could be in attendance as we worked. I didn't have any problems regarding anything like that and most were friendly and accommodating. There were others who insisted on having the curtains or windows permanently closed; I never did figure out why and as you'd expect the rooms could be like an oven in the summer. I arrived at such a flat late one morning where I had to adjust a kitchen cupboard door. I rattled the letterbox and knocked on the entrance door and after a while it was opened by a dishevelled young chap of Eastern appearance (it was obvious he'd just got out of bed as he was yawning and scratching). I showed him my ID and the job ticket and was invited in. There were piles of dirty plates and saucepans in the sink and on the worktops. The small kitchen table was full of plates of half-eaten food and there were discarded clothes everywhere. As the windows were closed and it was a hot day, it isn't difficult to imagine what the smell was like. I crouched down to have a look at the broken cupboard door and pulled it open to reveal opened boxes and packets of assorted food. There were bottles of cooking oil as well which had leaked and left a film all over the shelves where spilled rice and a variety of herbs and spices had become firmly embedded. The door had broken because it had been forced closed onto the protruding boxes. I managed to get it rehung and then reorganised the many boxes and packets so it wouldn't happen again, it was then that I spotted the cockroaches. The student had gone back to bed so I couldn't say anything to him, but I did give a report to the manager of the building, who when I showed him the ticket raised his eyebrows and said,

"Not him again, I'll have a word."

Luckily this was a rare occurrence and most of the students lived their lives in a way that was pretty much acceptable, for a student.

Some students coped better than others with life at Cranfield. There was a lot of support for them if they were struggling with homesickness or indeed anything else. If they happened to be in the room while I was working, they would often chat and practise their English and occasionally offer food. I wasn't in a position to refuse in case they were offended, well that was my excuse but it did have some merit. I sampled food from all over the world during my time there, all of it lovely. Other students weren't particularly friendly and one or two were totally up themselves and at times we were treated like skivvies or servants. I ignored them and just got on with the work. There was one occasion though when I was doing a job in one of the laboratories. A rather snide student really annoyed me - a condescending little twat. I didn't say anything to him directly, but I did have a word with the facilities manager.

"Oh him," he said, "Don't worry, I'll sort him out."

The next day when I went back to finish off, the student came up to me and rather sheepishly apologised for the patronising way he spoke to me the day before. He'd obviously had a severe bollocking and I'd have loved to have been a fly on the wall when that was going on. The facilities managers at Cranfield were always kind and supportive and ran their departments really well - I owed them a lot.

In June I had a few days off work and went for a walk, found in one of my books.

June 20th, 2012: *On a bit of a whim I decided to drive out to the small village of Brill which is between Aylesbury and Oxford. It's where my ancestors came from, and it was fascinating to walk through the same fields and woodland that perhaps they had over a hundred years ago. It was a 6-mile circular walk beginning and ending at the famous old windmill, and taking in the 646ft Muswell Hill where the view was spectacular. While I was there, I explored the old church and graveyard and sure enough I found a Hawes. A good day.*

There is nothing quite like walking in the English countryside. A month later I went on another one from the same Readers Digest book. This one took me to the Prime Minister's residence, Chequers. I would like to point out, I wasn't invited.

July 27th, 2012: *A lovely day today. I set off for the Chequers walk at about 10.00 o'clock this morning and arrived at about 12.00 after struggling to find the car park. The map was pretty good, and I was able to find my way round the route fairly easily.*

Luckily the weather stayed fine and I had a great time. The scenery there is lovely - lush meadows, unspoilt beech woodland, and glorious views from the hills. I managed to get myself to the top of two of them and was able to get quite close to a red kite that was floating on the thermals. The final part took me to the top of Coombe Hill which is 842ft high. When I got back to the car park, there was an ice-cream van parked up. The best I've ever tasted! I got home around 4.00 o'clock and after a shower went to the pub where I sat with Graham and Sue for a couple of hours. I got back in time for the Olympic Games opening ceremony but fell asleep before the end.

It looked as if I was getting used to living on my own; it didn't take long and some ten years later I wouldn't have it any other way. I was still doing odd jobs for Ben, including fitting a new toilet seat. We went to B&Q to have a look and were both surprised at the huge range of shapes and styles available.

"What do you reckon then"? I asked.

"Nothing too fancy, anything cheap and cheerful will do," he replied.

"Bog standard it is then."

In October my line manager had his Hearing, some 15 months after I and several others had made our complaints. I have no idea why it took so long, and it would be some time yet before we'd know the outcome. Anyway I was still very much counting the days before retirement and on the 9th October, hit a milestone - only 800 days to go, and counting!

There was a fair amount of work to do at home most of it the aftermath from the boys leaving. Both of their rooms needed decorating as did the hall stairs and landing and not to mention the front room. I've always called it that, even though it's at the back of the house. It originates from my childhood where we never did use the word 'lounge' which always sounded pretentious to me and it's certainly a word my Dad wouldn't have used. Anyway I decided all the decorating could wait until another 799 days had passed and I was happily retired. There was one job that I had to get done though, which was a broken double-glazed unit in Jay's old room. Strangely enough, it wasn't cracked but there was a small hole bang in the middle of it. There is something about that particular window that appears to be attractive to pigeons. To this day, once or twice a year the outline of a flattened bird can clearly be seen emblazoned on the glass, often with considerable detail. I've yet to see a dead or injured one, so can only assume that they hobble off to fly another day.

Magic jobs were still coming in, most of them ordinary and predictable but also some nice ones, including a lady's 90th birthday party in an old church hall in Northamptonshire. It was a large family gathering with people of all ages sitting around typical church wooden trestle tables. And there was loads of food! At one end of the hall several tables were groaning under the weight of sandwiches, homemade cakes, and even bowls of trifle.

"Do take some food home with you," said one of the ladies as I was leaving.

"Oh, alright then, shame to waste it."

(Don't you just love homemade cake?)

Friday nights in the Cross Keys was a regular thing now and soon became the highlight of my week. I would sit in the small bar with my pal Roy who was about 80 at the time and an ex regular soldier. Invariably he would be in before me sitting on his usual stool in the corner. When I'd arrive, he'd say,

"Hello Sunshine, what are you having, and how many days to go?" He always called me Sunshine, no idea why. Once we'd got settled, I would tell him about my week, and he'd tell me about his and invariably (after the third pint) he would tell me stories about his exploits in the army - of raw recruits doing their National Service which for many was their first time away from home. For some, from deep in rural England they were like fish out of water. When asked to take a shower they would look blank and have no idea what a shower was.

"They'd been bought up with an old tin bath in front of the fire which would be shared with the rest of the family, usually on a Friday night," said Roy.

"And another thing," he continued, "You'd be surprised how many couldn't march. They had no coordination whatsoever; their arms and legs were all over the place."

I did point out to Roy that surely marching works automatically and arms and legs coordinate naturally.

"That is true for most people," said Roy, "You can't do it wrong even if you want to - try it."

I heaved myself off my stool and tried marching up and down the pub with arms swinging trying to do it wrong (much to the amusement of other customers) and I just couldn't.

Roy would speak of his childhood in New Brighton and Birkenhead and tell me about his family's small claim to fame.

"My Dad was a bus driver and was the first to drive his bus through the Mersey Tunnel," he said, still proud after all those years.

Roy was evacuated to The New Forest in Hampshire during the war, and he said to me one night, "Have you have ever eaten hedgehog, Sunshine?"

Obviously, I hadn't, and he went on to explain how he had learned the perfect way to cook hedgehog shown to him by the gypsies in Ringwood. He was always interesting company, and we had a lot of laughs. One night there was a new and very attractive black barmaid behind the bar. Her name was Ebony and of course it was inevitable that at some point me and Roy would begin crooning the song Ebony and Ivory. Towards the end of the evening we were about to have our final pint and she was nowhere to be seen. I asked Roy to give Ebony a call into the other bar, "Ok Sunshine," he said, and leaning over the bar, called out, "Ivory, can we have some service in here?!"

Oops, she wasn't best pleased.

On another night Roy was buying a round and another friend, Phil, came in, just in time, "And what are you having, Phil?" asked Roy.

"I'll have an Eagle, please. Thanks Roy."

"And another Eagle," said Roy to the barmaid.

"She was a good actress," I said.

They both looked at me blankly and said, "What are you on about"?

"Anna Neagle," I said.

"You silly sod," they laughed.

There were many instances like that.

Roy had a wealth of life experiences and to be in his company was an absolute joy. He would talk about his large family and the pleasure they gave him, and also the sad times he'd suffered over recent years. Even through his final illness, he had the amazing sense of courage and fortitude that seems prevalent with his generation, he never complained.

"As long as I can hold my pint, Sunshine!"

Roy passed away in January of 2017, sadly the same week as my old friend Deke Leonard.

I was able to meet and chat with Roy's family at his funeral and I asked his wife how they'd met. She told me she lived a few doors away from Roy and one day she called into his house and noticed a photograph of a young Roy, smart and uniformed on the mantelpiece. She picked it up and looked at it and said, "One day I'm going to marry this chap." She did of course and they went on to spend many happy years together with children, grandchildren, and great grandchildren.

Now that the boys had left home, I was able to cope reasonably well with my finances. The earnings I made with the magic helped and I was still able to put money away each week into my ISA or pension pot. One day at the end of November I found two brown envelopes on the doormat. I opened the first one which notified me that I was now eligible for the government Winter Fuel Payment, £200! Then I opened the other one which was from the taxman with a bill of £246. The phrase giving it with the left hand and taking it away with the right sprang to mind. Luckily, I had a gig soon after which compensated a bit. It was a wedding and came from a chap I hadn't seen for over 40 years. He was a former junior member of the club back in the 60s and the last time I saw him he was about 15, and that's how I pictured him. The gig was for his son's wedding. How time flies. I set off early for the venue which was a country club/stately home in deepest Northamptonshire. It wasn't easy to find, and it was raining heavily for the entire journey. I got a bit lost in the vast grounds and when I did find the correct road (or track) it was under water with flood signs in place. I phoned the venue, and a chap came out in a Land Rover to make sure I could get through it ok, and I followed him to the rather grand house. It wasn't a particularly good night as there seemed to be a misunderstanding of what I was booked for - I realised that as soon as the Best Man came over to me and said, "The children are over there." I somehow got through it, and it was nice to meet the former youngster again (who I never would have recognised) and have a bit of a catch up - he's probably a Granddad now.

The year ended yet again with me and Tommy working at Buckingham Town Hall and Villiers Restaurant. As usual I popped down to the pub to see the new year in and at a minute past midnight, I said to myself. "I'm retiring next year!"

I had a nice magic job a couple of days later. It was in a village hall and was the 80th birthday party for the father of a chap I'd played table tennis with. Both father and son were builders and the family-run firm had been established for many years in the local area. As I walked into the small foyer, I couldn't help noticing the many photos on display and I stopped to have a browse. Many were of family members both past and present. Weddings and Christmas gatherings and the like. There were also pictures of successful building projects completed by the firm, going back decades. On a small table at the front there was a bunch of balloons tied down with string and anchored with a short rough-cut length of 4" x 2" and a brick. It was a great night.

Mum was 95 this year and inevitability her health began to decline. Due to poor eyesight cooking for herself was not only beyond her but potentially dangerous too. That being the case, hot ready meals were delivered daily and before the end of the year carers would visit regularly. She kept cheerful and was visited by my sisters and her grandchildren throughout the week. The neighbours in the small secluded close where she lived would look out for her as well and I'd go and see her every Sunday morning and Wednesday evenings. I'd sit and chat with her rather than have the TV on, which she couldn't see anyway. I'd often read stuff out to her - amusing quotes I'd glean from the internet, including this one from Delia Smith: "If you sometimes feel depressed or let down, if you're suffering from the pressure of life, or simply having a plain old grey day, my advice is to roast a chicken." - That one made her laugh. Other times we would chat about anything and everything and I was often astounded by her knowledge and memory going back many years.

I had a week off at the end of March and spent some time having a bit of a clear out and got rid of a load of stuff at the council tip. It took a couple of days and after that I thought I deserved a day out. I had another look through my Readers Digest book of walks and decided to go further afield. What better place to go on a bleak and cold day in late March (snow was on the ground) than the Norfolk coast? However, I was a bit wary about the car and being able to get there and back without something else going wrong - the latest thing was the cam belt a few weeks previously. That had cost me £750 which in all honesty was probably more than the car was worth. Anyway, I was still a member of the RAC, so I went for it. I set off early for the small hamlet of Shepherd's Port and had a trouble-free journey arriving at about 10.30. After a drink and an apple I looked at my photocopied page from the book, grabbed my rucksack, and set off on the 4-mile circular walk around Snettisham Common. I walked through woodland and open fields and crossed the site of an old railway line which was still visible. I carried on through a meadow and over the old sea defences and then walked along the embankment of the new ones. As I walked, I looked out across mudflats and sandbanks to The Wash in the distance. This is one of the most important sites for waders and wildfowl in Britain with more than 100,000 birds passing through over winter. I got back to the car some 2 hours later and went in search of a pub for some lunch before travelling home in the late afternoon hazy sunshine. I had a great time and the bleakness somehow added to the beauty of the place, it was nice just to get away for a while.

As well as walking regularly I was also going to the Milton Keynes Theatre quite often to see all sorts of things. There was one play in June of 2013 that had quite an effect on me. It was, 'Being Tommy Cooper' by Tom Green, with Damian Williams playing the lead. It was as much about Tommy the man as it was Tommy the entertainer. It not only captured the humour and style of his performances but also his vulnerability. I did meet Tommy a couple of times a year or two before he died when his health wasn't good. I asked him when he was going to retire, he answered in his own inevitable style,

"When they stop laughing son, when they stop laughing!"

They never did stop laughing, and they're still laughing now. I thought both the play and the performance by the cast was outstanding. A good night out.

Work carried on much as before with the usual number of familiar jobs - curtain track to fit, door closers to replace and adjust, and an assortment of windows and doors to sort out. I did have an unusual job to do in one of the accommodation block toilets one day. I had to box in a pipe that was attached to the ceiling. This sort of work is usually done for cosmetic reasons, purely to hide the pipe. In this case though there was a more practical aspect. A student (apparently worse for drink) had spotted the said pipe and couldn't resist leaping up to swing on it, no doubt to try and impress his fellow students. The end result was the pipe was wrenched from its fittings and fell to the floor along with the student. It gave me a couple of hours work.

Before I knew it summer had arrived and with 541 days to go before retirement, I had another week off. It turned out to be much the same as the previous one, with lots of clearing out and tidying up of the boys' rooms to do. By now I'd made a definite dent in the piles of mostly crap the boys had left behind. The final thing that was left in Jay's room was his old fitness bench which he told me to hang onto it in case he moved into a bigger house at some point in the future. Among the old magazines he'd left was a couple of 'Men's Health' which he used to have when he went through his "regular visit to the gym" phase. Both magazines had photographs on the front cover of blokes posing with impossibly defined 8 packs (certainly more than 6). I looked at the photos, then the fitness bench, then at the chart that fell out of one of the magazines. This was an eight-week course utilising a fitness bench as used by the chap on the front cover and guaranteeing a six pack just like his at the end of it. I looked down at my slowly growing paunch and thought sod it I'll give it a go. I wasn't expecting a miracle, after all I was 63, I'd be happy just to lose an inch off my waistline. To give myself a bit of credit I did manage to stick to it for almost two weeks but all I seemed to have lost during that time was a fortnight. There was no sign of anything like a six pack or even a two pack and I gave up. Anyway it was giving me a backache.

The week ended with a wedding gig. It was for Pete, a mate of mind who I'd known for years. I'd worked with him and his Dad at Llewellyn back in the 80s, and after that our paths had crossed many times as he worked for one of the local timber merchants. I didn't realise until I got there that I was also familiar with the bride's family, her late father was my youth club leader back in the late 60s. What a small world. It was a good afternoon and rounded off the week off quite nicely.

June 23rd, 2013: *I got up quite early this morning and got the bed linen changed. The weather forecast was for rain, so I didn't put it on the line. As it happened it would have dried anyway. I got to Mum's at about half past nine and she was ok. I did a bit of housework, and we had a nice chat for a while. Luckily her meal arrived early so I was able to get home with plenty of time to get myself ready for Pete's wedding. It went really well particularly with one of the bridesmaids who was almost hysterical with laughter. I got home at about six o'clock and after doing some hoovering, I sat in front of the TV for a couple of hours. I watched bits of Diehard 2, bits of the Isle of Wight festival and then The Who from 1970. I'm knackered now. It's been a good week.*

I can't say I'm surprised at the amount of trivia displayed here that I often wrote in my diaries. The fact that the washing could have dried had I put it on the line, or I did some hoovering is hardly earth-shattering stuff, but I still do it to this day, "I did the ironing after breakfast" is a fairly recent one. The reason is that I'm still following what I set out to do all those years ago which is to fill every line of every diary, even if it is mind numbing and of little importance.

The summer of 2013 was a hot one which often made work uncomfortable and not helped by the 'no shorts' rule. I had a couple of days of removing old floor tiles which may have contained asbestos so I couldn't have worn shorts anyway. I had to wear all in one disposable overalls, gloves, and a specialised mask as well. I sweated buckets and had to take a change of T-shirts to replace the sweat-sodden ones. The upside to that was I did lose a couple of pounds in weight and an inch or two from my waistline which was ironic, bearing in mind my failure on the fitness bench.

The Health and Safety department did have some concerns about the effect of the hot weather, as they posted small colour charts above the urinals informing us of the dangers of dehydration. The darker the pee the more dehydrated you were and therefore it was recommended we drink more water. As mine was the colour of an over ripe tangerine I had to do something about it. I used to carry an old empty fruit squash bottle around with me all the time and would refill it throughout the day. If I was working in the workshop, it was always within easy reach. That was stopped though, "In case I confused it with a bottle of white spirit" (which we didn't have in the workshop anyway). More could have been done to help prevent us suffering with the heat, rather than informing us of the symptoms which we were aware of anyway, including sweating profusely, having a headache, and peeing interesting shades of orange. The least they could have done was to allow us to wear shorts whenever it was safe to do so, as we would have been more comfortable and therefore more efficient. Oh well, not long to go now.

On August 4th I hit another milestone 500 days before retirement. It still seemed a long time but obviously considerably shorter than the 1311 when I first started counting. I even looked back 500 days to give me some idea of scale.

A few days later I had a magic job in one of the large hotels in Central Milton Keynes It was a black-tie charity event and a first for me as it was a masked ball. Not everybody wore a mask (me included), but many did and entered into the spirit of it. I had a surreal experience when one of the organisers tapped me on the shoulder and asked me if I would show some stuff for some friends of his. I turned round to be confronted with a lady holding a very ornate mask attached to a stick. Her partner didn't have a mask but did have an extremely realistic and lifelike horses head over the top of his own. It was bizarre trying to show tricks to what to me was a horse. I could just about make out his eyes through a couple of slits but not enough to see or tell if he was actually interested in what I was doing. I asked his partner if he could hear what I was saying, and the horse replied, "Neigh". True story.

The summer came to an end with the late August bank holiday. I had a nice time as can be seen from my diary, and again it appeared I aspired of becoming a writer.

August 26th, 2013: *A really good day today. I went for a long walk along the river all the way to Fenny Lock and then back home along the canal. Radio 4 was just great with a programme about internet dating, then one about a 100 mile walk in Cornwall, and finally part 1 of the Bonnie Parker story (Bonnie & Clyde). The weather was just wonderful, and I took another photo of another music-inspired boat, "Cecelia". I got home at lunchtime, had some lunch, and then went over to the Milton Keynes Museum which I loved. I might just write up my Wolverton Works experiences. After dinner I went for a walk around the lakes and saw cousin Terry halfway round. It was dark when I got in at nine o'clock. I did the ironing, posted some pictures onto Facebook, and had a chat to various people.*

The boat names inspired by music is a series of photos I continue to post on Facebook to this day, the title of which is self-explanatory. Over the years I've spotted lots of them - Dire Straits, Comfortably Numb, Glad All Over, Red Red Wine, and many more. It shows how important music can be to people who name their homes after a song or band that has touched them in some way. Also, absolutely fascinating that I did the ironing when I got home.

The following day wasn't so good according to my diary. It begins "What a crap day!!" Oh well, that's life, 478 days to go. I got through most of September unscathed and on the 14th had a lovely magic job at our local family church hall. It was a traditional Harvest supper followed by me performing close-up magic around the tables. It went really well and it's always nice to perform for family and friends even if they have seen me many times before. In the large glass fronted noticeboard at the front of the church (made by me), there was a huge beautifully hand-painted poster which said, 'Harvest Supper, With Entertainment' (me being the entertainment) - one of the few times I've been featured on a poster.

A couple of weeks later on the 28th, a large marquee was erected in the gardens of The Cross Keys for a special event. A gig from one of Ireland's finest rock/blues guitarists and founder member of Thin Lizzy, Eric Bell. A great night of blues and booze ending with his own version of Whiskey in the Jar (what else?). A brilliant night which I paid for with a bit of a hangover the following day.

October arrived and with it some interesting news regarding my line manager. We were told that he'd be off work until further notice due to personal reasons, then two weeks later on the 15th we had an update and were told he'd decided to leave. That was that, we never did hear any more. That same evening I went to see Wishbone Ash at The Stables along with my cousins Terry and Jeff. Another great night of guitar virtuosity with a packed house of diehard fans all singing along to songs many of us had grown up with. The band still play there to this day pretty much every year in October or November and it's always a sellout. Another sold out show I managed to get a ticket for was for the infamous Australian superstar, Dame Edna Everage. Two hours of hilarious mayhem with a lot of audience participation. What a performance that was.

November dawned and I was looking forward to a trouble and stress free run up to Christmas. Following that of course would be my final year of employment at Cranfield and at long last, retirement. The first job was to get my boiler serviced. I'd decided to have a change from the usual chap I used and went instead for a free one from my supplier at the time N Power. Once that was done and dusted, I'd make a start on my Christmas shopping at a very leisurely pace. That was the plan, but as the old saying goes even the best thought-out plans can go tits up.

November 8th, 2013: *What a bloody crap day!!! I went to the OK Garage to get a fuse for the car first thing this morning which didn't work. Then the chap from N Power came to service the boiler and condemned it because the flue had come adrift and it's horizontal and should be vertical! He suggested that I find out who installed it and get them to put it right. I phoned my usual plumber who didn't get back to me, then I spent a couple of hours trawling through my diaries trying to find out who did install it some ten years ago. I phoned them but they didn't answer. Next, I sent an email to the boiler manufacturer which they haven't replied to.*

From that entry you can see my anger and frustration, which continued for a four-week period during which time I had no heating or hot water. It was four weeks of pulling my hair out. I'd arrange for a plumber to come out who didn't arrive, and there were others who didn't reply, and I left many messages on answer machines all of which went unanswered. Meanwhile the weather was getting colder and colder. I got in touch with N Power who told me the engineer would give me a call and that didn't happen either. Finally in a state of desperation I went down to the biggest heating engineer and supplier in Milton Keynes and told them what the problem was and asked for a recommendation, "This chap will sort you out," said the assistant behind the counter as he handed me a business card. I glanced at it, and he appeared to be a one-man-band who lived locally which was good news. I gave him (Nick) a call as soon as I got home, and he came over to have a look (on time) a few days later. He phoned the manufacturer while I was there who said the flue *can* be adapted to go vertically through the roof (let's hope the price doesn't go the same way I thought, but what a relief). He ordered the parts, and it was arranged for him to fit them on Monday 25th. I gave him the key the day before and was looking forward to a warm house later that day when I got home from work. Halfway through that Monday morning he gave me a call and told me that the original flue had been put in wrong and there was a piece missing. He'd been in touch with the manufacturer and was told the part was now obsolete. He had also phoned around trying to trace and obtain the part all to no avail.

"What are my options then?" I asked.

"You've only got one," came back the reply.

"And what's that?"

"A new boiler," said Nick.

"How much will that cost?" I asked, more than aware Christmas was only weeks away.

"About £1,500."

"Do it," I said.

The gigs will pay for it, I thought hopefully.

On December 6th for the first time in weeks I came home to a warm house. It took one more visit to drain the system with a special chemical and that was that, and almost ten years later and an annual service from Nick, the boiler is as good as ever. A lesson I learned from the whole often traumatic experience is that a good and reliable plumber is worth his weight in gold.

I spent Christmas Day with my sister Jean and her husband Steve at the home of their daughter Kathryn. We picked up Mum on the way and managed to get her from bungalow to car to house in her wheelchair. It was a lovely day with plenty of food and laughter. The only time the TV went on was for the Queen at 3.00 o'clock. There is one comment in my diary that refers to a game of Scrabble, which is always very competitive.

December 25th, 2013: *...Then it was time for the Christmas game of Scrabble which Jean won quite easily. How could I compete with the word "estuary" on a triple word score, using up all her letters and scoring 87 points?!!*

For what it's worth, I rarely beat either Jean or Steve.

2013 came to an end with yet another gig for me and Tommy at Buckingham Town Hall and Villiers Restaurant, followed by a walk down to The Cross Keys to see the New Year in. The year sped by. One more to go.

2014 was an eventful year in many ways and certainly not the trouble and stress free run up to retirement I was hoping for. By now several of us had been employed via an agency at the university for about 5 years and despite being told many times that we'd be taken on directly it never did happen. What did happen was that we had to apply for our own jobs. It was by no means a foregone conclusion either that we'd be successful despite proving that we were more than capable based on our time and experience there. If three or four carpenters were required why not directly employ the ones they already had? It seemed crazy to us. Anyway it was all out of our hands. The jobs were advertised both internally and externally to a response of about 80 applicants. The application form was online, and we could write up to 900 words on why we thought we'd be good enough to be employed as carpenters. We were also told we'd have to do a woodwork skills test presumably to prove that we knew how to use our tools. I found that surprising and unnecessary as we were all qualified with years of experience, five of them working at the university! As well as the written statement and the skills test there was also a formal interview conducted by a panel of three members of staff. The whole process took about 3 months and despite a positive interview, I didn't get the job. I did make it clear from the start that I would be retiring at Christmas whatever happened which was only ten months away, so perhaps that was the reason, and they wanted it to be a more permanent position. I didn't ask. I was a bit surprised however as my interview seemed to go really well (not that that counted for much based on previous interviews I'd had). I was asked all sorts of things, including whether I preferred working as an individual or as part of a team. My immediate response was to say that I worked better on my own proved by 50 years of experience based on doing exactly that. Perhaps it would have been better had I told them what they probably wanted to hear, "Being a team player is one of my great strengths." Too late now though. After the interview and the decision, I began to work out my notice. A week later I was summoned to the office where I was offered a job (still with the agency) upgrading fire doors that would take me to July. I would be working as part of a team.

I accepted the offer as it would give me about four months extra work which would be guaranteed with loads of doors to sort out. I may well have been part of a team, but hanging a door is a solitary occupation anyway. In all honesty I just wanted to be left alone to see out my time there, however long it took.

I was asked at my interview what I enjoyed most about working at Cranfield. I told them with no hesitation that it was the people. I gave the following two examples. I had a job ticket one day to repair a window. It was a tilt and turn type which took ages to sort out over two visits. The first to try and improvise with a spare part that came from another type of mechanism which half worked. The second was to fit another part I found in a drawer in the workshop. The young African couple were in the flat on both occasions and watched me struggle with small nuts, bolts, and springs, and then Bingo! It worked. I made sure they were familiar with the working of it (three different handle positions) and then started to pack up my tools. They thanked me for my hard work and were over the moon that they now had a fully working window.

"We must give you something," said the young lady as she searched inside mostly empty cupboards.

"Not at all," I said, "You don't have to give me anything, I do get paid you know!"

"We must, we must," they insisted as the final cupboard was opened to reveal two small tins of baked beans.

"Please take these with our thanks," she said, as she handed me both tins which I felt I had to accept.

They thanked me again shook my hand and wished me well. Here were two young students obviously struggling, had virtually nothing, yet were prepared to give me everything.

As well as working in student accommodation, the job also involved maintenance and odd jobs in offices and laboratories and even out on the airfield. There are some really clever people at Cranfield, many of them distinguished professors and scientists, all of them at the cutting edge of modern technology. The university has a worldwide reputation for research in engineering, agriculture, management, and a host of other things. I was always fascinated with some of the stuff I saw there and was never shy about asking the question, "What do you do here then?" Sometimes I'd have an explanation and other times it would be a non-committal, "Oh well, you know, a bit of this and that." There was a certain amount of secrecy in some departments, which I understood and just got on with what I had to do. One day I had to hang a fire door in an office in the School of Engineering. The doors were heavy as they were thicker than a conventional door with a lot of work involved. The top and sides had to be machined with a groove for the insertion of intumescent fireproof strips. These had a furry protrusion which acted as a smoke seal. It was vital that the doors were a good fit as the strips when confronted with heat would swell up and seal the gap all around the door so preventing smoke and fire from spreading. They were hard work, so it paid to get it right first time to save heaving the door off and on several times. As I worked, the professor sat at his desk with his computer apparently engrossed in whatever it was he was doing. Finally the door was on with the door closer attached, and as I opened and let it go, the door closed with a satisfying whoosh as the furry material brushed the frame and finally closed with an even more satisfying click. I pulled the handle to make sure there was no movement and opened it a second time let it go, and again the whoosh and the click.

"You're really proud of that aren't you?" said the professor.

"Relieved would be a better word," I replied.

"I've been watching you work," he continued, "I can't do anything like that, and much to my wife's disappointment I'm absolutely useless with DIY."

He rose from his desk to have a look at the door and commented on the nice even gap all round. I told him that years ago when I was an apprentice the gap would have to be the thickness of an old penny and woe betide if it wasn't. I explained about the smoke seal as he opened the door and let it go and said,

"Perfect, I'm full of admiration."

"Nice of you to say so, if you don't mind me asking what do you do here?"

"Oh, nothing much really, I design lunar modules."

"Each to his own," I laughed as I collected my tools together and carried them out via the new door. I stopped and listened a few feet down the corridor until I heard it close behind me with a whoosh and a soft click. Relieved certainly and yes, proud.

I reached a bit of a milestone on February 1st - it was 50 years continuous membership of the Northamptonshire Magicians Club. Who'd have thought that as a 14-year-old lad I'd achieve something like that? 50 years man and boy. Three days later I gave yet another lecture there, this time on that wonderful little device, 'The Topit Vanisher'. I bought my first one from Pat Page in Davenports some 30 years previously. The Topit is a bit of kit that has a lot of uses and has been a godsend for me many times over the years. It makes things disappear, from coins to cards and thimbles and a host of other things. Around that time I did the magic at one of my favourite venues, The Old Shanghai Restaurant in Olney, on two consecutive nights. On my final table of the final evening sat three young men in their twenties. After I'd performed my last trick, they had a whip round and put three pound coins on the table.

"If you can make all three disappear, you can have them," was the challenge.

A few minutes later, thanks to the Topit, I was three quid better off.

"Where are they?" they asked.

I looked to my left and then to my right, tapped my nose and whispered, "They've gone to another dimension."

After my lecture at the club I was presented with a rather nice trophy to mark the occasion of my 50 years membership, which was an unexpected and lovely gesture. I have a lot to thank the club for and to this day I continue to go along to meetings and lectures and am now an Honorary Life Vice President (another unexpected honour).

On the 20th of February I reached another milestone, 300 days to go before retirement. This was assuming of course I'd still be there on December 19th which was still a possibility depending on work staffing levels and the unpredictability of management. At least I was guaranteed employment until July and as always, I'd just keep my head down and get stuck in and carry on counting the days.

Having reached the age of almost 64 and spending years lifting and heaving timber and heavy doors it was inevitable that all of this would take a toll on my body. My lower back was beginning to ache quite regularly, so I decided to invest in a new mattress. It cost me about two hundred quid weighed a ton and almost gave me a hernia heaving it up the stairs and manoeuvring it onto the bed.

February 22nd, 2014: *I woke up with a backache this morning, in the usual place but on the left side. I thought I'd seen the last of that since I bought my expensive orthopaedic mattress. I got up ok but struggled a bit to walk up to the Centre. I called into the Building Society to put the cheque in and then walked around looking at suits. They don't seem to make them now with deep pockets. I went to the market to get fruit and veg and as usual heaved my bag over my left shoulder. As I walked away, I noticed my backache had gone!*

Who'd have thought that five pounds of spuds, two of carrots, four pounds of apples and a large cauliflower could have cured a poorly back. It did though.

A few weeks later I had trouble with my elbow. It was painful and tender on the inside joint which was quite unusual. Had it been on the outside then it could quite easily have been diagnosed as Tennis Elbow. I can't say I was too surprised when I Googled my symptoms and discovered I was suffering with Golfers Elbow which, "isn't limited to golfers." (I sort of guessed that, as the last time I handled a golf club was when I played Crazy Golf with the boys in 1996.) I wasn't surprised either when I checked out the one-word symptom - pain. As with most joint and muscle problems I treated it successfully with ice and Ibuprofen. It did occur to me that there may be other aptly named sport related injuries. My mind went back to the seventies when hair was long and track suits (jogging bottoms) were a bit on the tight side. I was at the table tennis club one night when a chap came in wearing a pair that left little to the imagination and bizarrely, he had put a couple of balls in one of the pockets. I had an idea.

"What are those?" I asked pointing to his nether regions.

"Table tennis balls," he replied looking at me as if I was an idiot.

"I bet they're painful," I said, "I had tennis elbow once."

As well as a poorly back and elbow I was also starting to get a lot of headaches. They were worrying because my head was also tender to touch. Every time I lifted a door, a pain would shoot through my elbow and then zip across my forehead leaving me with a dull ache in my lower back. After a call to my doctor I was diagnosed with sinusitis which I was able to treat with a couple of over-the-counter nasal sprays and paracetamol. Luckily my elbow cleared up as well and by now my back was only giving me the odd twinge. Once spring had arrived, I began to feel better and got stuck into the door job. Meanwhile new carpenters had started and were struggling to settle in. I had to smile when one of them asked me what to put on the time sheet if you run out of work. I told him to have a word with his supervisor.

Summer arrived and I had a week off and stayed with Jean and Steve who had moved to the small town of Stonehouse in Gloucestershire. It's a lovely area and we spent a lot of time walking round Stroud and the surrounding countryside. The views in that part of the world are quite spectacular particularly when viewed from on high; the waterways too presented relaxing walks along the towpath and as we strolled, I couldn't help but think of the miles I would be able to walk once I had the freedom of retirement. Soon after I'd returned to work after my week off, the door job finally came to an end, and I was told by the university enough work would be available to last until Christmas. That was a huge relief.

Mid July also saw the arrival of The Milton Keynes International Festival. This happens every two years and I love it. Acts and performers from all over the world descend on Campbell Park and other venues in the city to entertain and amaze. One of the highlights for me was the Gilded Lili Revue which took place in the spectacular Spiegeltent. It took the form of a burlesque cabaret and was hosted by the beautiful Lili La Scala. As the audience walked in taking their seats and getting the drinks in, she was wandering around with a microphone commenting and ad libbing as she went, sometimes saying nice things but mostly outrageously taking the piss. She looked me up and down and said, "Mmm, nice haircut." I'm not sure if that was a compliment or not, I was just happy she spoke to me. Not only was she funny but she also had a remarkable voice, powerful and almost operatic. Her choice of songs for that type of voice was interesting too. Who'd have thought the David Bowie classic 'Space Oddity' would have worked, but it did, as did her stunning version of Radiohead's, 'Creep'. I just loved it, as did the entire audience. Lili compered the show in her own inimitable style which featured different and unusual acts, including strippers (tastefully and artistically done) and one or two that just defy description. It was a great show.

Work continued at a steady plod with regular health and safety courses including another one on working at height. The upshot of that was we were stopped from working on roofs. That decision I suppose was the ultimate in risk assessment. It did raise a comment from one of the chaps though, "How will they be repaired then, with sky hooks?" It seemed the risk was deemed too high for us employees and specialist contractors would be bought in. It suited me, I never was particularly happy about working at height. A couple of months later we were informed about the latest COSHH (Control Of Substances Hazardous to Health) regulations. We were told that we had to wear gloves and goggles whenever we used a spray lubricant. A bit extreme we thought. For most of us commonsense prevailed in as much as a quick squirt into a rusty lock at arms-length wouldn't cause a lot of damage. It was getting to the point when we were being over-protected, and things were beginning to get a bit silly. Another rule that was applied happened when I only had 85 days to go. During my five years of working there I must have fixed hundreds of whiteboards and pinboards to various walls all over the university (in fact I was known as the Pinboard Wizard). They were all sorts of shapes and sizes, and I never had any problems. I'd mark out the walls, drill the holes, put the plugs in, and then screw the boards into position. The new rule was that we had to use an electronic pipe and wire locator to make sure we didn't drill into anything hazardous. I was given one of the gadgets and used it for the first time in the Health and Safety office where a pinboard was required above a desk. I marked out the position of the holes and read the instructions of the locator and placed it on the wall where I was about to drill. It lit up and buzzed like a Christmas tree. Wherever I put it on the wall, it lit up. It seemed impossible to me that the entire wall could be criss-crossed with cables or pipes buried into it. It was obviously a faulty locator, so I drilled the first hole. As the drill went in, I heard a voice behind me,

"My computer's just gone off."

"So has mine," said somebody else.

To cut a long and embarrassing story short, I had indeed drilled through a cable, electricians had to be called out, and a part of the wall had to be dug out and new cable inserted. The irony wasn't lost on me that it was the first time I'd used the gadget after five years of drilling hundreds of holes without incident and why did it have to be in the H&S office?! The next day I went back and apologised to the staff once again and fixed the pinboard to the wall this time with heavy duty self-adhesive pads, hoping it would last and stay up for the 84 days I had left. That was the last pinboard I fixed at Cranfield.

At the end of August I met up with my two childhood chums Roger Tarbox and Ken Rainey. I'd met Roger for the first time in about 40 years in 2012. He came down to The Cross Keys from his home in Northamptonshire and we had a great time catching up and talking about what we'd been up to during all that time. When Ken joined us two years later it was more of the same. It was lovely to rekindle that childhood friendship and reminisce about life in the 60s and 70s before we went our separate ways.

In mid-October I had a week off work and spent much of it pottering about at home, but I did have a nice day out in London.

October 16th, 2014: *A good day out today. I got a National Express coach at about 9.40 which got me into Victoria at 11.15. I had a tour of the Royal Mews of Buckingham Palace. It was really interesting looking at the beautiful old coaches. From there I walked up The Mall to Westminster Abbey and Parliament and then up The Strand to Covent Garden where I watched the street performers. After that it was past The Royal Courts of Justice via the church of St. Clemence* *which played Oranges and Lemons as I walked past. From there it was up towards the Old Bailey, round past St. Pauls Cathedral and into Threadneedle Street and the Bank of England. After that a slow stroll back to Victoria.*

As usual on my trips to London, I walked miles. The highlight was when the church bells of St. Clemence sounded. I stopped for a while just to listen. It took me straight back to my childhood and singing Oranges and Lemons at Manor Road Infants school. A lovely moment.

On November 10th I heard the sad news that my old friend and mentor Bobby Bernard had passed away. The funeral was at Golders Green Crematorium and the hour-long service was full of genuinely felt tributes from the magic fraternity, including former Magic Circle president David Berglas. Bobby would have loved it all. I smiled to myself as I remembered the laughs we'd had over the years and the arguments too as we'd trade insults and still end up laughing. I sat next to my friend from the club at Northampton, Colin Hooton. Colin was the last surviving member of the club who was there at my audition in 1964. After the service, and as we made our way down the road towards the bus/tube station, we swapped stories and anecdotes about the man who was one of magic's most endearing and knowledgeable characters. He had touched both of our lives in such a positive way. I certainly wouldn't have had the success with the magic that I've enjoyed for almost a lifetime without his advice and friendship. I owed him pretty much everything.

The day after the funeral (29th November) I had a magic job in a small church hall in Stony Stratford. I arrived in plenty of time but still struggled to get parked as for some reason the town was really busy. The job was for a gentleman's 70th birthday party. I hoped this one would go better than my two previous gigs, which were for a 30th and 40th respectively - for those two yet again I had to compete with a disco. The fact that this was for somebody older did give me some hope. It turned out to be a lovely family affair which went really well. I discovered that the son of the birthday boy was one of the lads who had shared a caravan with me and a bunch of 7 others on that memorable school trip to Bude. He was married now, and it was nice to have a catch up and discover what had become of the other lads, some of whom he knew others he didn't, but at least I could tell him how Ben was doing. I worked my way around the hall for about an hour until it was time to go. It had been a good one and I thought about Bobby as I continued to perform with his advice ringing in my ears, "The audience must want to watch you." Thankfully on that day they did. At the end of my allotted time I said my goodbyes and wished everybody well and stepped out onto the street. There were crowds of people lining the pavement as I made my way to the car park. I realised then it was the annual lantern parade and I stopped to watch. It was a joy to experience the parade of mostly youngsters as they walked excitedly up the High Street. Their homemade and often spectacular lanterns glowing and lighting up the darkness.

The following Monday I phoned the agency to find out if I had any holiday owing. I was pleasantly surprised when I was told that I had 5.39 days left. Heaven knows how that was worked out but in real terms it meant I could retire a week earlier than I had originally planned. I would now finish on Friday the 12th of December and not the 19th. The fact that I should have begun my countdown at 1,304 days and not 1,311 suddenly didn't seem important anymore. Time suddenly seemed to go faster. On my final Wednesday I went to the canteen at lunchtime as usual and was touched to discover that a surprise presentation lunch had been organised, including a huge cake. I had no idea, and it was totally unexpected. I opened the large card to find it full of signatures and messages of good luck from friends and colleagues from all over the site, with many commenting on the fact that I can stop counting the days at last. There had also been a collection and I was given a voucher for B&Q and with that I was able to buy myself a good quality battery drill - my workmates and the staff there had been very generous.

My final days were quite full with plenty to do. On my last day I worked until lunchtime and then went round the campus to say goodbye to the many friends I'd made during the past five years. I ended up back at the workshop and showed the electricians a couple of tricks, and then after a final goodbye to the office staff and Tim the supervisor, I loaded the car with my tools and drove home for the last time. After parking and heaving out my toolbox I opened the front door and on the doormat was the buff envelope I'd been waiting for. The letter inside explained all about my pension and how much I'd have to live on for the foreseeable future. It was more than I thought, and it was reassuring to know that money wouldn't be a problem. Anything I made with the magic or odd bits of carpentry would be icing on the (retirement) cake. I went to the pub as usual on a Friday night to a nice welcome from the regulars and a lot of piss taking as well. After a couple of hours I staggered home happy, slightly merry, relieved, and extremely grateful.

The next day I was invited out for a meal with Ben and Jay to celebrate my retirement and the future. Ben was saving up for yet another trip, and Jay had just split up from his long-term girlfriend and was now living in rented accommodation, so when it came to paying the bill, they looked at each other and then at me. I didn't mind, especially when they produced a small, wrapped box containing a really good quality wristwatch, something I will always treasure.

In the days that followed I thought back through my 50 years of almost continuous employment. I had been really lucky to have experienced all that I had and appeared to have made the right decisions at the right time. I don't regret anything, even on the one or two occasions when jobs didn't work out, at least I tried. The best decision I ever made was to try my luck at Wolverton Works Training School when I was a lad. My apprenticeship there was the perfect beginning and gave me the groundwork for all that was to follow and for that I'll always be grateful. My experience in the furniture trade has given me the knowledge to design and make all my own cabinets, bookcases, beds, and other things in between and has given me a creative hobby too. My time at Cranfield was sometimes stressful with some of that due to me and a lack of confidence, other times it was due to other things that I had to struggle with. All in all though I did enjoy my five-year stint there and met some lovely people, and thanks to Tony and Colin I learned a lot too.

Throughout my working life I've worked hard and inspired by my Mum and Dad have always earned enough money to support my family and save a bit along the way too. I reckon I'd paid my dues and earned my retirement. The future looked good, I was optimistic and healthy and looked forward to whatever life threw at me in the years that lay ahead. I had projects in mind to keep me busy which I was looking forward to. I couldn't wait to get started!

I had a good Christmas with the boys and yet again the year ended with the 10th consecutive year at Buckingham Town Hall and Villiers Restaurant with singer and guitarist, Tommy. 2015 dawned to the next phase of my life.

CHAPTER 34

Mum

Mum's health declined slowly over the following four years. Her mental state was by no means dementia related and although her short-term memory was poor, she could remember things from as far back as her childhood with amazing clarity. One day I showed her a photograph which was taken of her ninety years ago when she was ten years old - not only could she remember it being taken, but she even knew the name of the photographer! As time passed though she would often get confused and began to wander from her bungalow. Her sight had virtually gone but her hearing wasn't too bad with the help of her state-of-the-art aids. She eventually became housebound, and carers and family had to visit more and more often. Sadly at the end of 2017 we came to the decision it would be in her best interests to move out of her bungalow and into a care home. It wasn't an easy decision to make, and we visited several before making the final choice. Mum settled in quite well to begin with but after a couple of falls she began to go downhill. In March of 2018 she had another fall which was more serious, resulting in a broken hip. As you'd expect we thought the worst and doubted she'd survive what we considered to be a major trauma. We were really surprised when the doctors decided to operate, bearing in mind she was 99 years old. It was explained to us that the operation would make her more comfortable and be less painful than it would to treat a broken hip for any length of time. Again Mum got through it and after about ten days she was back in her care home. The following two months were difficult. On good days she was coherent and able to chat and listen to music, other times she was just too sleepy and confused.

On April 22nd along with staff at the care home we organised a small family party to celebrate her 100th birthday. My sisters and the carers managed to get her ready and into the function room in her wheelchair where the family were already waiting. It was a really happy occasion and she coped well and was able to pose for photographs with children, grandchildren, and great grandchildren. It was lovely to see so many people there.

Her actual birthday was two days later on the 24th when she had a huge number of cards, including the big one from the Queen. She understood all that was going on and was quite bemused at being 100 years old. Mum had been through a lot in recent months, and it was remarkable she actually made it to such a milestone. We decorated her room and strung the cards all the way around and it looked great. We continued to visit her every day and things appeared to be going well in the days and weeks that followed, but on May 15th she passed peacefully away in her sleep.

Mum was the sweetest kindest most beautiful human being I have ever known. As with my Dad, she dedicated her life to her family. Without her love and support I doubt I'd have coped with those early years of single parenthood. During my eulogy at her funeral I commented on the fact that the world would be a much better place if we could all at least aspire to be as beautiful as she was - to be as caring, as generous, as tolerant, as forgiving, as loving.

I can hear her now with that lovely Welsh lilt as she would always end her conversations with us,

"Bye love, take care, and love to all."

CHAPTER 35

And Finally...

Retirement suits me. In fact I often say to people it was the best career move I ever made. I can always find something to do, and I'm never bored. I still have my workshop at the bottom of the garden where I do bits of cabinet making (at my own pace and thankfully no more time sheets). I play table tennis regularly, write stuff, read an enormous amount, have a strum on the guitar, have a go on the harmonica, take photographs, play about with cards and coins, and do a lot of walking. I just love the beauty of the English countryside and how good it makes me feel. The walks are for the most part circular and cover a distance of about 6 miles. I try and time them to finish at lunchtime close to a pub. After walking 6 miles, I'm ready for a pint. Then in the afternoon I'll adjourn to my library and have a read and a doze for an hour or two until dinner time. Perfect.

Jay is still a teacher at Bourton Meadow school in Buckingham and several times a year I volunteer as a parent helper. I go on various trips to help look after groups of children aged from five to eleven. They're great fun to do and the children are just wonderful. Some of them are funny, often when I'm introduced to them as Mr. Hawes; they have a good look at me, then at Jay, whisper between themselves and as the penny drops, they realise who I might possibly be. On one occasion a little lad asked me if

I was Mr Hawes' Daddy. When I answered, "Yes", he said, "No you're not!"

If me and Jay happen to be in the same group, I'm known as Mr Hawes senior or Old Mr Hawes, I'm happy with either. A regular outing is to Buckingham Fire Station which I've done several times. The first one was memorable with a large group of five-year-olds. We walked together across a small park with the children hand in hand in pairs and arrived at the Fire Station some 15 minutes later. We were welcomed by a group of firefighters into a large open area where the children were told what to do if ever their clothes caught fire. The three words to remember are Stop, Drop, and Roll. The children then had great fun rolling on the floor putting it to the test. Next up was a demonstration of the protective clothing firefighters have to wear, including breathing apparatus, and finally a look at the considerable amount of equipment carried by the fire engines. After a short snack break, we went out into the yard where the children were lined up to await the arrival of the fire engine. It soon came round the corner with lights flashing and a short burst from the siren. After that came a demonstration with ladders, hoses, and even a dummy (which was rescued). The final event was to be the children having a go with the hoses. While preparations were being made for that, a teacher went to the first group and began to sing London's Burning and the children soon joined in. She went to the next group and started them off, and the group after that. Soon the yard echoed to the sound of 50 five-year-old children giving it their all. It was beautiful. The highlight of the visit came next with each child having a go with a huge hose spraying it across the yard, supported by a friendly fireman. Then it was all over and after thanking everybody we walked back to school with many of the children chanting, Stop, Drop, and Roll! Stop, Drop, and Roll! Job done I reckon.

I still live in the same house I moved into with Babs, Clare and Jeff, and later Ben and Jay in 1980. I haven't moved, never felt the need. The house is ideally positioned with Campbell Park and the City Centre a short walk away at the top of the road, and the Ouzel Valley Park down the road at the bottom. Halfway down, turn left and a ten-minute walk away takes me to The Cross Keys. As I said, ideally positioned! Ben's old room and studio is now my spare room and office, and I converted Jay's old room into a library and rehearsal room and is where I spend most of my evenings. I live alone and am as happy and independent now as I was all those years ago when I was 11 years old.

I visit my childhood hometown of Bletchley at least once a week. It's a lovely three-and-a-half-mile walk along the canal which takes about an hour. I try and do it every Sunday morning to attend the service at Queensway Methodist Church. This is where I was christened, went to Sunday School, joined the Cubs and Scouts, and where I performed my first ever magic show as a shy 12-year-old in 1962. It's a place steeped in memories and has been a part of my life for 70 years.

Writing this book for almost three years has been quite an experience. Thanks to my diaries, I've relived every day of my life from a twelve-year- old lad to a sixty-five-year-old pensioner. As you can imagine, at times it has been a roller coaster of emotions as memories both good and bad came flooding back. But then again, youthful naivety, broken relationships, and bereavements are things most of us have to suffer and get through and ultimately survive, all are part of life's rich pageant that make us what we are. Reliving my wonderful childhood and teenage years in the 60s and 70s brought back many happy memories. I'd often laugh out loud at my childhood innocence as I re-read some of the early diaries. Reading them again has also given me a fresh perspective. I feel so grateful now to my Mum and Dad and family and friends who made a lot of things possible, and am more aware now of some of the sacrifices they made for my benefit. Writing the diaries each night has sometimes been a chore but I'm certainly glad now that I persevered. The 50 plus years portrayed in this book is a long time but in the great scheme of things it is only a snapshot. The diaries have obviously been useful to glean information but also to remind me of the many wonderful people I have admired along the way – teachers, magicians of course, and musicians too, people who have shaped and guided me in all aspects of my life; I'm grateful to them all and owe them everything.

I have many interests and hobbies, but magic has been intertwined in my life for over half a century like the word Blackpool in a stick of rock. Magic has given me confidence and joy along with the satisfaction of being able to spread entertainment and laughter to an audience. It has also given me the opportunity to visit some beautiful places and meet many wonderful people. That being the case I have decided to leave the final words to a man whose methods of performing have shaped me into the performer I am today. Dai Vernon, 'The Professor'.

Magic is the Absence of Moves,
It happens, then fades away like a quiet wind.

Love to all.

Ken Hawes
July 2023.

The End

I found myself alone in a small wooden boat. It was early morning in the summer. I was surrounded by the sort of mist that promises a beautiful day. The sun was just about visible in the silence, the only sound the gentle slapping of water on wood as the boat moved quietly in the gentle breeze. As the mist began to clear, things became visible. I could see a small wooden landing stage a short distance away, and soon a well-kept lawn came into view, the distinctive lines leading down towards the water's edge. Further up stood a large, beautiful house with outbuildings on either side. On the edges of the lawn were deep borders full of an assortment of colourful flowers and plants. A greenhouse came into view along with a thriving and well-kept vegetable patch. As the breeze quickened, the final remnants of mist disappeared, and as the sun rose into a cloudless sky, figures emerged from the house. Tables, chairs, and umbrellas were brought from one of the outbuildings and positioned around the lawn. The people who carried them looked familiar somehow but I couldn't place them. More figures emerged, some older than others, all of them smiling. One or two carried garden implements as they made their way to the borders. Three of them were elderly and one was a young woman of about 25. They walked to the edge of the landing stage and looked directly at me, smiling, and looking well. I recognised them all. Clare, her Nanny and Grandad Holmes, and my Dad. They didn't wave or beckon, they just stood there for a while looking happy and at peace.

Soon they were busily working on the garden, tending plants, and pulling weeds. More people came out and sat at the tables under the umbrellas, two of them strumming guitars. I watched as Deke Leonard and Micky Jones turned around to look at me and smile. Close by was a group of men deep in conversation holding coins and packs of cards. They paused for a moment and looked in my direction, all of them smiling... Bobby Bernard, Pat Page, Albert Goshman, and the unmistakable figures of John Ramsay and Dai Vernon. A tray of tea and cake was delivered by a small lady wearing an apron. John made a coin disappear into thin air! And Mum laughed! She looked out towards me, her hand across her forehead to create some shade, still smiling, always smiling. Around another table, more familiar figures were gathered... Bill Middleton, David Parriss, Norman Woodger, and Reg Gayton, all from the magic club. They too turned around to face me and smile. I could hear familiar sounds too, the unmistakable noise of an electric table saw from one of the outbuildings. The door opened with a cloud of dust and there stood Colin from Cranfield University, looking at me with his toothy grin. Then... the sound of a ping pong ball, bouncing with a steady rhythm onto a bat held by Bill Wooding, in his baggy shorts, still with an inch of underpants showing beneath. He caught the ball and mimed a classic forehand top spin loop with his bat, and smiled.

After a while, and as the mist came down, garden implements were carried back to the house; cards, coins, and guitars were put away; crockery was taken to be washed up; machinery was turned off; and bat and ball stored away. I sat in the boat surrounded by the now descending mist and happy memories, feeling peaceful, my mind at rest and unafraid of what comes to us all - The End...

Acknowledgements

A huge thank you to: My sister Jean Peck for teaching me things about the apostrophe I didn't know and for working tirelessly as my editor checking every single word. My neice Kathryn Myers for designing the wonderful cover. The team at Publishing Push for their invaluable help and guidance. And for my wonderful family who made it all possible.